Jewels of the Qila

Jewels of the Qila

The Remarkable Story of an Indo-Canadian Family

HUGH J.M. JOHNSTON

UBC Press • Vancouver • Toronto

20 19 18 17 16 15 14 13 5 4 3 2

Printed in Canada on FSC-certified ancient-forest-free paper (100 percent post-consumer recycled) that is processed chlorine- and acid-free.

Library and Archives Canada Cataloguing in Publication

Johnston, Hugh J. M., 1939-
Jewels of the Qila : the remarkable story of an Indo-Canadian family / Hugh J.M. Johnston.

Includes bibliographical references and index.
Also issued in electronic format.
ISBN 978-0-7748-2216-9 (bound); ISBN 978-0-7748-2217-6 (pbk.)

1. Siddoo family. 2. Sikh Canadians – British Columbia – Biography. 3. East Indian Canadians – British Columbia – Biography. I. Title.

FC106.S55J64 2011 294.6092'2711 C2011-906619-X

Canada

UBC Press gratefully acknowledges the financial support for our publishing program of the Government of Canada (through the Canada Book Fund), the Canada Council for the Arts, and the British Columbia Arts Council.

This book has been published with the help of a grant from the Canadian Federation for the Humanities and Social Sciences, through the Aid to Scholarly Publications Program, using funds provided by the Social Sciences and Humanities Research Council of Canada, and with the help of the K.D. Srivastava Fund.

UBC Press
The University of British Columbia
2029 West Mall
Vancouver, BC V6T 1Z2
www.ubcpress.ca

From the memories and manuscripts of

JAGDIS K. SIDDOO *and* SARJIT K. SIDDOO

Contents

Illustrations

Maps

Photographs

Preface

This is a family history about members of a minority community that has enjoyed remarkable success despite weathering decades of social and legal discrimination. It has taken fifty years and several contributors to bring this book to its present form. And it would not exist had the second generation – the children of immigrant parents – not realized that they had a story to tell and worked to preserve it. The primary locales are British Columbia and Punjab, places of dramatic contrast in climate, topography, flora, fauna, culture, tradition, and history, and yet linked in the lives of immigrants and the relatives they left behind. The family's background is Sikh, which means that it has belonged to a distinctive and visible minority both in India and in Canada. Its story is about change, challenge, trauma, foresight, confidence, and achievement in two countries that are half a world apart.

This is not a typical Sikh family – if such a thing exists – but it is a family whose lives and actions reflected and affected what happened in their expatriate world as well as their ancestral home. The surname, as it appears in print, tells us something. When writing in English the family spells it as Siddoo, although the common English version is Sidhu. Kapoor Singh Siddoo, the family's first immigrant to Canada, changed the spelling at the beginning of the First World War after he had been in North America for nearly eight years. He did so because he reasoned that it would help English speakers to get the pronunciation right; and he was being pragmatic in a way that was entirely consistent with his approach to life.

But one should not think he ever turned his back on his past or encouraged his two daughters to do so. As an immigrant who did very well in Canada, he was always mindful of what was going on at home and concerned to help. That attitude ensured not only his continuing involvement with India, but enabled the charity work of his wife and daughters.

His daughter Sarjit Kaur Siddoo began assembling material for a family history in 1959. A letter from an old family friend, William H. Moore of Pickering, Ontario, got her started; and she had time on her hands because she was waiting impatiently for patients to turn up at the charity hospital her family had built in rural Punjab. Moore, her correspondent, was a multi-faceted individual – writer, lecturer, farmer, politician – for whom her father had worked back in the summer of 1914. He and Moore had stayed in touch, and in December 1959, Moore had written to Sarjit after an article appeared in the Canadian edition of *Time Magazine* about the family's hospital. "You should write a book," he said, adding that it was a "must" and that she should do it "now." She immediately began to write about the struggle to launch the hospital. Intending to carry on with the writing, she preserved her notes, her diary, and correspondence from this period of her life.

Over the years, both Sarjit and her sister, Jackie (Jagdis), worked together on the family history, setting down what they knew, keeping clippings of magazine and newspaper articles, saving correspondence (although, with their constant movement from Canada to India, much was lost), retrieving business records, and exchanging information with relatives and friends. In the early 1980s, Sarjit and her husband, Avtar, taped several interviews with relatives and others who knew her parents. Twenty years later, with the project still unfinished, they hired a researcher who collected more material and added a few more interviews. They had a growing manuscript of recollections, descriptions, extracts from periodicals, portions of interviews, and chronologies, which they passed back and forth, adding and correcting. Nonetheless, though the manuscript, as they recognized, was material for a book, it was not a book yet.

I first met Sarjit in 1990 when looking for multiple copies of Mary Lutyen's biography of Jiddu Krishnamurti for a class I was teaching. She was able to get the copies for me, and at the same time she invited me and my wife for a weekend retreat at the Krishnamurti Centre that she and her sister maintained – and still maintain – on Swanwick Road near Victoria. We had a delightful time there, and for long afterward we received notices of coming events at the centre, but we let time slip without following up. Some years later, Sarjit invited the two of us for lunch at her home in the Vancouver area. I don't think she remembered me from the previous occasion. Instead, she had been told that I was an expert whom she could consult about the history of the Sikh community. That first lunch led to many more, spaced at six-month intervals. Over that time, my role in the Siddoo family history evolved from consultant to author, from making minor suggestions to taking on the writing, expanding the research in a major way, and constructing the story as I thought most useful, which was to supply as much context as I could without losing the thread of a family story.

Two earlier books of mine, one on the infamous voyage of the Sikh emigrant ship the *Komagata Maru,* and another on the life experiences of a Sikh immigrant of the 1950s, provide slices of the story that binds India and Canada. This book has a longer sweep, and writing it has added considerably to the complexity of my own understanding of a now prospering minority with roots in two countries.

Acknowledgments

My great thanks go to my good friend Sohan Singh Pooni for reading this manuscript in his always informed and attentive way, and for passing on documents that he collected and translated – the results of his years of searching for material for his recent book on Gadar heroes, *Canada de Gadri Yodhe,* a work that his fellow Punjabis have welcomed with spontaneous, enthusiastic, and deserved applause. My former student Archana Verma added greatly to my understanding of the Paldi/Mayo Siding community with interviews that she conducted twenty years ago in India and in Canada for her book *The Making of Little Punjab in Canada.* One of the people who helped her at that time was a member of the Mayo family, Joan Mayo, who was then looking for someone to write about Mayo Singh and Paldi, and who finally took on the job herself, producing a most readable and informative account.

It was after meeting Joan Mayo that I had a chance to talk with Mayo Singh's son-in-law Joe Soroya, who subsequently gave the Simon Fraser University Archives his personal papers and photographs. Some of what he shared has found its way into this book. Also, as I worked my way through my filing cabinet of material acquired over many years, I was repeatedly thankful to Sarj Singh Jagpal, not just for his invaluable *Becoming Canadians,* based on the stories of his father's generation of Sikh immigrants, but also for some of the documents he retrieved from the closets and cupboards of people he interviewed, documents that he long ago generously helped me to photocopy. In the past few years, I've enjoyed the very special experience of spending time with Durai Pal

Pandia's daughter, Aruna, and her friend from childhood, Ishar Singh Banns' daughter Chandra Raglin, as well as with Ishar's adopted son, Paul Banns, who freely shared what they knew and some of what Paul in particular had researched. Amarjit Hundle, a grandnephew of Kartar Singh Hundal, is another keen family historian whose help I appreciate. My friend Terry Aman kindly read my manuscript in its early stages, and I was glad to have his encouragement.

I give special thanks to my wife, Patricia, who has enthusiastically joined in my involvement with Sikhs and their history, attending *gurdwaras* (temples), visiting families and friends, scribbling as my unpaid assistant in the archives, listening to what I have written or wanted to talk about, travelling with me to India more than once, living there many months, and charming and befriending the many remarkable people who have come into our lives as a consequence. My three energetic and caring daughters, Megan, Caitlin, and Sian, have given help and encouragement throughout, and Sian has found the time to read and correct each chapter of this book as it emerged.

I am deeply grateful to Jackie, Sarjit, Avtar, and Chanda for the opportunity to write their story using their materials, their carefully written as well as their off-the-cuff recollections, their documents, and their pictures and interviews. I am also grateful for the research that a former student at UBC, Ranbir Johal, did for them a number of years ago while she was in graduate school. For many months I took up daytime residence in Sarjit, Avtar, and Chanda's Canadian home, and I was with them for a month in India, sharing their meals and their spirited conversations and feeling as welcome as any family member. It was in the comfort of their homes in Canada and India that I talked to many of their relatives and got a rich sense of their lives, which made writing this book a wonderfully inviting and rewarding undertaking.

The maps and the indexing for this book have been paid for with a grant from the Simon Fraser University Publications Fund, which I greatly appreciate.

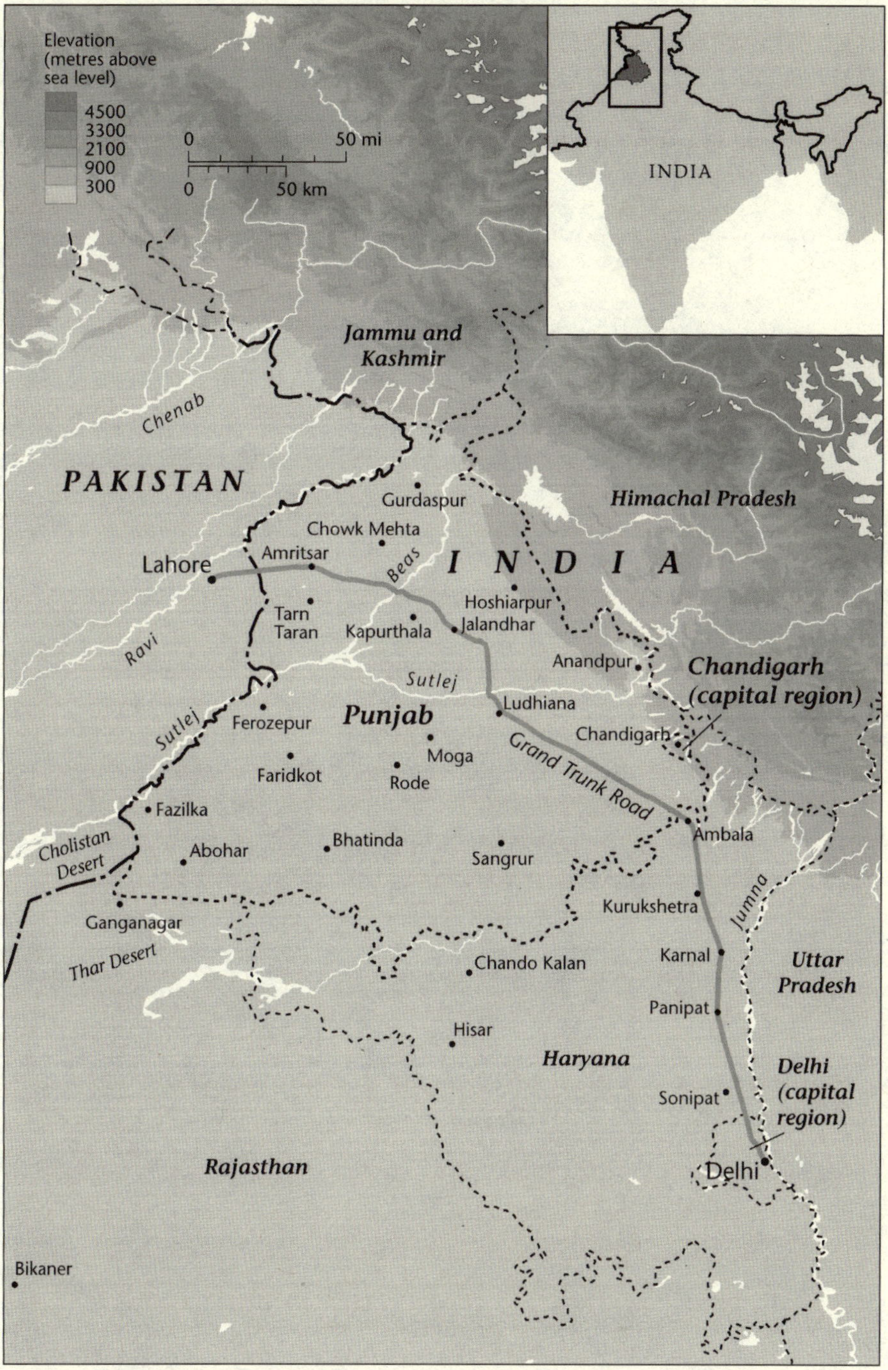

Punjab today and neighbouring states

The districts of the province of Punjab under British rule

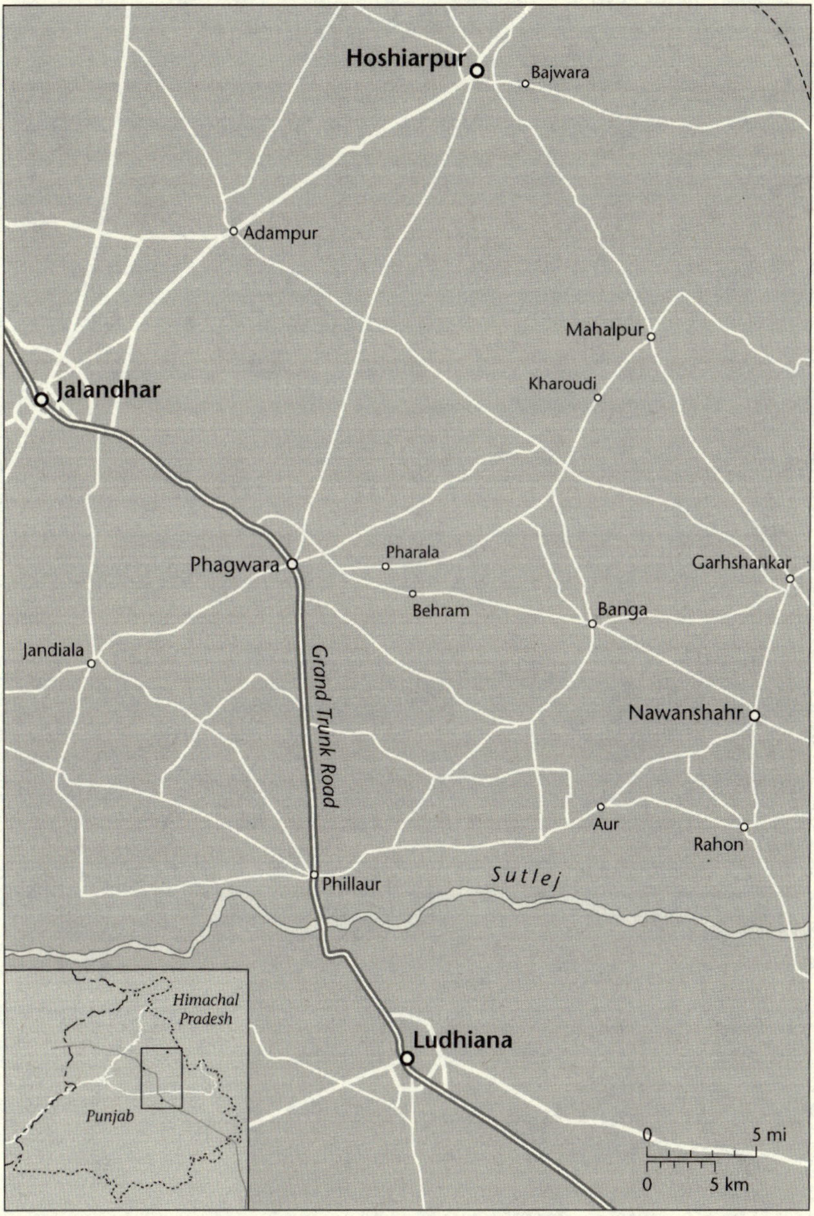

Aur, Kharoudhi, and nearby towns

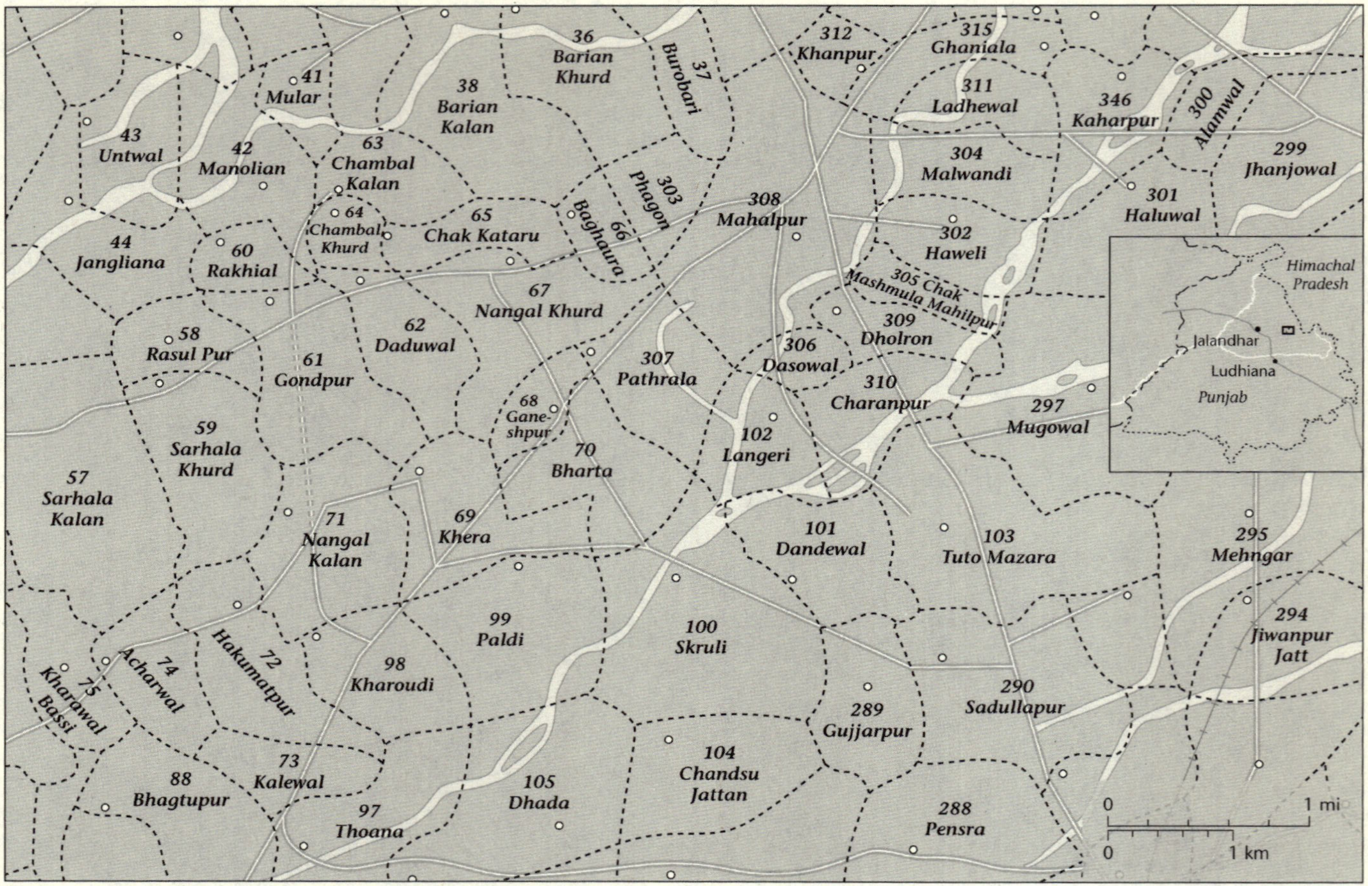

Mahalpur-area villages including Kharoudhi, Paldi, and Skrooli

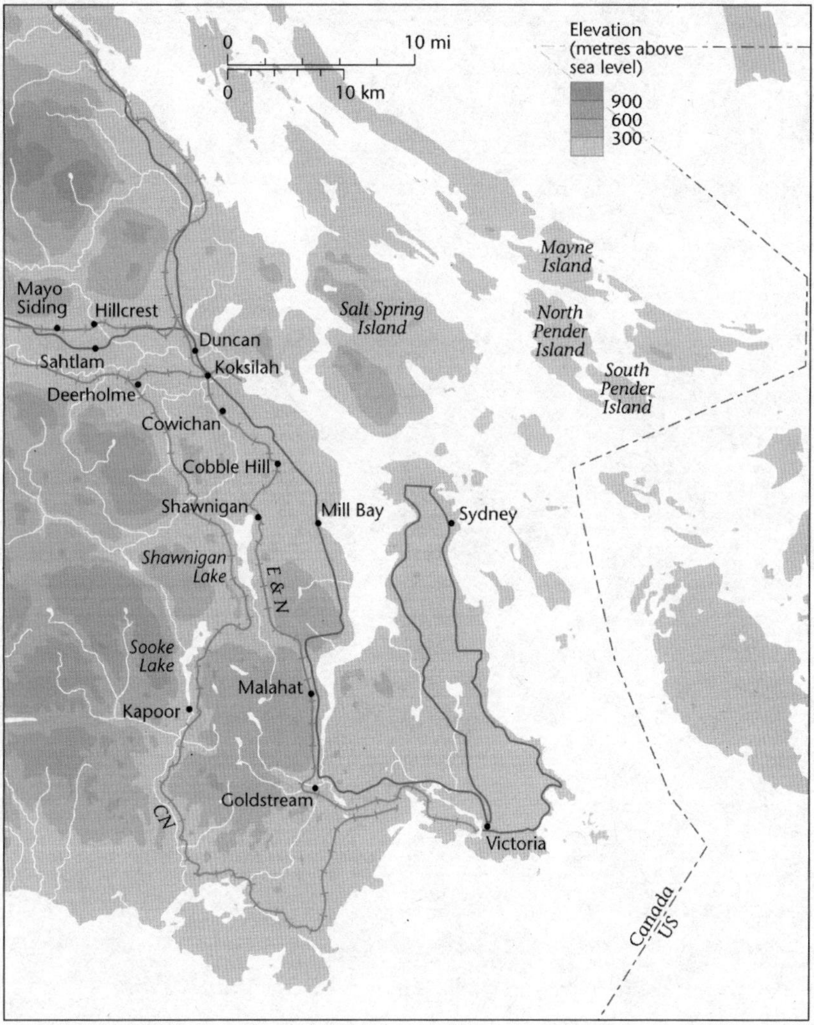

Kapoor's world on Vancouver Island

The Indian state of Punjab in South Asia

Jewels of the Qila

1
Pioneers

When Vancouver journalist Art McKenzie described Kapoor Singh Siddoo in a 1956 weekend magazine article, his lead adjective was "modest."[1] Kapoor was then seventy-one. McKenzie had been impressed by the quiet and gracious dignity of someone who was arguably the most influential and successful person in the local Punjabi community. When he did the research for his article, he found Kapoor living in a comfortable but unpretentious two-story house in a mixed middle-class/working-class Vancouver neighbourhood. Kapoor had occupied that house for twenty years, and McKenzie asked why he didn't build something grander. Kapoor said he had neither the need nor the interest. He had the money, but an ostentatious house he did not want.

By 1956 Kapoor could look back on fifty years in North America. He had been one of seven or eight thousand in the first wave of South Asian immigrants who crossed the Pacific, seeking fortunes in Canada and the United States.[2] The India he left behind was under British rule, but as he later explained, he was not abandoning his native country. His emigration was part adventure, part political act, inspired by a nationalistic teacher who told his students, "Boys, if you ever get the chance, go to America and make lots of money, and come back and free India." That exhortation was in the back of Kapoor's mind when, as a young man, he took passage from Calcutta (Kolkata). When he arrived in America and rubbed shoulders in the South Asian emigrant community, Kapoor got to know a mix of students and labourers – Hindus, Sikhs, and Muslims. Most were Punjabis but some came from other parts of India. Among them were political refugees and other fervent nationalists who coalesced in 1913 in the Gadar (Mutiny) Party, which they formed to wage a war of independence for India. Kapoor had Gadar friends but was not an activist. His daughters, growing up years later, were unaware of his Gadar connection, although they knew he had Gadar sympathies; they did not suspect his involvement until, in their late seventies, they were shown a reprint of an Indian police directory that listed his name.[3] He had not talked about the subject to them. Even so, the police in India believed he was dangerous and kept a dossier on him for decades, as they did with hundreds of other overseas Indians. This had consequences when he returned to India for the first time in 1931, after an absence of a quarter of a century. Although the reasons for his return were innocent and unremarkable, the police kept track of him. He had arrived at Kolkata on the Japanese liner *Yuen Sang* on 9 November, and the police knew it. He didn't intend to hurry back to Canada, but after fourteen months a police agent turned up and asked for his passport "for verification." Fearing that it would be confiscated, Kapoor refused to give it up and returned immediately to Vancouver with his family.

By then, Kapoor's home and heart were in Canada. This was in spite of the extreme prejudice and discrimination that he and other South Asians faced. He had seen the prejudice of the white community produce severe immigration restrictions against South Asians, and yet he had prospered and made friends beyond his *apnai* – his own people. He was one of an exceptional few who had landed in North America without difficulty early in the twentieth century and who had stayed and put down roots. In 1906 he had stepped ashore in San Francisco with as little hassle as any European. But he was enjoying a short-lived opportunity. He had not been in North America long before Canadian and American ports began turning back nearly every South Asian immigrant who tried to enter. Immigration barriers had gone up in both countries to exclude all but a few of his countrymen. And that became the pattern of the next forty to fifty years. People managed to get in with false papers and by indirect routes – via the Philippines, Mexico, and Europe – but their numbers were small.

Kapoor had remained in North America when a majority of his compatriots had returned to India. There were about seventy-five hundred on the Pacific Coast of Canada and the US in 1910, and less than three thousand ten years later. In British Columbia the number had dropped below a thousand.[4] Among them was Kapoor, and he was doing well. Men left North America for many reasons. One was the call of home; one was the conviction that they could help drive the British out of India; and one was loss of employment. The normal economic cycle had forced men out during recessions, and immigration restrictions made it difficult for new men to come in during periods of expansion. But besides this, the job market for Indian labourers was shrinking, a direct consequence of the anti-Asian lobby among white workers and the pressure they put on governments and employers to exclude Asians. By the time Kapoor had been in North America for five years, the alternatives for his people had become starkly simple: farming or working in the lumber industry. For those who stayed in California, it was mostly farming, and in British Columbia it was mostly the lumber industry. During the First World War, with a consortium of his countrymen, Kapoor became a sawmill operator, beginning with a small and marginal mill. So it was that he established the basis of a small fortune while most of his compatriots were leaving.

At the peak of his business, in the 1930s, '40s, and '50s, Kapoor employed hundreds of white, Punjabi, Chinese, and Japanese men. Among his own people, he was respectfully called Babu ji, a Punjabi form of address for a genteel and educated person, which he was. Whites called him Kapoor or Mr. Kapoor, treating his first name as his last. As a child, his youngest daughter, Sarjit, thought that her surname was Kapoor, and she confused her teachers at Henry Hudson Elementary School by saying that she was Sarjit Kapoor while her sister, a year older, was correctly telling them she was Jagdis Siddoo. The girls saw their father always being treated with respect. He was a handsome man, well spoken, well groomed, and impeccably dressed. A tailored three-piece blue suit was standard for him. Sarjit and Jagdis, or Jackie as everyone always called her, remembered with pride the question many people asked when their parents took them on a tour of Europe: "Is your father a diplomat?" He didn't look like an immigrant sawmill operator from BC.

Kartar Singh Hundal, who knew Kapoor for decades, and who worked with and for him, was one of the greatest advocates for South Asian rights that his community ever produced. When he was called upon to comment for the newspapers after Kapoor's death, he described Kapoor as a quiet and humble man who said only what he meant. Kapoor's daughters state that he was shy, in contrast to his youngest daughter, Sarjit, who has always been outspoken. When the family met with the prime minister of India, Jawaharlal Nehru, she did most of the talking. This was in 1957, when they were encountering innumerable obstacles in an attempt to establish a charity hospital in Punjab. They had come down to Delhi from Punjab for an audience with Nehru in his residence. When he entered the small study where they waited for him, it was Sarjit who spoke up. She was thirty at the time and a medical doctor, and she had been dealing with the problems first-hand. And yet her personality and her father's led her to take the lead while he sat back.

But his own people listened when Kapoor spoke, and he did not have to shout. Gurdial Singh Teja was one of the kinsmen he brought to Canada during the late 1920s to work in the Mayo mill at Mayo Siding, near Duncan on Vancouver Island. Gurdial was a big man: six foot two and 225 pounds or more, and the tough guy in the Siddoo clan when factional fights broke out among Punjabis. His son Dave Teja has told the story of one fight at the Mayo mill involving his father, which ended with Kapoor's intervention. Someone hit Gurdial so hard with a bottle that it dented his skull, and he had to be hospitalized. When he was released, he sought out his assailant, beat him up, and put a pistol to his head, threatening to kill him. Dave Teja said that his father was not proud of this act but had to show that he could not be pushed around. A circle of Punjabis gathered. Kapoor elbowed his way through and told Gurdial to hand over the gun. Dave Teja said that Kapoor was cool and effective. His father surrendered the gun, and though he did have to serve jail time, Kapoor managed to get him released on a bond.

This story becomes more meaningful when one understands that there were two Punjabi factions at the Mayo mill – two groups of kinsfolk who had joined forces to operate a sawmilling business. Kapoor was the principal figure in one group, and Maiya Singh – also known as Mayo Singh – was his counterpart in the other. They were the leaders in a masculine world, an isolated bunkhouse community located on a railway that ran through the old-growth forest of Vancouver Island. In their off-hours, this group spent a lot of time together, sleeping and eating in the "Hindu" bunkhouse and the cookhouse, whereas whites, Chinese, and Japanese went to their own buildings – four ethnic groups, four languages, four cuisines and bunkhouses sleeping fifty or sixty men each. Occasional flare-ups and tensions among the Punjabis were inevitable – as among other bunkhouse men. Remarkably, the Mayo-Kapoor business alliance survived for twenty years before it dissolved.

As an emigrant in North America, Kapoor lived for sixteen years in the rough company of men. He was nearly thirty-eight before he brought his wife, Besant Kaur, from India, and only then did they begin their domestic life together. It happened like this: after they married, she stayed with her own family, which was not unusual for a fifteen-year-old Punjabi wife at the time, and which required no discussion because Kapoor was still a student and not living at home. But then he had emigrated and stayed abroad, and they had been separated by Canada's anti-Indian immigration regulations. In 1919 the Canadian government finally relented and let Punjabi men such as Kapoor sponsor their wives and children. It took some correspondence and planning to bring Besant Kaur over, but she finally arrived early in 1923, escorted by Kapoor's older brother. Several other women came at the same time, and they made up the second small group of Punjabi wives to come to Canada in a twelve-month period. Others followed. After a couple of years, Kapoor's partner, Mayo Singh, returned from India with a bride who was nineteen years his junior. And Mayo's older brother, Ganeya, also brought his wife. Now, in the neat little community at Mayo Siding, with four large bunkhouses and over twenty individual houses, three large family homes stood out. First was Mayo's house, next to it was Ganeya's, and then after a space Kapoor's house – all wood-frame constructions built on the same scale, though Kapoor's had a different design.

Beginning married life late as they did, Kapoor and Besant Kaur expected no children, but they were blessed with two daughters born during their first three years at Mayo Siding. And they seemed to have surmounted the challenge of starting married life late by creating a very strong union. Kapoor turned out to be a wonderfully domesticated husband and Besant Kaur a supportive wife who brought a mature woman's leadership and guidance to the little community at Mayo. Jackie and Sarjit remembered with affection their family's early morning routine, one that shaped itself in Mayo and continued later at their Kitsilano home in Vancouver. "Daddy" would be up at 4:00 a.m., lighting the wood stove, which also heated the water tank. Then he began his prayers. "Mother" would be awake at the same time but, engrossed in her daily prayers, did not get up until she had finished. Before leaving for the mill, Kapoor peeled and chopped whatever food they would eat that day so that Besant Kaur's work would be lessened. She was a vegetarian, so if meat were on the menu – usually chicken – he cooked it. She did not cook meat, except for the dogs. For them she boiled chicken. Sikh women of her generation were commonly very fond of animals, and she was typical.[5]

It was a very close family circle that Kapoor and Besant Kaur created with their daughters, who grew up to be strong, capable, and accomplished women with a lifetime's devotion to their parents and their memories. Besant Kaur made no great effort to speak English – she had enough for shopping but not conversation – but she was one of the few literate Punjabi women of her generation and knew four written languages: English at a minimal level and Punjabi, Hindi, and Urdu very well. When Besant Kaur came out from India, she brought books in the last three languages and attempted to teach the girls to read them. The books were all religious in nature, for faith was the foundation of her life. The girls knew she did not want to be disturbed while at her prayers. That was the most important part of her day. What she could and did share were stories from the Hindu and Sikh traditions, from the Ramayana and the *Janamsakhi*s (narratives) of Guru Nanak, the first Sikh guru. She had a wonderful memory for these stories and a gift for telling them, which she used to mesmerize her daughters and others, leaving the stories themselves deeply and affectionately imprinted in their minds.

Kapoor and Besant Kaur impressed on their daughters the importance of following a spiritual path in life and also of giving back to society, not just in money but in service. Both parents were ecumenical in their view of religion. Besant Kaur's stock response to anyone of another faith was "Your God is my God." When it came to service, they wanted their daughters to become doctors, and Besant Kaur particularly wanted them to practise medicine in rural Punjab. The girls were still in school when she and Kapoor bought a lot in the Punjabi town of Phagwara, about twenty-five kilometres from her ancestral village of Aur. It was intended to be the site for a charity hospital that Jackie and Sarjit were to run once they had finished their medical training. The girls' futures had been mapped out long before they entered medical school.

The sisters grew up with a love of India. From their parents, they knew it as a country rich in history and tradition. From their mother, they understood that Sikhism, their family faith, was a path of respect for all people, men and women, high caste and out-caste; and from their father, they absorbed the idea that the world would be a much happier and more peaceful place if it combined the science of the West with the ancient wisdom of India. At Kitsilano High School, Sarjit was outraged by a social studies class on ancient history – taught by a very nice teacher – in which India was not mentioned. Asia was covered by a single sentence on Assyria, and then it was on to Egypt and Europe. This was just the way it was in Canada, her father explained: "They don't teach anything else." Also, Sarjit objected strenuously after attending a lecture by a Christian evangelist. The sisters had been sent by their parents only to be dismayed when the lecturer represented the Indian religious tradition with lantern slides of a hooded cobra, a sacred cow, and a fakir (Sufi saint) on a bed of nails. Sarjit found it degrading and protested to her parents when they got home. On these occasions, "Daddy" would explain that white men used such images to justify their hold on colonials. But they did not seem to disturb him, although he was passionate about Indian independence. In dealing with whites he had long since recognized that they were simply ignorant about India, not deliberately insulting, and he conveyed this moderating sense of things to his daughters.

Perhaps the most valued book in the family library was *The Wisdom of China and India,* edited by the Chinese American author Lin Yutang, with excerpts from the great Hindu, Buddhist, and Confucian classics. Kapoor bought it newly published in the early 1940s and prized it because it illustrated the wisdom of so many spiritual paths. What he said about spiritual matters, Besant Kaur reinforced, and vice versa. She wanted her daughters to know about religion but did not distinguish between faiths. In her home village of Aur, she donated to both Hindus and Sikhs when they came collecting for their separate causes; and when she was challenged about it by Sikhs, she would say, "What is it to you? We are all one." So, when the girls had their tonsils out at St. Joseph's Hospital in Victoria, and a nun invited her to pray in the hospital chapel, accepting the invitation was very natural for her. The nun had seen her at her favourite pastime, telling the beads of her *mala* – her rosary. They spoke a common language that needed no translation.

Jackie and Sarjit remembered that moment in a Roman Catholic chapel for what it said about their mother: her openness to other faiths – transcending her limited English. She wasn't putting up barriers, although barriers did surround her family and her community. At that time, Sikhs and other South Asians were still second-class citizens in British Columbia: they were denied the vote in provincial, federal, and municipal elections, excluded from several fields of employment, unable to sponsor their relatives as immigrants on the same terms as other Canadians, and refused service in local barbershops or made to sit in the balcony in movie theatres. Kapoor himself took a leading role in campaigning for change. One of the proud pictures preserved in the Siddoo family album from 1939 is of four men who financed and led the fight for the rights of Sikhs and other Indo-Canadians in Canada. Kapoor is one of the four, sharing the moment with his former business partner, Mayo Singh, and their spokesmen and strategists Dr. Durai Pal Pandia and Kartar Singh Hundal.

That picture marked a huge victory in a long struggle for acceptance and fair treatment. Immigration still remained an issue; and public ignorance and intolerance of visual minorities like South Asians was sometimes unpleasantly obvious – although generally kept in the background. But Kapoor's family, and others in the tiny post-war South Asian community, had done well in a material sense. Kapoor particularly had embraced a social and business world that gave him access to the Canadian mainstream. Canada, he remarked more than once, "was a United Nations in practice."[6] He made several lasting friendships with Anglo-Canadians, influential and humble, people to whom he could turn for help in business or family matters, and people whom he helped. When he and other South Asians won the right to vote, his daughters were medical students in Toronto, and the family was looking forward to the service they could offer in India. They were in a position to give back to society in both India and Canada, and that was to be a large chapter in their family story. But Kapoor's success in business had made it all possible. Theirs was an exceptional experience, and at the same time central to the general story of immigrants from India who found their way to Canada a century ago.

2
Jagirdar Families

Family defined Kapoor and Besant Kaur in ways they could not easily have explained to Anglo-Canadians. They would have had too much to tell them. They came from Sikh families, from a small but conspicuous minority in the predominantly Muslim and Hindu province of Punjab under the British. Their families had lost status when the British took over Punjab, but they still had a special place in village society thanks to the position and rank that their ancestors had possessed under the nineteenth-century Sikh ruler Maharaja Ranjit Singh. Kapoor's and Besant's families could trace their ancestry back for generations, and he could connect his to the lineage of princes. Their families belonged to the upper gentry of rural Punjab; they numbered among its "grandees," and villagers around them respectfully remembered the feudal title of *jagirdar,* which their recent ancestors had held when the Sikh maharaja ruled much of what is now northern India and Pakistan.

Kapoor was born in Punjab in 1885. He was from the village of Kharoudi, only twenty kilometres from the Shivalik Hills, the foothills that skirt the Himalayas. As a boy, looking to the northeast, he could see the low profile of the Shivaliks. To the south and west, the flat plains stretched out indefinitely, a continuous panorama of fields and villages. One can see much the same view today, making allowances for modernization and greater affluence, for tarred roads, motorized traffic, power lines, cell phone transmission towers, new masonry buildings, and a plethora of brick kilns to supply the building boom now under way. It still remains the case that the farther one goes from the mountains, the drier it gets, until three hundred kilometres away one reaches the thorny growth of the Thar Desert in Rajasthan and the Cholistan Desert in Pakistan.

The farming families of Kharoudi have been fortunate to toil in the "the garden of Punjab" – the green sub-Shivalik region where modest rainfall is supplemented by abundant groundwater from the subterranean run-off from the foothills and mountains. With water from wells and three hundred days of sunshine a year, wheat, maize, millet, rice, and sugar cane all thrive. In the last half century, dug wells have given way to deep drilled wells, and the water table is dropping, but it remains higher than it is farther away, where agriculture depends entirely on irrigation canals that bring water from the distant mountains.[1]

When Kapoor left Kharoudi, it was about the size it is today, a modest Punjabi village of about 150 homes surrounded by 135 hectares of village land. A Canadian prairie farmer might be surprised to see so many people living within a cultivated area smaller than his own one-family property. Of course, he could not harvest three crops a year as they do; and the economics of farming in Punjab differ greatly from that in Canada – more human labour and less machinery. And villagers today can earn money outside the village or receive support from relatives abroad, so not all are directly dependent on agriculture, although they once were, as landowners and cultivators or as their dependent servants.

Fields and crops, however, dominate the landscape, sweeping out to the horizon. Kharoudi's fields extend to meet those of adjoining villages: Paldi to the east, Hakumatpur to the west, Nangal Kalan to the north, and Thoana to the south. Beyond these villages and their fields are others. From the *abadi,* or residential area of one village, to the abadi of the next is less than two kilometres by footpath or track though the fields. Like the Canadian prairie, the countryside is extremely flat, although around Kharoudhi it slopes imperceptibly away from the Shivalik Hills so that, if you go a kilometre to the west, you drop ten feet in elevation; and if you go another kilometre, another ten feet. There are slight rises of land, a matter of a few metres, and here the village elites built their homes for good drainage and to catch the breezes from the west. Other village homes clustered in an extending circle to the east, with the lowest land assigned to the least powerful and most dependent villagers. This process might have started hundreds of years ago, as in the case of Aur, Besant Kaur's home, or more recently, as with Kharoudi, where the villagers moved the abadi after an outbreak of bubonic plague. The old abadi, with homes built mostly of mud, has since melted away without a trace into the fields.

Kapoor's family owned land, which still describes 40 percent of the families in Kharoudi today. The remaining families were either tenant-cultivators or servants who worked for the landowners.[2] Among the latter, there were four kinship groups, or clans, and among these the members of Kapoor's Siddoo clan were the most recent and most important arrivals. An abandoned brick ruin in the heart of the village was once the family home. Its high-walled courtyard is now filled with weeds and crumbling bricks, and the main structure is unsafe to enter, but this was once the domestic space of a one-time feudal fief-holder, a jagirdar, whom local people always addressed respectfully as Sardar ji, a title suggesting military rank. Kapoor's ancestors were from Harikapattan, a village some distance away. Early in the nineteenth century, Kapoor's great-grandfather, Sardar Nihal Singh, had been rewarded for his military service to Maharaja Ranjit Singh with a *jagir* (or fiefdom) of two villages in the Hoshiarpur District, Fatehpur and Kharoudi. When Kapoor's great-grandfather came to claim the Kharoudi part of his jagir – according to the family story – he stopped to ask for directions at a small village that he thought was on the way. "Sardar ji," he was told, "You have arrived in Kharoudi."[3]

During a 1982 interview, Kapoor's sister-in-law remembered that the revenue from the two villages was a handsome five hundred rupees a year. She was referring to a situation long before her time and passing on information told to her by family members. As jagirdar, Kapoor's great-grandfather, Sardar Nihal Singh, would have collected what was due him either in cash or in kind, depending on what the village cultivators could muster. He paid an eighth to the state, and the rest was his. He and his family enjoyed this income until the British arrived in the mid-nineteenth century. They changed the revenue system throughout Punjab, eliminating jagirs, appointing village headmen as revenue officers, and paying them just 5 percent of the village revenue. In mixed English-Punjabi parlance, the tax-collecting headmen became known as *number-dars,* or, slightly corrupted, as *lambardars.* A sense of the rivalry between the old jagirdars and the new lambardars survives to the present. When Kapoor's daughter Sarjit married Avtar Atwal, a professor of agriculture at the Punjab Agricultural University at Ludhiana, in 1964, this was a union of jagirdar and lambardar families. Their daughter, Chanda, growing up mostly in Canada but also in India, says she always identified with the jagirdar side of her family because they were servants of the Sikh maharaja, not of the British.

In Punjab, jagirdar families married among themselves, which explains the marriage of Kapoor Singh Sidhu (or Siddoo as he chose to spell it in Canada) and Besant Kaur Sandhu. First came their engagement ceremony when they were children in 1894 and then their marriage eleven years later.[4] Her father had taken the initiative in negotiating the engagement after a relative had seen "a bright and beautiful curly-haired boy" from a village twenty kilometres away. It was usual for the girl's side to make the first approach, and in other respects as well the two families followed traditional guidelines. They would not match a boy and girl from the same village or the same clan. A Sidhu could not marry another Sidhu or even a Brar, because the latter were really Sidhus. (In reaction to a dispute in the distant past, some Sidhus had changed their name to Brar.) Both families would have looked for someone from their own Jat background – descendants of the Scythian tribesmen who had invaded the plains from the west more than a thousand years earlier and who remained the dominant rural landowning caste in Punjab.[5] In addition, a good Sikh family would want a match with another Sikh family. And both sides would insist on an alliance with a family of equal status and reputation, all of which drew jagirdar families together.

One of the family stories that Kapoor and Besant Kaur later told was that, at the engagement ceremony, when she was four and he was nine, she had pinched him and made him cry, and everyone had laughed. Later in life, when it came to gentle teasing or boasting, she had certain advantages. She came from a big village, a town with a large market, and he was from a small one. He was a country boy by comparison. She could trace her family back seven generations, which was more than he could do, although he knew he belonged to the Harike branch of the royal Sidhu clan, who still ruled in the princely state of Patiala. Her ancestor had also fought for Maharaja Ranjit Singh and had been awarded a jagir, but theirs was five villages, not two. Aur was one of these, and when they had moved to Aur from their former military headquarters at Una in the Shivalik Hills, they built a *qila,* or fort, with a courtyard large enough to keep twenty-five horses and five elephants. Part of this fort remains the family home in Aur today, although in two centuries it has been so subdivided and built against that tracing its complete outline is now impossible.

Although stripped by the British of his jagirdar's income and military function, Besant Kaur's father, Hakim Singh Sandhu, had become the *patwari* (land record officer) at Aur. In this role he kept the village's landownership and production records, including a map of its lands and an exact reporting of its cultivation. In every crop season, fall, spring, and summer, he inspected the fields and enumerated the data, and he carried out his duties with such efficiency that he was offered a promotion in the revenue service to *naib tehsildar* (sub-district revenue officer), supervising the work of many village patwaris. The promotion meant a transfer away from Aur and out of the Jalandhar District, and he declined it because he did not want to leave his village.

Hakim Singh was both educated and pious. His family remembered that he was especially fond of his daughter, Besant Kaur – even fonder of her than of his son, Sundar Singh, who, following family tradition, was to become a *unani* doctor, practising a medical tradition that went back to ancient Greece and that had reached India through the Arabs. At a time when there was practically no formal female education in rural Punjab, Hakim Singh taught his daughter at home. From him, she learned the Gurmukhi script of the Sikhs as well as Devanagri and Urdu and acquired an impressive understanding of Sikh, Hindu, Muslim, and Christian teachings.

Her mother, Bishan Kaur, was from Makrayree, a village in the Shivalik Hills near the jagirdar's headquarters at Una. She had grown up making no distinction between Hindu and Sikh teachings, and she held that view throughout her life. She had a strong constitution and her life was a long one, ending in 1956 when she was ninety-six. By then she had been a widow for more than fifty years, because Hakim Singh had died prematurely of the bubonic plague when it swept Punjab during the first decade of the twentieth century.

The story of his death is one that Jackie and Sarjit know well, although he died long before they were born. Their mother told them that he rested his head on her lap as he lay dying and asked her to recite prayers. This was a family that loved animals, and his little dog was with him on the bed. As death approached, he said, "See, they have come to take me." Besant Kaur asked "Who?" He answered that two horses stood at the front door, one with a rider dressed in white and the other with an empty saddle. "That one is for me," he said. She continued reciting, and as she finished, he closed his eyes and was gone. His little dog refused to eat after that and died within three weeks.

Besant Kaur said that she was distraught when her father died, and that she wept until she had a dream in which he told her to go to the *diwan khana,* where she would find two *ladoos* (sweets) as *prasad* (holy food). He warned her not to say anything to anyone, or she would not see him again. In the village home of a jagirdar, as in the great aristocratic homes of Lahore and Delhi, the diwan khana was a room for the men of the household, which opened off the courtyard. Besant Kaur hurried across the courtyard to find the ladoos but was so overcome by excitement and emotion that she immediately told her sister-in-law; and her father never again appeared in her dreams.

Kapoor and his two brothers did not have the same warm memory of their father, Sardar Sham Singh Sidhu, who was six feet four inches tall, a disciplinarian, and away for much of their childhood. When the boys saw his stern figure looming in the distance after a long absence, they ran into the fields to avoid him. Kapoor's younger brother, Tara, remembered him chiefly for his hard slaps, administered without a word when they were working in the field if Tara had not listened or had touched something he shouldn't. This was after their father had retired and was living on a meagre army pension of seven rupees. He had been a non-commissioned officer – a *havaldar* – in the Second Sikh Lancers under the British, serving all of his time within the boundaries of British India. Unfortunately, he was not a dog lover, a fact that had cost him a promotion to *subedar* (sergeant-major). His English superior officer had gone on holiday with his wife, leaving their dog in Sham Singh's care. When they came back, the dog had been so neglected and was in such poor shape that the officer rescinded the promotion.

Sham Singh was a sick man during his few years of retirement before dying at about age sixty of pulmonary tuberculosis. As a dying man, he was attended by his daughter-in-law's brother, Sundar, the unani doctor. Tara, his youngest son, was still a boy at the time. Decades later, as an old man himself, he recalled the moment when the doctor told him that his father would not live and asked if he wanted to go in to speak to him. The boy didn't. "I was a kid," he remembered. "What was I going to say?"

The three sons, Tara, Kapoor, and their older brother, Bhagwan, had already lost their mother, Ossie Kaur. When Tara was small, she had visited her home village of Samari and fallen ill with the plague. Tara barely remembered her. She was nice, he could recall, but "*katar*" (strict). After her death, he sometimes stayed with his *massi,* his mother's youngest sister in Fatehpur, sometimes with his father, and after the death of both parents, for a long time with a *bhooa,* an aunt on his father's side. Kapoor, on the other hand, was old enough to be deeply attached to his mother and to feel her loss. The aunt who looked after him and treated him as her own was Nikko, another of his mother's sisters.

Kapoor was the one son chosen to go to school. He was obviously an intelligent and attractive child, his parents' favourite, and later his aunt's – even over her own children. When Sarjit interviewed her Uncle Tara while researching her family history, she asked him which of his siblings his mother liked the most, and he answered without hesitation, "The one who went to school." Sometimes Tara's father would send him nearly thirty kilometres to the high school in Bajwara, carrying special food for Kapoor – fruit, yogourt, butter, and *roti* (bread). Sarjit asked Tara if he ever felt angry that his family gave Kapoor the best clothes and food. "No," he replied, "he was entitled to it." Tara himself had never expected to go to school. If a family did educate a son, it was generally just one, and Tara thought his father was exceptional in doing even that. He said that, had his father not been exposed to the world beyond the village, thanks to the army, he might not have educated any of his sons. That was how Tara explained the thinking of his father's generation and, he admitted, his own as well.

For Tara, the idea of going to school never came up. His duty was to watch his father's cattle where they grazed in the village common field. That had been Kapoor's duty too until he reached the age of six. Then he became the *para* (the one who studies). To attend primary school, he walked eight kilometres to Mahalpur, which was a police headquarters and a town of a few thousand people on the main road to the district capital of Hoshiarpur. At school he did his lessons sitting on a grass mat under the open sky, after leaving his sandals outside the entrance to the walled school compound. He enjoyed school and never described the walk there as a hardship. Instead, he set off in the morning with distinction, wearing a shirt and shorts made of homespun cotton *(khadi),* but most importantly a coloured turban, not a *keski,* the simple head-covering worn by boys, but a complete turban, with the colour – pink, blue, yellow, or purple – denoting his grade at school. He always remembered with pleasure the morning and afternoon walk through the countryside, passing through a shady mango orchard at one point and a small bit of jungle or wooded area at another. On the way to Mahalpur, he was steadily angling closer to the Shivalik Hills and to the wooded gullies of the streams flowing out of the Shivaliks, which were conduits for wildlife. There he saw deer, rabbits, and quail, and from time to time, wolves or jackals, which sparked a lifelong identification with nature.

In the orchard that he passed through twice a day was a spiritual teacher, a guru, with a company of his devotees. Kapoor regularly paid his respects to the guru, performing an obeisance, a *mattha tekda,* getting down on his hands and knees and pressing his forehead to the ground. This regular encounter was significant for Kapoor because it was full of promise. The guru took an interest in the boy and on one occasion read the soles of his feet. "You have a *padam* here," he exclaimed – a lotus. "Either you will be a raja or a fakir" – a ruler or a mystic.

He was ten years old and in the fifth grade when he had a passionately nationalistic teacher who told his students they should go to America and make lots of money so they could come back and free India. A year later Kapoor elected to study English, a prerequisite for a career in the British Indian civil service, which seemed to be the best option for a boy like himself. Like many educated Punjabis of his generation, he was learning to write beautifully in three languages, the Gurmukhi script of Punjabi, Urdu, and English; and he maintained his fluency in all three for the rest of his life.[6] As it turned out, his ability to speak English also helped him to go to America. For high school, starting with grade nine, Kapoor went to Bajwara, which was near the district capital of Hoshiarpur. It was too far away to walk from Kharoudi, but by then his aunt Nikko was looking after him, and he could stay in her village. His mother had died and his father did not live long enough to see him graduate from high school.

After high school, Kapoor attended a business college in Kolkata for training in shorthand and bookkeeping.[7] Given his family's meagre income, he would not have expected support from his father – had he lived – and did not expect it from his older brother, Bhagwan; but he was helped by his future father-in-law, Hakim Singh Sandhu, who sent him spending money. Hakim Singh, being a good Punjabi father, looked after the boy his daughter was engaged to marry. Soon after she reached age fifteen and Kapoor was twenty, they were married in Aur.[8] She remained there with her family while he pursued his studies eighteen hundred kilometres away in an urban environment that was very different from rural Punjab. He was in Kolkata during an intense period of protest against British rule by the local Bengalis and by Bengali students in particular. If that was an important part of his Kolkata experience, he did not speak about it in later years. What he did talk about were two young English ladies who took a great interest in him and spent time with him reading English literature and poetry.

Punjabis have a strong sense of marriage as an alliance of families, not just of husband and wife. This sense helped Kapoor and Besant Kaur maintain a bond while separated. Even before they married, their two families were turning to each other. When Sham Singh Sidhu was dying, it was Hakim Singh Sandhu's son, the doctor, who attended him. And after her marriage, Besant Kaur made a regular practice of riding to Kharoudi, with a family retainer holding the horse's bridle and walking alongside, to visit the women of Kapoor's extended family. She was a great favourite because she was the only literate woman among them and a storyteller. When she arrived, they hurried to finish their chores and gather in the courtyard to listen to her tales from the Ramayana and the Mahabharata and her stories of Guru Nanak.

In a natural and spontaneous way, she kept up her connection with her husband's family during his long absence. He must have appreciated it. In an interview he gave for a Canadian paper in 1953, Kapoor said, "The harsh Canadian immigration restriction that kept us apart for 16 years might have wrecked other marriages, but not ours."[9] When they finally got together, their marriage worked because they were wonderfully compatible, but in the years of separation, her efforts to visit his people made a difference, and their social and cultural environment helped to preserve their bond even when they were on opposite sides of the world.

3
Emigrant *Jatha*s

When Kapoor was growing up, emigration was the great dream of ambitious and adventurous young men in his district. Every village around had men who had been abroad or families whose men were still employed in some distant place – Malaya, Singapore, Hong Kong, or Shanghai, and in recent years, Australia. Many emigrants had returned to their families after a few years away and lived out their lives in their home villages. Some continued to shuttle between their Punjabi home and one they had adopted overseas. Others never returned, but their collective story motivated young men, if they were free to leave and had the means to travel. Getting permission to go was not automatic; in patriarchal families, the elders ruled and the needs of the family came first. And the farther abroad a young man proposed to go, the more it cost, and raising and spending that money was generally a matter decided by elders.

The situation was a little different for Kapoor, whose education set him apart from other villagers and made him more independent than most. When he left for North America, he turned for help not to his elders but to his teenage wife, who was still living with her family and who – unquestionably – would not be going with him. This was in 1906, the year Kapoor joined a gang of men – a *jatha* – from the Mahalpur area, one of a number of such gangs that set out on foot for the nearest railway station to take the train to Kolkata. He went with these men because they wanted him, but it was his young wife who made it possible.

Kapoor had worked a short time in Kolkata as a clerk for an Englishman whom he met while he was attending business college. From the good accounts he later gave of this man, he must have enjoyed his employment, but he stayed with him for only eighteen or twenty days. He decided to leave after listening to an enterprising young man from his home area, Piara Singh Langeri, from the village of Langeri near Mahalpur. Piara Singh was a natural leader and organizer for twenty would-be emigrants from neighbouring villages who wanted to go to America to make money. He was slightly older than Kapoor, a good athlete and an army veteran, but he was literate only in Punjabi, and none of his group spoke English. So he made a special trip from Punjab to Kolkata to ask Kapoor to come with them to America, knowing him only by reputation. Kapoor initially refused, saying he had been a student all his life and could not do manual labour, which was the kind of work they would get in the US. Piara's response was that if Kapoor acted as their interpreter, the others would do the heavy work and pass on a portion of their wages to him.[1] This was how Punjabi-speaking villagers figured they could manage in North America without having any English themselves.

North America was a new destination for men from the Mahalpur area, and for Punjabis generally, although generations of them had been going abroad as soldiers, tradesmen, entrepreneurs, and labourers. Besant Kaur's own uncle, her father's younger brother, Atma Singh Sandhu, was a great traveller who found his way to Malaya, Australia, and ultimately to Argentina. Of course, he had education and medical skills as a unani doctor, dentist, and surgeon. In Malaya he treated a member of a sultan's family and received two solid gold trays as a reward. In Australia in the 1890s, he encountered a small immigrant community of his own people. That had its disadvantages. Besant Kaur's father heard a rumour that Atma had shaved his beard and cut his hair. He was so disturbed that he took a steamship out to Australia to see if it were true, only to discover that it was not. He had returned from Australia long before Kapoor ever thought of going to North America.

Until 1900 North America lay largely beyond the ambitions of Punjabi villagers. Four turbaned Sikhs landing in San Francisco in April 1899 were enough of a curiosity to be worth a short article in the *San Francisco Chronicle,* which described them as "the most picturesque group" seen in a long time.[2] They had come via China, where they had spent twenty years in the police and the army. After that, other Sikhs arrived in California, a handful at a time over the next few years, mostly men who had served under the British in Shanghai or Hong Kong. In early 1904, Vancouver papers began reporting arrivals of five or ten Punjabis at a time, and then the numbers crept up. As these men succeeded in finding work, the news percolated back to Punjab, but Piara Singh Langeri and many others in 1906 and 1907 seem to have been stimulated by Canadian Pacific Steamship Company (CPS) circulars and notices in the Punjabi language, distributed by steamship agents in Kolkata and posted in Punjab on village walls or at police stations such as the one at Mahalpur. These notices were addressed directly to Punjabi men who wanted to come to Vancouver, and they spelled out the route, the fares, the cost of food along the way, the medical procedures, and the amount of money they must bring to satisfy the Canadian immigration officials. The Canadian Pacific Steamship Company saw a future business in carrying Punjabis to Canada and was seeking to encourage it.[3]

Kapoor might have encountered one of these notices in a Kolkata post office. An imagined scene of Kapoor in Kolkata looking at a CPS poster was incorporated into a CBC Radio play based on his history and produced in 1941.[4] But he told his daughters that until Piara Singh recruited him, he had not thought of emigrating. When he did agree to go, he wrote to his younger brother, Tara, who was just seventeen and living in Kharoudi, telling him to come along. He mailed this letter and took the train from Kolkata to Punjab. This was in the midsummer of 1906. His first destination was his in-laws' qila in Aur, where he talked to Besant Kaur. Taking her with him would have made little sense, and at the age of sixteen, she did not want to go; but he needed money and she gave him some of her chunky gold jewellery to sell to pay for his ticket and expenses. Throughout her life, Besant Kaur showed little interest in jewellery, and her daughters never saw her wearing any. But as a traditional Punjabi bride, she had worn heavy gold ornaments for her wedding ceremony – rings, bangles, a nose piece, pendants, necklaces, anklets – that were to be her *stridhan* (woman's wealth) to keep for herself in marriage. On a jeweller's scales her gold jewellery would have weighed two and a half or three pounds, and she reached into this treasure for her wandering husband so he could embark on his great adventure.

While Kapoor was in Aur, his younger brother, Tara, took a train to Kolkata, expecting to join him there. As a result the two missed each other, and a long time passed before they discovered what had happened to each other. Tara has told of some of his adventure, and other parts can be pieced together. His account, which is fuller than Kapoor's, enriches Kapoor's own story.[5] Tara had borrowed the money required to emigrate to Canada. For that, he had to approach his oldest brother, Bhagwan, who arranged the loan from a village moneylender. He had also picked up ten or fifteen travel companions from the Mahalpur area, and so he set off with his own jatha. This came about as a consequence of his inability to read. When he asked an educated person to read Kapoor's letter to him, its contents became public, and many people in the Mahalpur area learned that a group was going to Canada, that the trip cost about three hundred rupees, and that one could earn seven rupees a day in Canada. To understand what that meant, one need simply reflect that a sepoy in the Indian army then earned nine rupees a month. Several young men from Kharoudi and nearby villages said "Let's go." When they started off, they gathered at 3:00 or 4:00 in the morning at the Mahalpur police station, where they had already picked up their clearance papers. Like peasants in empires through the ages, they were closely controlled by their rulers and needed official permission to travel. From Mahalpur they walked for several hours to Hoshiarpur city in time for the morning opening of the *kacheri* (court) in the deputy commissioner's office. There they had to get approval for travel overseas. From Hoshiarpur they walked a day and a half to the nearest railway station at Jalandhar. There they went into the passport office for their "British Indian/Indian Empire" passports before catching a third-class carriage on a train that took at least two days to reach Howrah station in Kolkata.[6] All along, they imagined that they would be joining Kapoor's group before it sailed.

In Kolkata they discovered that Kapoor had gone back to Punjab. They did not know why exactly – perhaps a holiday or a visit. Some favoured returning home, but others wished to carry on, saying they had come this far and were not going back. It was a point of pride not to turn around before reaching Hong Kong, which was at least halfway. What would they say to people at home if they abandoned their great adventure so quickly? Young Tara was borne along by a sense of group solidarity and pride. If some went, all should go. That was the core of the discussion. The voyage to Hong Kong was rough, as many other Punjabis were to find over the years. Tara and his companions were aboard what he called a small ship, and he remembered that it took fifteen or sixteen days to reach Hong Kong, which suggests that it went there directly, without lengthy stops at ports such as Rangoon and Singapore.[7] Travelling in unfurnished steerage, they slept on cotton bedding rolls spread on the surface of the deck, which was frequently wet because the ship rolled heavily and took on water.

From the Hong Kong harbour, they walked a dozen blocks to Queen's Road East, where they found the Sikh gurdwara (temple), which had been built by Hong Kong Sikhs five years earlier. They stayed in the gurdwara dormitories and cooked and ate their meals, as many Sikh travellers have done since. They had arrived after dark, so Tara's first amazed view of a harbour choked with sampans was on the next morning. They remained in Hong Kong for about a week before catching a steamship for Vancouver. Their previous ship had been Japanese. This one, he said, was run by *gore log* (white people). In fact it was a Canadian Pacific steamship, the coal-burning *Empress of Japan,* in its sixteenth year of service and already dwarfed by newer passenger ships. Even so, the *Empress of Japan* carried 93 first- and second-class cabin passengers, mostly European, and 394 in steerage – mostly Chinese.[8] Tara paid about 150 rupees (thirty dollars) to go steerage. With him were 103 Punjabis – nearly all Sikhs – many of whom had started their journey at Hong Kong or Singapore. The steerage deck had bunks but in an open plan without compartments. The twenty- or twenty-five-day Pacific crossing was a long time for boisterous young men in close quarters, and Tara said there were fights between his people and other Punjabis. He said his cousin from Kharoudi, Natha Singh, was especially quarrelsome and got into several fights. But many on board were in no mood for this, because they were seasick. The price of their ticket included meals, but many did not make it to the dining area and regularly sent others to bring food back for them.

Some of the men knew what to expect in Canada, and as the *Empress* approached Vancouver in October 1906, they warned Tara to say he was eighteen – adding a year to his age. He was the youngest of them, except for one other boy. When the ship tied up next to downtown Vancouver at the Canadian Pacific wharf at 2:00 p.m. on a Monday afternoon, all 103 of the "Hindoos" (as they were called in the Canadian newspapers) were put into quarantine in the wood-frame immigrant detention hospital at dockside. It had regular accommodation for about fifty but overflow space in the attic.[9] The doctor reported that twelve of the Punjabis had trachoma, an infection of the eye. And he said that a few had fever, which he imputed to "sudden climatic change." But most were perfectly healthy and being kept in detention until jobs could be found for them outside the city. According to the daily newspapers, all but sixteen were "liberated" by Friday and taken to adjoining municipalities to clear land for building lots or far into the Interior to work on a railway.[10] In Tara's memory, the stay in the detention hospital lasted for about a week before he and his companions were released and relieved of five dollars each (twenty-five rupees) for the food they had received while confined. The hospital was like a jail, he said. They were given food but told to cook it themselves, and much of it was of no use to them; they did not eat the meat and they rejected the biscuits because they feared they contained cow fat. Sometimes, looking out the hospital windows, they would spot a countryman and shout "Is there anyone from our village there?" But when they got out, they found very few apnai – very few of their own people.

Of the 103 from the *Empress of Japan,* Tara said, "some went here and some went there," but his companions from Mahalpur stuck together. Lacking English, he would have had little sense of the stir his arrival caused in BC, where a strong lobby against the Chinese and Japanese already existed. Immigration from India had started slowly. Before August 1906, months might pass without any new men coming. Then, thanks to the advertising of steamship agents in Punjab, hundreds of "Hindoos" began disembarking from Canadian Pacific steamships. Tara had come in the midst of this. There had been 250 on the *Empress of China* in August, 300 on the *Tartar* and 250 on the *Empress of India* in September, and then 120 on the *Athenian* at the beginning of October; a fortnight later, the *Empress of Japan* docked with Tara and his group. Finally, there was the big arrival of the year, the *Tartar* with 696. Long afterward, the Punjabi community in British Columbia spoke of that voyage as the "seven hundred ship," just as it called the *Monteagle* a year later the "nine hundred ship."[11]

When nearly seven hundred Punjabis disembarked from the *Tartar* a month after Tara arrived, most of them had nowhere to go for their first night: no accommodation, no dry place to sleep. They trooped into the city and camped where they could. On the second night the police found eighty men in a cove, lying on bare ground that was covered with hoar frost, trying to sleep under a black sky. Then began an immediate scramble by city authorities to improvise shelters – for which they charged the immigrants.[12] Conditions had been better for Tara and his companions when they had arrived in October. After they walked out of the detention hospital with their bedrolls over their shoulders, they found a rooming house run by a white woman and settled in there. Some of them knew English and asked around for work, and everyone who managed to earn something bought provisions and shared with the rest. Young Tara and a couple of others were sent to cut firewood for a white man and his family on the outskirts of the city, where there were few houses.

This was Tara's introduction to working for hire. It did not go well: he was in a strange country, he was scarcely more than a boy, and he was being asked to do servants' work. In his mind, the white man was thinking dismissively, "Poor people have come; they can cut wood." When the wife of the house brought out milk and bread, Tara and his companions, although hungry, did not know what to do, because the bread might contain cow fat. With the children of the household, there was an interplay that began with strangeness and ended with horsing around. The children laughed at the Sikhs with their turbans. One of Tara's well-muscled companions, Ganga Singh, discovered that he could scare the children into the house by snapping his fingers. But soon, overcome by curiosity, they would creep out again. This interaction progressed into general play for most of the day. The woodpile was forgotten. At the end of the afternoon, one of the parents gave the young Sikhs a note. Tara and his companions were pleased until they took it back to their rooming house and showed it to Asa Singh from Kharoudi, who could read English. "You didn't work," he said. "There is no work for tomorrow."[13]

The fall and winter were tough times to look for employment in British Columbia. Some men from Tara's ship had been dispatched six hundred kilometres to Revelstoke as labourers for the Canadian Pacific Railway, only to encounter snow and head back for Vancouver within days. The arrival two weeks later of seven hundred Punjabis on the *Monteagle* did not improve matters. Tara and his companions were scrambling from job to job, sometimes at one place and sometimes at another, and the seven rupees a day that they'd hoped to earn were not materializing. Through their compatriot network, they heard that America offered lots of railway work, so around the end of the year or early in 1907, they crossed to Victoria by the twice daily ferry service and took a Pacific Coast Steamship boat from Victoria to San Francisco. The fare, Tara remembered, was $12.50 each. In San Francisco they went straight to an employment office, and from there they were sent three hundred kilometres – presumably by rail – passing through Sacramento, California, and going into the Sierra Nevada Mountains to work on the Southern Pacific Railway, repairing the main line by replacing and resetting rails. A photograph taken on the Southern Pacific about that time shows twenty-eight bearded and turbaned Sikhs organized for a group picture and standing above the tracks on the steep slope of a railway cutting, with pickaxes and shovels in their hands. This had become Tara's world.

Tara's group initially consisted of only ten or fifteen men, but other Sikhs joined and it expanded. There was a major surprise for Tara in the collection of Sikhs who joined his group, for Kapoor was among them. Tara and his companions were camping in tents supplied by the contractor alongside the railway, doing their own washing and cooking. Their white bosses told them to erect more tents because more of their own people were coming, some apnai men as Tara put it. This was an unwelcome development because the newcomers might compete for their jobs. When the new men arrived, it was raining, and Tara was sitting in his tent. Some of the new men poked their heads through the flaps, and introductions began with the question that one Punjabi asks another: "Where are you from?" Tara asked this of Kapoor without recognizing him. The two had matured in appearance, with Kapoor now fully bearded and Tara looking like a man. They had not seen each other for a long time and had not lived together for years. Asa Singh from Kharoudi had to tell Tara "That is your brother."[14]

Kapoor and his group had left Kolkata a few weeks behind Tara. From Hong Kong they had taken third-class steerage to San Francisco, probably on a Japanese steamship service operating via Yokohama.[15] The voyage lasted a month, which was longer than the crossing to Vancouver, but they had chosen the first ship available rather than waiting for one to Canada. When they reached San Francisco in November, they looked for work there, and like Tara and his group were directed inland, initially to the Western Pacific Railway's right of way in the mountains beyond the Sacramento Valley town of Oroville. Kapoor walked sixty-five kilometres to the site to get the job for his companions and then brought them in on three horse-drawn wagons supplied by the contractor – a team of horses per wagon.[16] At this point they were about a hundred kilometres on a straight line from Tara and his gang, but with no notion that they were in the same country. Kapoor continued scouting for other work and found it on the rival Southern Pacific Railway. When he and his gang quit their jobs, the contractor refused to let them use his wagons, so they walked to Oroville. From there they made their way south until they reached the point where the main line of the Western Pacific intersected with the Southern. All this adventure was behind them when they appeared at Tara's encampment.

The brothers were together in California for the next five years, constantly moving from job to job, with Kapoor finding the employment and acting as interpreter, foreman, and timekeeper. He was not expected to do physical work, but he did that as well. His function has been described in a massive American congressional inquiry into immigration conducted at the time. South Asians, although not numerous, were among the multitude of immigrant workers that the inquiry's researchers investigated. These researchers noted that South Asians went about as gangs looking for work and had headmen to deal with employers but that their gangs were less organized than, for example, those of the Japanese or Chinese: their members were much more individualistic, and their headmen did not take commissions from them, as did happen with the Japanese. As a foreman, Kapoor got more than the others: he told a journalist many years later that he received $2.00 a day instead of the $1.75 that the others were paid.[17] At that rate he could save $50.00 a month. The challenge was to stay continuously employed and save $600.00 in a year.

The Southern Pacific job lasted a few months. Then the whole gang tied up its bedrolls and headed for Marysville, where a branch line of the Southern Pacific and the main line of the Western Pacific crossed. This was to be the gang's main centre as long as it was in California. Tara and some of his companions ended up in jail the first night in Marysville when they camped on open ground and lit a cooking fire. The police arrived immediately, held them till morning, and released them after fining them five dollars each. Kapoor continued hunting for work, and as other Punjabis turned up, the number in his gang rose to a peak of 150. He found Tara jobs on railways, on ranches, and in a lumber mill.

After the completion of the Western Pacific main line in November 1909, however, work became scarcer. One reads about it in official reports and correspondence, which begin to mention a movement of South Asians back into Canada. Officials on both sides of the border attributed this not just to the loss of railway jobs, but to the hostility of white workers in California, Oregon, and Washington. This made employers increasingly unwilling to hire South Asians. On top of this, Tara had an accident at a mill where he was stacking lumber, severely injuring his back. Part of his recuperation, under Kapoor's direction, was a diet of chicken soup stewed in the fresh air of their camp, nourishment that Tara remembered into his old age. As work petered out in 1912, a day here and a day there, Kapoor decided that there was no point in two of them using up their savings, so he sent Tara back to Punjab. According to Tara, this was Kapoor's decision, and the brothers were not reunited for another fourteen years.

Between them, the brothers tell the story of early Punjabi immigration to North America. A majority of the pioneers went home within a decade, and in that sense, Tara was typical. But those who stayed, like Kapoor, put down roots that ensured a permanent Punjabi presence in Canada and the United States. Kapoor's family network bridged the globe, linking as it did Kapoor in North America with his relations in India – Tara, brother Bhagwan, and all their relatives, as well as Besant Kaur and her kin. The North American connection was hugely important to the family in India, and family ties stayed strong despite distance and passing time. This was common among Punjabi families like Kapoor's, whose members were oceans apart and yet bound by the loyalties and expectations of kinship and marriage.

4
Settling in Canada

The British Empire cast a shadow everywhere that Kapoor and his emigrant compatriots went. Whether they wished the British gone from India or were willing to accept the fact of their presence, they could not ignore it. And when they travelled outside India, the lines of commerce and travel they followed, the ports and colonies that served as stepping stones to their destinations, were generally within the empire. If not, they were diplomatically tied to it. Even when they reached the United States, the empire still echoed in their lives because, far from home, they began to talk about British rule in India with new intensity, and they differed among themselves about the solution: whether it should consist of patient waiting or armed action. Being abroad with other young men from home – free to read, publish, lecture, discuss, and plan far from the censorship of their village elders, their families, and the Indian police – was a powerful political experience. Their closest friends abroad were young men from their home localities, those who had gone ahead of them, travelled with them, or arrived later. But their closest friends were also people with whom they could agree on the great political question of their day – independence and how to get it. As they moved from here to there, looking for work, they depended on people of common background and common thinking. The individuals who made up Kapoor's social network were a varied group with diverse experiences, but most came from his part of Punjab and shared his moderate political views.

During their early years in North America, Tara and Kapoor were great adventurers – like all Punjabi emigrants of that era. Setting off for San

Francisco from Victoria had been a small move for Tara after he had already come halfway around the world. His willingness to travel was a common trait among his companions. What they were looking for was opportunity. If they were disappointed in one place, they listened readily to stories of another. They trusted what they heard from people they knew. What they wanted was to see for themselves. They also followed great individualists, those who explored ambitiously on their own. Kapoor's own questing took him far into northern Ontario to a place that few Canadian visited then or now. He did not stay, but he showed that all of North America lay within his range and that of others like himself.

In time Kapoor put down roots in British Columbia, choosing the Pacific West over the country east of the Rockies like the great majority of fellow Punjabi pioneers, who saw the Rockies as a greater barrier than the Canada-US border. Most of these pioneers had landed at Vancouver and Victoria during an eighteen-month period between the summer of 1906 and late autumn 1907.[1] Like Tara, a majority had quickly decamped for more rewarding prospects in the US. The groups that went ahead of Tara kept pushing south, finding railway work in Washington and then in Oregon and California. And in California they discovered farm work that paid almost as well as the railways. Tara and Kapoor arrived in Marysville in the Sacramento Valley about the time that Punjabis were first being hired there as fruit pickers, and within a year some were working much farther south on sugar beet farms and orange groves in the Imperial and San Joachim Valleys.[2] Then, after that rapid dispersal from Vancouver Island to the San Joachim Valley, Punjabi pioneers settled into farming in California and the lumber industry in British Columbia. Very few ventured further after that; but it was not because they lacked the spirit of adventure."

When Kapoor went to Ontario in 1914, his short-term employer and exceptionally interested friend William H. Moore urged him to stay because South Asians received fair treatment there, at least in the law. They had been stripped of full citizenship in BC, but BC was the province in Canada where they were choosing to live. In California they faced a vociferous anti-Asian lobby and found themselves excluded from citizenship and landownership, yet the largest number chose California in which to settle. How do we explain this? First, Punjabi pioneers depended on each other to make their way, so they stuck together. If more had been allowed to land in Canada or the United States, moving into other industries and spreading out geographically would have been easier. But BC and California were particularly attractive frontier environments. They were new and rapidly growing economies, with wide-open opportunities that Punjabi pioneers were ready to seize.

Communication was the key to knowing where the best prospects lay. By letter, telegram, and word of mouth, friends, relatives, and fellow villagers kept in touch. During the First World War, the Canadian immigration department used the government's wartime powers to intercept telegrams sent by Punjabis and other South Asians in Canada. The department was looking for evidence of anti-British activity, but it found none in the telegrams it intercepted, which were all about work and jobs: "Come to Wardner quick. Have job for you and Jagat Singh," or "Send four more men," or "Yourself and Dhampol come quick. Mill starts Monday." For three years the department filed away telegrams like this, but all it had uncovered – with this evidence – was a job-finding network among Punjabi pioneers in British Columbia.[3]

From the beginning, the Punjabi network extended from BC to California. Kapoor was plugged into the BC scene long before he arrived there. An important connection for him at that time was the Sikh missionary and community worker Prof. Teja Singh, or as he was known later in his life, Sant (Saint) Teja Singh. He and his five-man missionary jatha visited Marysville in May 1909 as part of a tour of Punjabi worker communities on the Pacific Coast. Kapoor was one of the people whom he involved in his projects.[4]

Prof. Teja Singh had arrived on the east coast of North America as a student, and Vancouver Sikhs had invited him to the coast after seeing a newspaper article about two lectures on Sikhism that he had given at Columbia University in the summer of 1908. Punjabi-speaking labourers on the coast would never have seen that story had it not been for an educated Bengali activist, Taraknath Das, who was then living in Seattle. Das told his Sikh friends about Teja Singh, and they wrote to him because they were looking for an organizer who could help them petition the Canadian government for fair treatment, especially with immigration.

Teja Singh was admirably qualified for this. He had a law degree and a master's degree from Government College Lahore; he had briefly practised law in Lahore; he had served in the British India civil service as a revenue officer in the Northern Indian Salt Department; and in his late twenties, he had been the vice-principal and then the acting principal of the most important English-language educational institution for Sikhs in Punjab, Khalsa College in Amritsar. He had gone abroad for higher education and had enrolled in a teacher-training program at Columbia. Before that, he had spent five terms at Cambridge in the United Kingdom.

He had also been granted admission to Harvard, which he was deferring for the time being, but which he eventually accepted. This was his history up to the age of thirty-two.

Teja Singh had another dimension that served him well in North America. He had a number of loyal white friends and followers, people attracted to Eastern religions, some of them through Theosophy, the thirty-year-old esoteric science of the Russian-born spiritualist Madame Helena Blavatsky. He collected some white followers in New York, and others gravitated to him in Vancouver, treating him as a guru and inviting him to their homes for intimate philosophical talks. He seems to have impressed them with his superb English, his clarity and erudition, and his intense earnestness conveyed with an unsmiling but animated expression. Singh's own spiritual journey had begun in his twenties while he was vice-principal of Khalsa College. Previously, he had been unreligious and even agnostic. His own family belonged to a clean-shaven non-Khalsa Sikh tradition, although he was raised as *keshdhari* (keeping uncut hair). While in Amritsar he had found a spiritual mentor, a Sikh sant, or holy man, who had initiated him as a Khalsa Sikh wearing the Sikh symbols – the five K's (*kes, kanga, kara, kirpan,* and *kachh,* or uncut hair, comb, bangle, dagger or sword, and soldier's undershorts). This sant had sent him abroad for higher education and to serve as a Sikh missionary to Sikhs abroad. The sant had given him 125 rupees to help pay his passage as well as a set of instructions: to keep his Khalsa form, to live a spiritual life, to found Sikh gurdwaras, and not to waste time on unreceptive audiences.[5]

One of Teja Singh's white followers was a middle-aged and distinguished-looking English American mining promoter named T.C. Crawford, whose business ventures took him from California to Alaska to London. Crawford lived in Pasadena, California, but travelled incessantly. He met Teja Singh in London and saw him in New York, where he joined him so devotedly for daily Sikh prayer and meditation that Singh renamed him Himmat Das – "courage" and "servant (of God)." Crawford owned a gold mine in Jacksonville, California, an investment that was going sour. He persuaded Teja Singh to back it, displaying a surprisingly adept understanding of the power of gestures in Punjabi culture. In his plea for financial help, he placed his cap at Teja Singh's feet, an act of humility and self-abasement that did the trick.

Crawford was counting on Teja Singh's ability to raise money among his countrymen even if Singh himself had no money. This was the genesis of the Guru Nanak Mining and Trust Company, created by Teja Singh in Vancouver in December 1908 as an investment vehicle for Sikh immigrants. From men earning $1.50 or $2.00 a day, he raised $50,000.00. The main asset he bought on their behalf was a quarter of a million shares of Crawford's mine, although he also purchased a 152-acre prime waterfront property on the north shore of Burrard Inlet, across from Vancouver, and he bought other assets as well. He set up the Guru Nanak Mining and Trust Company as a registered British Columbia company and then secured investments from Punjabi immigrants up and down the Pacific Coast. He went down to Jacksonville to see Crawford's mine, and on the same trip in May 1909, he went to Marysville. About this time he recruited Kapoor as a company director representing Sikh investors from California. Along with Piara Singh Langeri and others, Kapoor had been raising money among the California emigrants for village schools in Punjab and a high school in the city of Jalandhar. They were the kind of people the Guru Nanak Mining and Trust Company needed.[6]

Teja Singh had no money of his own to invest and no personal profit to make. His aim was to create an investment vehicle for Punjabi immigrants that they controlled. He was able to set it up quickly because, in his early days on the West Coast, he was esteemed and revered by all. The Sikh and Punjabi community stood in awe of him, as a man of education and profound spirituality, and it readily followed his lead and advice. But bitter critics soon emerged. Even a spiritual leader could not escape complaint and censure when money was involved and when some people in the community believed that their investment had been mishandled or even misappropriated. Teja Singh was never more than a visiting presence in British Columbia. He set a great deal in motion within a few weeks, but his base was in New York and then Cambridge, Massachusetts, where he was a student, and he finally left for India in 1913, a year and a half after completing his master's degree at Harvard. Kapoor could not have spent much time with him, but the loyalties and differences that he inspired and provoked did affect Kapoor's last years in California and his first years in Canada.

In 1910 Kapoor tried three times to get to Vancouver on Guru Nanak Mining and Trust Company business, and each time Canadian immigration officials refused him entry.[7] His association with Teja Singh did not help. Among Indian activists, Teja Singh was a moderate; in fact he had ties to the conservative Sikh elite in Punjab, which was both strongly Sikh and unmistakably dependent on the British rulers. He accepted the British presence in India, but he called on Britain to give Indians a large measure of self-government. That call was enough to put him in the bad books of pro-empire officers in the Canadian immigration department. Teja Singh had said publicly in Vancouver that Britain needed to concede home rule in India to avert armed uprising. He was not advocating violence, simply warning that it would come if Britain failed to honour its professed standards of justice and democracy. Officials in the immigration department saw no difference between warning of violence and promoting it. They viewed Teja Singh as a dangerous person but let him come and go from Canada because he had a white and South Asian following capable of generating a large fuss. Kapoor, who was less prominent, got no concessions.

Kapoor finally moved to Canada in 1912, but only after two attempts to do so. He had sent his brother, Tara, back to India after work dried up in California, and then he had attempted to enter BC at the Blaine border (south of Vancouver), only to be refused. When he returned to California, other Punjabis advised him to use a borrowed alias and identity. Many had done it, including his friend Piara Singh Langeri, who had originally talked him into leaving India and to whom he had grown so close in California that they had declared themselves *dharam* brothers – brothers in spirit. Piara Singh was now in Victoria, living under the name of Karam Singh. He had come to Canada to be managing director of the Guru Nanak Mining and Trust Company, and he encouraged Kapoor to follow, describing Canada as a beautiful country with wonderful mountains. Kapoor, however, was determined to enter under his own name or not at all. He probably understood that Canadian immigration officers had a lot of personal discretion regarding who got in. Much depended on the judgment of an individual officer, on the attitude of the immigration office within which an officer worked, or on the information he had at hand. The Vancouver immigration office, which was responsible for the Blaine border crossing, had blacklisted Kapoor. Victoria had not, and in the Christmas season of 1912, he landed there without difficulty.

The small provincial capital of Victoria on Vancouver Island was Kapoor's home for the next year and a half. He had savings from his five years in California, and he made a number of investments in British Columbia. With separate cheques for a total of $750.80, made out to two Punjabis named Laboo and Lall Singh, he bought a dairy operation on rented land with a small herd of cows, a barn, hay, and a pony and a mare for transportation.[8] He also bought real estate in Victoria and Vancouver, and had money invested in the Guru Nanak Mining and Trust Company. His dairy operation records for two months show that he cleared about eighty or ninety dollars a month, which means he was making more than an ordinary lumber worker's income on this business alone. A single milk contractor took most of the milk, but Kapoor also sold to a few individuals and houses, customers he recorded idiosyncratically as "red house," "white house," "old lady," "some white man," and in a mix of Punjabi and English, "*ronewali* lady" (crying lady). The crying lady appears once in the accounts, paying $1.75 for milk on 1 September 1913.[9]

In Victoria, Kapoor's circle included his dharam brother, Piara Singh Langeri, as well as Kartar Singh Hundal and Dr. Sundar Singh, all committed activists but moderates in comparison with some of their contemporaries. Kartar was zealously labouring as a journalist in a low-roofed one-story frame cottage at 630 Speed Avenue in Victoria, just off the main road leading into the centre of the city. From there he was managing the production of a quarterly newspaper in Punjabi and English that he and Dr. Sundar Singh advertised as "The Only Hindustani Paper in Canada." It was called *Sansar,* or the "World." The first few issues of *Sansar,* in 1912, were handwritten in Punjabi and run off on a cyclostyle duplicating machine, but by 1913 the paper had a press with Punjabi type imported from England (which had to be set by hand). Sundar and Kartar had collected money in the South Asian community among Sikhs, Hindus, and Muslims, and were producing a secular paper. Sundar wrote the English copy and clipped relevant stories in English from mainstream Canadian papers. Kartar wrote the Punjabi copy with help from Piara Singh Langeri. When Kapoor settled in Victoria, he joined the effort.[10]

This group brought together four men of different personalities and experience who shared a common goal – to persuade the British and the Canadians to honour the promise made by Queen Victoria to the people of India a half century earlier – to be equally dutiful to all her subjects. As a reminder, they ran Victoria's promise on the masthead of their English-language monthly, the *Aryan,* which they had started before *Sansar.* Of the four men, Piara Singh was the most pious and best versed in Sikh scriptures. In respect for his religiousness, his Punjabi companions called him Bhai, or Brother. His 1953 memoir claims that he was once a *sharabi* (heavy drinking) and quarrelsome person who changed as an emigrant in a foreign land after reading an inspirational novel by the Punjabi writer Bhai Vir Singh and a history of the Sikh Khalsa, *Tavarikh Khalsa*. Becoming both religious and political, he took an oath to devote his time to his *quom,* or community. In California, when Kapoor and his gang returned to camp at the end of a ten-hour day, and after they had cooked and eaten their rotis, Bhai Piara Singh Langeri was one of two men among them who recited the evening prayer, *kirtan sohila.* He did it every evening while the others sat cross-legged and listened.[11]

He later found his way to Victoria, arriving there before the Sikhs finished building its red brick gurdwara – the third gurdwara erected in British Columbia and in Canada. When it opened in October 1912, he became the first priest, occupying the small house provided behind the gurdwara.[12] The location, at 1210 Topaz Avenue, was a brisk twenty-minute walk uphill from Kartar Singh Hundal's printing establishment on Speed Avenue. The gurdwara was a place of worship, but it was also a forum for Piara Singh and his friends, and what they said at special meetings there, they reported in *Sansar,* which they distributed as widely as they could. Even though Bhai Piara Singh could not read English, he knew enough about St. Paul to make a political point – that St. Paul could travel freely in all parts of the Roman Empire, whereas British subjects could not do the same in the British Empire. He was addressing Punjabis in the Victoria gurdwara, but what he said appeared in *Sansar,* translated into English for an English-speaking audience.[13]

Kartar Singh Hundal, also known among Punjabis by his nickname Kainchi (scissors), was the member of this group who made the most remarkable entry into mainstream Canadian society. For Punjabis, his nickname signalled his anglicization. The name came about through a curious linguistic transformation as he accepted the English pronunciation of his first name and then as his Punjabi countrymen translated that back into their language. Kartar (KrTAR) had become Carter, which Punjabis heard as Cutter and turned into Scissors, or Kainchi. Like Kapoor and Bhai Piara Singh Langeri, he came from near the Shivalik Hills, from the town of Mahalpur, where Kapoor had gone to school. His mother was from Mahalpur. His father belonged to the village of Bandala Guru, near Amritsar. When his mother died, Kartar and his three younger brothers were shunted off to their maternal grandparents in Mahalpur.[14] So, though he was properly a son of the Amritsar District, his formative years were spent in Mahalpur. These separate affiliations were significant in rural Punjabi society.

In the 1960s, when Kartar Singh's nephew Talminder had just arrived in Vancouver, Kartar told him his own early story over apple pie and ice cream served with coffee at a cafeteria on Pender Street, near Kartar's office. This was exotic food for Talminder, but he liked it immediately. What follows is what he later remembered from these conversations with his uncle, supplemented by his own research. When Kartar Singh was eighteen, he matriculated from Khalsa College in Amritsar – where Prof.

Teja Singh was vice-principal and then principal. Students at Khalsa College got an excellent education in English while absorbing the conservative teachings of a Sikh revival movement. The college was closely tied to the British regime, and until that time, the principals had been British. After graduation Kartar Singh returned to Mahalpur to found a Khalsa elementary school, and after a couple of years, he decided to go to America, ostensibly to study agriculture at Cornell. His connection with Teja Singh soon brought him to Victoria.

American immigration officers on the Pacific Coast were turning away most South Asians, but it was easier for students to get in than for labourers, and easier through Atlantic ports. Kartar Singh took advantage of this. In the spring of 1911, with four or five other Sikhs from Mahalpur, he worked his passage on a coal freighter from Mumbai (Bombay) to Marseilles and then to New York. He told his nephew Talminder that he and his companions chanted the names of God – Satnam, Wahiguru – night and day for the entire passage. They worried about three cows tethered on the deck, food to be butchered for the crew, but despite their prayers the cows had been consumed by the time they docked in New York. The first thing they did in America after they got their pay was to prepare for travel by buying backpacks, cups, spoons, forks, soap, and towels – and shirts and pants because the clothes they brought from Mahalpur were eaten away by coal dust. From New York they made their way to California, arriving in Stockton, which had become a centre for Sikhs in the Sacramento Valley. There, at the home of the Stockton area's most successful Sikh farmer, Jawala Singh, Kartar met his former teacher Prof. Teja Singh, who had just finished his Harvard degree and was lingering in California, planning to return to India. He brought Kartar Singh to Victoria, found him a job in a local mill, and introduced him to Dr. Sundar Singh. At the age of twenty-two, under Dr. Sundar Singh's guidance, Kartar Singh began to learn the art of publication: writing, editing, printing, and distribution. It was to be a lifetime activity.[15]

Dr. Sundar Singh was a medical doctor who had trained at Glasgow Medical College in Scotland and then qualified before the medical licence board in London. He was a young man in 1911, only three years older than Kapoor and Piara Singh and seven years older than Kartar, yet he was living in retirement on Homer Street in Vancouver. This is what he told American immigration officers when he tried to cross the border in 1910.[16] The only business he then admitted to was real estate, not as a broker but buying and selling for himself. He claimed a net worth of about five thousand dollars. He said he had practised medicine in London and then spent two years as a ship's surgeon earning eight to ten pounds a month before giving it up because he did not like the sea. For someone so active in Canada over a five-year period, Dr. Sundar Singh's story is now surprisingly hard to trace. Part of the explanation is that he dropped out of the BC Sikh community in 1914 and never returned. But even when he was there, he was a mystery to many, including the Vancouver immigration department. Its inspector W.C. Hopkinson, an Anglo-Indian (mixed-race) who had served in the police in Punjab and in Kolkata and who spoke Hindi and some Punjabi, spent much of his time tracing the backgrounds of the main actors in the local South Asian community and figuring out what they were up to. When he became aware that Dr. Sundar Singh had settled in Vancouver, he asked his Punjabi informants about him, but they had little to report.

Hopkinson may have asked the wrong people. When Dr. Sundar Singh came to Canada in 1909, he made a bee-line for Vancouver as if he already knew people there. He landed in Halifax on 5 March on an Allan line steamer from Liverpool, crossed the continent to reach Vancouver by the middle of the month, and shortly afterward opened a bank account in the Fairview area, where most South Asians lived. He may have had some family connections in the Mahalpur area, although he himself was from Amritsar and had left a wife and child there – not an uncommon thing for a Punjabi man of the era to do. In any case, even after he disappeared from Vancouver, he stayed in touch with his Mahalpur friends, and fifteen years later, possibly in Toronto, he joined Piara and Kartar for a formal portrait of the three of them in a photography studio.

Sundar Singh maintained a beard and turban for two or three years in Canada. Then he began cropping the hair on his head and trimming and shaving his facial hair. He typically wore a hat, but on special occasions and for show he would wear a turban. He wore one at the opening ceremonies for the new Sikh gurdwara in Victoria, and he donned a conspicuous yellow turban as the only Sikh in a party of Toronto businessmen on a day's outing to a prison farm and an agricultural college in Guelph. He liked to be noticed. He impressed Canadians as singularly bright and articulate, although, some thought, a bit too keen for attention.[17] His experience – his time in Glasgow and London and on a British freighter running between Liverpool and Argentina – contributed to his confidence in conversing with Anglo-Canadians. This confidence helped him to make a remarkable splash on his first trip to the east.

For immigration officers in Vancouver, he was just another Sikh troublemaker. Upon learning that he was in the city, they wanted to deport him but held off after he was hospitalized with appendicitis in Vancouver and then sent to the Kamloops Sanatorium after a mistaken diagnosis of tuberculosis.[18] They must have doubted the strength of their deportation case, because he had been freely admitted by a Halifax immigration officer, who applied the same rules to him as to all other immigrants. When he was discharged from the sanatorium, the Vancouver immigration office decided to drop its deportation order, and he stayed in Canada. That left him free to go to Ottawa in November 1911 in a delegation of four: himself, Prof. Teja Singh, Louis W. Hall (a Presbyterian missionary from Victoria), and Rajah Singh, another educated Sikh who had served on a British hospital ship in China during the Boxer Rebellion.[19] They were lobbying the government to let South Asian pioneers bring their wives to Canada. This was the most emotive issue they could raise in trying to get Ottawa to soften its harsh immigration restrictions. They reached Ottawa by train on a Friday and saw the minister of the interior on the following Monday. They met him again that Wednesday along with BC members of parliament and officials. Two weeks later they saw him once more, but the net result was no concession, and when they returned to Vancouver, they had to admit that their mission had been a failure.

Sundar Singh stayed in the east longer than the others and attracted an amazing amount of attention. He was the featured speaker at the Canadian Club on 28 December 1911 and at the rival Empire Club of Canada on 25 January. At these clubs he addressed the elite of the city in forums that had national attention. A month later he spoke at the Labour Temple in Toronto, and that speech was also widely reported. He may not have convinced many of his point of view, but he got good coverage in the Ottawa, Montreal, and Toronto papers: "courteous and sympathetic" he called the reporting and the editorial comment that appeared in these papers.[20] And he found many friends and supporters in eastern Canada, particularly in Toronto, among Theosophists and in various Christian church groups, Quakers, Unitarians, and Presbyterians. At the same time and through some of the same people, he met leading businessmen and professionals in Toronto.[21] The connections that Dr. Sundar Singh made in Toronto over the Christmas season 1911-12 were the source of a long friendship that Kapoor later established with a Toronto businessman turned writer and lecturer, William H. Moore. And it was probably thanks to Moore that Kapoor later got to know the bitter cold of northern Ontario.

The city of Victoria had been Kapoor's introduction to Canada, and from the moment he arrived there, he defined himself by the company he kept. Nearly all of his friends and companions were from the Mahalpur area, but each brought a different quality. Piara Singh Langeri had been as close as a brother for five years, providing Kapoor with a constant example of devotion to the Sikh tradition. With Kapoor he shared a connection with Prof. Teja Singh, and that shaped their circle in Victoria. The link with Teja Singh drew them into partnership with Dr. Sundar Singh and Kartar Singh Hundal, and through this partnership they got to know a number of sympathetic Anglo-Canadians. In Victoria Kapoor had a Mahalpur social network plus a means of reaching out beyond it. And through his social network, he was able to pursue business interests (a dairy and real estate) while supporting causes he cared about deeply – Indian independence and fair play for Indian immigrants in Canada.

5
Trouble in British Columbia

Threats and violence that erupted in his own community not long after Kapoor arrived in British Columbia made his first stay a short one – only eighteen months. In a material sense, he did well in Victoria with property investments and small business ventures, but he found himself in the midst of people roiled up by militants who put the cause of India ahead of everything else and who spoke with menace of anyone who seemed to differ. When militants threatened his friends, Kapoor left with those who were closest to him. The community – moderates and militants – might have come together to fight Canada's race-based immigration policy. But, at a critical moment, Kapoor and his friends found themselves excluded from the struggle by their own compatriots. And at this moment, with their personal situations becoming more dangerous, they chose to remove themselves to eastern Canada.

When he first arrived in Victoria, Kapoor got involved through Piara Singh Langeri, Kartar Singh Hundal, and Dr. Sundar Singh with the short-lived English and Punjabi paper, *Sansar.* They sought to persuade rather than threaten; that was the politics of their paper. By helping with its English-language content, Kapoor was supporting a reasoned appeal to Canadian politicians and to the Canadian public – an appeal that the delegation to Ottawa had used and that Dr. Sundar Singh had delivered to the Canadian Club, the Empire Club, and the Labour Temple. It was the same appeal that Sundar Singh and Kartar Hundal voiced in the *Aryan,* and it was the main argument that their community would make over the next forty years.

They were asking Canadians for fairness and justice for Sikhs and spelling out their special merits – their status as British subjects, the sacrifices their fighting men had made for the empire, their loyalty to the British, the hard work they did in Canada, and the economic contribution they had already made. In the right setting, Kapoor's associate Dr. Sundar Singh could make a Canadian audience sit up and listen. At the Empire Club, when he said that men were being refused permission to bring their wives to Canada for no other reason than that they were Sikhs, his criticism sparked spontaneous applause.[1]

But applause was easier to get from a well-heeled Canadian audience in Toronto than on the streets of Vancouver. Too many British Columbians subscribed to the rhetoric of the anti-Asian campaigner H.H. (Harry) Stevens. A Conservative member of parliament for Vancouver who had been elected in 1911, he stood out as a dominating voice from BC, even in his freshman term. A lay preacher and small businessman, he was a man of the people, a successful self-made son of struggling British immigrant parents, and he spoke for a broad section of BC's white society. At twenty-two, he had gone to China during the Boxer Rebellion – as a volunteer with auxiliary services accompanying American troops – and what he saw of a "foreign and crowded" country made him an unrelenting opponent of Asian immigration. This was his main issue when he was elected to parliament in 1911, and it was the central point of his maiden speech in the House of Commons when he repeated the popular claim that Canada was "a white man's country" and that government must keep it that way. He was the source of some extremely derogatory public comments about India and Indian people. *Sansar* responded by describing Stevens' abuse as nothing better than "colour prejudice."[2]

Kapoor's activist friends were trying to counter men like Stevens. That was the mission of the *Aryan* and of *Sansar;* and it was the purpose of the Hindu Friend Society of Victoria, which was fostered by Kapoor and his companions. They did gain a few energetic allies among whites in Victoria, and none more dedicated than Louis W. Hall, the missionary at the First Presbyterian Chinese Church in downtown Victoria. Louis Hall was a sixty-year-old American, married to a Canadian, who had lived in Victoria from 1892 when the Chinese mission first opened. He had known Prof. Teja Singh from 1908 when the professor first visited Victoria. With Teja Singh, Dr. Sundar Singh, and Rajah Singh, Hall had gone to Ottawa in 1911 to argue with the government – unsuccessfully – against the exclusion of South Asian wives and children. The Sikhs of Victoria also sent Hall to Seattle in 1913 to petition American officials – unsuccessfully again – on behalf of 197 Punjabi immigrants who were being deported from the US.[3]

When Hall made the 1911 trip by train to Ottawa with three Sikhs, he got a crash course on Sikhism. He had four days in a railway coach to read about Sikhs, and he had a spiritual teacher to talk to in Teja Singh. In his autobiography, Teja Singh says that on the eastbound trip Hall finished a book on the tenth Sikh guru and said, "Guru Gobind Singh! Guru Gobind Singh!! If I had come across this book as a young man, I would have become a Sikh of Gobind Singh."[4] Hall did not actually offer to change his religion, for in his maturity he did not see that as necessary, but back in Victoria, he began speaking of the Sikh faith with such enthusiasm that he gained a reputation among whites as a convert. That was how the immigration department's Anglo-Indian immigration inspector, Hopkinson, described him in a report to Ottawa.

Hall may have introduced Isabella Ross Broad to the Hindu Friend Society of Victoria. She had arrived in the city in 1913 and immediately felt disturbed by the "un-Christian attitude" toward the Sikhs that she witnessed. Previously, she had lived in rural and small-town Ontario within a Presbyterian and Scottish Canadian environment. Her husband, considerably younger than herself, had been a Presbyterian minister. After his death, she had come to Victoria to live in a house near the harbour, a block away from the legislative buildings. As a churchgoer, she was well aware of the money that Canadian Christians gave to overseas missions, and she was quick to believe that unfairness to the Sikhs damaged the mission effort in India. It was from this viewpoint that she published a pamphlet addressed to Canadian Christian churches, calling for fair play for Sikhs and making wholesale use of Dr. Sundar Singh's words and material. She asked if they realized how serious the situation was "when the heathen in India can say to the missionary, your message is not true, you treat the Hindus in your country unjustly."[5]

The Presbyterian Church had a closer relationship to the Vancouver and Victoria Sikhs than any other church. This was because the Presbyterians in Canada included several retired missionaries who had served in India or among the descendents of South Asian immigrants in the West Indies and who took a personal interest in Sikhs, and because of the encouragement of Kapoor's associates, Sundar Singh and Kartar Hundal, who wanted someone with status in white society who would speak up for South Asians. They contacted the national organization of the Presbyterian Church because they were impressed by Hall and by his example as Presbyterian missionary who helped the Sikhs without trying to convert them.[6] The Presbyterian Foreign Missions Board, based in Toronto, eventually sent two retired ministers to BC. These ministers had learned Hindi while working among South Asians in Trinidad. They were willing to work long and hard for a few converts, but conversion was nonetheless their primary objective – not what Dr. Sundar Singh and Kartar Singh had in mind.

One of these ministers came to Vancouver in 1913 and the other to Victoria in 1914. If they did not perceive it right away, they quickly realized that they had taken on a tough, unrewarding assignment. William L. Macrae, a Scots Canadian from Nova Scotia, stuck it out for more than a decade, steadfastly offering regular English and Bible classes as well as worship for the scanty dozen or so Sikhs and Hindus who showed up. Macrae recognized a lot of truth in the Sikh faith, and he saw that as an obstacle. He put it this way: the more truth a non-Christian religion possessed, "the more tenaciously its devotees cling to it." But this was not his only problem. His Christian mission was a provocation for many Sikhs, especially for the gurdwara leadership, which was becoming fiercely militant at the very moment he set up shop.[7]

The Presbyterian missions in Vancouver and Victoria were just a sideshow in an intense political storm that overtook the Sikh community as Kapoor settled in Victoria. A shift in the local Sikh leadership had begun before Teja Singh returned to India in March 1913. He had already lost influence, and so had Dr. Sundar Singh, to so-called uneducated men who did not speak English and who were passionately militant in their politics. Three months after Teja Singh sailed from Vancouver, the militant party gained immense strength and momentum with the arrival of a charismatic radical, Bhagwan Singh Jakh, who landed in Victoria in early June. He happened to be on the maiden voyage of the *Empress of Russia,* which carried a holiday crowd of prosperous globetrotters who disembarked in Victoria with great fanfare after crossing the Pacific in a record-breaking nine days. Bhagwan Singh Jakh was one of five South Asians among the thousand passengers on board, and he slipped through the immigration net without difficulty.[8]

Bhagwan Singh Jakh was a Brahman (priestly caste) Sikh from Amritsar. His Brahman identity made him slightly suspect in the minds of some Sikhs, and the fact that he was from Amritsar also provoked distrust arising from Punjabi regional rivalries. But at the age of thirty, he had a well-earned reputation among Punjabis as a fiery fighter against British rule. He entered Canada using another man's identity – a man who had lived in the country. W.C. Hopkinson, the immigration inspector who interviewed him when he landed, had no idea who he was, although Bhagwan Singh had already cut a prominent swath through Sikh communities across southeast Asia, from Burma to Thailand, the Malay Straits, Java, Sumatra, Borneo, Singapore, and Hong Kong. He was a powerful speaker, versed in Hindu, Muslim, and Sikh texts, who had boldly braved government censure in colonies and countries where the British had influence or jurisdiction. He did so in a spoken Punjabi rich in suggestive metaphor and obvious analogy. During his three years as chief priest in the Hong Kong gurdwara, the British arrested him twice for preaching sedition, only to drop the charges both times. From Hong Kong, where he had a grand send-off from friends and supporters, he had come to British Columbia and began organizing his countrymen there, using the Vancouver Sikh gurdwara as his platform and base, holding weekly political meetings in the basement.[9]

Bhagwan Singh lasted less than six months in Canada before he was physically thrown out by immigration officials and police. His departure, as described in the Vancouver and Victoria newspapers, was an extraordinary affair. He had been packed off without time to get his luggage or even a change of clothes. On the wharf he fought back physically, and several policemen wrestled him handcuffed up the gangway and onto the outbound *Empress of Japan,* while his lawyer was trying to serve a writ of habeas corpus to set him free. The chief immigration officer in Vancouver personally oversaw Bhagwan Singh's deportation. A few Canadians worried about the rough and arbitrary approach of this official and the injury he had done to relations with the Sikhs.[10] But Bhagwan Singh Jakh was a divisive force within his own community, and some of his countrymen were relieved to see him go. Kapoor and his friends were among them.

The issue with Bhagwan Singh was one of methods, not goals. He was a disruptive presence even though he was a nationalist fighting for the common cause of all Indians, not just the freedom of the Sikhs. Speaking as a nationalist, he told Sikhs in BC to use the pan-Indian greeting "Bande Mataram," a declaration of respect for Mother India, instead of the Sikh "Fateh," a faith-specific invocation of the Great Guru. By strength of personality he persuaded the majority of them to do it.[11] He used the Vancouver Sikh gurdwara as his main political base, and he set out to expand its sphere of authority. That forced a split in the community. *Sansar* was one of his targets. The Guru Nanak Mining and Trust Company was another, and Kapoor and Piara Singh Langeri came into his line of fire because they were involved with both. The stakes were high because

Bhagwan Singh Jakh and his many followers were calling their opponents "traitors." They accepted no middle ground.

Kapoor's closest friend, Bhai Piara Singh Langeri, has left a memoir of what happened with *Sansar*. In it, he wrote that his group – Dr. Sundar Singh, Kartar Singh Hundal, himself, and others – had approached all segments of the South Asian community for help to start a Punjabi-language press. With that money they bought the Speed Avenue property in Victoria, where they housed their office and the printing press. Bhai Piara Singh stated that they promised to publish a newspaper that was not *phirkaprast,* or faith-based – that did not promote any particular religious perspective. This stance encouraged Hindus, Sikhs, and Muslims to contribute funds and take out subscriptions. Trouble began when Bhagwan Singh Jakh came to Victoria in person, bringing militant articles he wanted *Sansar* to print. As editor, Kartar Singh refused because he feared that the Canadian government would shut *Sansar* down if it ran openly seditious material, anti-British material. Bjagwan Singh responded by trying to take over *Sansar* and its Speed Avenue property, seeking to bring them under the control of Vancouver's Khalsa Diwan Society, the oldest of the three BC gurdwara societies. Initially, Dr. Sundar Singh, Kartar Singh Hundal, Piara Singh, and their supporters refused to relinquish their secular newspaper to a religious society.[12]

Bhai Piara Singh's brief memoir adds to what one reads in *Sansar* and in a brief-lived and antagonistic rival, the *Hindustanee.*[13] A bitter factional fight, already under way when Bhagwan Singh Jakh was in Canada, got hotter after his deportation. His friends were sure that he had been reported to the immigration department by informants among his own countrymen. He spoke only in Punjabi, they said, so how could the immigration department know what he had been saying – whether or not it had been seditious? And how did the department know that he entered the country with a false identity?[14] Fingers pointed at Bela Singh, a former signaller in the British India army who spoke fluent English. He had returned to Canada in 1913 on the *Empress of Russia* with Bhagwan Singh and had then spent much time at the Vancouver immigration office, making himself so useful that he was put on the payroll.

In the two months following Bhagwan Singh Jakh's deportation, *Sansar* appeared twice, defiantly standing up to the militants, and after a gap of three months, it appeared one last time.[15] In the first of these issues, it listed Bela Singh as one of eleven new members of an organization called the United Indian Association, whose principal officers were Kapoor's friends Dr. Sundar Singh, Kartar Singh, and Piara Singh. In retrospect admitting any connection with Bela Singh seems rash, as only a few months later he became infamous for shooting nine Sikhs, killing two of them, in the Vancouver gurdwara. But they could not have anticipated what was going to happen. The Bela Singh shooting was the culmination of a drift to violence that began when Bhagwan Singh Jakh arrived. Bela Singh claimed that he acted in fear for his own life. The situation made Vancouver and Victoria dangerous for militants, moderates, and suspected informants alike. All of this is a vital part of Kapoor's story because it affected his friends and finally led him to leave British Columbia.

Bhai Piara Singh says that the quarrel over *Sansar* became so heated and *Sansar* staff so unpopular in the community that people were making alarming threats to shoot them. On 9 January 1914, he and Kapoor tried to calm things down, joining a delegation from *Sansar* that met with representatives of the Khalsa Diwan Society in the basement of the Vancouver Sikh gurdwara. Kapoor and Piara both spoke for *Sansar,* and both were clearly searching for peace and conciliation. Neither Sundar Singh nor Kartar Hundal was there, so the matter could not be resolved on the spot. All this was recorded in the minutes of the Khalsa Diwan Society, but what happened next, the minutes do not show.[16] Two months later, *Sansar* published its final issue. It was the last because someone set fire to the Speed Avenue office. Piara was sleeping in the building at the time and ran out after the arsonists, only to see their retreating shapes. After that, continuing the newspaper was impossible.[17]

The death of *Sansar* came a few months after the appearance in San Francisco of a new weekly revolutionary paper called *Gadar* (mutiny), which was published in Urdu and Punjabi. This paper and the revolutionary movement it engendered among overseas Sikhs constituted the most alarming threat to British rule during the years that Gandhi and passive resistance dominated the Indian independence movement. *Gadar* was produced by a number of Indian expatriates in California – Sikh, Hindu, and Muslim. Their circle included Bhagwan Singh Jakh, who had eventually made his way to back to North America to join them in San Francisco. On their masthead, they exhorted young Indian men to pick up their weapons quickly. The first Punjabi issue came out on 9 December 1913; within days, copies had reached Vancouver and were being read out in its gurdwara, where militant Hindus and Muslims would join assembled Sikhs.[18]

Gadar extolled the work of bomb makers and bomb throwers, and spoke of the courage that young men gained by killing oppressors. It described itself as the proponent of a rebellion that was spreading like the wind and that had patriots in London, Paris, Geneva, New York, San Francisco, Vancouver, Fiji, and Natal, all working together "with singleness of purpose." Ominously, its editors singled out "a disloyal party" in Canada. They meant the group around Sundar Singh, whom they described as "educated Hindustanis" who were pretending to help the cause but who were actually "cutting at the roots." The editors of *Gadar* used language designed to escalate an already angry situation.[19]

All this was brewing when, during the night of 21 May 1914, the immigrant ship *Komagata Maru* from Hong Kong steamed into Canadian waters with 376 Punjabis on board. This ship is bitterly remembered by Punjabis, not just because the Canadian government refused to let the passengers disembark (except a small number who were already residents of Canada), but because it confined them on the ship in Vancouver harbour for two months, with casual regard for their health and welfare, and then chased them away with a naval gunboat. The Khalsa Diwan Society leadership had encouraged the passengers of the *Komagata Maru* to challenge Canada's discriminatory immigration regulations, and while the ship was still crossing the Pacific, had set up a committee in Vancouver to support them. Kapoor and his friends must have had a sense of how isolated they were when everyone associated with *Sansar* was excluded from this committee – the antagonism of the militants was too intense for the *Sansar* group to be included.

Nonetheless, Kapoor and his friends did what they could. The first glimpse of the *Komagata Maru* for anyone onshore came early in the morning of 22 May as it approached the William Head Quarantine Station, near Victoria. A large launch full of South Asians from Victoria circled the ship, trying to communicate by loud hailer, until immigration officials ordered them to move off. One assumes that Kapoor was among them. Next day the *Komagata Maru* reached Vancouver. From then on, until the ship and its passengers returned to Asia, the militants of the Khalsa Diwan Society and the Shore Committee took charge of all aspects – legal, political, and financial – of an ultimately futile battle to get the passengers ashore.

Kapoor's friend Dr. Sundar Singh headed for Ottawa within days of the ship's arrival. On 29 May, he gained an interview with Loring Christie, legal advisor to the Department of External Affairs. In Christie, he was speaking to an influential government lawyer who had direct access to the prime minister. But he walked into an adverse situation because at Christie's elbow was an immigration official named Frederick Charles

Blair, who had strong and negative opinions about the Sikhs in Vancouver. The interview was a failure from the start, as can been seen in a lengthy memo that Christie wrote afterwards. He took the doctor to be a typical "Hindu" agitator, "tricky but not particularly clever or shrewd." And Blair had reported that Sundar Singh was discredited in his own community because he had shaved his beard, so Christie discounted him as representing nobody but himself or at best a minority faction. He dismissed Singh's visit as a grandstanding attempt to regain favour in his community. Perhaps there was some truth in that, but what the doctor had to say deserved a more serious hearing than it got.[20]

The doctor came to the interview with two proposals. He wanted Ottawa to let the passengers go ashore on bail while their case was in the courts, a move that would spare them the expense of staying on the ship, which they were renting on charter; and he wanted a general inquiry into the whole question of immigration from India, bringing together all interested parties – trade unions, municipalities, immigrants from India – to work out a policy. He did not say what the outcome should be but thought a middle course could be found between absolute exclusion and unrestricted right of entry. For his part, Christie suspected everything Singh said, reading hidden motives and objectives into his mission, and he transformed the interview into such a vigorous cross-examination that Singh must have come away knowing he would receive no help there.

Dr. Sundar Singh left Ottawa for Toronto, where he knew influential Anglo-Canadians from his visit there two years earlier. By June of 1914, he had taken up residence at 261 Church Street in downtown Toronto.[21] He may have hoped to return to British Columbia brandishing concessions from the government, but that had not worked out. Bhai Piara Singh and Kapoor joined him a few weeks later. Kartar Singh Hundal also came that summer, as did other members of their group. In his memoir, Bhai Piara says that he went "helplessly" to Toronto after it became impossible to produce *Sansar* and after he and his friends had done as much as they could for the *Komagata Maru.* Many years later, Kapoor explained that he went to Ontario seeking a place that was more hospitable than British Columbia. He also mentioned the internal dissension that was tearing up the South Asian community, leading to beatings and murders. He and his friends had gone underground and did not want to be found by the wrong people among their own countrymen.

A letter written to Kartar Singh in Toronto that September makes this clear.[22] The writer, Battan Singh, had been the assistant compositor for *Sansar,* and he was still living on the *Sansar* property at 630 Speed Avenue.

When Kartar Singh left Victoria for the east via Vancouver and Calgary, Battan had seen him off at the dock and had subsequently kept Kartar's whereabouts a secret. His letter mentions the six or seven Sikhs they had seen at the dock whom Kartar Singh had warned him of. Since then, other Sikhs had come to Speed Avenue asking for Editor ji, which was the name they used for Kartar Singh. Although they seemed friendly enough, Battan had put them off, saying that Editor ji had just stepped out or gone on an errand, not admitting that he had left town. Dr. Sundar Singh's absence could not be denied, but Battan was not giving up his address or Kartar's. Someone asked for back copies of *Sansar,* and Battan told him that Dr. Sundar Singh had burned them. In the weeks before he wrote this letter, the Sikh community had been shaken by a succession of retaliatory murders and assaults, including the immigration informer Bela Singh's bloody outburst in the Vancouver gurdwara. Since then, Battan wrote, there had been no more disturbances, and though he sensed no danger to himself, he was staying close to home and planning to come east when he could.

Kapoor left British Columbia because he found the environment hostile – the attitude of whites and the anger dividing his own people – and he left because his friends were going. The radicals in his community had not singled him out as they did Kartar Singh Hundal and Dr. Sundar Singh, and he never faced the same hostility, but he belonged to their camp. Like nearly all his countrymen in Canada, he believed that British rule in India was the root cause of their problems at home and abroad. But in the struggle for change, he had cast his lot with moderates and his loyalty was with them. He chose to follow Bhai Piara Singh to Ontario because he had not given up on Canada and it was not a good time to return home. In fact, neither British Columbia nor Punjab was safe or inviting. Ontario gave him the hopeful prospect of a fresh place and a new start.

6
Refuge in Ontario

The 1914 outbreak of war in Europe confronted Punjabis in Canada with unavoidable choices with radically different consequences. Some were swept up in a wave of nationalistic zeal and set off for India, hoping to strike against the British to liberate their homeland; others went home during the opening months of the war after losing their jobs during a brief downturn of the BC economy. Still others, including Kapoor, elected to stay in Canada and to make the most of whatever opportunities presented themselves. At a historic moment such as this, friends could differ profoundly on what to do. This was the case with Kapoor and his closest friend, Bhai Piara Singh, but remarkably their friendship survived intact. They were together and newly arrived in Ontario when the war started, but a difference had already arisen between them because Kapoor had just shaved his beard and discarded his turban, whereas Piara Singh had not.

Soon after he stepped down from the train at Union Station in Toronto, Kapoor walked into a barbershop in the downtown business core. He had already taken scissors and a razor to his beard, so his face was roughly shaven, but he was wearing his turban, and to the delight and entertainment of everyone in the shop, he proceeded to unwind it – all four and a half metres of material – to expose hair that had never been cut and that was arranged in the customary style, carefully combed and twisted in a knot on the top of his head. Then he asked for his first haircut.[1]

When he told this story forty-two years later, the journalist interviewing him jotted down King Street as the location of the barbershop and 14 June 1914 as the date. What this journalist wrote is the only account we have of this most important moment in Kapoor's life. The date may be incorrect because that day was a Sunday, and in a city famously called "Toronto the Good," barbershops would have been closed. Perhaps Kapoor trimmed his beard on the Sunday and went into the shop on Monday for the full treatment of haircut and shave. What is striking, although not surprising, is that he had a very specific memory of the place and time of that haircut. It had been an immensely significant declaration for him.

We get an idea of what it meant from Kapoor's friend Kartar Singh Hundal, who also discarded his beard and turban about the same time and also after coming to Toronto. A perpetual journalist, he described his experiences in print in a way that Kapoor never did. Giving up his beard and turban was a great sacrifice, he wrote, one at several levels. He had always considered himself a "militant" Sikh, by which he meant one who was serious about his faith and its commitments. To compound his dilemma, he was a community leader and he was well known. And like all initiated or baptized Sikh men, he had pledged to keep the beard and turban as visible symbols of his faith.[2] By shaving and cutting his hair, he was dishonouring this pledge and abandoning a brotherhood of co-religionists. He later got to know Canadian society well enough to realize that most Canadians – had they been told about his scruples – would find it "ridiculous" for him to agonize about shaving and cutting his hair. But he did agonize.

The other side of the issue for Kartar Singh – what made him give up his beard and turban – was what he called "the problem of the Sikh in Canada." He was troubled by the Canadian argument that Sikhs would never adopt the Canadian way of life, because they insisted on keeping their own customs and dress. As Kartar Singh explained it, he felt he could not refute that argument while he retained the beard and turban, so he sacrificed them as an "initiation" into the life of Canada. Pledging to keep them had been part of his initiation as a Sikh. Giving them up would be his initiation as a Canadian. When he did so, he said, he entered a new world and launched himself into a demanding and difficult exploration of what it was to be Canadian.

Kapoor and Kartar Singh cut their hair at much the same time. Dr. Sundar Singh had done it in Vancouver or Victoria two years earlier, just as his relations with militant Sikhs were deteriorating.[3] Kapoor and Kartar Singh did it in the emotionally charged aftermath of the *Komagata Maru* episode. When Kapoor entered the King Street barbershop and asked the barber cut his hair, its passengers were still waiting to disembark. He had been active on their behalf in British Columbia. Then he had left and for the rest of the summer, he followed their story from a distance.

The ship had been forced to return to India. In early October 1914, he read reports that the passengers had rioted at the port of Budge Budge, near Kolkata (Calcutta), upon disembarking at the end of their long voyage back to India. Troops had fired on them, and according to the first official reports, sixteen passengers had been killed. In later reports the figure rose to twenty. After the riot and the shooting, most of the passengers had been arrested and imprisoned or sent back to their villages and put under village arrest.[4] The Indian government suspected nearly all of them of being revolutionaries or their sympathizers. Years later, when Kapoor talked to his daughters about the *Komagata Maru,* he emphasized the frustration of Punjabi pioneers in Canada, who were unable to help the people detained on board. He also spoke of the splits in the community that summer, which he attributed mainly to the manipulations of the immigration department, particularly the Anglo-Indian immigration inspector W.C. Hopkinson. In the midst of that crisis, he made his decision to become a Canadian, which brought him to Toronto and the barbershop on King Street.[5]

Bhai Piara Singh Langeri had come to Ontario a little ahead of Kapoor after hostile militants set fire to the *Sansar* office and after the *Komagata Maru* berthed in Vancouver's harbour. He had urged Kapoor to follow and when Kapoor did so, he was already working on a lakeshore country estate at Rosebank, thirty kilometres east of Toronto, near the town of Pickering. He had kept his beard and turban, and would never give them up, but that did not affect his close friendship with Kapoor. They were always "dharam brothers." Kapoor joined him and got to know his employer, William Moore, a Toronto lawyer and railway executive who was developing his Rosebank property as a holiday and weekend retreat with the intent of eventually retiring there and devoting himself to writing. He had built a great home high over the lake just the previous year, a home so imposing that as long as it lasted – fire destroyed it in its old age – local children knew it as the castle.[6]

Moore employed several Sikhs that summer, all refugees from BC. He was especially fond of Bhai Piara Singh, whom he knew as Karam – the name that Piara had used to get into Canada – and that friendship quickly included Kapoor. Bhai Piara was an excellent horseman whose three years in the Indian army included one in the cavalry, and that alone might have been enough to win over the Moore family. He was also good with children, and he taught the two Moore boys, then nine and fourteen, how to ride. He may have tried to teach their four-year-old daughter as well. In the Moores, he had connected with an old established Ontario family but one with an open-minded outlook on the world. Moore was the son of a well-known Baptist preacher who also bred prize-winning thoroughbred horses.[7] His wife was a Unitarian, which then as now was a small Christian sect that attracted people of liberal and independent views. It says something about Moore himself that after a few years of marriage, he shifted to his wife's Unitarian congregation. One can see from the books that Moore later wrote that he was widely read and large-minded, with many interests, including Eastern religions.[8]

Moore's friends in Toronto included a small group of Theosophists who had been attracted to Hinduism and Buddhism by Helena Blavatsky's influential and controversial book on the ancient knowledge of the East, *The Secret Doctrine,* that was published nearly a quarter of a century earlier. One of Moore's friends, George McMurtrie, was the Toronto member of the Theosophical Society who regularly ordered copies of *The Secret Doctrine* and other Theosophical literature for anyone who might ask for it.[9] Moore shared the friendly interest that Theosophists like McMurtrie had in the handful of Sikhs who turned up in Toronto in the summer of 1914 in the company of Dr. Sundar Singh. Whether Moore met Dr. Sundar Singh through the Theosophists, the Empire Club, the Canadian Club, or all three, their meeting must have been the crucial event that brought Piara Singh to Moore and then placed him on Moore's farm well outside Toronto soon after he arrived from Vancouver. Kapoor, following in his wake, found a respectful and supportive friendship with Moore that lasted a lifetime. He also formed a lasting association with the Theosophists based on the value they placed in the traditions of India.

Neither Bhai Piara Singh nor Kapoor stayed long with Moore, but Moore continued to help them, even after they left his farm for radically different destinations. Dealing out jobs was not hard for Moore. He was a senior executive with the Canadian Northern Railway and the right-hand man for its owner William Mackenzie, one of Canada's great capitalists and railway builders. In the summer of 1914, Canadian Northern was months from completion as a transcontinental system rivalling the CPR. And Moore's boss, Mackenzie, also owned the private company that operated Toronto's urban and interurban electric railway system. Moore was the secretary of the Toronto Railway Company and responsible for its operations.[10] When Kapoor decided to leave the farm, Moore must have directed him to his next job, which was on a section gang building the interurban line from Toronto to Newmarket, part of the electric railway system that Moore ran. Kartar Singh Hundal also worked for a while at Toronto's Union Station, another railway job probably found with the help of Moore.[11] Neither Kartar nor Kapoor nor Piara ever forgot the support that Moore gave them from the moment they turned up in Toronto.

When war broke out that summer in Europe, the Gadar Party leadership, without pause or reflection, called for a mass return of Indian emigrants to fight for India's freedom. Within hours of Britain's declaration of war on 4 August, Gadar leaders held public meetings in California. Their rhetoric was stirring and fierce, but as one participant recalled, no one had a clear idea of how to start the revolution once they got back. There was nothing secretive about their meetings or plans; it was all freely reported in American newspapers. And the *Gadar* newspaper published a call to arms in its first August issue, which was distributed far and wide, making it easy for British government agents to know what the party was doing.[12]

When Bhai Piara Singh heard the Gadar call, he instantly decided to take part, and he urged Kapoor to return to India with him. Kapoor refused. He said he had become Canadian when he shaved his beard and discarded his turban, and Canada was where he wanted to stay. But he told his friend that he would support him morally and financially, and over the following years he did.[13] Their conversation was short because Piara was impatient to join the first group of Gadarites who planned to sail from San Francisco on 15 August. From Toronto, he made the five-thousand-kilometre trip by rail to California, where he waited for two weeks until the group finally left on 29 August aboard the steamship *Korea.* While he waited, he stayed at the gurdwara in Stockton, California, where he met Bhagwan Singh Jakh, the firebrand who had been deported from Canada in 1913 and who was now touring the West Coast promoting the return of revolutionary patriots to India. Like the other chief Gadar leaders, Bahgwan Singh was not going himself, but conducting the revolution from a distance. The police in India came to know of Piara Singh's contact with Bhagwan Singh thanks to informers among the men going back to India. This information went into his police file in Delhi.[14]

The Gadarites were organizing so openly that the British consul-general in San Francisco and W.C. Hopkinson, the Canadian immigration officer in Vancouver, were able to report to India the name of everyone who left and the ship they took. Those who sailed on the Nippon Yusen Kaisa line from San Francisco to Kolkata disembarked directly into the arms of waiting police, who arrested them on the spot. Fortunately for Bhai Piara

Singh, the *Korea* was a Pacific Mail steamship on a run that ended at Hong Kong, and he left it early at Nagasaki along with two friends so they could come by way of Shanghai. The police had no idea when he would arrive. In mid-October, he and his friends disembarked in Kolkata from a small Hong Kong–based steamer, the *Fau Sang,* without attracting any special attention. Later that day, they ran into police in the bazaar and were in danger of detention but did some quick talking and got away.

On 12 April 1915, the Indian police finally arrested Bhai Piara Singh about eight kilometres south of his village of Langeri, after they received a tip from the *zaildar* (headman) of a village he had repeatedly visited. By then, he had been in India for six months, always on the move but mostly close to home. He had waited for three months before reporting to the Mahalpur police, and then, after being placed under village arrest, he disappeared, or "absconded" as the police put in their report. His wandering, sometimes in the dress of a *sadhu,* or holy man, supported their suspicions. They assumed he was consorting with other Gadarites, preaching mutiny to Sikh regiments, or planning robberies or raids on armouries, dressing as a sadhu as a cover. He denied this at his subsequent trial but confirmed it many years later in his memoir. He had been active mostly within a ten-kilometre radius of Langeri, never staying two days in the same place, slipping in and out of villages by night to give revolutionary lectures in homes. Once he spent two weeks in Kohat, in the Northwest Frontier Province, to preach sedition to sepoys and cavalrymen from the Mahalpur area who were stationed there. Otherwise he kept to the countryside he knew best.[15] Even there, he was moving among villagers whom he could not always trust.

Two weeks after his arrest, the police brought him to trial in old Punjab's capital of Lahore. The court noted that he had been injured during his arrest. At the approach of a mounted posse of villagers and a police sub-inspector, he had run out of a sadhu's hut and had continued running for miles through fields. But he could not evade men on horseback forever and took a brutal beating when he was finally trapped between the sub-inspector's horse and a thorn hedge. His captors delivered him to jail, shackled in chains, with eyes swollen shut and a fractured leg bound in splints. During his arrest, he had struck back at the sub-inspector, driving a long-handled hatchet into his thigh, and the judges added that to the list of his offences. His sentence was life imprisonment, which he began to serve in Rawalpindi in West Punjab before being transferred to the massive Kalapani Cellular Jail at Port Blair in the Andaman Islands. His was one of a long series of sedition cases tried in the Lahore courts between that April and 1917, which resulted in twenty-three hangings.[16]

Kapoor's daughters got to know Piara Singh Langeri in India during the 1950s. Jackie thought he had the softest and sweetest voice she had ever heard. Sarjit felt her heart touched when she heard him reciting his prayers. She asked him to pray, and he responded by praying aloud with a power she found deeply moving. He described the beating he had taken during his capture and the privations he suffered in his isolated cell at Port Blair. He stated that he had survived through prayer and meditation, and that during his time in jail, he had begun to levitate while saying his prayers.[17]

After serving five years of his life sentence, Piara Singh was released from prison under a general amnesty in 1920. He continued his anti-government activity, which led to two and a half years of incarceration between 1923 and 1926. At the time of his 1920 release, a number of Gadarites were let go, but others remained in jail for many more years. One person who spoke up for Piara was his former employer on the Pickering, Ontario, dairy farm, William Moore. While Piara suffered in prison, Moore had launched a movement that aimed, unsuccessfully, to bridge a bitter division between English and French Canada regarding the war. The movement was called Bonne Entente, and it put Moore's name in the news. By then, Kapoor was back in British Columbia, but when he saw Moore's name in the newspaper, he decided to write him to ask him to help Bhai Piara Singh; and Moore, who had connections with the Liberals in Canada's wartime Union government, did what he could. Piara's friends were certain that Moore's intervention made all the difference. And their feeling was not fleeting. Kapoor remembered Moore's kindness twenty-five years later when he wrote him a thank-you note after a visit to the farm near Pickering: he felt compelled to mention again what Moore had done for Karam – the name by which Moore still knew Bhai Piara Singh.[18]

Kapoor and Bhai Piara Singh were friends who went different ways at a historic fork in the road. The latter was a vital part of Kapoor's story and not solely because he was a close friend. He represented a choice that Kapoor did not make and an experience he did not seek, but a choice and an experience that he nonetheless respected. And Kapoor had other options because, at the moment of the Gadar call to arms, his other associates from *Sansar,* Dr. Sundar Singh and Kartar Singh Hundal, were finding their own direction, also with a mission. In their case, the mission was to win fair opportunity for their countrymen in Canada. Kapoor's life was interwoven with theirs as well, and particularly with Kartar Singh's.

Dr. Sundar Singh eventually dropped out of sight but not immediately. After settling in Toronto, he continued to work energetically for his countrymen in British Columbia. He campaigned from Ontario but with the advantage of being closer to Ottawa, the national seat of power. Together with Kartar Singh, he established the Canada-India Committee, involving Kapoor and the small band of their Sikh friends who had come east to Toronto, as well as a number of prominent Toronto citizens. They were replicating what they had done in Victoria with the Hindu Friend Society. The *Sansar* had died, but now Sundar Singh and Kartar Singh had a new publication, *Canada and India: A Journal of Information and Conciliation,* as well as pamphlets, all part of a continuing lobby effort. They needed help and they were immensely grateful to a few Torontonians who opened doors for them. Besides Moore these included Arthur Hawke, Samuel Thomas Wood, Dr. Lelia Davis, Albert Stafford Smythe, and many others. Their main effort lasted though the war years from 1915 to 1918.[19]

Hawke was a journalist and former publicity man for the Canadian Northern Railway, where he had worked alongside Moore; his friendship with Moore was the basis of their wartime initiative with the Bonne Entente movement. Wood was also a journalist, well known through the *Toronto Globe* as a nature writer and a dedicated laissez-faire liberal and single tax advocate. As a young man he had founded the Toronto Anti-Poverty Society. Lelia Davis was a lecturer in microscopic anatomy at the Ontario Medical College of Women, and like the college founder, Emily Stowe – the activist and suffragette – she was a Theosophist and a socialist. And Albert Stafford Smythe was the founder of the Theosophical movement in Canada. He was yet another journalist, former president of the Toronto Press Club, much later the editor of the *Hamilton Spectator,* and a man of great energy who was active in many of the city's literary groups. It was his son Conn Smythe whose name came to mean hockey for generations of Canadian sports fans after he purchased a Toronto hockey team and renamed it the Maple Leafs.[20]

The Theosophists were immensely important to Kartar Singh Hundal, and he devoted much of the next fourteen years to the Toronto group, particularly as the editor of its newsletter. For a time he and Dr. Sundar Singh stayed in touch with the Presbyterian Foreign Missions Board, one of the voices supporting their effort. But the Presbyterians developed a jaundiced view of Dr. Sundar Singh, the product of stories they heard from Sikhs in British Columbia and Toronto. He had briefly shared a Toronto house with a Gainda Singh, a newly converted Christian Sikh from Victoria, but the two had differences over money; the Presbyterians knew Gainda Singh's side of the story, and it helped sour their attitude toward Sundar Singh. Nonetheless, he seemed irrepressible. From the Presbyterians he turned to the Quakers, who invited him to speak every Sunday afternoon on the religions of India at their Maitland Street meeting house. This was in the summer of 1915. After that, he disappeared from view, and Kartar Hundal became the main focus of the effort that had begun with *Sansar.*[21]

Sundar Singh and Kartar Singh met the Quakers through the Theosophists, who were their main window into Toronto society. Through the Theosophists, they got to know people who shared an interest in psychic phenomena and Eastern religions yet belonged to many different Christian traditions. A stalwart of the Toronto group, and one most helpful to the South Asians, was Felix Belcher, a Quaker by conversion and continuing practice. Others in the Toronto society attended mainstream churches such as the Presbyterian, Methodist, and Reformed Episcopal. They also belonged to fraternal orders such as the Masons and the Orange Order. And they represented a diversity of experience in business, the professions, and the arts. Toward the end of his long residence in Toronto, Kartar Singh was the pallbearer at a funeral for a long-time member of the Toronto Theosophical Society. Shouldering the casket alongside him was Lawren Harris, the Group of Seven painter. The image of the two of them on that occasion was a fair indication of how far Kartar Singh had penetrated to the centre of an Anglo-Canadian world. And the Theosophical Society was the home that helped him do it.[22]

For most of his time in Toronto, Kartar worked as an accountant and office manager. But even in his earliest years, when he earned his living by scrubbing office floors or by shovelling snow on Toronto streets – when he found a "blessing" on a winter day "in two plain buns for a nickel at Jacob's coffee shop on York St." – Kartar knew people who could feed his interest in the arts and literature. On one occasion in 1916, Augustus Bridle, the editor of the weekly *Canadian Courier* and later the *Toronto Star* music critic, gave Kartar tickets to *Chitra,* a play written by Rabindranath Tagore. The performance was at Bridle's Arts and Letters Club in an attic over the County Court Building, where Kartar saw and got to know the pioneers of Toronto theatre and of the Canadian Little Theatre movement. Through his Theosophical Society friend and mentor Albert

Stafford Smythe – the father of the hockey czar – Kartar met the poet Bliss Carman at Toronto Literature Club meetings in a school near Spadina Crescent, where they were joined by Donald French, the influential editor of McClelland and Stewart. At those meetings, he understood that he was witnessing the birth of Canadian literature, and he identified with its development.[23]

That was Kartar's story during the First World War. Kapoor was exploring Canada in yet another way. In 1915, with a few of his Sikh friends, he headed north seven hundred kilometres to what people were then calling "the new Ontario." The just completed transcontinental railway line that Moore had helped to manage ran through parts of northern Ontario and Quebec that seemed to have an exciting agricultural potential. This was the Great Clay Belt, with an estimated 12 million hectares of level terrain and grey clay soils. It was being promoted as a new agricultural frontier, the first great tract of farmland in eastern Canada to be opened in fifty years. Time has shown these early expectations to have been grossly unrealistic. Summers were short and broken by occasional penetrating frosts; winters were bitterly cold; and under the forest, much of the land was muskeg bog. Settlers never succeeded in transforming more than 3 percent of the Great Clay Belt into farmland. What land they did develop was good for hay, barley, oats, and pasture but not wheat; and within a couple of generations, their frontier was in retreat. An American geographer surveying the decaying margins of the settled area in the 1950s saw fenced land returning to weeds and forest, wheeled hay rakes rusting in forgotten fields, and crumbling homes, schools, and churches, all abandoned by settlers who had given up.[24]

The earliest settlers in the Great Clay Belt had started clearing land only four or five years ahead of Kapoor. Most of them were French Canadians, and Kapoor got to know some of them as neighbours. A few began clearing their land just before the transcontinental railway pushed through the area; more came as the railway advanced; and Kapoor and his Sikh friends were among those who arrived shortly after the railway was complete. After travelling through hundreds of kilometres of rocky woodland, Kapoor got off the train at the first ribbon of settlement he saw. This was at Nellie Lake, a railway stop near a northern lake of the same name, where a network of rough roads and raw clearings branched out on either side of the track. Near the railway line at Nellie Lake, Kapoor pre-empted a 160-acre (65-hectare) lot and started clearing its mixed forest of spruce, pine, speckled alder, and birch. The provincial government had laid out the area in square-mile blocks, divided into four lots each, which ensured that the country would be lonely, even in its most settled state. A lucky settler might have a neighbour half a kilometre away, but the topography was so broken by swamps and areas of poor drainage that neighbours could be separated by kilometres of bush. Moore was probably the person who inspired Kapoor to go to this new frontier, where he could acquire title to a large acreage by clearing and farming some of it. The real estate he could claim as a new settler in the Clay Belt seemed a princely territory to an emigrant from Punjab, where the same amount of land could sustain several hundred people. Of course, Kapoor had spent enough time on Moore's farm to know that the economics of Canadian agriculture were very different from those of Punjab. But Moore himself believed in the potential of the Clay Belt and foresaw a time when it would be a region of "contented farm homes." He saw it from the perspective of the railway that had opened it up. But he also approached it as someone who built bridges between Canadian solitudes, after observing that English Canadians were more reluctant than French Canadians to settle in the north. His interest in the subject meant that he had booklets about the Clay Belt on his desk for Kapoor to see. They were written in French and intended for French Canadians but had beautifully coloured maps that explained the geography.[25] These maps and Moore's enthusiasm must have been selling points for Kapoor.

In that part of the country, one worked in the winter and rested in the spring while waiting for the ground to dry out. Work resumed in the summer and fall. Kapoor set about meeting the government's settlement requirements, which meant building a log cabin of at least 370 square feet, living in it at least six months of the year, and clearing and planting two acres each year until he had fifteen under cultivation. Then he could apply for his title to the land. Twelve kilometres away, in the rising village of Iroquois Falls, the Abitibi Power and Paper Company had just built a pulp and paper mill, which had produced its first newsprint in August 1914. At the mill, Kapoor had a market for his softwood timber. As the seasons changed, he cut pulpwood, extracted tree stumps, cleared brush, and planted and harvested. He lived through the summer's mosquito season and the minus forty winter temperatures. And in sharing his habitat with moose, black bear, lynx, and red fox, he saw northern nature up close. One story he later told his daughters was of a night that a huge snorting and stamping bull moose made such an angry racket in the creek nearby that he half-expected it to come up and demolish his cabin.[26]

In 1916 Kapoor accepted a call back to British Columbia, ending his Ontario adventure. During his time at Nellie Lake, he was probably unaware of the wartime detention camp at Kapuskasing, 140 kilometres farther up the railway line. Had he known of it, he might have felt sympathy for the men in the camp. While he was falling trees on his lot, over a thousand Ukrainian detainees were clearing land for a government experimental farm that was supposed to demonstrate the agricultural potential of the Clay Belt. They were in a minimum security camp with no chance of escape, surrounded by hundreds of kilometres of boggy forest, full of mosquitoes in the summer and dangerously cold in the winter. The railway was the only way out and too public for them to attempt. After the war, the government sent soldier-settlers to the Clay Belt; and during the Depression of the 1930s, it did the same with unemployed tradesmen from southern cities. Years later, in 1947, Kapoor hired a young war veteran from Ontario named Eric Smith. Smith's father had lost his Toronto job at the onset of the Depression and had taken his family homesteading in the Kapuskasing area. When Smith and Kapoor talked about the Clay Belt, there was no doubt that Kapoor had not liked the country, especially the grim winter. And he got no argument from Smith.[27]

Kapoor has left behind a rough summary of his financial history over the forty-five years that followed his emigration to North America. According to this summary, he accumulated $4,000 during his five years in the United States and another $3,400 during a year and a half in Victoria. And his assets continued to grow from the moment he returned to BC in 1916. But he had nothing to show for his time in Ontario. Yet Ontario was the place where he decided to make Canada his permanent home, in spite of Bhai Piara Singh's urgent suggestion that he return to India. Kapoor did not go as far as Kartar Hundal in assimilating Anglo-Canadian values, but he did find a way to balance the best and worst of what Canada had to offer.[28]

Although Kapoor, Kartar, and Piara Singh pursued different paths during their summer of refuge in Ontario, their choices did not encompass all the possible options. Also working on Moore's estate that summer and fall was young Bukkan Singh Bains, another of the Mahalpur-area Sikhs who had come to Toronto from Vancouver. His history has only recently been recovered by Sandeep Singh Brar, a Toronto-based photographer and researcher who collects Indian war medals. From a British dealer, Brar obtained a Victory medal inscribed with Bains' name, rank, and serial number. When he realized that this medal belonged to a Sikh who had served in the Canadian army during the First World War, he started looking for his war record in the Ottawa archives and asking questions of his family.[29]

What Brar discovered was the story of a fourteen-year-old who had joined one of the emigrant jathas that left Mahalpur in 1907, a year after Kapoor. In British Columbia this boy – growing to be a young man – had worked in the mines; and in Ontario he worked for Moore. He left Moore's employ in the spring of 1915 to join an infantry battalion mobilizing among the Scots Canadians of eastern Ontario. At the end of August, he was on the Canadian troop ship *Scandinavian,* bound for England. Six months later, he was in the trenches in Flanders with the Canadian Expeditionary Force. He served 100 days at the front in the Ypres sector and was wounded twice within the space of a month, taking shrapnel to the side of the head and then a bullet through the knee and lower leg. He was out of action through the late summer, fall, and winter of 1915-16, convalescing in English military hospitals, but he would have been sent back to the front had he not shown signs of tuberculosis. The diagnosis was confirmed at the end of March 1916, and he languished in a small convalescent hospital at Hastings on the English south coast for the next fifteen months. When he returned to Canada in August 1917, it was in a hospital ship. He spent the last year of his life in a military hospital in Kitchener, Ontario, and after dying at the age of twenty-four in August 1918, he was buried in a soldier's grave in Kitchener. His Mahalpur relatives had not heard from him since he left as a boy in 1907, and their first news of him was the Canadian army death notice they received as next of kin.

Three weeks after Bukkan Singh Bains was wounded for the second time, his name appeared in the Canadian army's daily casualty list. The *Toronto Star* published a brief story about him along with accounts of all the local men on that day's list – a regular feature of Canadian papers during the First World War.[30] From the details, it is clear that much of the *Star*'s information about Bains – when he came to Ontario, where he worked, and that he was the first Sikh to volunteer for the Canadian army – came from William H. Moore, and it is likely that Moore prompted the paper to do a piece on him. Moore would have followed with interest and concern whatever he heard or saw of the Sikhs who had appeared so suddenly in Toronto and come to work for him. Whether he influenced Bains to join the army, we do not know. He did think that Ontario was a better, less-prejudiced place than BC for immigrants from India, and his advice to Kapoor had been to stay there. But Kapoor, like the others, had his own course to follow.

Unless otherwise noted,
the photographs have been provided by Sarjit K. Siddoo

Kapoor's father, Sham Singh Sidhu, in uniform, with the chevron of a lance-naik (lance-corporal) on his sleeve.

Besant Kaur's brother, Sundar Singh Sandhu, who died in Africa in 1920. This photograph was taken in Punjab, ca. 1900.

Besant Kaur's uncle, Atma Singh Sandhu, who died in Argentina in 1922. This photograph was taken in Punjab, ca. 1900

Clockwise, from top left:

The qila in Aur, looking south from the upper-level patio, March 2006.

The ancient tank in Aur, looking southeast, March 2006. *Photographed by author*

Sikhs disembarking from the seven-thousand-ton steamer *Monteagle* at the foot of Granville Street, Vancouver, September 1907. *Vancouver Public Library*

Sikh pedestrians at the intersection of Granville and West Hastings, Vancouver, 1908. *Vancouver Public Library*

Mayo Siding, with Kapoor's house behind on right, 1920s.

H. McDOWELL & CO.

Sikh workers on the Southern Pacific Railway near the California-Nevada border, ca. 1907.

FACING PAGE:

Hundal boys (Atma, Iqbal, Teja, and Jemeja) and their grandmother Bishen Kaur after their arrival in Vancouver from Hong Kong, 1913.

Mayo's house in 2007, unoccupied and the last house standing in what was Mayo Siding. *Photographed by author*

Original Sikh temple at Mayo Siding, 1920s. *Joe Soroya Collection, SFU Archives*

Besant Kaur, shortly after arriving in Canada, ca. 1923.

Besant Kaur, Jackie, and Prince the dog on the porch of the first house in Mayo Siding, ca. 1927.

Mayo, Kapoor, and Doman Singh in front of Kapoor's first house in Mayo Siding, 1925.

Facing page:

The entrance to Kapoor's village of Kharoudi, 2006.
Photographed by author

Isabella and George Bovyer, Duncan, BC, ca. 1940.

19 ਸਵਾ ਕਰਾਈ ਰਛਪਾਲ ਸਿਘ ਗਿਲ ਸ੍ਰ ਮਈਆ ਸਿੰਘ

Counterclockwise, from top

Sarjit and Jackie, aged about one and two, Mayo Siding, 1927.

Kapoor's 1923 Chev at the Mayo mill.

The Siddoo family with Cousin Kashmir (at left) on the porch of their first house at Mayo Siding, 1928.

MAYO LUMBER COMPANY

Div. 2
Mayo School
1934-35.

Facing page

The 1934-35 Division 1 class at Mayo Siding with Miss Winstanley on the left and Miss Ferguson on the right. In a class full of boys, Jackie sits with the other two girls.

Miss Winstanley and her 1934-35 Division 2 students at Mayo Siding. Sarjit is on the steps, back row, left.

The extended Siddoo family in Mayo Siding, ca. 1930. Kapoor's brothers Tara and Bhagwan are in the back row, second and third from the left. Cousin Kashmir is to the right of his father Bhagwan. Naranjan, Ajaib's father, is second from right in the back row. Jackie, Ajaib, and Sarjit are in the front to the right.

The Japanese of Mayo Siding, 1924. *Joe Soroya Collection, SFU Archives*

Reunion photograph of Sundar Singh, Kartar Singh Hundal, and Piara Singh Langeri, spring 1929.

7
The Lumber Business

Punjabis came to North America to get ahead – materially. Kapoor was typical, in that he was in no way a displaced person, but someone with status in rural Punjabi society, with an education, a job, prospects, and property (through his family). As an educated individual from a landowning family, he belonged to Punjab's rural elite. He was assured of a life that would be more rewarding than that of millions of Indians, but he had ambition. When he emigrated, he and his companions were looking for something with a greater return than the labouring jobs they accepted in the beginning. While they moved from job to job, they learned how things worked in North America and where they had the best chance of getting ahead. This unsystematic but collective search soon identified the areas where prospects were best. In British Columbia, this was the forest and lumber industry. After working in this industry for several years, a number of men – some of those who had stayed behind when war broke out – were ready to go into business for themselves. Their initiative brought Kapoor back to BC, where things had calmed down with the departure of militants for India in the fall of 1914.

He was back in BC by October 1916, in partnership with a group of Sikh sawmill workers and bunkhouse men. They had acquired a sawmill and asked him to manage their accounts. The group's leader was the bunkhouse cook, whose kitchen was the magnetic place where Sikh mill workers lingered after meals to talk and plan. His name was Mayo Singh, and he and his closest companions were from Paldi, the village immediately east of Kapoor's village of Kharoudhi.

In 1906 and 1907, Paldi men had set off for North America with Kharoudi men and others from the Mahalpur area. Like Kapoor, Mayo went to California and then made his way north to Canada. He was a small man, not well suited to heavy work, but shrewd, outgoing, and enterprising. Unlike Kapoor, he had little formal education, although he began teaching himself English soon after arriving in BC. When Kapoor came on the scene, Mayo was already carrying a newspaper in his back pocket so he could ask any available English speaker the meaning of words that stumped him. His main teacher was Clarence Martin, a fourteen-year-old boy from a large fatherless Protestant Irish family, whom he had hired to do odd jobs around the mill. Mayo must have practised his writing assiduously, because his signature on early documents is well formed and fluid. His name had been Maiya, but he had anglicized it to make it easier for Anglo-Canadians to remember and repeat, thinking it was good for business. The sixth earl of Mayo had been a viceroy of India, so the name may have had some resonance for him.[1]

Mayo Singh and a mixed gang of Punjabis and Japanese had been working at Fernridge Lumber, a sawmill on the Fraser River that supplied lumber and shingles to farmers in the surrounding rural community of Rosedale, ninety kilometres east of Vancouver. They lost their jobs in 1913 when the mill shut down during a protracted collapse of the lumber market. The next spring, Mayo rented a forty-acre farm in the Rosedale area, and the thirty-five men in his gang planted potatoes as a joint venture. What Mayo did next proved his ability to keep going after a failure. At the end of the season, unable to sell the potatoes, he left them in the field for the owner's pigs to root up, offering that as his payment on the rent. On behalf of his gang – which was still living at the mill-site bunkhouse and picking up occasional work on farms – he went back to the owners of Fernridge Lumber and persuaded them to lease their sawmill. Mayo and his consortium operated there as Cheam Lumber Company – borrowing the name from Mount Cheam, which they could see to the east. When he and his gang took over the mill on 1 October 1915, their timing was good. They hit a resurgence in the lumber business, and they made money. They were just getting into this business when they wrote to Kapoor, asking him to join them as a full partner.[2]

Initially, Mayo and his partners took strategic advice from Husain Rahim, a fifty-year-old educated Gujarati businessman who was fluent in English. In Canada – where he landed in 1910 – Rahim claimed to be a Muslim, but word circulated among the Punjabis that he was really a

Hindu who had changed his name to escape creditors in Kobe, Japan, where he had been in the cotton trade for fifteen years.[3] In Vancouver, he pushed himself to the forefront as an active champion for his countrymen, playing a highly visible role on the Shore Committee that tried to help the *Komagata Maru* passengers. Mayo and his partners trusted Rahim. Unfortunately, he smoked, whereas, as Sikhs, they did not. He was talking and puffing cigarettes at a prolonged meeting in Mayo's office until Mayo told him to quit smoking or stay away. Rahim chose to stay away. But he does deserve credit for suggesting that Kapoor be asked to return from Ontario so the group would have a partner who spoke English fluently and who knew how to keep accounts.[4]

Kapoor kept for posterity two cancelled cheques that he wrote in January 1917, after returning to British Columbia. One was made out for steel purchased from Fernridge Lumber, the owner of the Rosedale mill.[5] The second was for expenses at a sawmill on the CNR line at Strawberry Hill, south of New Westminster, much closer to Vancouver.[6] The two cheques, written within days of each other, are evidence that Kapoor, Mayo, and their partners had a long-term business plan. They knew that the timber at Rosedale was exhausted; they planned to keep going a couple of years longer by acquiring the mill at Strawberry Hill; and they were actively searching for better locations with more potential.

Before they found what they wanted, Kapoor and Mayo set up several companies – the Pacific Great Lumber and Shingle Company, the Cooperative Timber and Logging Company, and the Mayo Lumber Company. The last one became a large and durable enterprise, whereas the others soon disappeared without a trace. In October 1916, Kapoor, Mayo, and three other investors from the Mahalpur area each put $4,000 into the Mayo Lumber Company to manufacture lumber "at places to be selected." They used this company to run the mill at Strawberry Hill while they prepared for something bigger. It was Husain Rahim who suggested they look at railway land on Vancouver Island.[7]

In BC, logging was easiest on the coast. There, loggers dropped trees straight into the water or used donkey engines on the shore to winch logs out of the woods, and then floated log booms and rafts to the nearest sawmill. In this era, they took only the most accessible timber near the shore, and they operated this way on hundreds of kilometres of isolated coast on the Inside Passage, north of Vancouver, and on the far side of Vancouver Island, avoiding the expense of logging roads and overland transport. Coastal logging attracted both large- and small-scale operators, but it was a domain that South Asians could not enter, because the coastal forests were on provincially controlled Crown land. South Asians could not cut timber on Crown land in BC, because they were not voting citizens; and that was because Victoria had taken the franchise away from them. Their exclusion from coastal forests was no accident but a deliberate measure by provincial politicians who catered to the anti-Asian sentiment of white voters.

In the Fraser Valley, most of the prime timber stood in the Dominion Railway Belt, consisting of more than over forty-four thousand square kilometres of choice land that the province had turned over to Ottawa back in 1871 to finance the Canadian Pacific Railway. Provincial regulations did not apply there, so South Asian loggers were not excluded. But Mayo, Kapoor, and their partners were concerned about their long-term prospects. The issue was not the future of the forest industry in the Fraser Valley, where over a hundred sawmills, shingle mills, tie mills, and pulp mills, big and small, would be operating for years to come.[8] The issue was what kind of stake they could get in an area where most of the forest was already in the hands of other companies. At Rosedale and Strawberry Hill, they got a start with marginal mills that were reaching the end of their economic lives. This was why they paid attention when Rahim told them of railway land on Vancouver Island, where they could acquire timber rights with a long future.

In 1912 the CPR had completed a railway line that ran thirty-seven kilometres west from Duncan, then a village of about six hundred people, to Cowichan Lake. The CPR was already operating the Esquimalt and Nanaimo Railway, which ran along the southeast side of Vancouver Island. The branch line to Cowichan Lake gave access to old-growth Douglas fir, western red cedar, and Sitka spruce, the best timber in the province, growing in mixed stands with western white fir and western hemlock. And for fifteen miles on either side of the track, this timber was on railway property and therefore available to South Asians. At Nellie Lake, in Ontario, Kapoor had been clearing land where the tallest trees were seventy or one hundred feet high. In the Cowichan Lake area, the average tree was 150 feet high and produced massive timber of exceptional value on the international market. The logs were so huge that moving a twenty-four-foot length along a logging track could require a dozen horses in harness. The business of carrying these logs to coastal mills made this the most profitable line in the CPR service. And the line opened the country to sawmillers as well as loggers. Kapoor, Mayo, and their partners were quick to take advantage of the opportunity in a rebounding lumber market.[9]

Mayo found a desirable location for a mill west of Duncan on the Lake Cowichan branch of the Esquimalt and Nanaimo Railway. This was to be the site of the Mayo mill and village, right in the heart of the heavy timber. Mayo later described a dismal introduction to the area. He had taken a bus from Victoria to Duncan and spent a night in a railway section man's shack after the two Duncan hotels turned him away; apparently they had no room for a turbaned "Hindu." Someone sent him walking down the track in the dark to find the section man, who, he was told, was another Hindu. The man turned out to be a Sikh who lived in such disorder that when Mayo shook the blanket from the only bed, a mouse dropped out. Mayo had never met this Sikh before but accepted his offer the next day to take him along the track toward Lake Cowichan on his four-wheeled hand trolley. Twelve kilometres up the line, on the south side of the track, Mayo spotted his future mill site by a creek that could be dammed to form a pond for sorting logs. At this site the Mayo Lumber Company purchased timber tracts from the CPR – initially 400 acres at ten dollars an acre, then another 250 acres, and after that cutting rights to an expanding territory north of the railway.[10] In the fall of 1917, the Mayo Company bought machinery at auction from the Island Lumber Company, which had closed its mill in Duncan the year before. During the winter of 1917-18, Kapoor, Mayo, and their partners pitched a tent for shelter while they built their mill; and in early March 1918, they started production. From the defunct Island Lumber Company, they had also picked up a Chinese labour force of mill workers, fallers, road workers, and rail crew.[11]

When it opened, the steam-powered mill could produce forty to fifty thousand board feet a day and ship seventy-five rail cars of lumber a month. It was a good-sized mill by BC standards, which is saying a lot because BC was becoming the country's principal lumber-producing province, with the largest and most efficient mills. The Mayo logging operation would have impressed a timber expert from eastern Canada, given the size of the logs and the steam-powered donkey engines and steam locomotive employed to bring them out of the woods. Railway logging in BC dated from the 1880s, but with the opening of areas such as the Lake Cowichan district, it was assuming a new importance. In most of the country, logging was still a fall and winter activity employing horses and sleighs to draw logs over the snow to the nearest lake or river, where they would wait for the spring thaw to be floated to a mill. In BC, the size of the timber and the difficult terrain demanded a more industrial approach, and more capital. The Mayo operation used horses and trucks to bring out its logs, but that was in conjunction with a rail line that snaked its way farther and farther through the harvested forest. Within twenty months of starting production, the Mayo Company had three kilometres of railway over which it ran flatcars pulled by an eighteen-ton Shay locomotive – geared for light track and steep grades. A gravel road ran parallel to the railway, and a network of logging roads fed into it, with six trucks to navigate them. The Mayo Lumber Company was moving with the times in an expanding BC lumber industry.[12]

The Mayo lumber mill burned down during its first year of operation, but the partners rebuilt it the following year. Then, in the third year, in March 1920, the Duncan volunteer fire brigade was back to put out a fire that destroyed a new lath mill and much of the lumber in the yard. During the fire, help came five kilometres from the neighbouring mill at Hillcrest, where Carlton Stone, the English-born owner, employed a large contingent of Sikhs. The Nanaimo and Esquimalt Railway also sent a locomotive to pull three loaded cars out of danger. The losses were considerable and the local newspaper, the *Cowichan Leader*, reported that the owners were only partially insured. For Kapoor, Mayo, and partners, these fires were setbacks at the very moment that lumber prices peaked at an unprecedented thirty-five dollars per thousand board feet. For the rest of the decade, prices ran about fourteen to eighteen dollars. Nonetheless, they had the money, the credit, and the potential production to survive the fire and carry on.[13]

In 1920 Kapoor and Mayo bought a second – smaller – mill near Duncan. It was called Tansor Lumber and had belonged to a Duncan firm, an Anglo-Canadian concern. After taking it over, Kapoor and Mayo ran it for four years as an adjunct to the Mayo Lumber Company, barely covering operating expenses but turning a profit on the capital investment, presumably in transfers of equipment and machinery to Mayo Lumber. Mayo was the major partner in Tansor, but Kapoor had a substantial share, and in four years he cleared $2,000.[14]

At the same time, Kapoor was involved with a third mill on Vancouver Island. From 1917 to 1924, he was a major shareholder in the Virginia Lumber Company near Coombs, about ninety kilometres northwest of the Mayo mill. A short spur line connected the Virginia mill to the branch of the Esquimalt and Nanaimo Railway that had reached Port Alberni in 1914. The manager of this mill and a major shareholder was Amar Singh

Sangha, who was also a partner in the Mayo mill. He was a year older than Kapoor, who would have known him from his youth.

Like Kapoor, Amar Singh Sangha had attended primary school in Mahalpur and secondary school in Bajwara. Then their paths had parted. Amar trained as an engineer in Lahore, worked in East Africa, and then owned a flour mill in Mahalpur before emigrating to Canada in 1914, landing in Victoria on 28 July. At that moment the passengers of the *Komagata Maru* were on their way back to Asia, after their failed bid to land in Canada. Amar seems to have immigrated with false papers, and he used two names in Canada – Jawalla Singh and Amar Singh. In Victoria he and a man named Wilson went into business, with a blacksmith and carriage repair shop on Herald Street, near the harbour. He had friends in the Gadar Party, and in January 1915 he turned up in Fresno, California, to speak at a Gadar meeting, a fact that was duly reported to the police in India. By 1916, however, his attention had turned to the lumber business, and that led to a reconnection with Kapoor.[15]

Amar Singh Sangha came from the village of Skrooli, and for that reason he was well known to his partners in the Mayo and Virginia Lumber Companies. The principal partners in these companies were from three adjacent villages – Kharoudi to the west, Paldi in the middle, and Skrooli to the east. They are numbered villages 98, 99, and 100 on a contemporary government map of the Garshankar *tehsil* (subdistrict) of the Hoshiarpur District. (This tehsil has over three hundred villages, and the district itself has more than thirteen hundred.) Skrooli, Paldi, and Kharoudhi fall within a compass of six kilometres – a tiny neighbourhood of large importance for Punjabis in Canada. Besides Mayo, several other men from Paldi were involved in the Mayo mill. One of them was Doman Singh, whose son Herb (Harbans) Doman later established himself as a giant of the BC forest industry. Both Mayo and Doman held shares on behalf of other Paldi men. At Virginia Lumber, two Skrooli men were principal partners – Amar Sangha and a Brahman named Pandit Bal Makand. Other partners came from neighbouring Garshankar villages, such as Mahalpur, Langeri, Maranwali, and Maili, and one from the Jalandhar District was tied in by family. Locality and family were the bonds that linked the members of these partnerships.

Most of the partners were Sikhs, but a couple, such as the sweet-mannered Pandit Bal Makand, were Hindus. And the Mayo Company brought together Sikhs from two caste communities – Jat and Manhas Rajput – whose families never intermarried though they had long lived in adjoining villages. Like Kapoor, Amar Singh Sangha was a Jat, but Mayo Singh, Doman Singh, and the other partners from Paldi were Manhas Rajputs. The differences were unimportant in everyday relations, in business, work, eating together, socializing, and worship. In Paldi, Manhas Rajput families owned the land and employed fellow villagers from subordinate caste groups. It was the same with the Jats of Kharoudi and Skrooli: they were the landowners and employers of their villages. But the two groups, Kapoor's Jats and Mayo's Manhas Rajputs, were conscious of their separate pedigrees; and that was a source of rivalry and potential tension – the rivalry of people with more common characteristics than differences.

Of the many landowning caste communities of Punjab, the Jats were the most numerous, generally the most successful, and for these reasons, the most potent politically. All these factors contributed to their prestige. The Rajputs, who claimed descent from ancient warriors and rulers, enjoyed an equal status. But the Manhas Rajput subgroup was not considered by its Punjabi neighbours to be truly Rajput, just a low-caste group with Rajput pretensions. For proof, they cited the fact that Manhas Rajputs did not intermarry with Rajputs. And their marriage customs differed from those of the Rajputs: their families exchanged brides and allowed widows to remarry, which the Rajputs did not do. The name the Jats applied to them was Mahton, not Rajput, and they used it in a derogatory way. When the British conducted their earliest ethnographic surveys of Punjab, they associated the "Mahton" with a low-caste group bearing a similar name. But British officials also identified them as exceptionally fine farmers.

In contrast to the Jats, the Manhas Rajputs were a microscopic minority in Punjab. They occupied a belt of just twenty villages across the Garshankar *tehsil* and running into the Jalandhar District. Even there, where they were concentrated, their villages occupied just 7 percent of the land. They were surrounded by Jats as well as "real" Rajputs and by other farming castes. But, though they were a minority among Punjab's farmers, their villages had long been some of the most prosperous. When Mayo and his fellow villagers came to Canada, they brought the confidence and enterprise of that background with them. Kapoor, having grown up near them, did not hesitate to join them in business.[16]

Kapoor and his partners were investing in BC while many of their countrymen were leaving. By the time Kapoor returned from Ontario in 1916, the Punjabi population in BC had fallen to less than eleven hundred – a fraction of the more than five thousand who had entered the country before 1908. Half of the original immigrants had gone to the United States, many more left Canada during the recession that began in 1913, and others, such as Piara Singh Langeri, went home in 1914 and 1915 in response to the Gadar call to arms. The last group had little chance of returning to Canada, because Canadian immigration officials had black marks opposite the names of suspected revolutionaries. During the war years, men left without being replaced, and by 1918 the community had fallen to about seven hundred.[17] Some men did return once the war was over, but they came from a few specific localities in Punjab. The Mahalpur area was one of these, and the Mayo and Virginia Lumber Companies were a large part of the reason.

Mahalpur lies within a triangular area known in Punjab as Doaba (Two Rivers) because its boundaries are defined by two rivers, the Beas and the Sutlej. Kapoor naturally associated with others from that area, commonly called Doabis. And he was living in an emigrant community that never forgot the local rivalries and prejudices it brought from home. From south of the Sutlej were the Malwais, and from west of the Beas were the Majhails. Each thought themselves better than the other.[18] In Punjab, families would not marry across these boundaries, and emigrants retained that attitude. Among Punjabis it made a difference whether one was from Doaba, Malwa, or Majha, whether one was Jat, Rajput, or Manhas Rajput, and whether one was Hindu, Sikh, or Muslim. Circumstances threw Kapoor into the company of his fellow Doabis, both Jats and Manhas Rajputs, although he was personally open-minded in the friendships he formed.

Punjab was always on Kapoor's mind and on the minds of his compatriots, and they responded to their families' appeals for help or aided village and district projects or the nationalist cause. During the war years, the BC Punjabi community began gathering annually for ceremonies and speeches to commemorate Mewa Singh, who had been hanged in January 1915 at the federal penitentiary in New Westminster for shooting and killing immigration inspector W.C. Hopkinson in a corridor in the Vancouver courthouse. The community also remembered seven compatriot revolutionaries who had embarked from Vancouver in the fall of 1914 only to be arrested, tried, and hanged by the British. The first of these was executed on 16 November 1915, and the last in June 1917, all but one in the Central Jail of Lahore. Among them was Balwant Singh Khurdpur, the former *granthi* (priest) at the Vancouver Sikh gurdwara, who shipped out of Vancouver in December 1914 and got as far as Bangkok, where he became sick enough to be hospitalized.[19] The Thai police arrested him in hospital and turned him over to the British in Singapore, who sent him back to India. In the Lahore court he was tried, convicted, and sentenced for his activities in Canada and the Far East – for the inflammatory speeches he made and the company he kept.[20]

Canadian Sikhs were still angry about these hangings when they refused to register for Canadian military service in the winter of 1917-18, six months after Canada introduced conscription. In a small community the issue was personal. Kapoor knew Balwant Singh Khurdpur, who was from the same village in Jalandhar as Lashman Singh, one of Kapoor's Virginia Lumber Company partners. And though the community had been divided when Kapoor and his friends were targeted by extremists in 1913 and 1914, he strongly sympathized with those who fought for India's freedom. His closest friend, Bhai Piara Singh Langeri, was a freedom fighter, and Kapoor admired all who sacrificed themselves for India. His countrymen expected him to take a leading role in recognizing its heroes, and he accepted that duty.

The gurdwara at Fraser Mills outside New Westminster was the usual place for the annual gathering for the martyr Mewa Singh, but in January 1918, the community met at the Strawberry Hill mill owned by Mayo, Kapoor, and partners, this time to remember all the Canadian martyrs in the struggle against the British. When the Canadian Sikh community formed a committee in 1921 to raise money for the families of imprisoned Gadarites, Kapoor stepped forward as a committee member and played a leading role.[21] By then, Gandhi was the unquestioned leader in India of the All-India Congress movement, and from his Canadian vantage point, Kapoor had become a Gandhi supporter. He admired heroes who stood up for their country, and at the same time he identified with the nonviolence that Gandhi embodied. In January 1922, Kapoor spoke at a meeting of the United India Home Rule League in appreciation of the work that Gandhi's Congress was doing. A month later, while presiding over a meeting of another Punjabi emigrant organization, the Doaba Press Association of America, he read out letters from Piara Singh Langeri, his revolutionary friend who had been released from prison two years earlier. Whatever was going on, Kapoor was at the centre, in partnership with Malwais and Doabis, militants and moderates, and always challenged by the need to smooth out differences in a small emigrant community facing adversity.

In early July 1920, Kapoor had been elected as the first president of the BC branch of the United India Home Rule League, which was aligned with Gandhi's Congress movement. Organizations like this could be formed quickly and expire early, even without the high challenge of sticking to Gandhi's principles, and this one was tested within a year when the South Indian founder of the United India Home Rule League in India, R.S. Hardikar, toured North America to raise money. During his tour, Hardikar spoke at the Vancouver gurdwara and at the Labour Temple in Seattle. A Punjabi-speaking agent of the Canadian government did everything he could to stir up division, pretending to be a Hardikar supporter while getting his Punjabi informants to agitate against him.[22] But Hardikar himself confused whites in his audiences by speaking ambivalently about non-violence. At the Seattle Labour Temple, when an American asked how Americans could help the Indian cause, Hardikar answered "With ammunition, revolvers, guns, cannons" before adjusting to what he *should* say, explaining that his movement was non-violent and would *not* use weapons to gain India's freedom. The BC branch of the home rule league collapsed after that visit, but a year later, the Hindustani Sabraj Society took its place, again with Kapoor as president. Several years later, he headed the Canadian Hindustani Congress, yet another organization supporting Gandhian ideals and objectives.[23]

When Hardikar visited BC in 1921, there were scarcely 950 Punjabis in the province, only a few of whom were women. Most of the men were labourers – about half worked in the lumber industry and the rest in construction, for the railways, or in food processing. Within two years, nearly all of them would be working in sawmills, and the success of entrepreneurs like Kapoor and Mayo was a prime reason for this. And smaller-scale entrepreneurs were also finding their way. In 1922 an Indian scholar spent some time in British Columbia documenting the activity of Punjabis and other South Asians settled there. He counted two grocery stores, two shingle mills, fifty firewood outlets, and twenty-five farms owned by South Asians. And he counted six lumber companies and seven logging camps.[24] Kapoor, with a major share in three of those lumber companies, each with its own logging operation, was a big operator, but the Canadian earnings of this community were the envy of relatives and fellow villagers at home in Punjab.

By the end of 1922, Kapoor had been in North America for sixteen years. He had stayed when most of his countrymen went home, and he had been successful despite the hostility and prejudice toward South Asians that was so prevalent in British Columbia at the time. Early on, he had decided that he would make a life in North America, and his actions were consistent with that objective. He never lost his affection for India and Indian culture or his dedication to the cause of Indian independence. The small Punjabi emigrant group was the heart of his world in Canada, but he made good friends among Anglo-Canadians, and he served as a vital bridge between his compatriots and the Canadian mainstream. Remarkably, he was living out his conviction that there was a future for himself and his community in Canada.

8
Women and Children at Mayo Siding

The women of Kapoor's generation were home- and village-bound, whereas many of the men were travellers. Like women of a seafaring community, they were used to seeing fathers and husbands disappear over the horizon while they waited for their return. However, their men could be gone for years, and some failed to come back. Kapoor's friend Kartar Singh Hundal left behind a teenaged wife whom he never saw again. When it became obvious that he would not return, his father placed a *chadar* (shawl) over his abandoned wife, ceremonially transferring her to Kartar's younger brother, a customary provision for widows among Jat Sikhs.[1] But the strength of village society kept most marriages intact, even though husbands were long gone. Women enjoyed the community of an extended family household – either that of their husband, as with Kartar Singh's wife, or their own, as with Besant Kaur. Eventually, most husbands did return, or some eventually sought to bring their wives to join them. In either case, the women helped reconnect their husbands with the village values they had left behind or let slip.

The right to have their wives with them was an emotional issue for South Asians in Canada and one that took years to resolve. While Kapoor was still in California, two activists, Balwant Singh Khurdpur and Bhag Singh Bhikhiwind had gone back to India for their families and made a highly publicized effort to get them into Canada. The intent of this was to benefit their community. A noisy crowd of seven hundred Sikh supporters had greeted their ship when it docked in Vancouver in January 1912, and their countrymen in Canada had agitated for the next six months until Ottawa at last relented and let the families stay, while insisting that no one else in the community could expect such treatment. In truth, the government backed down whenever challengers had the resources to fight its rulings and if those challengers showed enough determination and persistence. When the Department of Immigration relented, it allowed women to land as "an act of grace" to avoid a legal confrontation and precedent while still refusing to concede that they had any right of entry. Official figures show that only seven women and twelve children entered the country in the six years before the outbreak of the First World War.[2] Some of these women and children subsequently left Canada, so until the end of the war, there were never more than three or four families at any one time. This was a small group, with remarkable and, in some cases, tragic stories. Among those who left for India after a couple of years were the wife of the activist Balwant Singh and their three small children. In the fall of 1914, they sailed with him from San Francisco and continued as far as Singapore, where he set about his Gadar work while they went on to India, never to see him again. Bhag Singh's wife, Harnam Kaur, died of medical complications early in 1914, nine days after the birth of her second child and only seven months before Bhag Singh himself was killed in the notorious Bela Singh shooting. Her cremation was a front-page sensation in the Vancouver papers.

These papers might – but did not – have tried to follow what happened to Harnam Kaur's children, who were orphans in a community consisting almost entirely of men. Had the papers investigated, they would have discovered that the Vancouver gurdwara, having inherited responsibility for a newborn baby girl and a little boy, found a home for them with "a white woman" – as she was described in the gurdwara minute book. This woman was Annie Wright, or, by her Punjabi name, Bibi Labh Kaur, who six years earlier, despite the objections of some of her relatives, had married Munsha Singh, a young Sikh who spoke fluent English. Annie Wright was the best foster mother available for two orphaned Sikh children, but the gurdwara management committee worried about a girl growing up without a Punjabi mother, and when she was six, it took her from Annie's home and sent her back to Punjab.[3]

Among the two or three South Asian women living in Canada throughout the First World War were the wife of Hira Singh and the mother of Hakam Singh Hundal. These men were Indian army veterans and founding directors of the Guru Nanak Mining and Trust Company. After building up property assets in British Columbia, they went home to collect their families. On return in 1911, Hira Singh had a three-month struggle with the immigration department, fighting a deportation order and eventually getting his wife and three-year-old daughter landed "as an act of grace." In the late spring of 1912, at the Salvation Army Maternity Home in Vancouver, his wife gave birth to their second child, who was also the third South Asian born in Canada.[4]

That was the beginning of one Canadian family. The landing of Hakam Singh Hundal's children was another. His mother, Bishan Kaur, and his four underaged sons had languished for eighteen months in Hong Kong, living in its gurdwara while waiting for Canadian government permission to proceed.[5] That permission finally came in July 1913, again as an act of grace. Hakam Singh Hundal had a home ready for them in Point Grey, Vancouver, where the boys attended the local elementary school, the high school, and eventually the University of British Columbia, showing the way for later generations of Indo-Canadian students.[6]

Kapoor knew these people well. During his time in Victoria on the staff of *Sansar,* that paper ran several reports on them and their struggles with the immigration department. *Sansar* editor, Kapoor's associate and friend Kartar Singh Hundal, was related to Hakam. Moreover, like Kapoor, Hakam Singh belonged to a jagirdar family, and their shared gentry status was the basis of a personal relationship. When Kapoor and his family later lived in Kitsilano, Hakam Singh (who was old by then) regularly came over from his home to theirs, walking twenty blocks from Alma Street to York Avenue for a visit. He always had a dog with him and a short walking stick with a knob at the top. Kapoor's children learned from their mother that in Punjab one could recognize a jagirdar by his horse, dog, and walking stick. These were his *nishan* – his emblems. In Vancouver by then, a jagirdar did not have a horse but still went about with a dog and a stick.[7]

Kapoor was still living in Ontario in the winter of 1915-16 when he first applied to the Canadian government for permission for Besant Kaur to join him. This was a little more than a year after he had walked into the Toronto barbershop for his dramatic first shave and haircut, resolving to stay in Canada and to change his appearance to fit with Canadian society. One suspects that his politically connected friend William Moore, who was encouraging him to settle in Ontario, also encouraged him to petition the Department of Immigration for Besant Kaur's admission. She was now twenty-five, and though they had been married for ten years, they had yet to live together.

In early January 1916, Kapoor's petition reached the desk of the superintendent of immigration in Ottawa, William Duncan Scott, a bureaucrat who had held his job for so long that he knew the South Asian file intimately from the moment when the Punjabis landed in Canada and when public pressure built to have them shut out. In wartime, Scott began rethinking the South Asian case and – in memos to his superiors – advocating the admission of wives and children. Kapoor could not know it, but Scott supported his petition and used it as an argument for a broad review of Canada's South Asian immigration policy. Kapoor's history as a political moderate and success story made his case a good one to put forward. But that was as far as it went. The political chiefs in government were not yet willing to risk antagonizing white voters in BC.[8]

Seven more years passed before Besant Kaur could join Kapoor. In the early years of the war, his friends Kartar Singh Hundal, Dr. Sundar Singh, and their small band of Anglo-Canadian allies had argued in the press and in interviews with officials that, with Canadians and Indians fighting side by side in the trenches of Europe, Indians deserved better treatment in Canada.[9] Scott was one of the people whom they had persuaded. And from London, the Canadian prime minister was getting the message that Canada's immigration policy was such an aggravation to Sikhs in Punjab and in the Indian army that it threatened the welfare of the British Empire in India.

Only in the fall of 1917 did bureaucrats and politicians in Ottawa agree on the wording of a concession allowing the entry of wives and children, but this did not become policy for another sixteen months. And when it finally did, in March 1919, without any fanfare or publicity – so as not to cause controversy among whites in BC – it contained a huge obstacle for Kapoor and Besant Kaur, and for every other Asian couple in their situation. The Canadian government demanded that a wife or child must have a certificate from a commissioner or deputy commissioner in Punjab to prove the marital or parental relationship claimed by the sponsoring husband or father. This was one more document to be wrested from a district deputy commissioner's office in Punjab and another source of delay that kept women waiting from one year to the next for permission to sail. The Canadian immigration department was aware of the problem and of the frustration for Punjabis in Canada, but two years later, it was still not talking with Indian bureaucrats to resolve it.[10]

The first two women to immigrate under the new policy came in 1921.[11] The next year, Besant Kaur left India with seven other women, several men, and a number of children. They travelled in a group, as Punjabi villagers normally did, leaving from different villages but planning the trip together, coordinating departures, and staying with each other throughout the journey. Some women were accompanied by their husbands, who had returned from Canada to get them and who had the travel experience to guide the party. Kapoor's older brother, Bhagwan, who was back in India after some time in Canada, travelled as Besant Kaur's escort. On this journey, he betrayed his trust in one critical respect that Kapoor could never forget. Kapoor sent him money for two first-class passages by way of Europe, but Bhagwan pocketed the difference and brought Besant Kaur by steerage class and through Hong Kong – which he may have justified to himself because he went with others who chose that route. But he knew it was not what Kapoor expected. Nearly thirty years later, when Kapoor's daughters were visiting India as young adults, Bhagwan told them that in 1906 he had paid for their father to go to North America on a first-class ticket via Europe. This was not true; and for the first time in their lives, Jackie and Sarjit heard their father explode with anger. "Don't tell these girls lies," he said.[12]

When Besant Kaur left India, she still wore the *jhund,* or headcloth, that Punjabi women used in the purdah tradition to veil their faces in public or respectfully in the presence of the senior men of their families. In Canada, Kapoor urged her to drop the custom, and she agreed without argument. However, on the way to Canada, as she followed Bhagwan through the congested streets of Hong Kong, with the jhund impairing her vision, she bumped into iron rails loaded on a bullock cart and cut a deep gash in her forehead. She heard a passerby saying, "Beti (child), there is blood on your head."[13]

When Besant Kaur told her daughters this story years later, she said that she feared she would fail her medical examination as a result of the injury. All immigrants were required to pass a medical exam in Hong Kong before boarding a ship bound for Canada. As it happened, the gash was not a concern, but she failed her exam nonetheless because her eyes were red from crying. She had felt emotionally prepared to leave her village and country because she had so few close relatives there. Her father had passed away many years before, and her brother, Sundar, had emigrated to Africa, where he had died in 1920. Her uncle, Atma Singh Sandhu, had gone to Argentina, and news of his death had recently reached Aur. Her mother was the only immediate family she left behind. But in foreign surroundings en route to Canada, she was terribly homesick. When the Hong Kong doctor saw the redness of her eyes, he identified it as trachoma, an infectious form of conjunctivitis that both Canadian and

American immigration doctors looked for in Asian immigrants and used intentionally to disqualify them. The Hong Kong doctor also found trachoma in four other women in Besant Kaur's party, and the five of them had to remain for treatment (eye washes, vasoline, and antiseptic applications) while the others went on. The experience of this unexpected protracted sojourn in Hong Kong, staying at the gurdwara – the hostel for every Sikh traveller passing through – made them life-long friends. It also extended their journey to six months. They left home in 1922 but reached BC in 1923.

Kapoor did not know what ship they were on, and so was not there to greet them when they anchored at William Head Quarantine Station, the first call for all vessels approaching Victoria and Vancouver. There they could see the narrow peninsula of William Head, with a collection of staff and hospital buildings and a groomed lawn that contrasted with the wild, forested BC coastline in the background. Besant Kaur and Bhagwan disembarked there and spent the night at the quarantine hospital after sending a telegram to Kapoor at Mayo Siding, eighty kilometres away. He arrived the next morning with a choice for Besant Kaur. He had already purchased a property on York Avenue in Vancouver and built a house there with a view of the sea and the mountains. He also had a house in Mayo Siding but suspected that, having grown up in a village the size of a small city, she would not be happy in a remote sawmill community. When asked where she wanted to live, Besaunt Kaur gave an answer that defined their relationship from then on. She had come to Canada for the *darshan* (blessed sight) of her husband, she said, and she was content with that. Wherever he stayed, she wished to be.[14]

The choice that Kapoor offered Besant Kaur was considerate but unrealistic in that it assumed she might want to live among strangers in a foreign city with only his visits to look forward to. Still his desire to give her a choice was special and not what every new Punjabi wife could expect of her husband or his relatives, however affectionate. It could be quite different. Dhan Kaur Johl was one of the other women who came to Canada at that time. Her husband was the youngest of three brothers living in a sawmill bunkhouse in Vancouver while running a business with fifteen trucks that employed twenty-five men. The older brothers, all with wives in their village in Punjab, sent the youngest back to India to get married, and in 1923 – after an absence of two years – he returned with his new wife, Dhan Kaur, and their baby girl. When their ship docked in Japan, and people from the bazaar came on board, he bought a skirt and insisted that she wear it when they disembarked in Vancouver. For days after their arrival in Canada, she persisted in wearing her Punjabi suits (her *salwar kameez*) until her older brother-in-law, the head of the household, burned them in a wood stove.

The brothers had purchased a house for them all to live in, they had employed a Japanese girl to cook and to look after the baby, and three days after Dhan Kaur arrived, they bought a new 1923 Chevrolet sedan. The next day her brother-in-law taught her to drive, and every day after that, she drove the ten blocks to the sawmill to deliver lunches to the men. Later, she picked up the friends she eventually made, four other young Punjabi women who settled in Vancouver, and took them to the beach, or shopping at Woodward's Department store, or perhaps just to look around. That was life in the city. For Dhan Kaur, it began with loneliness and tears but thrived with a loving marriage and a growing family. The insistence on Western clothing came from the men in her household, who did not want her to attract hostile attention in a narrow-minded Anglo-Canadian environment.[15]

In Mayo Siding, Besant Kaur wore her Punjabi suits, although in time she also adopted Western dresses while keeping her headscarf, or *dupatta,* as other Punjabi women of her generation in Canada also did. This was a practical adaptation: making up Punjabi outfits was a problem in a country where there were no tailors who knew how to do it.

At Mayo Siding, Kapoor had employed Japanese workers to build his house, a large two-story clapboard structure in a classic Canadian farmhouse style. It had a veranda on three sides and sat on a three-acre lot surrounded by a picket fence with a stand of second-growth western hemlock behind. Mayo, his older brother, Ganeya, and Doman Singh soon began building their own houses, using a design with more complex rooflines and a covered front porch. But when Besant Kaur first arrived, Kapoor's house dominated, with nothing behind it except trees and the two-kilometre-distant profile of Hill 60, where lumbermen were felling trees for the mill. Hill 60 was the destination of the logging trains that climbed out of Mayo Siding on tracks that ran ninety metres east of the house.

From the front of the house, one looked at rough-built unpainted garages, the company office building, bunkhouses, wash-houses, and cookhouses for single men, and homes for the families of some of the workers. Many of these buildings were clustered along the CPR's Esquimalt and Nanaimo Railway. The biggest was the two-story lumber office and store, where several hundred Mayo Company workers – counting those in the mill and in the bush – could get supplies in exchange for coupons. Near the junction of the CPR line and the logging railway was a small frame shelter on stilts that served as the railway switchman's station. Across the CPR tracks were the chimney stacks, lumber piles, and the sheds of the planing, lathe, and sawmills. A single-unit passenger train came through once or twice a day, providing the easiest way in and out of Mayo Siding, if one could afford the ticket. Some workers and some Japanese women and children walked the thirteen kilometres from Duncan along the railway track to save the money. Alternatively, one could walk a winding route through the forest to catch a bus on the Cowichan Road. This access route had only recently been widened and upgraded to let motor vehicles through; and Kapoor had purchased a car, the first in a succession of Chevrolets. This was life in an industrial village in a partially logged-off countryside.[16]

In 1923 Besant Kaur was the first South Asian woman in an overwhelmingly male multi-racial community. Her female company consisted of a few white and Japanese women, with whom she had a great language barrier to overcome. Some were mothers whose children attended a small frame school, surrounded by huge stumps, that lay across the logging railway tracks, east of the mill. The Mayo Company had donated the lumber for the school two years earlier, and the first to attend it were white children, soon joined by a few Japanese. In their area in the west of the village, the Japanese families erected a separate schoolhouse for after-hours classes in Japanese and to use as a Japanese community centre. In a place where the rain transformed walkways into mud, the children of Mayo Siding made their way to school over boardwalks and, when they passed near the mill, a planked road. This was a morning and afternoon procession that Besant Kaur could observe from her house. When she left it, she usually headed a short distance to the west, past the lots where Mayo and his brother would build their homes, on her way to the gurdwara, which was one of the earliest buildings in the village. This was a one-story frame structure with a veranda and, in the Sikh tradition, entrances on all four sides. The gurdwara and her home quickly became the mainstays of her life.

The partnership that Besant Kaur created with Kapoor was one of equals, with her strong values and sense of self undiminished. Kapoor himself was a modern man, ahead of his time in many respects, although from a traditional culture. He took the unusual step, during their first few years together, of making her a shareholder in the Mayo Lumber

Company. Mayo Singh and Kapoor together held three-quarters of the shares in equal amounts, with the rest divided among fourteen people. Of the fourteen, only one was a woman, Besant Kaur. Kapoor was respectfully and affectionately including her in his world. He also worried about her health, which was poor for a long time after she arrived. She refused most of the food, so he took her to a Duncan doctor, who told her that in a cold climate she must eat meat and eggs. Like almost all Punjabi women of her time, she was a vegetarian, and her vegetarianism was too essential for her to give up on a Western doctor's advice. Kapoor, however, took instruction from her in the matter of prayer, which was her bedrock. In his sixteen years in North America, he had forgotten his Sikh prayers. She taught him the thirty-eight *pauris* (parts) of the morning meditation, or Japji, and for the rest of his life, he rose early to recite it.

In late March of 1925, with three feet of snow on the ground – which was extraordinary in an area famous for its mild winters – Kapoor rushed Besant Kaur to King's Daughter's Hospital in Duncan for the birth of their first daughter, Jagdis, or Jackie as everyone was to call her. A year and a half later, their second daughter, Sarjit, was born in Mayo Siding, her delivery coming too quickly for Kapoor to drive Besant Kaur into Duncan. As a young mother, Besant had the frequent and willing help of Auntie Bovyer (as the children knew her), the childless middle-aged wife of the mild-mannered office manager at Mayo Lumber. George and Isabella Bovyer lived in Duncan, but Isabella spent a lot of time with Jackie when Jackie was small and became very fond of her. The Bovyers were Methodists – George's younger brother, who was named John Wesley after the early Methodist leader, was a missionary in China. As Sarjit recalls, the Bovyers regularly brought Christian evangelicals to Mayo to visit the Kapoor home and the school. These evangelicals would crank up a portable gramophone and play hymns while the family or the schoolchildren sang along. Besant Kaur welcomed them warmly, but when they asked her to convert, she put the matter to rest with the answer, "No. Your God is my God." Auntie Bovyer never said anything to Kapoor about converting, and the memory that the girls had of her was of a warm, affectionate, and outgoing person, somewhat in contrast to her kind but shy and silent husband.

Auntie Bovyer helped during Jackie's infancy, but when Sarjit was born, Besant Kaur employed a Japanese woman, Kiku Urabe. Her husband, Toeman, had belonged to the gang of Punjabis and Japanese at Rosedale. At Mayo Siding, he helped build Kapoor's house and then Mayo's and Ganeya's. The Urabes had three children, and their youngest, Shigeko, born in 1921, who had a slight limp from polio, tagged along when her mother worked in the Kapoor house. Shigeko, or Jean as she was known outside her family, remembered Mrs. Kapoor as a fastidious housewife. One specific incident shaped this impression. Besant Kaur had offered her an orange but made her sit on a newspaper to peel it to protect a prized Indian carpet.

The Urabes already had a young family when Kapoor and Besant Kaur were just starting theirs, and that earlier start in raising children said something about the situation of the Japanese and the South Asians in Canada. Japanese men had begun bringing their women to Canada before the First World War – more than a decade ahead of the South Asians. They did so within the framework of an agreement negotiated between Canada and Japan in 1908 and honoured for twenty years. For the Chinese, the situation was different again. In the Chinatowns of Vancouver, Victoria, or Nanaimo, a few Chinese merchants had their wives and families with them, but the vast majority of the Chinese in the province did not; and the immigrant head tax – which only the Chinese had to pay – was a big factor in this. Men could not afford to bring their wives into the country. Canada's immigration regime imposed an unmistakable pattern on the development of Mayo Siding. The first few families were white and Japanese. For the Punjabis who ran the place, family life began with the household created by Kapoor and Besant Kaur, after Canada gave the green light to the immigration of women and children from India. The Chinese, who made up nearly half the workforce at Mayo Siding, were all men without families, living in bunkhouses in their own part of the village near the mill pond.[17]

Besant Kaur urged Kapoor to bring over his relatives, and he began to do it in the years that followed. His brother Tara came in 1926, fourteen years after leaving California. He did not have landed status or residence in Canada, but he managed to get in anyway and to bring his new wife, Balwant Kaur.[18] Others followed, and in their coming and going from Kapoor's house, they kept Besant Kaur cheerfully busy, prepared to serve food at any time for anyone in her circle of friends and family who might turn up. In the autumn of 1925, Mayo Singh left for India, returning nearly two years later with a nineteen-year-old bride, Bishen Kaur. And Mayo's older brother, Ganeya, and their fellow villager Doman Singh also brought back wives in subsequent years. More relatives came and Mayo Siding witnessed more births, beginning with Mayo and Bishen's first child in 1927. In these years, Mayo Siding was becoming an extension of

Paldi and Kharoudi in Punjab, the villages of Mayo and Kapoor. Kapoor's daughters had the comforting presence of relatives from Kharoudi all around them. In front of their house was Aunt Daleep's house; across the tracks of the logging railway were Aunt Harnam's house, Aunt Mauan Kaur's, and Uncle Balwant's sister's house, all in a row. South of that, across the CPR line, was Uncle Daleep's.

Every few weeks Kapoor drove the two hours into Victoria, taking Besant and the girls with him. Before they left, Besant asked their relatives for a list of the special supplies they wanted from Victoria. Once she was old enough, Sarjit took on the job of going to these homes to ask for the list. Everyday supplies were available at the Mayo Siding company store and from a Chinese fruit and vegetable vendor, Bing Chong, who brought his rickety black truck to the mill once a week, where it was greeted by a crowd of women who lifted the rubbery sheets along on the sides of the truck and peeked at his produce before he had time to switch off his engine.[19] And at Mayo Siding, households also had their own food supplies. Behind Kapoor's house was a garden and a barn with cows, goats, and chickens, all the domain of the cook, a Punjabi named Kabli. But when Kapoor had business in Victoria, that provided an opportunity for shopping. The family usually went to the big David Spencer department store that spanned an entire business block in downtown Victoria. Besant Kaur had enough English to shop but not much more than that. She would pack a special lunch, which they enjoyed during a stop en route, but sometimes the girls were treated to a restaurant lunch of onion soup with croutons and fish and chips, while their mother watched, not relaxing her vegetarian principles. If Kapoor's business was prolonged, he would leave Besant and the girls at Beacon Hill Park, where Sarjit and Jackie played on the swings.

Kapoor built swings for them in their own yard at home, and their strongest early memories of Mayo Siding were of that yard and those swings. Bhai ji, or Kabli, the bachelor cook who maintained a large garden and looked after the livestock, was not very friendly – aloof in the company of women or children – although the girls watched him in fascination as he butchered chickens, which would run around headless. Twice a day he entered the house with pails of milk, some of it goat's milk for Jackie, who was allergic to cow's milk. On the advice of the doctor in Duncan, Kapoor had purchased goats and the few he bought grew under Kabli's care to a herd of more than a hundred, all white. Much more welcoming than Kabli was "Daddy" Maclean, the railway switchman who watched the intersection of the main line and the logging line. He exuded a love for children and was a lot of fun when the girls went down to his shack to collect buttercups or on some other pretext. They were visiting him when they had the shock of seeing a Japanese logger's body brought out on a flatbed railway car, covered except for his spiked boots. But the logging railway had much happier associations for them because their father sometimes took them on excursions up the line. They would ride on a flatcar, and he would spread sheets of newspaper on the narrow cast-iron plates at each end so they could hang their feet over the track without getting their cotton dresses dirty. After a slow trip of forty-five minutes – almost forever in a child's mind – they arrived at the logging camp with its small collection of bunkhouses and a stream to splash in.

Kapoor and Besant Kaur spent over a decade at Mayo Siding, a decade broken in the middle by a year in India, and besides books and the stories their mother told them, this mill setting was the world that Jackie and Sarjit knew until they were nine and ten. At Mayo Siding they had a sheltered family life, playing with their cousins and two white girls. Their mother would not let them play with any of the boys in Mayo Siding except their cousins. Their constant backdrop was an operating sawmill and a great beckoning outdoors. Before their front door, a multi-racial, multicultural village went about its business, with their father and his partners its employers and chief benefactors. The town existed for one purpose, and they learned to recognize as music the high-pitched whine of the saw as a fresh log made its first passage through the mill. But the wilderness was not far away, and they fondly remembered their blackberry-picking expeditions along the railway with their cousins. In one favourite moment, they stood in the forest with their father, eyes fixed on a deer. This is what they had come looking for, and their father was armed with a rifle. "Shoot Daddy," they said, and he fired and missed; they never shook the thought that he had missed deliberately because he was too kind to aim to kill.

Their mother told them that, had her brother and uncle been living in Aur when Kapoor called her to Canada, she would not have come. She was too attached to her own family and too removed from him. But she did come, and at Mayo Siding the two of them replicated the close family she had enjoyed at home. For years he had suppressed his own family instincts while building assets in Canada. When the Canadian government finally let his wife into the country, and when she chose to live by his side rather than in the city, he committed himself to domestic life. It may have been his nature or her guidance or a mutual wisdom, but after a marriage that began with years of separation, they moved into a united partnership to raise two children who were equally fond and proud of both parents, and unable ever – even in the smallest thing – to get one to say yes when the other had said no.

9
Village Life in Canada and India

Life in a lumber village for Kapoor, the businessman, family man, and community leader, was wonderfully varied. And it was probably more rewarding for Besant Kaur than the city would have been at that stage in her life. For the girls, it was full of stimulation even though their parents were protective – very strict to use Jackie's words. The girls were growing up as Canadians, but in an ethnically diverse community unlike most of Canada at that time. They had a father who wanted to teach them about the world, through books and travel and by encouraging them to sit in on adult discussion and conversation. And the world beyond reached into the lumber community, when Kapoor hosted some quite extraordinary people. They had a mother who taught them, by example and through storytelling, about matters of faith. Through their father, they learned of the big issues in their community – the independence movement in India and the campaign for rights in Canada. They grew up loving nature, which lay at their doorstep, and they had the Mayo mill in full view of the house, taking it for granted as much as the forest and mountains.

The lumber business was the sole reason for their presence at Mayo Siding, and it was doing well in the boom times of the 1920s. By the end of the decade, Kapoor, Mayo, and their associates employed nearly four hundred men at Mayo, they had a second mill of the same size at Sooke Lake, fifty kilometres to the south, and they were planning a third at the foot of Cowichan Lake, eighteen kilometres to the west, where they had timber land. At Mayo they continued to operate as the Mayo Lumber

Company. At Sooke and Cowichan Lakes, they were the Kapoor Lumber Company, and at all three locations, Kapoor and Mayo were the principal partners. They had subsidiary companies, Tansor Lumber and Maroka Lumber, through which they owned other mill properties, machinery, and lumber, but the mill and forest at Mayo, and the mill and forest at Sooke Lake were their main assets. Kapoor was no longer involved with the Virginia Lumber Company, but the expansion that he and Mayo undertook together more than made up the difference.[1]

The Kapoor Lumber Company began operating in the Sooke Lake area in October 1927 with the purchase of five thousand acres of virgin timber, mostly fir. Its mill was at mile thirty-five of a new CNR line from Victoria to Cowichan Lake, and it sat alongside an abandoned horse-and-buggy road that once ran from Victoria to Duncan, passing east of Sooke Lake. The logging camp was a two-kilometre climb by logging railway to a small scenic lake in a long valley enclosed by mountainous ridges. This was Wolf Lake, two hundred metres in elevation above the mill. At the mill site, the company built a village like the one at Mayo, a cluster of sixty or seventy buildings: frame bunkhouses with detached washrooms, a store, and four cookhouses – for whites, Japanese, South Asians, and Chinese. Set against the forest was a little one-room frame schoolhouse with a pitched roof and windows along one side, an entry at one end, and a chimney at the other for the cast-iron wood-burning stove inside. On arrival at the village by automobile, one rattled and bumped over a plank road fronting the fifteen wooden garages that serviced the mill's logging trucks and Mayo and Kapoor's cars. Most of the Japanese working at Sooke had families who kept attractive gardens in front of their houses. Mayo had a house there, although Kapoor did not until he took over the house that had been occupied by Sam Cowan, the accountant. The village of Kapoor at Sooke Lake was even more isolated than Mayo Siding. It was fifty kilometres from Victoria, but the trip by motor vehicle was an all-day adventure over logging roads, rising, falling, twisting, turning, and skirting boulders.

The Kapoor mill had been operating for a year and a half when the Bengali poet and Nobel laureate, Rabindranath Tagore, visited BC as the headline speaker at a conference of the National Council of Education (an influential Canadian association concerned with patriotism, curriculum, and citizenship). Attending the conference in April 1929 constituted Tagore's one and only trip to Canada, although he was a world traveller whose lecture tours often took him to Europe and the US. On this trip he stopped only in Victoria and Vancouver before going on to California.

Tagore was an Indian national icon, lionized abroad and loved at home. The Sikhs of BC claimed him enthusiastically; although his Bengali culture was as different from theirs as French from English, they shared his Indian sentiments and enjoyed his acclaim. He spoke four times in Vancouver and once in Victoria, and on those nights the queues of Anglo-Canadian Vancouverites or Victorians wanting to hear him stretched for blocks. While in Vancouver, he went to the gurdwara for an evening of sacred Sikh music in his honour, and he was supposed to go to the Victoria gurdwara for its Baisakhi Day celebrations but had to cancel at the last moment after he became ill. He was apologetic, but he was nearly seventy, and keeping up a hectic schedule was no longer easy. A crowd of Sikhs had waited to greet him and garland him at the Victoria docks when he first arrived, and before he left, a delegation of Sikhs called on him at the Empress Hotel in Victoria with a farewell address and a purse of gold, which they asked him to use as he chose for his own good works in India.[2]

Kapoor had no reason to write about Tagore's visit, but his friend Kartar Singh Hundal, the editor and journalist, did, and we get a sense of the occasion from him. In a group photograph taken then, Kartar stands immediately behind Tagore. Also in the photograph are members of the Vancouver and Victoria gurdwara executives, but Kartar Singh is there because he was Tagore's guide in BC.[3] And he was simultaneously hosting the famous missionary and Gandhi companion Charles Freer Andrews, who was also a translator and editor of Tagore's poetry.[4] Andrews had come to BC from New York at the end of a North American tour after he learned that Tagore would be there, and it fell to the highly literate and bicultural Kartar Singh to look after both men. (Tagore and Andrews knew each other well.) While in Victoria, Andrews finished the preface to a book he was publishing on Mahatma Gandhi, drawing on his years of working with Gandhi in South Africa and India.[5] For a moment, the Sikhs of BC had the attention of two internationally renowned and respected advocates of Indian independence. The advice they received from Tagore at the moment he left was to embrace the country in which they had settled: "Do your very best to prove yourselves 'Good Canadians.'" Their formal reply, written certainly by Kartar Singh, was an echo of the same thought – they would strive to be worthy citizens of the country in which they lived and of India whence they came.[6]

The words came agreeably and naturally after the Bengali poet and the Punjabi activist had spent a few days together. They expressed Kartar Singh's sentiments exactly. No one in the South Asian community had plunged farther into Anglo-Canadian life and culture than he, and yet his concern for India and his desire to serve India's people burned on. This desire remained alive after his long exile in Toronto, away from his own countrymen, when he had found a spiritual and intellectual home in Toronto's small but active Theosophical Society. He had been a mainstay of the society for years, a volunteer for its many tasks – librarian, secretary, treasurer, and dedicated editor of its newsletter. When he first spoke of leaving, Albert E.S. Smythe (the founder of the Theosophical movement in Canada) expressed his regrets in the *Canadian Theosophist,* describing Kartar as nothing short of a saint.[7] Kartar had announced he was going back to India but changed his mind and settled in BC to work for his countrymen there. Kapoor, who gave him employment, may have influenced his decision. In any case, Kartar Singh told his Toronto friends that he considered himself a Canadian and that he intended to find a way to interpret the Sikhs to the rest of Canada and Canada to the Sikhs.[8]

With Kapoor's backing, Kartar Singh made a valiant attempt by publishing another English and Punjabi newspaper titled *India and Canada: A Journal of Interpretation and Information.* This was a single-handed effort that he composed and typeset in the partitioned-off back room of a store on Fourth Avenue in Vancouver and then in slightly roomier premises at the corner of Fourth and Vine. He depended on Kapoor for some funding, while also raising what he could through subscriptions and a few advertisements. Mayo was a generous subscriber. Kartar Singh's first issue in English gained some gratifying attention in the mainstream press, and he produced seven monthly issues in 1929 and 1930 before letting the bilingual effort lapse and putting his energy into a fortnightly Punjabi edition, in which he wrote explicitly about the internal affairs of the community, family scandals that everyone was talking about, personal jealousies, and public altercations, as well as community achievements and celebrations. His purpose was to educate. In the Punjabi edition, he could be scathing when he thought community standards had dropped too low or that people were too grasping, petty, and self-serving, or too caught up in narrow regional and sectarian differences. In English, he always presented the community in an entirely positive light.[9]

Before he launched his newspaper, he toured the Sikh settlements of the BC Lower Mainland and the island, and during this trip he saw the Mayo and Kapoor mills. In his third issue, he ran a biography of Kapoor in English. Here was an immigrant, he wrote, who had been tremendously successful in the lumber industry, who was employing hundreds of men, who was highly cultured, and who had a great stake in BC, but who could not vote and did not have the full rights of citizenship. He asked,

"Why should Canada treat an East-Indian Canadian who had adopted Canada and fulfilled all of the requirements of true Canadianism in such a way?" This was Kartar Singh's central point, and Kapoor was his best illustration.

Also in Canada at that time was Kapoor's friend and dharam brother Bhai Piara Singh Langeri, who had been released from jail in India – his second prison term – in June 1926. He had come to Canada via San Francisco in May 1928, and as a major figure in the community, he spoke in the Victoria gurdwara on Baisakhi Day in April 1929 when Tagore had to cancel. Police files in India listed him as dangerous, still working with Gadar Party activists in California and with revolutionary and anti-government organizations in India. Kapoor, Kartar Singh, and nearly all Canadian Sikhs welcomed him. Some skeptics did question his loyalty and integrity, asking why he was free when other Gadar heroes remained in jail. But both Kapoor and Kartar Singh admired him as a friend, a great human, and a warrior in the national cause. On the eve of Bhai Piara Singh's return to India, Kartar Singh ran his picture on the front page of *India and Canada*'s Punjabi edition and described him as a "pure and brave servant" who worked incessantly for his community and country. That feeling was shared by the Victoria Sikhs, who presented him with a sword and several purses at a farewell gathering.[10]

During this period, Kapoor himself was active in two locally based Indian independence organizations – the Canadian branch of the Indian National Congress party and the War Council of the Hindustani Congress. With Kartar Singh Hundal, he also collected funds for the legal defence of Bhagat Singh, the twenty-one-year-old Punjabi revolutionary who, with his associate B.K. Dutt, had thrown two bombs from the visitors gallery in the Central Assembly Hall in Delhi.[11] The bombs caused little damage, and he openly courted arrest only to be betrayed by some of his associates on the serious charge of previously murdering a police officer. He was famous throughout India and among Indians abroad by the time of his murder trial in July 1929, a legendary patriot and martyr who would not disown his actions to avoid the hangman's noose. Kapoor and Kartar Singh worked together in Canada, raising money to help pay for the best possible lawyers for Bhagat Singh's initial trial and for his unsuccessful appeal to the Privy Council in London. Informants duly reported this fundraising to the Indian police for their files.[12]

The police in India had reports of Kapoor's involvement with the revolutionary Gadar Party, now centred among Sikhs in Stockton, California. These sprang from his efforts with Kartar to raise funds for publications and for community work, which led him to talk to South Asian leaders on both sides of the border. When Kapoor went to Seattle in 1928 and met with Gadar representatives, the Indian police learned about it. And they learned of a trip that he, Kartar, and two other Canadian Sikhs took late in 1929 that again involved conversations with Gadar leaders. According to the files of the director of intelligence in New Delhi, the Gadar leadership wanted several Canadian Sikhs to go to India to do Gadar Party work, and Kapoor refused, saying he did not want to leave Canada. But the situation had an ominous backdrop that this brief summary misses.

A couple of years earlier, the Gadar Party had turned toward the Soviet Union and Marxism. This shift and the resulting secretive revival of party activity produced two dozen murders or more among California's South Asians in a four-year period from 1927 to 1931.[13] Militants were targeting suspected informers in their community. Kapoor and Kartar Singh managed to keep their distance and were able to do so because the violence fortunately was confined to Punjabis in California. As always, Kapoor maintained a consistent line. Much as he admired his friend Bhai Piara Singh Langeri and the sacrifices of patriots like Bhagat Singh, his goals had not wavered from the moment in 1914 when he shaved his beard and discarded his turban. He still saw his work, his contribution, and his future in Canada.

In the fall of 1931, he did take his family to India, but that was after a Depression-induced collapse of the international market for BC lumber, not for political reasons. The Depression had taken a while to settle into the lumber market, which had remained reasonably healthy for several months after the Wall Street crash of October 1929. Even in the summer of 1930, despite the increasing cost of logging in a diminishing forest and a drop in log prices that shut down most logging operations, nearly all the important mills in the Cowichan district were still working. In June, Mayo's neighbour at Hillcrest was among the first to close, and mills throughout the West Coast lumber industry began scaling back production.[14] Then, in August 1930, fire totally destroyed the Kapoor mill at Sooke and part of its lumber stock. The fire had started on the CNR right of way, perhaps sparked by a railway engine, and it had burned in the brush on CNR property for a day before charging across the tracks and through the mill and mill yard. The Kapoor Company sued the CNR for $150,000 (starting a lengthy legal battle) and within a month optimistically began rebuilding the mill.[15] But the Depression spread and deepened, and the main international markets for BC lumber – the eastern US, Japan, the UK, and Europe – collapsed. On 31 October 1930, the Mayo

Company closed its mill and laid off its workers except a few who shared the watchman's job. Everyone knew that conditions might remain poor for a long time, and many Mayo employees headed home to their villages in India, where they could live for less.

The mill had been shut for almost a year when the Siddoos left Canada to visit Besant Kaur's seventy-year-old mother in India. Grandmother Bishan Kaur Sandhu was in Aur with her widowed and childless daughter-in-law, Pritam Kaur, and though she was unwilling to come to Canada, she corresponded regularly with Besant. This visit would be her opportunity to get to know her granddaughters. Kapoor's brothers and their families were in Canada, and Kharoudi was empty of relatives, so he and Besant Kaur felt no need to divide their time between his village and hers.

Jackie was six and Sarjit just past her fifth birthday when they left by steamship from Victoria on 3 October 1931, bound for India via Japan. Jackie was old enough to remember a full moon shining when they docked in Kobe, Japan, and both girls remembered the narrow Kobe bazaar decorated with balloons and streamers that led to a beautiful Buddhist temple, which they entered to the sound of drums and where their mother, always open to other faiths, prayed. But they remembered little else of a journey that took over a month to reach Kolkata (Calcutta) by way of Hong Kong and Ceylon, except the lessons in English that Kapoor gave them as part of the daily shipboard routine. While they were engaged in this way, the police intelligence bureau in India was tracking them and knew the dates of their departure from Canada and arrival in India.

They spent fifteen months in Aur in the village house that had once been their great-grandfather's qila, or fort, where, as a jagirdar in the service of Maharaja Ranjit Singh, he kept his elephants and horses. Although the qila had been subdivided and its wall incorporated into adjoining houses, the family retained a considerable part of it including a large walled and paved courtyard. From the upper part of their house, they could look beyond the courtyard to green village fields in the midst of which sat a beautiful half-acre reservoir, or tank, built on a perfect square by a villager who had risen to the rank of *vazir* (chief minister) under the Mughal emperor Jahangir. After nearly three centuries, it was still in good condition, preserving all the Persian brickwork of the fourteen steps that ran along three sides and led down to the water.[16] The antiquity of the village was also evident in the Persian brickwork, elaborate entries, and great carved wooden doors of the homes of the leading village families, homes that were adjacent to the Sandhu qila.

They stayed in Aur for more than the full cycle of Sikh and Hindu religious holidays. The girls never forgot the play performed in July in the narrow alley running by their home – a dramatization of Lord Krishna's birth in a prison and his rescue from the evil ruler who would have slain him as a newborn – or the festival of Dussehra in October when villagers re-enacted the story of Rama and Sita and their crossing of the River Ganga, using the ancient half-acre reservoir to represent the river. They became familiar with the rhythm of village life and the steady stream of hawkers and peddlers bringing all manner of treats to their door. And they went to the noisy bazaar, crowded with Muslims, Sikhs, and Hindus, a meeting place for people from the plains and the hills. Sarjit would ride on the shoulders of a family friend, Harnam Singh, who was over six feet tall, and their grandmother spoiled them by buying whatever they asked for. They acquired a great collection of traditional India clay toys, low-fired brightly painted miniatures of birds, animals, deities, heroes, and carts and other implements common in village life.

All through those months in Aur, their father gave them daily English lessons and their mother taught them Punjabi, supplemented with tales from the Hindu epics the Ramayana and Mahabharata, and from Sikh tradition and history. The girls were always in the protective care of their parents or grandmother, never free to wander beyond the courtyard gate to play with the local children. Instead, their mother invited neighbouring children into the courtyard to play with them while she watched.

With Aur as their base, their parents toured Sikh and Hindu shrines such as Anandpur and Nankana, Haridwar and Rishikesh. Sometimes they left the girls with their grandmother, and sometimes they took them along. The girls went to Anandpur Sahib, the shrine associated with the tenth Sikh guru. On that excursion, they travelled by bus as far as the Sutlej River and spent the night on its banks – there were no hotels – before crossing by ferry barge the next day and proceeding a short distance to the gleaming white shrine that sits on the edge of the Punjab plains, with the Shivalik Hills rising behind. They also accompanied their parents to Nankana Sahib, the birthplace of Guru Nanak, the first Sikh guru, and they ventured farther into the Muslim country of West Punjab. Most memorable for the girls was the occasion in the Peshawar Valley when two passengers started fighting and creating chaos on the bus. A European policeman boarded and six-year-old Jackie announced to everyone from her seat at the front, "Now that the Englishman is here, everything will be alright."

A trip into the Shivalik Hills also made an impression that the family kept alive by repeating the story many times. It had to do with an otherworldly phenomenon. They had taken a bus to Una to find the village in which Grandmother Sandhu was born. They got off the bus as darkness fell in the midst of a thunderstorm. The girls were frightened and Besant Kaur was unsure of which path led to her mother's village. A big black dog appeared, wagging its tail, and Besant Kaur said to Kapoor, "Let us follow that dog." It led them to the family home, where her relatives answered the door. Wishing to reward the dog with milk, Besant Kaur discovered that it had vanished. Her relatives recognized it from her description and marvelled because it had died several years before but was known to turn up whenever someone was in distress.

Kapoor had been too successful an emigrant for people not to know he had returned to Punjab. One consequence of this was an invitation to a tea party in the state of Patiala with Maharaja Bhupinder Singh, a prince of immense influence under the British, the most noteworthy Sikh of the day, a sportsman, diplomat, military man, and a Sidhu from the same branch of the Sidhu *got* (clan) as Kapoor. But a Sikh from Canada who was prominent enough to receive an invitation from a famous maharaja was bound to attract police attention. Early in 1933, an agent of the Intelligence Bureau came to Aur to demand Kapoor's passport "for verification." Kapoor refused to surrender it, expecting he would not get it back – his association with the Gadar Party and his friendship with Bhai Piara Singh were too well known. Rather than risk being trapped in India without a passport, he made immediate plans to leave. He and the family returned to Canada in February 1933 to be greeted when they stepped ashore in Victoria with a heavy fall of snow. He did not return to India for nineteen years, until after the British had gone.[17]

At Mayo they found a new house in the place of their old one, which had burned down while they were away. They had left the house in the care of Harnam Kaur, the teenage wife of Kapoor's fellow villager Narang Singh Gill. She had gone every day to feed Prince, the family dog, let it out for a run, and make sure everything was alright. How the fire started, she did not know. It had happened during the night, possibly someone's *shararit* (mischief), and the house had been a total loss.[18] Mayo had built a new one for Kapoor's family, patterning it after his own. So now there were two similar houses near each other. Kapoor's family had established itself in this new house in time for the reopening of the Mayo mill on 15 March 1933. The lumber business was improving, and the Kapoor mill began operating as well. If Kapoor needed reassurance, he got it from

William Moore, his old friend from Pickering, now a Liberal MP and an economic analyst, who came to Vancouver that fall to speak to BC businessmen about a lifting world depression.[19]

For the next two and a half years, Kapoor kept his family at Mayo, where the girls went to school, with Sarjit going straight into grade two and Jackie into grade three on the strength of the teaching they had received from him. Although they lived in Mayo, the family spent enough time at Kapoor during Christmas and summer holidays for Jackie to make friends with Barbara Cowan, the accountant's impish daughter. And the girls, young as they were, remembered the visits of two scholars who used the Kapoor village at Sooke Lake as a place of study and retreat. One of them was an exceptional Sikh from Piplanwala, Hoshiarpur, named Sadhu Singh Dhami, who arrived in Canada in 1922 as a boy of sixteen to work in Vancouver sawmills while attending John Oliver High School. He went on to university in BC and then Alberta, Berkeley, and Toronto. By 1937 he had earned a PhD in philosophy at Toronto with a thesis on John Dewey. During these years, the village of Kapoor was a kind of resort for Dhami, an ideal place to study and write. Five years after earning his PhD, he secured a job, thanks to Trade Commissioner Mool Raj Ahuja, British India's first diplomatic representative in Ottawa, with the International Labour Organization (then temporarily headquartered in Montreal). Years later, in retirement in Geneva, he wrote an evocative novel in English, *Maluka*, about the Punjabis he knew as a young man while working in a sawmill on the Fraser River, some of whom were illiterate and who needed his help to read their letters from home and to write their replies.

Whenever Dhami was in residence at Kapoor village, the cookhouse became the centre for lively discussions on all manner of subjects, whether religious, literary, or political. Kapoor encouraged his daughters to sit in and listen, which they were keen to do.[20] Dhami himself later said that the Sikh cookhouse was his own first university. As he knew from personal experience, a cookhouse audience was tough to handle. Sitting together were Gadarite revolutionaries who espoused communism and admired the Soviet Union, moderates like Kapoor who revered Gandhi, and religious nationalists who were firmly attached to the Sikh way. None were deferential. An uninspired delivery or a commonplace bit of information would prompt shouts of "Sit down! Even the boards of the cookhouse know that." And a speaker who relied on a prepared text would hear "Throw away the papers! Give us something out of your head." And though poetry reading was popular, and aspiring Punjabi lumber-worker poets were keen to recite, a cookhouse audience would not put up with weak rhymes or foreign notions such as blank verse. "That's not poetry," they would say. "That is prose run wild."[21]

The other scholar who visited Kapoor village was Anup Singh Dhillon from Jhabal, Amritsar, who was writing a PhD dissertation in political science for Harvard, which he finished in 1935. His subject was the International Labour Organization, which may have influenced his friend Dhami's eventual career choice. Dhillon had arrived in North America at the same time as Dhami, but being five years older, he was farther along in his studies. He had gone to Berkeley and Kansas before enrolling at Harvard. While conducting his PhD research and afterward while living in New York, he made two trips to Ottawa on behalf of South Asians in Canada, lobbying for their rights as he did for South Asians in the US. One contact to whom Dhillon and Dhami jointly turned was Hugh Keenleyside, a sympathetic senior official in External Affairs who had taught history for two years at UBC and whose childhood roots were in BC. Through Dhillon and Dhami, the village of Kapoor briefly became a command post in the long campaign for equal rights for South Asians in BC.[22]

Among the children at Kapoor was Ajaib Siddoo, who arrived in Canada in 1930 at the age of seven to join his father, Naranjan, an uneducated sawmill worker and a cousin to Kapoor (he was the son of Kapoor's maternal aunt Nikko). Naranjan had been in Canada for three years while little Ajaib had been living in Kharoudi with his mother, grandmother, and three-year-old brother and, for a year, attending school in a nearby village. Like Kapoor a generation earlier, he had walked to class, going several kilometres daily with a group of Kharoudi schoolboys. He never knew why his family decided to send him to Canada; nor did he have a chance to ask. His mother was not going and never did, and as a small boy he found himself travelling with Narang Singh Gill, from Kharoudi, Narang's new sixteen-year-old wife, Harnam Kaur, and Doman Singh from Mayo's village of Paldi and his wife, Prabhi. Both men were middle-aged, having spent many years in Canada, and they had gone home to Punjab purposefully to bring back young wives. Doman Singh was also taking a nephew with him, Meetu, whom he described to officials as his son; and while on board, Ajaib and Meetu explored the ship more adventurously than the adults, getting to know some of the other passengers and the crew, who produced toys for them to play with. (Like many Punjabis, these families did not eat in the ship's dining room but cooked separately.) The route was the usual one: train to Kolkata, boat to Hong

Kong, a month in its gurdwara, and a large ship to Canada. Ajaib knew that it was an American ship, belonging to the President's line, and it docked in Victoria late in January 1930.[23] On arrival he went to Mayo Siding and then Kapoor village, and in the years that followed, he attended school at both places.

In Kapoor, Ajaib stayed with his father at the house of Sam Cowan the accountant and for a period in the bunkhouse. He took his meals at the South Asian cookhouse, where the cook would feed him ahead of the main rush. And he ate many times with the Chalmers, one of the white families at Kapoor, who invited him because they had a son of his age. In their house, he learned to eat European food; and for one highly enjoyable holiday, he went up island with the Chalmers on a two-week camping trip. Kapoor itself offered much for boys to explore: When no one was looking, they played with the hand-operated trolley that ran on the railway line. Sooke Lake, protected by a live-in guard because it was the source of Victoria's drinking water, was out of bounds though not inaccessible to boys who found gaps in the fencing, not to swim but just to enter forbidden territory. A natural pool in the river that flowed into Sooke Lake provided a good spot to splash about and build rafts, and they helped themselves to apples from the orchard of a nearby farm.

Ajaib acquired a newspaper route and delivered to about fifteen homes. The route was not easy because it required a lot of strenuous walking in steep terrain, and the newspapers came with the mail just three times a week, so he carried three days of papers at a time. He also delivered milk from a local dairy farm to the Chinese workers at Kapoor, and by the time he was fifteen, he felt rich enough to buy a car for twenty-eight dollars, paid for in two instalments. This was an old thirty-five horsepower Durant Motor Company Model T Star, which, when new, had been worth ten or twelve times what he paid for it. He taught himself to steer and shift by quietly observing what drivers did and by practising on his own with his car. To get a licence, he drove into Duncan with a friend and presented himself for the exam. After he had passed, a policeman asked how he got there, and he said that the person he came with was shopping in a store, not mentioning that this was another unlicensed youth like himself.[24]

As a boy, and especially a boy who was in the general care of everyone and the special care of no one, Ajaib enjoyed a lot of freedom, far more than Kapoor's daughters. But they were close to his age and they were cousins, so they spent time with him whenever they were in Kapoor or he was in Mayo. Later he lived with Kapoor's family in Vancouver while attending high school there. The three of them grew up with shared memories of family drives to the sea at Maple Bay east of Duncan where they sat on the beach and enjoyed the sliced ham sandwiches that Kapoor made for them – Besant Kaur would not prepare meat – stopping in town on the way back for an ice cream cone.

They were fascinated by the same people: Johindsa, the white-bearded priest at Mayo, who enunciated beautifully but spoke rapidly during gurdwara services and who demanded focus and attention, which he got by shouting at the women to stop their talking and take their restless children outside; Kabli, Mayo's aloof cook, who tended his vegetable garden and kept a herd of white goats; Gurbachan Singh, the lovely mannered cook at Kapoor, with his magnificent garden, love of flowers, and herd of goats stocked from Kabli's, which the boys would chase and try to ride, and his *dholki,* or drum, that he played during *kirtan,* the religious singing that he led in a special room in the bunkhouse basement; the bearded man Bhao, who lived in a railway boxcar; and the old Punjabi who claimed to have been a cowboy, whom Ajaib enjoyed talking to and who could be found with his cows, riding horse, and buggy by the sheds near the bridge, where people lowered their pails for drinking water.

They knew the same teachers, Miss Pollard at the tiny school at Kapoor, and Miss Winstanley and Miss Ferguson at Mayo, although Jackie and Sarjit knew Miss Pollard only at a distance. The girls had their schooling at Mayo. At first, it had one school, but a second one for the bigger children, up the hill and known as the "upper school," was added later. This was Miss Ferguson's domain where she was strict and feared and remembered without fondness by Sarjit, whom she once hit seven times with a ruler after hearing whispering and identifying the wrong girl. Miss Ferguson was a legitimate target for pranks, the best by a boy who presented her with a rose liberally sprinkled with pepper, which she received with a smile, then sniffed and went into a fit of sneezing. Miss Winstanley, who taught the smallest children, was young enough to be heckled with calls of "shame shame" by a group of Mayo children who were diverted from their after-class sport of catching tadpoles when they spotted her walking along the railway line with an older boy, who happened to be a notorious cut-up.

Miss Winstanley and Miss Ferguson had a respectful but reserved relationship with the Mayo Singh and Siddoo families, conscious that these people owned the village and employed them. Every morning Besant Kaur sent Jackie with fresh milk for the teachers, an intimidating job for a shy girl, even though they received the milk with a smile. With the full support of all the parents, the teachers celebrated Christmas annually in the school, with a Christmas tree, decorations, and an exchange of presents. But when Besant Kaur regularly came into the school in the mornings and rearranged the boys and girls to seat them separately, Miss Winstanley or Miss Ferguson simply waited until she left and put them back where they had been. Sometimes, the Siddoos took the two teachers along in the Chevrolet for their monthly or bi-weekly trips to Victoria. Jackie sat in the back with the teachers, terrified of Miss Ferguson, and Sarjit in the front with her parents. Miss Winstanley had lived in Alaska and she had a game: "Close your eyes," she would say, "we are going to Alaska." And she would describe the adventure. During one trip, on the winding road through the Malahat Pass, thirty kilometres out of Victoria, Miss Winstanley threw up into her handkerchief but said nothing about it, simply tossing the vomit out the small side window. Miss Ferguson kept silent, and Jackie was too constrained to speak up. Kapoor discovered what had happened only after they got home.

Nonetheless, the school and the teachers were an integral part of Mayo, and whenever Punjabi Sikhs held a festival in the village, the school was involved. Festivals were all-consuming events: the whole community would play the role of host to a great crowd of BC Sikhs. The Mayo gurdwara was one of six in British Columbia, three on the mainland and three on the island, six main gurdwaras for a BC community of fourteen hundred people. The nearest gurdwara was just five kilometres away along the CPR line at the Hillcrest Lumber mill. The farthest was at Abbotsford, seventy-five kilometres east of Vancouver, whose people would travel to Mayo by hired bus, cross the Strait of Georgia on a BC Coastal Steamship ferry, and then drive up the island highway. By agreement, nearly every gurdwara hosted one major Sikh festival during the year – Guru Nanak's birthday, Guru Gobind Singh's birthday, Baisakhi Day, or the martyrdom of Guru Arjan. The Mayo gurdwara had its festival on 1 July (Dominion Day as it was called), and people gathered from across the province for a procession to the gurdwara led by five bearded Sikhs and a band. After this came three days of devotional singing (kirtan), followed by a day of sports – trials of strength, wrestling, traditional swordplay, footraces for old and young, male and female, and team sports such as soccer, volleyball, and the energetic Punjabi running-wrestling-tag game of *kabadi*. At Mayo, these games had a special flavour because the teams included every local person who was willing to play, Punjabi, Chinese, Japanese, or white.[25]

Joan (Taylor) Mayo, who grew up on a farm near Nanaimo and married Mayo's oldest son, Rajindi, in 1953, eventually wrote a book about Mayo Siding from stories she collected from its old-timers. She described the excitement of the *jor melas* (community fairs) held there: the activity of the schoolchildren in the week ahead, making coloured flags from construction paper to hang on mill twine that they stretched from the gurdwara to the cookhouse and bunkhouses; the urgent cleaning and other preparations for the visiting men and boys who would stay on the ground floor of the gurdwara, and the women and girls who would be billeted in homes; the band of musicians who got time off from the mill to meet each group of visitors arriving by bus and escort it to the gurdwara; the special moment on a Friday evening when the saffron-coloured Sikh flag rose on the flagpole in front of the gurdwara in a formal outdoor ceremony of prayers and hymns; the constant conversation and story swapping in the cookhouse; and the exuberant children, running about the village as they renewed the friendships they made on these occasions. In that era, the Sikh community was a small one, although spread over a great area, and the visiting and sharing during jor melas helped to ensure that everyone knew everyone else.[26]

Their time at Mayo Siding also gave Jackie and Sarjit a few sobering and frightening moments: one night, the mill caught fire, and they could see the flames from their house. This was during a terrible windstorm when they stood with their parents and watched all kinds of things blow away. During the storm, Jackie impressed her mother and father by saying, "Do not be afraid. God takes care of everything." When Jackie was in grade four and Sarjit in grade three, they witnessed a cremation on the road to Duncan, only three hundred metres from the school. One of the Sikhs from Paldi had passed away. Jackie and Sarjit went up the road with their parents to attend the service and the cremation; and this first direct encounter with death made a deep impression. About the same time, they lost a delightful schoolmate who was slightly younger than they were. This was Rajinder, the second child of Mayo Singh and his wife, who was only six. She had come home from school, found the house empty, and tried to light the wood stove but had accidentally ignited her clothes and died from the burns she suffered.[27]

At Mayo Siding, Jackie and Sarjit learned geography from an oilcloth that covered their dining table. It had a world map on it, which Kapoor used to show them where they had been or where they had not been. As youngsters they had already travelled half the world and across Punjab. They lived sheltered lives, both in India and Canada, nurtured by protective parents who vetted their playmates and kept them as much as possible within the home and family circle. But Jackie and Sarjit had journeyed much farther than typical Canadian children of their age and seen countries that few Canadian children could imagine. And in the lumber villages of Kapoor and Mayo Siding, they lived in an international community. They had aunts, uncles, and cousins nearby, the relatives whom Kapoor had brought over, so they had an extended family as if they were growing up in his village of Kharoudi. But the population of Mayo Siding and of Kapoor was multi-racial and multi-national. In the 1934-35 school photos of the eighteen students in the Mayo lower school and the twenty in the upper, the beaming faces of the pupils on the wood steps outside each school are Japanese, white, and South Asian. They appear unconscious of the difference. Jackie is tucked comfortably between two Japanese girls, and Sarjit sits in a row with two Japanese boys, a white girl and another South Asian girl. This was normal in the village school of Mayo.

For Kapoor, the Depression years brought a break from the ambitious and demanding life he had led for many years, when he had been acquiring property, building a business, and playing a major role in his community. For nearly a year and a half, when his daughters were still at a formative age, he was able to spend much of his time with them and, together with Besant Kaur, to home-school them as they learned to read. During that time, he explored his native Punjab with Besant Kaur and with the girls as well. When he returned to Canada, he threw himself back into the lumber business alongside Mayo, but his sojourn in India made him ready for change, and change was to come.

10
Ending a Partnership: Life in the City

Kapoor prospered within a Punjabi partnership that depended on him to deal with English-speaking Canadians. He was probably effective in this role because he was, by nature, a quiet man. His own countrymen could be quick to quarrel, with family and clan divisions always a potential mischief. And the white world in which he worked erected stiff and antagonizing barriers for South Asians. It had been essential for Kapoor, Mayo, and their Punjabi partners to combine and work together to create a business, and they had done so successfully despite the obstacles. They could not have achieved it without helpful white Canadian friends and business partners, or without a forward-looking attitude, or without expecting success and achieving it by degrees. Persistence and decisiveness had carried them far, and they had to take reverses in stride without accepting defeat. Maintaining their own partnership as long as they did was an accomplishment in itself, but it was not destined to last forever, and a final destructive fire ultimately finished it off.

This fire struck the Mayo Lumber Company mill on 25 December 1934, twenty-one months after the mill reopened following Kapoor's return from India. It broke out on Christmas night in a raging windstorm that carried flames from nearby tree spars to the sawmill and the planing mill, completely destroying them as well as 2 million board feet of lumber stacked and ready for export. This was the fire that Jackie and Sarjit watched with their parents from their house. It was a greater setback than earlier fires at Mayo Siding because lumber prices were still far below the pre-Depression level, and rebuilding the mill was a more uncertain business than it had been in the early 1920s. Nonetheless, Mayo was determined to do it, and he got a new mill up and running within a year. Kapoor, however, was ready to withdraw. He wanted to put Jackie and Sarjit into city schools, and he was already contemplating a move to Vancouver, where he owned a house on York Avenue.[1]

Had their separation been friendly, Kapoor and Mayo, each with 40 percent of Mayo Lumber, should have wound up their partnership expeditiously. But there were fourteen other shareholders, most of them relatives from Paldi or Kharoudi, and marshalled behind them were other relatives and villagers who worked in the mills and logging camps at Mayo Siding and Kapoor. Ill-feeling had been festering for some time – one family group who happened to be Jats was pitted against another who were Manhas Rajputs. The Jats – Kapoor's people – suspected that the fire had been deliberately set to force them out of the business. The villages of Mayo Siding and Kapoor became places of raw feeling. Late on a cold starlit New Year's Eve, Jackie and Sarjit saw their mother set off with a servant, walking into the night along the railway track toward the Kapoor mill with a rifle in her hands. Kapoor had been at a meeting in the mill office for far too long, and she was worried – alarmed by the talk of one of Mayo's men who had implied that Kapoor would be an easy target for anyone with a gun. The girls remembered their mother's instant answer that if anything happened to Kapoor, she would kill ten men in exchange and then shoot herself. This was from a woman respected in the community as a mother figure, a peacemaker, who always kept the friendship of the women on the Mayo side.

Before the fire at the Mayo mill, the two sides had argued over the management of their companies, over who was getting jobs, over the allocation of profits, and over personal matters – a quarrel with many issues and many loud voices but two opposing camps. Ironically, only a month before the fire, Kapoor had thought that Mayo and his people were becoming more reasonable.[2] But the fire brought everything to a head. In an interview given decades later, Kapoor's younger brother, Tara, spoke of physical confrontations: of fights breaking out; of Kapoor arriving at Mayo Siding only to find himself blocked by a crowd of men who prevented him from driving to his own garage; of one of Mayo's biggest fighters striking Cousin Gurdial Singh Teja, a strong man on the Kapoor side, and of Gurdial returning with a revolver and coming perilously close to shooting him in retaliation; and of Tara himself provoked to anger, threatening to rip another man's beard. The priest Johindsa tried to arbitrate, but to Kapoor's people he seemed biased. Even the accountant at Kapoor, Sam Cowan, came under suspicion from Kapoor's side as an agent of Mayo.[3]

Business went on in spite of tempers. Logging operations at Mayo Siding and Kapoor continued, and the Kapoor mill kept up its output. But the principal partners had a complex business relationship to untangle and in a heated atmosphere. Mayo Singh had a large interest at Kapoor, just as Kapoor had a large interest at Mayo Siding, and in the management of forest land, the two men advocated contrary approaches. Mayo would happily accept the consequences for defaulting on taxes, letting the land revert to public ownership once it had been logged. Kapoor, looking to the future, believed in holding on to forest land and waiting for new trees to mature. That meant continuing to pay taxes on the land after the trees had been harvested. During his negotiations with Mayo, Kapoor took advice from L.C. Lytton, a staff member of the Esquimalt and Nanaimo Railway land department, a friend to whom he had generously lent money. It was Lytton who suggested a compromise that Kapoor successfully put to Mayo. In this negotiation, it helped that Mayo was anxious to get his new mill into production and wanted to put obstacles aside. In Kapoor's view, that helped bring him around to a reasonable settlement and pay-out.[4]

To operate the new mill at Mayo Siding, which he rebuilt by the end of 1935, Mayo created Mayo Brothers Timber Company; his older brother, Ganeya, was a minor shareholder, and Kapoor was excluded. But he and Kapoor continued as partners in the Kapoor Company at Sooke Lake until Mayo's death in February 1955.[5] Even so, their personal relationship remained purely formal, with no more contact than was necessary and mostly through people such as the Vancouver-based accountant Walter Jacklin or, for the sake of the community, when they co-sponsored lobbying efforts in Victoria and Ottawa. The active part of what had been an extremely successful business partnership ended in 1935.[6] Mayo signalled its conclusion by applying to the post office to change the name of Mayo Siding to Paldi for his home village in Punjab. The symmetry of a village named for each partner was over.

Kapoor moved his family to Vancouver in the summer of 1935, in time for the beginning of the school year. Sarjit was old enough to remember her last longing look at their house in Mayo Siding as they drove up the hill and away. Kapoor had built a house on York Avenue, Vancouver, back in 1921 and had been renting it to the manager of the Bank of Commerce branch with which he did business. The banker and his family were still occupying the house when Kapoor arrived with his own family via the

Vancouver Island ferry. For a few nights, the Siddoos slept in their Chevrolet beneath the steel truss bridge over the Capilano River in West Vancouver, and in the mornings they washed up at the edge of the river. Then, during renovations after the bank manager moved out, they spent some time with Punjabi friends who lived on West Second Avenue in Vancouver near their intended home.

The two nights in the Chevrolet were an austere start in Vancouver for the family of a man who had already been written up in the mainstream press as a Punjabi success story. But neither Kapoor nor Besant Kaur were afraid to rough it, and they may have preferred the car to the indignity of traipsing around the city, looking for a hotel that would accept them. In those years discrimination showed its face in many places – in barbershops that would not serve Asian customers, swimming pools that were closed to them, and hotels that refused them rooms.[7] On the ferry service from Vancouver Island, anyone who could afford it could get a stateroom – which is what Kapoor did – but the fifty-cent and one-dollar bunks in steerage were segregated, with Asians and Native people set apart from the whites. That was the background to the nights the Siddoos spent in their car under a bridge. Only after a prolonged wait did they get into their two-story frame home at 2416 York Avenue in the Kitsilano area. Once there, Kapoor and Besant Kaur stayed in that house for the rest of their lives.

Jackie and Sarjit enrolled at Henry Hudson Elementary, a sixteen-room brick school built before the First World War, which was only five and a half blocks from their home. Both parents walked them there on the first day. At Henry Hudson, Sarjit learned her real surname for the first time after she confused her teacher, Miss McGlashan, by giving it as Kapoor while her sister was telling *her* teacher that it was Siddoo. Sarjit had always heard white people address her father as "Mr. Kapoor." The girls were then nine and ten, and starting grades four and five. They had transferred from a tiny rural school, where three-quarters of the pupils were either Japanese or Punjabi, to a large city school with a distant and intimidating principal, Mr. Gordon, and a population that was three-quarters white. They were the only South Asians in their large classes, which numbered over forty students. And the Japanese girls who attended in those pre-war years did not live nearby, so getting to know them was difficult. Besant Kaur remained vigilant in her opposition to friendships with boys (other than cousins), and she would not let Jackie and Sarjit go to the houses of their girlfriends. "You have plenty of space here," she would say, "you don't have to go to other people's houses," and she would encourage them to bring their friends home. One favourite was Lisa Weber and another was Martha (Mattie) McKenzie, who lived at 1546 Yew Street, just off York Avenue, and who was Sarjit's age with wonderfully curly hair like Jackie's but bright red. Martha and Lisa were among the girls who played baseball on the street in front of the Siddoo home or other games in the basement. On the weekends, when their friends got money for the movies, Jackie and Sarjit asked their father if they could go too. He always said, "Ask your mother." And she nearly always said no.

The girls had no problem fitting in as students. Later, when attending junior high, they passed a small boy at one house who would call out "Hindu, Hindu." For a while their parents sent their young maid along with them for moral support. But that name calling was an isolated matter. The maid was one of a succession at their York Avenue home: first was a German girl, then Mary Loewen, whose family had immigrated from Russia, then another Mary, also German, followed by a Sylvia, and after that an untrained girl whom the family agreed was very stupid because she disposed of garbage by hiding it under a tub in the basement. One of their long-time York Avenue neighbours was a diminutive merchant seaman, Alfred J. Tremeer, or "Mr. Tremeer" as Jackie and Sarjit called him, who was away at sea much of the time during the early years and married to a cheerful good-looking woman who happened to be much larger than he. Sadly, she died and when Tremeer wanted to sell his house, Kapoor bought it. Then, when Tremeer returned after yet another absence and needed somewhere to live, he moved into the Siddoos' basement to become an integrated member of the household for several years.

In the city, the Siddoo family home remained the same secure nest it had been in Mayo, one that was open to visitors but a complete world for the family. One moment forever expressed Jackie's feelings for her father. On a winter's day, with two or three feet of snow on the ground, she walked with him along Balsam Street to the waterfront park where they could see people skating. She was holding his hand, and its warmth on a cold day conveyed the comfort she always felt with him. Sarjit had an almost identical memory but located it on a wintry day in the Kapoor forest at Deer Lake. And their bond with their mother was just as strong. They grew up with equal attachment and equal loyalty to both parents. When they were heading down York Avenue to buy groceries and – as happened more than once – a woman stopped to say "Your father is so handsome," they would answer, "So is our mother," and get the reply "Oh yes!"

Their house resembled others in the area, larger than its immediate neighbours but with a similar front porch reached by a flight of wooden steps. Most of the living space was on the main floor, which had a kitchen, living room, dining room, bathroom, and two bedrooms. The second floor was a half-story, with sloping ceilings in the two upstairs bedrooms and bathroom. Jackie slept there. Sarjit had her own room as well, but while she was in elementary school, she slept with her mother, always finding restoration in her calming presence after any childhood disturbance. Their father would be up early, reciting prayers in his separate bedroom and attending to the wood-burning kitchen stove that heated the water for family baths. On cold days in Kitsilano, the girls sat in the kitchen, studying, with the oven door open, their feet in the oven.

Singing was a family institution, with Sarjit on the dholki, the barrel-shaped North Indian hand drum, and either Kapoor or Jackie on the harmonium. Kapoor led, with a voice that impressed the girls as especially beautiful. They sang Sikh devotional songs and the old Urdu-language Indian anthem "Sare Jahan Se Acchha," warmed by the thought that a Muslim poet, Iqbal, had so beautifully expressed the pride of all Indians for their homeland. They were saddened when his language lost its status in India after the partition of the country in 1947 and he was appointed poet laureate of the new Pakistan. The Bengali-Sanskrit anthem that India adopted in 1947, "Bande Mataram," was never as moving for Jackie and Sarjit as the one they knew when growing up. But their tastes were broad, and their repertoire included songs that Canadian children learned from the radio, at school, or from friends – "Little Brown Jug," "Red River Valley," and "Springtime in the Rockies." These were favourites during car rides and most commonly requested by their Punjabi-speaking mother. At Christmas and Easter, the family gathered around the short-wave radio, purchased by Kapoor after they moved to Vancouver, to listen to the Catholic services in Latin, broadcast from Westminster Cathedral in London, and that sacred music could bring tears to their eyes.

The girls did struggle with the ignorance of India that was all around them. Throughout her school years, Sarjit felt on the defensive whenever the subject of India came up. This occurred when they went to Bible meetings on York Avenue and heard a lecturer applauding the work of Christian missionaries in dispelling the "superstition" and "backwardness" in India. And it happened at school. Mr. Shapiro, a teacher she liked a lot, devoted just one sentence to China and India when he described the rise of civilization in world history. And Mrs. Higgenbottom in grade nine social studies said disparagingly, "In India, of course, when a husband dies, the wife is burned with him." She had a confused notion of the practice of *sati,* something that Sarjit had never heard of. "Oh. Mrs. Higgenbottom," she said emphatically, "they do not!" Looking displeased, the teacher said, "You don't speak like that" and gave her a detention. Reassurance came at home when Kapoor reminded his daughters that Europeans were living in caves when India first had a flowering civilization.[8]

Kapoor continued going to Vancouver Island to oversee his mill and logging operations. During holidays, he took the family to Kapoor or later to Shawnigan Lake, where they had a cottage. They drove up from Victoria on the old, seldom used, horse-and-buggy road running through the Victoria watershed, which was the source area for the city's drinking water. No one was supposed to stop there, but they took a break at a beautiful waterfall on the way. They liked that road, the immense feeling of peace in the forest and the chance of seeing a deer, perhaps a doe and fawns, crossing the road. When they went to Kapoor, they walked along the tracks of the logging railway and followed little routes off the tracks. The two lakes on the Kapoor property, Wolf Lake and Deer Lake, were surrounded by trees, although they were soon logged off. One vivid memory for the girls was a hiking expedition from Kapoor with their father to cut a Christmas tree. On one famous summer occasion, when they were in high school, they brought three schoolmates to Vancouver Island. One was the red-haired Martha McKenzie. By then Cousin Ajaib was on his second car, an Oldsmobile, and he had a great time driving the girls around, going into Duncan and even down to Victoria.[9]

Kapoor never sought attention, and a bad experience on a March day in 1938 made him especially leery of it. In his mind, material success was not something to advertise, a feeling that strengthened after he was held at pistol point by two Punjabi men demanding money only four blocks from his house.[10] One of them wore a skimpy, roughly tied red-print turban and had a beard; the other, who was clean-shaven, had a dark-blue hat pulled down over his face, as if to avoid recognition. They were strangers to Kapoor, but they had been seen several times in the neighbourhood, and the police tracked them to temporary rooms within six days of the incident. It happened that the managers of their rooming houses were Japanese, Mrs. Yamashita and Mrs. Suzuki – a reflection of Vancouver's mosaic at the time.

At their preliminary trial, Sarjit and Martha McKenzie, then aged eleven, gave testimony because they had spoken to them only minutes before their extortion attempt. Their encounter occurred at 12:50 when they were walking back to Henry Hudson Elementary after lunch. A Ford coupe pulled up beside them and the man in the passenger seat asked Sarjit in Punjabi if her father was at home. Answering in the same language, she said "Yes." In the courtroom, she identified him as one of the arrested men.[11]

The men drove straight to the Siddoo home, where the one with the red turban rang the front doorbell. Kapoor answered the door, only to be disturbed by this man's suspicious behaviour – the uncivil way he rushed in, his explanation that he had a letter in English for Kapoor to read, his nervous search through his pockets for the letter, which he could not find, and his departure to retrieve it from his car. After five minutes, Kapoor went into the street to look for him, searching first on foot and then in his own car. Soon he found the two men parked at the corner of York and Arbutus. When Kapoor stopped his own car, the man in the red turban came to the passenger side. Kapoor, still not comprehending what they were after, opened the door only to have a pistol shoved into his ribs. The man had a small handwritten note and he now spoke in English in a low voice. He wanted Kapoor to drive immediately to a bank to get money, but Kapoor managed to twist the gun out of his assailant's hand and push him out of the car. The man ran back to the Ford Coupe and sped off with his accomplice, leaving behind in Kapoor's car the revolver, the note, some shells, and a cardboard briefcase, presumably for the money. The damage to Kapoor from the brief struggle was an injured index finger and bruising and cuts to his right hand. But he had taken down the licence number of the Ford Coupe, which had been rented from a local car dealer; and it was only a matter of time before the police made their arrests.

After the robbery scare, Kapoor decided to get a watchdog, and at a pet shop tucked in among the exclusive shops on South Granville Street, they bought a pedigreed Doberman Pinscher on the advice of the store owner. As much as both parents and children loved animals, this dog was not a good choice. It grew too big and active for their house and yard and needed more exercise and attention than they could give. Although the pet shop owner said it was trained, it attacked and mauled a neighbour's dog – which upset everyone – and Kapoor got rid of it by sending it to a farm. With the Doberman, the family had also acquired a small black pup with a docked tail that had been thrown into the purchase for free, and this dog was to enjoy a life of indulgence with them for another eighteen years. Unlike the Doberman, it was very bright, although of no breeding, a kind of miniature lab whom they called Prince, their favourite name for a dog. Its most famous exploit, many years later, was to escape from the open window of their parked car while Kapoor and Besant Kaur were shopping at Spencer's department store in downtown Vancouver and make its way through many kilometres of the city, turning up to everyone's surprise on their York Avenue front porch. This was one of several dogs over the years for whom Besant Kaur would prepare meat, although she would not cook it for her family.

At the preliminary trial of the two would-be extortionists, the prosecuting lawyer asked Kapoor if he knew them. At that time, only about 1,350 South Asians lived in British Columbia, so recognizing any given face or name was not an impossibility, especially because the community gathered regularly at one gurdwara or another for jor melas (fairs) and other functions. Kapoor allowed that he might previously have seen one of the men, but he was not sure. When the lawyer asked if either of them had ever worked for him, Kapoor explained that though he employed many men, he did not hire them himself, so he could not say. The Punjabis whom he knew well were relatives, fellow villagers, people from the Mahalpur area, or community leaders. And his life on York Avenue drew him away from an exclusively Punjabi environment, so he had a cross-section of Canadian friends and associates as well.

Kapoor's expanded circle included people whom Kartar Singh Hundal knew. For a period Kartar Singh was in the York Avenue house nearly every day, producing the last of the English-language editions of his periodical *India and Canada*. Initially, he had published it from commercial premises on Fourth and Vine, but in 1936, he moved his press into Kapoor's basement, where he spent long hours hand setting the type. For a while, he was Kapoor's manager-accountant at Sooke Lake. But his long-term residence was in the Granville Street area of Vancouver or in the village of Barnet, where he lived with Alice Marion Curtis, a slightly older woman from Ontario who was very fond of him and who mothered him like a son. (He was in his midforties by then.) He had met her through the Theosophical Society in Toronto, and she had come to Vancouver with him. The Siddoos got to know her as an outgoing person, a nice woman, recognizable at a distance by her short stature and her hair worn in a bun. Through Kartar and Alice, they became involved with the Theosophical group in Vancouver and also heard of the teacher Jiddu Krishnamurti, who was later to become an influential part of Jackie and Sarjit's lives.

Their family doctor, Washington E. Wilks, was a Theosophist whom they met through Kartar Singh. For medical consultations, they went to his office in the Medical Dental Building on Georgia Street, across from the Hotel Vancouver. But Wilks also ran the Orpheus Lodge of the Theosophical Society from the same address, and they attended Theosophical meetings and lectures there – that is, Jackie and Sarjit went with their father; their mother did not go, because the lectures were all in English. Wilks had been a key member of the Theosophical Society from his earliest days as a British immigrant doctor just before the First World War. He had a medical practice in Nanaimo for nearly a decade before moving to Vancouver in the early 1920s, and his involvement in the national Theosophical Society dated from his Nanaimo days. Kartar was still living in Toronto when he first knew Wilks as a fellow member of the national executive, and their relationship continued quite naturally after he returned to Vancouver.

In the 1930s, the Theosophical Society of Canada claimed about five hundred members, half of them in Toronto and the rest across the country.[12] Vancouver had two lodges, and the Orpheus Lodge led by Wilks for many years was the larger one, with thirty paid-up members. Among Theosophists he was a traditionalist in that he grounded his spiritual search on the revelations of Helena Blavatsky, the Russian countess who had launched the international Theosophical movement in the 1870s. None of the controversy around Blavatsky – the charges that she was a fraud and a charlatan – affected the lifelong excitement that Wilks felt in her "inspired" writings on the ancient wisdom of Egypt and India. He regretted that, after her death, the movement's new leadership had pushed her name and her publications from centre stage. And yet he still worked hard for a society that appealed to many *because* it was open to anyone of any creed, race, sex, caste, or colour and *because* it espoused no doctrine.[13]

It was open-minded inquiry into spiritual mysteries that brought Kapoor and his daughters to Wilks' Theosophical meetings. And, within the Theosophical Society, Kapoor – like Kartar – found people who were sympathetic to India's demands for independence, something that Canadians at the time generally did not understand. The formidable English-born activist Annie Besant, the international president of the Theosophical Society after Blavatsky's death, a post she held until her own death in 1933, had been interned in India during the First World War for campaigning for home rule. She set a powerful anti-colonial example for Theosophists, although few Canadian members shared her fire on the subject. They agreed it was only right that India should eventually be granted home rule, but they did not understand the urgency that justified rash or radical action. All would come to those who waited. They tended to think that Britain was providing fair and beneficent rule. Kapoor and Kartar had to overlook a great gulf in perceptions, even among their enlightened Theosophical friends.[14] Still, the society connected them with prominent, influential, and interesting Canadians, particularly in the arts.

It was not quite by coincidence that Kapoor became interested in Theosophy at the same time as two notable residents of Victoria, the artist Emily Carr and the novelist Ethel Wilson. Their common influence was the Group of Seven painter Lawren Harris, a friend to Carr and Wilson and also to Kartar Singh from his days in Toronto, where Harris used to teach a class on Theosophy and Art. Kartar Singh introduced Kapoor and his family to Harris shortly after Harris moved to Vancouver in 1940, taking them to visit him in his temporary residence in the British Properties in West Vancouver, an occasion made memorable because they were received so graciously by someone they understood to be a renowned and important Canadian. They were also conscious of the irony that homes and lots in the British Properties had a covenant against sales to Asians like themselves.[15] Kartar was familiar with the Canadian cultural scene, and through him, Kapoor and his daughters had an acquaintance with it. Visiting Harris in his home was one instance of this.

Kapoor also knew non-Sikhs through his business, and not just on Vancouver Island but in the Vancouver area as well. In the summer of 1938, anticipating the end of the Sooke Lake timber stand, he started looking for a mill site in the Vancouver area. In August, he incorporated a new company, which he called Modern Sawmills. His younger brother, Tara, had just gone back to India with his family, but he wanted to be included, and Kapoor assigned 40 percent of the shares to him while keeping 60 percent to himself. In fact, Tara did not have that amount of money to contribute, and Kapoor increased his own capital investment so that by 1940 he owned 78 percent, some of which he distributed to Besant Kaur, Jackie, and Sarjit. Modern Sawmills was a Siddoo family concern, with no other Punjabis involved, and keeping it that way was a joint decision of brothers and cousins. Altogether, eight Siddoos were shareholders: Kapoor and his immediate family, Tara, Cousin Kashmir, Cousin Ajaib, and his father, Naranjan. In addition, two Anglo-Canadians held one share each. These were Don Dewar, the company's accountant, and Jim Armstrong, an insurance and real estate agent. Kapoor felt particularly close to Armstrong, a clergyman's son from rural southern Ontario who was about his age. Armstrong and his wife, Olive, became warm and trusted friends in the years that followed.[16]

Armstrong found a magnificent mill site near the village of Barnet on Burrard Inlet in the shadow of Burnaby Mountain (then known as Snake Hill) – ideal because the property ran from the shore to the CPR main line and was only twenty-three kilometres east of Kapoor's home in Kitsilano. Logs could arrive by sea and finished lumber go out by rail. There was no local timber. It had all been logged off during the previous forty years. A large sawmill had operated at this site under a succession of owners from the beginning of the century to the First World War and then from the early 1920s until 1931, when it had shut down under the threat of a strike. The concrete mill structure on the western half of the site was being demolished. The site itself was available on a tax sale because the previous owners had not paid their taxes, and their property had reverted to the Municipality of Burnaby. What Kapoor wanted was the forty-five acres of the eastern half, a property that extended into the inlet and came with the right to maintain docks, floats, and log booms on 20 acres of water along the shoreline, along with the ownership of the sea bottom – not just rights at the surface. Because this land was municipal property and he was a South Asian, Kapoor could not purchase it directly – just one of the discriminatory features of life for South Asians in British Columbia at the time. But there was a way around the problem, and Armstrong exercised it by acting as the front man for Modern Sawmills. In that transaction alone, he earned his single share. Once the purchase had been accomplished, Kapoor changed the company's name from Modern Sawmills to Kapoor Sawmills, safely letting be it known that this company was owned by South Asians.[17]

Kapoor took over tenant houses that had belonged to the old mill, and he built a new bunkhouse and cookhouse in which he installed electricity and up-to-date plumbing. He bought logs for his mill on the open market until 1943 when he obtained timber-cutting rights on Vancouver Island from the CPR's Esquimalt and Nanaimo Railway. These cutting rights bordered on the nine-hundred-metre-high Koksilah Ridge a few kilometres from Shawnigan Lake, north and east of his old operation at Sooke Lake and closer to the east coast of the island. By increments, with scheduled annual purchases from the railway, he increased his tract to fourteen thousand acres within five years. He opened it with a ten-kilometre gravel road following a right of way through other properties along the Koksilah River. Building it got him into litigation with a well-known Vancouver journalist, impresario, and arts supporter, Lily Laverlock, who had a property on his route and who objected to the aesthetic impact of the road. But that did not stop Kapoor. He established a camp and began operating by employing loggers who commuted by car from Duncan as well as others who lived in bunkhouses at the camp. He had trucks and other gear at Sooke Lake, which he now transferred to this operation. His own men – who included a large number of Swedes – felled most of his timber, but he did subcontract some logging.

The logs from this Shawnigan Lake tract were trucked by gravel road to the nearest railway siding and then taken a very short distance by rail to the coast at Mill Bay and towed in log booms for 120 kilometres across the Georgia Strait and into the Burrard Inlet. When they arrived at Barnet, they floated in booms along the mill shoreline for most of a kilometre. Once milled, the lumber went out on CPR flatbed railway cars. That was part of the deal with the railway: lumber manufactured from logs from its lands had to be shipped over its lines.[18] To cut the expense of shipping by rail, Kapoor built a kiln at the Barnet mill so that he was not transporting heavy green lumber but lighter lumber that was kiln dried.

The mill at Barnet gave the family yet another destination for weekend outings. They had younger cousins there, sisters Diljeet, Gurmeet, and Harjeet, and their older half-brother, Hardev, whose father Gurdial Singh Teja – the same Gurdial who had been in the famous fracas at Mayo – worked at the mill for Kapoor. The Tejas had lived in Duncan and Port Alberni before the Barnet mill opened. At Barnet, they temporarily occupied a floating house on the mill's water property, one of two such houses surrounded by log booms. The children attended a one-room school in Barnet village on the highway, and they spent their spare time on the school grounds and in the planked yard of the mill, playing skipping games, games with bouncing balls, or games that involved searches and puzzles with hints or clues. They had a Jersey cow, which they liked to feed, although they initially refused to drink the milk.[19] They preferred the bottled version sold in stores. The cow was a pet that would walk along with its head on their mother's shoulder. At the little school, they were persistently excluded by the children of white working-class families. In the school yard, they joined softball games but were never given a turn to bat, which they assumed was because they were South Asian. Years later, when Diljeet spoke with a former schoolmate while contributing to a published collection of memories of Barnet village, she learned that the unfriendliness was related to money, not race. The white families had come through hard times during the Depression, and the Tejas, who were always neatly groomed and well dressed, appeared relatively well-off.[20]

On the weekends when Kapoor brought his family to the mill, Besant Kaur taught the Teja cousins Punjabi, sometimes sitting with them on a blanket spread on the stony beach of the mill property but usually in a room in a bunkhouse. Kapoor frequently asked them to wash his Chevrolet and rewarded them by paying for it. They also visited Kapoor's family by taking a Pacific Stage Coach bus into Vancouver and a streetcar to York Avenue – a major expedition but also a special day, which featured ice cream every time they went. For Jackie and Sarjit, their weekend visits to Barnet were also special, an outdoors experience at an industrial property that they found entertaining. They stepped on the floating logs, and Jackie would dive into the bracing water of Burrard Inlet, or they walked along the beach or played catch in the mill yard. On Sundays the mill was quiet, with only the millwrights working, and the empty yard with its piles of lumber became a children's playground. From time to time, they saw deer swimming across the inlet toward them, heading for the second-growth timber on Burnaby Mountain. It was a place to watch and listen to waterfowl and shorebirds. And they relished the time they spent with their father on those Sundays, walking with him to the edge of the property and listening as he talked about his future plans for the mill.[21]

On the wall of his office at the mill, Kapoor had a map of Vancouver Island, and he would readily show visitors the geography of his business, the source of his logs, and the route they took to Mill Bay. That map and the oilcloth world map on the dining table at Mayo were iconic images for Jackie and Sarjit, identifying their place in the universe. Kapoor and Besant Kaur had created a rich Canadian experience for them: city life and a city school, where they grew up with girlfriends such as Martha McKenzie, coupled with time spent close to nature at Sooke Lake, Shawnigan Lake, or even on Burrard Inlet, although always with an industrial backdrop that they readily accepted as part and parcel of the environment.

In the city they still visited the Punjabi friends of their parents and saw their uncles, aunts, and cousins; and they attended festivals at the Vancouver gurdwara on Second Avenue or in the outlying community of Abbotsford. On these special occasions, Besant Kaur joined the other women to prepare food in the gurdwara kitchen. Kapoor stayed clear of gurdwara politics; in any case, a clean-shaven Sikh could not serve on the management committee. But when the committee asked for money, he would step forward. Within a year of moving to Vancouver, he paid for a mosaic of Guru Nanak, the founder of Sikhism, crafted in Venetian glass against a background of French enamel.[22] The Sikhs installed it on the front of their twenty-eight-year-old gurdwara while refurbishing it for Vancouver's Golden Jubilee. That building has long since been sold and demolished, but the mosaic survives over the entrance to the gurdwara that replaced it in 1969.

Thanks to their parents, the girls grew up deeply attached to India and its culture, so they were Canadian children who knew and treasured their roots. They spoke Punjabi and from an early age could recite the morning and evening prayers of the Sikh faith, the Japji and the Sodar Rahiras, as well as the twenty-four stanzas of Guru Nanak's *Asa ki Var.* They had the constant devotional example of their mother and her familiar repose with the beads of her mala and her invariable practice whenever they drove anywhere of invoking the Creator with a low-voiced repetition of his/her name, Satnam. But both parents encouraged an ecumenical religious outlook, and as important as Sikhism was to them, they were not given to purely formal observance. Reflecting on her childhood, Sarjit could not remember whether they had the Sikh holy book, the *Guru Granth Sahib,* in their home.[23] What she could recall was a family library packed with books about Gandhi, Tagore, Sarojini Naidu, Vivekananda, and other eminent Indian poets and teachers; she also remembered listening to Christmas services on the radio and attending Theosophical meetings. Within their safe family circle, Jackie and Sarjit learned naturally to integrate the spiritual traditions of East and West.

11
Citizens without Votes

Making money and fighting for fair treatment were equal priorities for Kapoor and his compatriots from the time they arrived in Canada. Over the years, they did remarkably well, despite their second-class status, in generating income and acquiring property. And material success put them in a better position to campaign for fair treatment. It gave them the means to make themselves heard, and they were always prepared to lobby the most powerful officials in Ottawa. They were also mindful of the value of a good spokesperson, and they were perpetually on the lookout for someone from India with the personal qualities and the credentials to make a favourable impression on Canada's political leaders. They sent several missions to Ottawa over the decades and suffered disappointment every time one of these missions came back empty-handed. But history was on their side. Canadian attitudes would change, and India's independence would eventually make a difference. The beginning of the end was the outbreak of war in 1939, a moment whose potential they fully understood.

At the beginning of the Second World War, Cousin Ajaib – now sixteen – lived for a while at York Avenue. From the age of seven, he had grown up in Mayo Siding and in the village of Kapoor at Sooke Lake, and he had attended the one-room schools there. In September 1939, he came to Vancouver for a year of high school. His father, Naranjan, was living in a bunkhouse at the Barnet mill, but Ajaib stayed with Kapoor's family to be close to Kitsilano High.

As it happened, Ajaib left Victoria by ferry on 3 September, and when he landed in Vancouver, he saw the newspaper headlines about Britain's declaration of war on Germany. A few years later and before the war was over, he had graduated from Vancouver Technical School on Broadway and volunteered for the Royal Canadian Air Force, with which he served in Saskatchewan as a mechanic in support of the Commonwealth Air Training Program. Getting into the air force had taken strong backing from his principal, James Sinclair, who, to his credit, told the air force recruiters that if they wanted any of his boys, they would have to take this South Asian lad as well. Sinclair had to be firm because the Mobilization Board in BC had stopped signing up South Asian volunteers after their community had protested the draft. The board's feeble justification of its policy was that South Asians would not fit into the military, because they required special food.[1]

War solved a problem for Ajaib that as a youngster he scarcely knew about. He was an illegal immigrant, like his father and hundreds of other South Asians then living in BC. Some had crossed the Canada-US border surreptitiously, a few of them coming via Mexico then slipping into the United States and eventually reaching Canada. Others had landed at Victoria, Vancouver, or even Halifax and got by immigration officials by swearing an affidavit that they were simply visiting Canada when they actually intended to stay for years. Some had used assumed names backed by passports obtained with false declarations, forged documents, or travel permits purchased in India from men who had been in Canada. And some had claimed that they had immigrated years earlier and were returning to Canada from a recent visit to India. In some instances, the story had been a partial truth, because men did go back and forth between Canada and India – sometimes more than once – while using the fictitious identities they assumed on first arrival.

The couple who brought Ajaib to Canada when he was only seven were Narang Singh Gill from Kharoudi and his teenage wife, Harnam Kaur. When Sarjit – in pursuit of her family history – taped an interview with Harnam Kaur more than fifty years later, her elderly aunt dug into a drawer to find an old British-India passport with the 1930 date of her arrival in Victoria stamped on it. For a moment they were both surprised because the passport said "Harnam Kaur wife of Inder Singh," which was not her husband's name. But then memory immediately suggested the answer: he must have been using another name.[2] Such a thing was not extraordinary when so many of the men in the community had entered the country illegally. But it meant that Ajaib, when he landed in Canada as a boy, was joining a father who did not have legal landed status, and that he travelled as the purported son of a couple who also lacked legal landed status. Somehow immigration officials had let them all in anyway.

Ajaib was surrounded by illegal immigrants: his father, his uncle Tara (Kapoor's brother), Narang Gill, and many more. The immigration department really had little idea who was in the country, let alone how they got there, although reputedly it employed a number of officers to track illegal immigrants down. The situation was complicated by the power possessed by individual immigration officers. They could be firm and uncompromising, but they could also be flexible, and sometimes they would permit an individual to stay when a strict application of the rules dictated otherwise. In the Sikh community, the officials had a reputation for shielding some people rather than pursing them – especially those known in the community as informants – and the department's own files suggest that they applied different rules in different instances. For example, a case that began in 1937 was that of Rakha Singh, a fifty-one-year-old Sikh with a Mexican wife from Texas who had stolen across the US-Canada border only to be reported to the immigration department within a few months. The fact that he was accompanied by his wife was a mitigating factor for immigration officials, who, two years after they obtained it, still had not exercised a deportation order against him. But even in cases they pursued aggressively, the men they targeted were stubbornly resistant, appealing deportation orders at every stage and often disappearing when decisions went against them. In September 1939, the department had twenty-five active cases on its books, many going back several years. No one knew how many more there were, but Ajaib's was one of them.[3]

Mayo Singh's family has kept passports and correspondence that show how Punjabis got around the immigration barrier and how they often did it with the department's own help, and, in Mayo's case, with the written support of local notables in Duncan – the mayor, postmaster, bank manager, high school principal, and secretary of the merchants association – who understood what the Sikh mill did for the area's economy.[4]

In the late summer of 1927, when he came back from India with his new wife, Bishen Kaur, who was not yet twenty, Mayo brought two boys. He travelled by way of Europe and at the request of his travel agent, Thomas Cook and Sons of Berkeley Street, London, he left India carrying a letter from immigration in Ottawa stating that his whole party – another family was with him – would be allowed to land when their Cunard liner

Antonia docked at Quebec. Steamship companies regularly screened passengers who were likely to have trouble with immigration, so Mayo needed that letter to buy tickets to Canada for his wife and the other new immigrants he was bringing. He got the letter thanks to the support of an immigration officer in Victoria. It was a treasured document for him and his bride, a souvenir of her arrival in Canada, and they framed it for the living room wall of their home at Mayo Siding. The names listed in the letter include the other family, Mayo, his wife, and the two boys, Bishen and Shankar. Bishen, the older one, was sixteen and his passport photograph shows that he was already sporting a moustache and a wispy beard. Mayo claimed him and Shankar as his sons, presumably by saying that they were from a previous marriage.[5]

In fact, Bishen and Shankar were the sons of another villager from Paldi, Ganda Singh, who was himself an illegal immigrant. Mayo did Ganda Singh a favour by bringing his sons out for him. And he did it without any negative consequences for himself, even though the immigration department had evidence within a year that the boys were not his. The evidence came from India and from the government of India, but for whatever reason – lack of reliable testimony, shortage of personnel to investigate, or Mayo's friendship with people of influence – the department let the matter ride. After two years, Bishen made a return trip to India, registering under another name – Sohan – and now identifying himself as Ganda Singh's son. He re-entered Canada a year later without difficulty and attracted no attention from immigration officials for several years until a report from a Punjabi informant prompted them to review his file and decide they had a case of misrepresentation. Then followed a protracted struggle: a hearing, a deportation order, an appeal, a dismissal of the appeal, and a court-issued restraint order against the immigration department. That made Bishen Singh one of the twenty-five active cases on the department's books in September 1939.[6]

The department could not have taken on more than a few of these cases had people in the South Asian community not informed on each other. Informing was an unpleasant aspect of life in a small beleaguered immigrant group with sharp divisions and intense family, caste, and regional loyalties. When under attack from outside, it stood united, but when a personal quarrel or a motive for blackmail arose, someone from one faction would report on someone from another – a Doabi on a Malwai and vice versa – and they could do so with some impunity because the immigration department did not reveal its sources. Sometimes informants were illegal immigrants themselves but protected by immigration officials, or so the community thought. This unwholesome situation was a consequence of a leaky immigration barrier and the vulnerability of men who entered the country illegally. What the community wanted – if it could ever achieve it – was a fair right of entry for relatives and fellow villagers, not just for spouses and children but a much more extended group. But a more pressing concern was the protection of men already in the country who had been living and working for years under the potential threat of being reported and deported. This issue united Mayo and Kapoor, despite their differences, in backing efforts to lobby the government.[7]

Sadhu Singh Dhami and Anup Singh Dhillon, the two Sikh scholars and activists who visited Kapoor village at Sooke Lake, went to Ottawa in April 1938 to press for a halt to South Asian deportations. They talked to Frederick Charles Blair, the director of immigration, and to a friendlier Hugh Keenleyside in External Affairs without getting any results.[8] What seemed abundantly reasonable to Sikhs looked like special pleading to Blair, who headed a tough-minded department that had deported thousands of immigrants during the Depression – Germans, Scandinavians, Central and Eastern Europeans, and a great many British. These deportees had been unemployed and on relief, had engaged in radical political activity, had medical problems, or had run afoul of the law. In sending them packing, Blair's department had energetically served the interest of employers, labour, municipalities, and Ottawa, and it easily ignored the protests of unions, church groups, and even foreign governments.[9] Although Blair was familiar with only a few South Asian cases, he thought them politically significant because of the vocal anti-Asian lobby in BC. None of these considerations made him receptive to the South Asian case.

As war approached, and as the British worried about the loyalty of India, South Asians in Canada could make a stronger case for themselves. Indians in India were being called upon to support the British Empire in its hour of need, and neither the British nor Canadian governments desired bad publicity. Kapoor and other educated members of his community were quick to perceive this. In any event, they kept trying to get Ottawa to listen. And in the summer of 1939, they found a new spokesperson in Dr. Durai Pal Pandia, an impressively articulate and educated thirty-three-year-old Tamil from a village near the city of Tirunelveli in the southern tip of India, as far from Punjab as one could get and still be in the same country. Pandia had studied in England and confidently claimed to have an MA from Bailiol College, Oxford, a PhD from the University of London, and a barrister's training at the Middle Temple of the Inns of Court, London. He exaggerated, listing degrees he had started but not finished, but he had the erudition, bearing, and personality to carry it off.

In 1939 Pandia was based at the University of Ceylon, in Colombo. That year, he visited the Theosophical Society's headquarters just south of Chennai (Madras) at its expansive garden estate and mansion on the banks of the Adyar River. He had joined the society during his early student days in Chennai, and while staying at the Adyar headquarters, he agreed to go to Canada on a country-wide lecture tour under Theosophical Society auspices.[10] His tour began in May 1939 in Vancouver, where he gave thirty addresses to service clubs, church groups, political clubs, and the two local lodges of the Theosophical Society. In a two-month period, he went from Vancouver to Victoria, Calgary, Edmonton, Saskatoon, Winnipeg, Hamilton, Toronto, and finally Montreal, keeping an intense schedule, frequently with two engagements a day, lecturing, giving classes, and speaking on Theosophy and ethics, reincarnation, new trends in Eastern and Western civilization, India's spiritual tradition, and other similar subjects.

A member of the Indian National Congress party, Pandia had briefly been a secretary to Mahatma Gandhi. One of his standard lectures was "Gandhi as I Know Him," and he impressed his Canadian listeners with his description of Gandhi as a man who could transform humanity with the guidance of two books, the New Testament and the Bhagavad-Gita.[11] The mayor of Hamilton took Pandia in an aircraft over his city, the Toronto Rotary Club president drove him one hundred kilometres into the countryside to meet visiting Rotary dignitaries, and the ladies of the League for Peace and Reform organized a luncheon for him at the University of Toronto's Hart House. He became the subject of controversy in the Toronto Theosophical Society after some leading members wrote to Oxford and London to check his credentials and concluded that he was a fraud, but most people took him at his word, and his tour, which excited a lot of notice, was generally a great success.

In Vancouver, Dr. Pandia had attended the Sikh gurdwara, an obligatory stop for any distinguished visitor from India, and one he could not have overlooked after meeting Kapoor and Kartar Singh Hundal at the Orpheus Lodge of the Theosophical Society. When he talked to Sikh leaders in the gurdwara, they launched into their problem with deportations, and he promised to help. As he later remembered, the man who first raised the subject with him was Ishar Singh Banns, a friend of Kartar Singh's and Kapoor's who was known by his compatriots as Adaroo, the Flyer, because he was both an aviator and a parachutist. He was from the village of Kotla Naudh in the Hoshiarpur District – another Doabi – who, without telling anyone where he had gone, had run away as a thirteen-year-old in 1907 to emigrate with a distant cousin. (His parents were deceased, and fifty years passed before he wrote to his family.) When he arrived in Canada on the *Monteagle,* he had little English, but he did have a middle school education and a passion for things mechanical. Nearly thirty years later, he was an experienced mechanic, an avid reader of every English-language publication he could obtain on mechanics and aviation, a businessman – shop owner, lumber camp operator, manufacturer – and a graduate of the flying course at the Warren School of Aeronautics in California. Flying led to parachuting, and he had drawn a crowd in Victoria in April 1930 when he made a well-publicized jump.[12] Inspired by Lindbergh's famous trans-Atlantic flight of 1927, he had lost no time in taking to the air.

Ishar Banns led a delegation of three Sikhs who came by train from BC to Ottawa to meet Pandia at the end of his speaking tour in early July 1939. It was the first trip to eastern Canada for all of them. Ultimately, this delegation cost a lot of money – an estimated $6,000 to $7,000, which would have been several years' income for a single sawmill worker in BC. Kapoor and Mayo Singh contributed the largest amounts, making good on their support for Pandia and his mission. With this backing, and following Pandia's lead, the delegation stayed at the Chateau Laurier, the elite hotel in Ottawa. Pandia reasoned that people with power were impressed by things like that. He also believed in starting at the top, so he began with the prime minister, William Lyon Mackenzie King, in his office in the East Block on Parliament Hill. Pandia long after remembered the stares that he and his delegation attracted as they walked the short distance from the Chateau Laurier to Parliament Hill. On the small-town streets of the nation's capital, they felt hugely conspicuous with their brown skins and a couple of them with turbans.

Like Pandia, Ishar Banns was about five foot seven, but the other two, Naina Singh Kondola, a long-time Punjabi interpreter for the CPR, and Battan Singh Dhoot, were big turbaned Sikhs. Pandia thought that their size impressed and even shocked the prime minister, who seemed touched when told that robust men like these could be deported even though they had worked in Canada for years. King, of course, was thinking of the larger implications of any negative story about Sikhs. War now appeared close at hand, and he and his officials were conscious of the threat that Sikh disaffection had presented to the British in India during the First World War. Pandia had a sketchy sense of King's past experience with the

Sikh community, which went back to a one-man royal commission that King had conducted in Vancouver in 1907 after an anti-Asian riot. In fact, King had recommended the measures that Canada adopted in 1908 to stop immigration from India. But what Pandia read in King's face was respect and sympathy, qualities that turned out to be genuine.

When Pandia subsequently settled down to specifics with the director of immigration, Frederick Charles Blair, an Anglocentric veteran bureaucrat of hidebound opinions, he found him polite and attentive, asking many questions and willing to give a lot of his time but basically unhelpful: grudgingly accepting instructions from the prime minister and the minister of the interior to give this delegation a good hearing. To move things along, Pandia widened his efforts by lobbying members of parliament from all three parties and publicizing his story via the press and radio. Having rooms near Parliament Hill in the prestigious Chateau Laurier did help. Pandia also took time to return briefly to Vancouver and Victoria to consult with the community there and to speak with the premier of BC, Duff Patullo. Again, he did things in style, avoiding days of rail travel by boarding a twin-engine Lockheed aircraft for a fifteen-hour Trans-Canada Airlines flight to Vancouver, an option that had not existed three months earlier. In this way, July disappeared and August slipped by without a deal being made. Pandia wanted an end to deportations and Blair wanted an assurance that the community would stop bringing in illegal immigrants; and on these points they made no progress.

The impasse broke in September when Canada made its formal declaration of war on Germany. It was no coincidence. On the very day of the declaration, Secretary of State for External Affairs O.D. Skelton, the prime minister's chief adviser, wrote to Blair saying that the moment had come to resolve things with Canada's Sikhs. He used neutral language but left no doubt that the issue was serious: reminding Blair of the *Komagata Maru* in 1914. Skelton, and presumably the prime minister, did not want a repetition of what had happened in India, and particularly among Sikh troops, when Canada turned back a boatload of Punjabi passengers on the eve of the First World War. Blair took his point and within days, he stopped investigations and deportation proceedings against South Asians and assured Pandia that the government would not deport the illegal immigrants it knew about. At that point, Blair had a documented list of twenty-five cases, but his department was aware that there might be forty or fifty more. That was the estimate that Pandia had given.

Pandia took a train back to Vancouver and launched himself on a difficult but ultimately successful task that kept him in Canada until the end of November. The first problem was to get more people to come forward. He spoke to a naysayer, Gurdit Singh Bilga, a forceful personality and activist who had initially disparaged his mission to Ottawa as a waste of money, claiming that such delegations were futile. Now that Pandia had achieved success in twenty-five cases, he began expanding his list by asking Gurdit Singh if he himself had ever brought anyone's son into the country. Well, yes, he had brought his brother's son. So Pandia had this nephew's name added to the immigration department's list and advertised the fact that he had won a general amnesty, not one that applied solely to the cases with which the department was already familiar. Then people started registering in droves, and by the end of November Pandia had 218 names, all males except for one woman. His success was so great that he found it embarrassing. He had not expected so many to come forward and had not warned Blair. For a while the total seemed likely to reach 300, but some held back or were out of the country. Even 218 was an extraordinary figure when – according to the national census taken two years later – there were fewer than 750 South Asian males over fourteen years of age in the province.

Pandia left Vancouver for California at the end of November 1939, intending to spend the next several months advocating for the small South Asian community in the US. What he had achieved in Canada had helped many of Kapoor's closest relatives and friends. Eight of the men who registered as illegal immigrants came from Kapoor's village of Kharoudi; another eleven were from Mayo's village of Paldi. Kapoor's younger brother, Tara, registered, thanks to Pandia, as did Cousin Ajaib and Ajaib's father, Naranjan. A majority of the registrants were from villages within ten or fifteen kilometres of Mahalpur, where Kapoor had gone to school; two-thirds were from the districts of Hoshiarpur and Jalandhar, Kapoor's Doaba area.

Kapoor's brother Tara had a complicated story – like many others – and registration on the amnesty list did not immediately make his life easier. He had first immigrated when there were no regulations barring entry from India, but he had lost his landed status when he left for California and then returned to India. Somehow he had managed to get back into Canada in 1926 and then bring out Balwant Kaur, his young second wife (whom he habitually called Beant, his first wife's name). They began having children – three boys, Lakhbir, Gurdeb, Baldev – while he worked at Mayo Siding and Sooke Lake. And he did all this without being legitimately landed. Understandably, he was not committed to staying. In 1939 he took his family home to India, but when the Barnet mill opened, he returned without them. Later that year, when he registered as an illegal immigrant, he boxed himself in because the immigration department would not let anyone on the amnesty list sponsor their families. Throughout the war, he continued alone in Canada. Finally, two years after the war ended, with immigration department permission at last in hand, he wrote to his wife and family saying he was coming to get them. After spending two months in Kharoudi, he brought his family by air – increasingly the transportation of choice among Canadian Sikhs.[13]

Kapoor's older brother, Bhagwan, had gone back to India in the 1930s, although his son Kashmir, who came to Canada as a seventeen-year-old in 1928, had been back and forth since, returning most recently in 1940 to step in as the Barnet mill manager.[14] The business was doing well, which made it possible for family members to choose to live comfortably in India or in Canada. For Kapoor, it was different because, as the principal owner and manager, he had to be in Vancouver, but he found that no hardship, because his attachment to life in North America was so strong.

One way in which the country had taken hold of him was in his love of driving. This was an outlet for his passion for travel, an appetite that he sought to pass on to his daughters. The oilcloth map on the dining room table was a prized educational tool, but even better was the family car. Every summer when school was out, he drove his family down to California to visit the Teja cousins in Yuba City and Marysville, cousins from his father's sister's side. And in each of the first two summers of the war, before gas rationing made it impossible, he drove east to the Atlantic seaboard or the St. Lawrence.

In 1940 the family and the little dog Prince drove to New York City to catch the second summer of the New York World's Fair and its exhibits of recent marvels such as television. They took the northern route, through the Dakotas and Chicago. Coming back, they crossed the Pennsylvania-Maryland border and headed through the American South on their way to California for their annual visit with their cousins in Yuba City. As always, they passed the kilometres in singing *bhajans* (hymns) and American popular songs, or in listening as Kapoor told stories of his life and experiences. Besant Kaur would finger the beads of her mala and quietly recite her prayers. At that time she was the only vegetarian in the family and unable to find much to eat at roadside cafes except fried potatoes, but she did not complain. When night approached, they would find a motel. Sarjit, then fourteen, would go inside to ask for rooms. Her sister was now old enough to do some of the driving but too reserved to go into the motel office; her mother could not speak English; and her father would sit at the wheel with the motor running because some motels did not allow pets, and they might need to carry on. At one motel in the American South, the woman behind the counter dismissed Sarjit automatically: "We don't take coloured people." The woman was cross-eyed, which made the moment even more unforgettable. Her bluntness came as a shock to Sarjit, who had never encountered prejudice expressed in such an offhand manner and so directly.

The next summer they drove as far as Quebec City to see their own country. While they were passing through Medicine Hat, CBC Radio broadcast a play about Kapoor that had been researched and written by Toronto journalist Allister Grosart, later Senator Grosart. He was then in charge of the CBC's War Effort Programs, and his play was part of a series titled "New Canadians." It established the wartime connection with an introductory tribute to "the gallant soldiers of British India" who were then fighting alongside British, Australian, and Free French forces in Iraq and Syria. Before the broadcast, the CBC tried to contact Kapoor but failed to locate him, so he and his family missed it. What they did eventually see was Grossart's script, which he sent later. In the Rockies they stayed at the Chateau Lake Louise and the Banff Springs Hotel. In Toronto they stayed at the Royal York and in Ottawa the Chateau Laurier, all grand railway hotels in their mature glory. Few Canadians ever saw the country the way they did. Crossing the mountains of British Columbia was possible then only in summer; and it took a steady hand at the wheel on the switchbacks of the Fraser and Thompson Canyons, where the highway was often too narrow for automobiles to get by trucks and where there were many blind curves. They learned the conventions of the route, stopping on a blind curve, honking and listening for an answering honk, and then getting out to negotiate who should back up, depending on who was in the more difficult position. For a family that had already travelled by bus in the Shivalik Hills and in the Peshawar Valley near the Afghan border, it was all taken in the spirit of adventure.

Following the all-Canadian route, they had taken the new Ontario Highway 11 for seven hundred kilometres through northern Ontario, far north of Lake Superior, passing towering cliffs near Lake Nipigon and covering kilometres of muskeg and lake country on the way to the mining towns of Kapuskasing and Cochrane. Long stretches of the route were still under construction, dusty graded gravel roads that eventually gave way to a freshly asphalted two-lane highway with a clean white line down the middle. One of Kapoor's incentives in coming this way, besides the magnificent northern scenery, was to pass through Nellie Lake, where he had homesteaded in 1915 and 1916. Although the Siddoos never forgot his story of building a cabin and clearing land, what they actually saw at Nellie Lake was unmemorable. When they reached Quebec, they felt that they had arrived at a new place, one unlike the rest of Canada, an impression summed up by the sight of a man urinating against a tree. They are like Indians in India, they said to each other: "How terrible." In Quebec City, Sarjit and Jackie found they could manage well with their high school French. After that they turned around to go home the same way they had come.

That September, Sarjit entered grade ten at Kitsilano High and Jackie grade eleven. During that school year, the outside world intruded on their classrooms in a most disturbing way. Sarjit and Jackie had always had Japanese classmates, in Mayo and in their city schools. Several Japanese Canadians sat in their classes at Kitsilano High, but they were all gone by the summer of 1942, after the Canadian government had ordered Japanese Canadians away from coastal areas. For a while these evacuees were held at the Hastings Park fairgrounds, and Jackie and Sarjit could talk to classmates and friends through the fence. But they did not see them again after the government moved them to the interior of the province. This happened so abruptly and unexpectedly that it was hard to absorb or accept.

The girls knew that their parents expected them to become doctors, and they worked hard at school. Sarjit did so well that her teachers selected her for an accelerated class the next year when she did two years in one. This meant that she and her sister graduated from high school at the same time. But home always provided a balance for the information they got at school, especially when it came to current events and perspectives on the world. For international news, Kapoor regularly tuned in to the shortwave radio broadcast of the BBC world news, and he had a favourite news shop across from the CPR station, where he picked up the *Manchester Guardian* or the *Christian Science Monitor* to supplement his daily three Vancouver papers, the *Sun,* the *Province,* and the *News-Herald.*

Kapoor kept a file of newspaper cuttings, starting in December 1941 after the Japanese attack on Pearl Harbor. One week after Pearl Harbor, he set aside a full-page map of the Pacific theatre of war. But what he really cared about was evident in the cuttings he saved over the next few months and years. He was watching developments in India like a hawk. He kept every story that touched on the British promise of independence for India, on what the Americans were saying regarding the subject, on what Chiang Kai-shek and his Chinese government were saying, and on British efforts to win the wartime cooperation of India's national leaders, Nehru and Gandhi. As the Japanese slashed deep into Burma, Kapoor watched the progress of negotiations in Delhi between Sir Stafford Cripps for the British government and Mahatma Gandhi and Muhammad Ali Jinnah for the Indian National Congress and the Muslim League. In early April 1942, when the Vancouver papers headlined the shocking news that Japanese planes had sunk a British aircraft carrier near the coast of Ceylon (Sri Lanka) as well as two cruisers in the Bay of Bengal, the story that Kapoor circled dealt with the failure of the Cripps mission – the rejection by the Indian National Congress of Cripps' plan for Indian independence.

This was the pattern of Kapoor's reading throughout the war. Even in early June 1944, when the Allies opened up a second front in Europe, he combed the papers for news of India or stories with an Indian element. On 8 June 1944, two days after the D-Day landing, with huge headlines about the Canadian advance to the outskirts of the French town of Caen, the story that Kapoor marked was a few lines of type about Private Nand Singh, who had won a Victoria Cross for leading a platoon charge in Burma.

Kapoor naturally kept cuttings of stories about himself, his family, and his own community in Canada. In April 1942, he made a statement in the *Vancouver News-Herald*, the most sympathetic paper in town. Featured in the same article was a thirty-six-year-old educated Sikh, Jerry Hundal, a UBC graduate and one of the Hundal boys admitted to Canada as an act of grace back in 1913. Kapoor and Hundal were speaking out after Gandhi and the Indian National Congress rejected the Cripps plan for independence, hoping to assure Canadians that the Congress was antifascist and would fight the Japanese but that its leaders expected provisional self-government without further delay. Kapoor believed that talks had broken down because the British had not offered enough. Neither he nor Jerry Hundal thought that the demands of the Muslim League were reasonable or that religious and cultural divisions made India ungovernable. The *News-Herald* reporter, who described Kapoor as elderly and handsome, quoted him as saying that self-government would not bring chaos in India. "They (Indians) would not quarrel over religion," Kapoor told him. "They are hungry. They want bread and butter."[15] The implication of his remark was that they were not getting bread and butter under the British.

Kapoor and other prominent South Asians were also trying to get action on their own situation in Canada. For that purpose, they recruited one of Gandhi's long-time associates, who spoke to the Lions Club of

Vancouver at the Hotel Georgia in January 1942. This was Henry Polak, an English Jew and Gandhi follower of nearly forty years from the days of Phoenix Farm, Gandhi's experimental commune in South Africa. Polak was on a lecture tour in eastern Canada, and Kapoor, Mayo, and Kartar Singh invited him to BC to speak with members of the provincial government and to give several addresses. The invitation was probably Kartar Singh's idea, with Kapoor and Mayo putting up the money to bring him out. Kapoor kept a newspaper cutting of Polak's eloquent appeal before the Lions Club in the Hotel Georgia for British Columbia to give the franchise to its Sikh citizens. Polak put it this way: "If Sikhs were good enough to fight and die beside Canadians in Hong Kong, they were good enough to vote in Canada."[16] The Japanese had captured Hong Kong only a few weeks earlier, so Polak's comment was topical. As it happened, he was speaking in Vancouver just as Canadians launched themselves into a conscription debate that would bitterly divide the country along the lines of its two major solitudes, French and English. Only a week after Polak spoke, Prime Minister King announced a national plebiscite on conscription. Kapoor kept none of the stories on the conscription controversy. But after conscription came into effect, he began cutting out articles regarding what happened when young Sikhs received draft notices and about how they responded by becoming active in the fight for the franchise.

Many Sikhs were incensed by the draft. Young men wondered why they should fight for a country that wouldn't let them vote, and the gurdwara society turned to a law firm it had long trusted, Bird and Bird, to help those who were drafted. The first to get a notice was a twenty-four-year-old communist and union activist named Darshan Singh Sangha, who was from the village of Langeri, near Mahalpur. He had come to Canada as a student and, like Sadhu Singh Dhami and others, had worked in various sawmills to pay his way while enrolled at UBC. After graduation, he worked at Kapoor's Barnet mill. When he received his notice, he spoke to several people including Kapoor, who advised him to report for military duty while waiting for the lawyers to do what they could. So Darshan went to training camp in Vernon, BC, as the only non-white there and endured the life of a recruit until he was released four months later.[17]

Getting himself out of the Vernon training camp was not enough for Darshan Singh Sangha. Along with other educated South Asians of his generation, he took over the campaign for the end of racial barriers and for treatment as full citizens with the right to vote, or failing that, for exclusion from the draft. Nagindar Singh Gill, who at thirty-five was the secretary of the Khalsa Diwan Society, took a leading role in this campaign as did Jerry Hundal and Hazara Singh Garcha, who had recently finished his master's of science at the University of Alberta. They gave interviews to the press, talked to members of the Co-operative Commonwealth Federation (CCF, the socialist opposition party), and wrote to labour organizations and the governments in Ottawa and Victoria. Nagindar Gill put it simply for a reporter: "We are British subjects. We are ready to fight for Canada, but we can't understand why we are not entitled to vote."[18]

These men found a friend and counsellor in a seventy-year-old retired senior India Civil Service officer, Sir Robert Erskine Holland, who had once been Chief Commissioner of Rajputana and only recently had settled in Victoria. Holland helped them draft petitions to Victoria and Ottawa. In March 1943, he led a delegation that met with Irish-born premier John Hart and the provincial cabinet. The delegation included Harold Winch, the CCF leader of the Opposition, Harold Pritchett, the president of the lumber workers' union, and nine Sikhs. Two of the Sikhs were clean-shaven recruits in army uniform, and one was a veteran of the First World War in civilian jacket and tie but with his service medals prominently displayed on his chest. No one could miss the symbolism intended. These were people who served the nation and the empire.[19]

Six weeks earlier, these same Sikhs had booked Vancouver's largest and most magnificent theatre, the Orpheum, for a mass meeting of two thousand people. Most of the crowd came to the Orpheum from the gurdwara after a day of religious music and prayer celebrating the birthday of the tenth Sikh guru, one of the occasions on the Sikh calendar that brought Sikhs together from all over the province and that made it possible to assemble so many people at the same time. In the theatre, Darshan Sangha, Nagindar Gill, and Hazara Garcha were on the platform along with Elmore Philpott, the left-leaning editorial director of the upstart *Vancouver News-Herald,* CCF leader Harold Winch, union leader Harold Pritchett, and CCF legislative assembly member Dorothy Steeves. Philpott, a forty-seven-year-old war veteran who had to steady himself with two canes as a consequence of his war injuries, chaired the meeting. His words captured the mood of all present: "We ought to hang our heads in shame when we force a man to fight for Canada and refuse him the right to vote."[20]

Kapoor sat on the balcony with Sarjit and Jackie, characteristically avoiding the platform and the limelight. But he was vitally involved and wanted his daughters to participate as well. This was a night for his family and his community to enjoy the outspoken support of their white friends.

When the evening began, Jackie briefly appeared on stage in a trio of Sikh youngsters offering a short musical program. Noreen Johal was the vocalist; Buchan Singh Manhas had the accordion; and Jackie – Jagdis Kapoor as reported in the newspaper – played the piano.[21]

In 1943, however, it was not sufficient to have support and help from the socialist party, the woodworkers' union, the *News-Herald,* and a distinguished retiree from the British regime in India. Some members of the government were persuadable, but others were not, and the general public was on both sides of the fence, with many still seeing Canada as exclusively Christian, British, and white. The Reverend Canon G. Wilson, president of the Ministerial Association of Vancouver, told the press he would not support any petition for a vote for South Asians for two reasons: "heathens" from Asia were not easy to assimilate, and India was not demonstrating much loyalty to the empire.[22] Voices like this made a difference. While BC's premier, John Hart, and members of his coalition cabinet listened to the Sikhs who came to see them on a Tuesday morning in March 1943 and sent it off with a friendly promise, time revealed how little it meant.[23] Four more years of campaigning – two years beyond the end of the war – were required before John Hart's government finally granted the franchise.

It took patience as well as determination to keep up the long fight for full Canadian citizenship. And in Kapoor's case, that patience, and the generosity of spirit that went with it, characterized his ordinary daily exchanges with other Canadians. A letter to Kapoor written years later by an elderly man reaching back in his memory paints a vivid picture of the Punjabi-style hospitality typical of Kapoor and Besant Kaur. The writer, who signed himself Fred J. Lawrence, had been a primary school principal at Seaview School in Vancouver, and his connection with the family had begun via a chance encounter with Jackie. Neither she nor Sarjit attended his school, but he had talked to her in St. Paul's Hospital, where she was a patient and he a visitor. She had been hospitalized for seventeen days after painful and dangerous surgery for an infection of the mastoid bone behind her ear, and his friendly words had led to a dinner invitation to Kapoor's home. To make up a social evening, they had also invited two of the girls' regular schoolteachers and Jerry Hundal, who was then a law student. Lawrence never forgot the Indian curry that Besant Kaur served (and Kapoor helped to prepare), which was a first taste of Indian cuisine for him and his wife. And they were driven home, embarrassed by what they had received, with pockets full of oranges, a wristwatch for Lawrence, and what he remembered as "ornaments" for his wife. They came back a second time, invited for dinner and an entertainment program put on by Jackie, Sarjit, and some of their girlfriends from school in the family's basement rumpus room. He described those evenings as highlights of his long career as a teacher. To Lawrence and his wife, seeing these young people of different backgrounds, comfortable, unself-conscious, and natural with each other, seemed most remarkable and praiseworthy. He couldn't quite find the words for it, but tried anyway: "An immigrant family from half way around the world had been received with open arms by our own Canadian people who had so much to learn from the newcomers."[24]

Lawrence had no sense of irony in what he wrote. He was perhaps unaware of the legal barriers that South Asians faced as citizens without votes who were excluded from jury duty, from employment and contracts in the public sector, and from many clubs, cafes, movie theatres, beer halls, and dance halls, and who were refused service in some barbershops or turned away from some hotels. As a good host, Kapoor had not bothered his guests with the deportation issue, the franchise, the other grievances of his community, or even his concern for the future of India. Instead, he invited Lawrence into his home without barriers of race or religion and without inflicting political talk. Had Lawrence asked a few questions, he might have sensed how protective Kapoor and Besant Kaur were of their daughters, how happy they were to see Sarjit and Jackie bring home their Anglo-Canadian girlfriends and their teachers, and how unwilling they were to let them go to these same girlfriends' houses. They retained the values of Punjabi jagirdar families. It was exciting for Lawrence to be entertained by people from afar, even though his letter showed that he was not sure where they came from: he seemed to think it was the Middle East. It was the warmth and charm of their hospitality that impressed him and that he never forgot.

12
A Real United Nations in Practice

Jackie and Sarjit's generation of Indo-Canadians reached adulthood as Canada began moving – in small steps – toward full acknowledgment and acceptance of visible minorities. They were much freer to choose a variety of careers and occupations than their parents had been. And they had the skills, education, and outlook to do so, even as they kept their roots in Punjabi culture. With scarcely an exception, these young Indo-Canadians reached adulthood with the strong sense of family and family duty that one would have expected among villagers in Punjab. They accepted the direction of their parents to a degree that most young Canadian adults did not, even back in that wartime and early post-war world. That was most obvious when it came to marriages, which Punjabi parents in Canada continued to arrange for their children, seeking suitable matches by Punjabi standards. And it was apparent in other ways. Kapoor and Besant Kaur differed from other Punjabi parents in wanting their daughters to get an education and become doctors, and in considering that goal more important than getting them married. But they were like other Punjabi parents in keeping their daughters close to home. They retained this attitude when the girls graduated from high school and went to university.

Jackie and Sarjit started classes at the University of British Columbia in the fall of 1943. They went together because Sarjit had crammed grades eleven and twelve into one year, along with thirty-five other select students at Kitsilano High, so she left high school when Jackie did. There was no question about what they would study: their parents had decided that they should be doctors and practise in India – giving back to their ancestral country. With the help of Bhai Piara Singh Langeri, Kapoor had already purchased land in the town of Phagwara, near Besant Kaur's village of Aur, as grounds for a hospital for Jackie and Sarjit to run. The girls knew how immensely disappointed their parents would be if they deviated from this plan. Even so, during her last year in high school, Sarjit had announced another idea: she would be a lawyer. Kapoor said he did not mind but added in the next breath that he would be upset if his daughter lied for a living. Sarjit had too much regard for him to push her own idea further.

UBC was then a small university with a stable student population of about twenty-five hundred and a campus in arrested development, as it had been from the beginning of the Depression. When Jackie and Sarjit first attended it, UBC had not put up any new buildings for nearly twenty years. It had no medical program, and the sisters enrolled in a premed mix of arts and science courses, planning to go on either to McGill or Toronto. The campus was a half-hour by electric streetcar from their York Avenue home, so Sarjit, the agitator, asked for a car. Kapoor agreed but did not take them with him to choose what they wanted – something classy. Instead, he bought a large four-door Dodge with a stick shift on the floor and a black exterior that made it look to Sarjit like a hearse. She thought it the ugliest car she had ever seen. Of course she objected, but he said she could choose between this car and public transportation, so she and Jackie took the car.

During their two years at UBC, they studied chemistry, physics, zoology, math, and English. The teacher who left an indelible mark was Dean Mawdsley (Dorothy Mawdsley), dean of women and instructor in English. They saw her by appointment on their first day, and showed up in slacks, which their mother thought they should wear. All through school, they had worn skirts and dresses like their classmates, but Besant Kaur decided that as mature young women at university, they should cover their legs. As they entered Mawdsley's large office, she glanced at their slacks and said sharply, "I hope you are not going to start that racket here." She obviously did not approve: in the 1940s, North American women dressed up for office work, classes, or shopping excursions, wearing frocks or skirts and blouses with mandatory stockings; slacks were reserved solely for household, recreational, and informal wear. Humiliated, Jackie and Sarjit understood that they had made the wrong choice. They had a big discussion with their parents that evening. Their mother was shocked that the girls were expected to wear skirts and show their legs but did not argue, and from then on they dressed like other university women. Later, they found that Mawdsley, who gave the course on literature from Chaucer to Milton, was quite nice. But that first encounter ensured that they would never forget her, as they did many other instructors.

None of their girlfriends from Kitsilano High went past high school except Vivian Wong, the single Chinese girl in the group, who lived nearby on York Avenue and took rides with them to the university during their first year.[1] Mostly, they drove to and from campus on their own, with Sarjit at the wheel. They worked hard, assiduously attending classes and studying long hours, not wanting to let their parents down, and they did not join in extracurricular activities, go to dances, or attend any big functions on campus. Their parents would object if they began spending social time in the company of boys. And they did not make girlfriends during those two years, and did not worry about it. On weekends they went to Barnet with their parents and played football or basketball with their cousins in the mill yard. That was their relaxation away from studies. When they got into debates and discussions, it was in a family setting rather than at the university. This would happen regularly when their cousins from Barnet came visiting. Their uncle Gurdial Singh Teja, a college graduate in India and always outspoken in the gurdwara or the mill yard, was one of a number of staunch communists in the Punjabi community, and he would assert his views just to provoke Sarjit. She inevitably rose to the bait, and they would argue with relish while his wife, Harbans Kaur, and eldest daughter, eleven-year-old Diljeet, sat with heads down in embarrassment. They were guests and he was arguing with their host's daughter. Each time, as they drove over for a visit, Harbans Kaur asked Gurdial not to get Sarjit stirred up, but he could never resist it.[2]

Intensive study paid off in the second week of May 1945 when Jackie and Sarjit learned they had first-class standing for their final year at UBC. At that time, the *Vancouver Province* and the *Vancouver Sun* published the results for all UBC students, and Kapoor proudly kept the pages of both papers with the full list of names.

That same week, as the war ended in Europe, Kapoor paid close attention to the gathering of world leaders in San Francisco at the founding conference of the United Nations. His friend Elmore Philpott of the *Vancouver News-Advertiser,* who was among the journalists there, was giving a daily 10:00 p.m. analysis on local radio.[3] Kapoor followed the San Francisco conference for what it meant to India, and Philpott was not alone in giving him a personal connection. Anup Singh Dhillon, the scholar and activist who visited at Sooke and who had gone to Ottawa for Kapoor's community, was in San Francisco and being mentioned in the press. The issue was India's representation. India was one of the forty-six nations with a seat at the conference, but it was present as part of the British Empire, with delegates named by the British regime in New Delhi. The Indian National Congress was sending Jawaharlal Nehru's sister Vijaya Lakshmi Pandit to protest, and as the Congress representative in San Francisco, Anup Dhillon was preparing for her arrival. He called the seating of India's British-appointed delegation "a farce."[4] Kapoor could read about this with special appreciation, because the speaker was someone he knew well.

That fall, in September 1945, Jackie and Sarjit enrolled at the University of Toronto, far from home. They had to thank their father's old friend from the Toronto area, William Moore, for making the arrangements. In June, at the age of seventy, Moore had given up his seat in parliament after ten years as a Liberal MP and retired to Moorlands, his lakeside farm at Rosebank east of Toronto, where Kapoor and Piara Singh Langeri had worked for him in the summer of 1914. Of the Sikhs whom he had befriended then, he knew Kartar Singh Hundal best because Kartar Singh had stayed on in Toronto for many years. Kapoor asked Kartar Singh – by then both his friend and employee – to get in touch with Moore and ask him to arrange for Jackie and Sarjit to be admitted. The only hitch was the refusal of the medical school to take the two sisters at the same time, so Moore directed Sarjit to the smallest of Toronto's four arts colleges, the Anglican college of Trinity at the north end of the Toronto campus. Jackie went straight into medicine, and Sarjit followed a year later. Occasionally, while the sisters were in Toronto, Moore invited them to his farm, and they would take the hour-long bus ride to Pickering, where he met them, a big, broad-faced man, slightly stooped, both gracious and expansive and always visibly happy to see them. He would take them to his upstairs study and tell stories about their father, Kartar Hundal, and the horsemanship of Bhai Piara Singh Langeri, whom he still called Karam.

Moore was a member of the Toronto Hunt Club, which rode to hounds near the Scarborough Bluffs east of Toronto until its membership shifted exclusively to golf during the early 1930s. He belonged to the Toronto Club and the University Club in downtown Toronto; and he was active in the arts community. When he ran for re-election as an MP in 1940, he put a concert grand piano on the platform at a rally so that Norman Wilks, who was one of his supporters as well as a pianist and principal of the Toronto Conservatory of Music, could give a recital before presenting a political speech.[5] If anyone knew both the cultural and business elite of Toronto, Moore did. That included members of the Theosophical Society.

In the fall of 1945, as Jackie and Sarjit were just settling into their studies, Kapoor and Besant Kaur came from Vancouver to see how they were doing and paid an evening visit to Moore's country home, where they were entertained by Moore and his wife, Mabel. The person who drove them to the farm was George McMurtrie, Moore's and Kartar Singh's old friend from the Toronto Theosophical Society.[6]

Jackie and Sarjit were never sure how they ended up living in the home of Velma Wallace during their Toronto years. Possibly it was through Moore and his circle of friends and acquaintances that they found themselves with this gracious lady rather than in a boarding or rooming house nearer the campus. Or it might have been thanks to Kartar Singh, who had flown to Toronto that July to visit his old Theosophical friends – his very first flight and one that left him raving about the three-thousand-mile view of Canada from the air.[7] Auntie Velma had a three-story house on Foxbar Road, a genteel four-hundred-metre-long semi-circular enclave of thirty homes angled between two major traffic arteries, St. Clair and Avenue Road. A large Protestant church stood at the corner where Foxbar entered St. Clair. Auntie Velma attended this church every Sunday.

Velma was the widow of Edward Wilson Wallace, who had been president and chancellor of Victoria College, the United Church College at the University of Toronto. She was his second wife and had married him after he returned from China, where his first wife died. He had been a missionary in western China for over twenty years until 1927 when he had returned to Toronto with his eleven-year-old son, Eddie, after being evacuated during fighting between the Communists and Chiang Kai-shek.[8] From 1930 to 1941, he had been chancellor of Victoria College, and he was only sixty-one when he died. Velma was four years his junior. She had suffered a second loss in October 1942 when her stepson, Eddie, by then a flying officer in the Royal Canadian Air Force, was reported missing in action and presumed dead. Jackie and Sarjit came to know most of this history well during the years they lived with her.

In the mornings, at Jackie's insistence because she was a keen walker, they would walk south along Avenue Road and then University Avenue to the far side of the campus, a distance of three kilometres, all downhill and much shorter than a walk from York Avenue to UBC. In the evening they took the bus back to Foxbar Road. They had free use of Velma's kitchen to prepare breakfast or a light supper, and they took their main meal out, always at noon and generally in the cafeteria of the Toronto (Royal) Conservatory of Music, which was then near the Hygiene and Pathology Buildings, the Toronto General Hospital, and the Children's

Hospital, where they had lectures. On Sundays the three of them, Jackie, Sarjit, and Auntie Velma, prepared dinner together, which they ate at midday after Auntie Velma came back from church.

On Saturday afternoon Auntie Velma always tuned the radio to the local CBC station for the live Texaco-sponsored broadcast from the New York Metropolitan Opera. With the volume turned up, Berlioz, Bizet, Puccini, or Wagner reverberated through the house while Jackie and Sarjit tried to study. They found it a hardship but in spite of themselves learned to love the classical themes that became so familiar. And when they showed an interest, Auntie Velma happily took them to concerts at Toronto's Massey Hall or Eaton's Auditorium to introduce them to the Western classical music tradition. One summer the Siddoos invited her to Vancouver, and the relationship reached such a comfortable point that when Auntie Velma went on a long holiday to Florida, Besant Kaur came to Foxbar Road to stay with the girls for several months.[9]

They had been living with Auntie Velma for three years when she told them something about their father that took them by surprise. She had read an article by a Toronto-based freelance writer about the Sikhs of British Columbia, in *Saturday Night,* Toronto's premiere arts and public opinion magazine.[10] The article mentioned Kapoor and described him as a very wealthy man, the owner of an immense sawmill with hundreds of employees, Anglo-Saxon as well as South Asian. It was the wealthy part that surprised Jackie and Sarjit. Sarjit laughed and told Auntie Velma that the magazine had made a mistake: her father had never, even once, indicated that he was anything other than an ordinary person.

Sarjit and Jackie were themselves extraordinary as Indo-Canadian women in medicine at the University of Toronto. They looked around their classes and saw nine or ten men for every woman and no one else with their combination of Canadian upbringing and Indian heritage. Women had been studying medicine at Toronto for several generations but always in small numbers.[11] When Jackie and Sarjit were there, they did encounter a few women from India or Indian communities abroad. Sarjit's class had one Parsi woman from Mumbai (Bombay), Zinet Currimbhoy, who became a good friend; and at Trinity College, Sarjit got to know Lakshmi Rao, who was from a Hindu family in Puri on the Bay of Bengal but a convert to Christianity, which perhaps explained her presence at an Anglican college in Toronto. Lakshimi Rao was a graduate student in public health and lived at the Trinity women's residence as a don, which involved being a guide or chaperon for the undergraduate students staying there.

Two other friends were sisters from Trinidad, Agnes and Sylvia Ramcharan, who were also studying medicine and who were outstanding students: Sylvia was the gold medallist in her year. These sisters were Christians from a Presbyterian school in Trinidad, who began to emphasize their Hindu heritage while in Toronto and changed their names to Amala and Savitri, although Jackie and Sarjit went on calling them Agnes and Sylvia. Jackie and Sarjit were naturally drawn to this group of Indian women, although they also found it easy to be with their female Anglo-Canadian classmates. Outside class they did not mix with the male students, either the younger ones or the considerable number who were several years older. They still depended tremendously on each other, while finding a comfortable home with Auntie Velma.

What distinguished Sarjit's class at Toronto Medical School from those of previous years, including Jackie's, were the veterans returning to their studies after the war. Sarjit's class was already being called "the veterans' class." Some students had come straight from high school to medical school, but the war veterans created a different atmosphere, adding a leavening of maturity and also irreverence. In fact, it was reassuring for Sarjit to see that even older and war-experienced students could clam up in front of a professor. When doing hospital rounds in groups of ten with the cardiologist at Toronto General, Sarjit noticed that everyone was too intimidated to ask a single question. And yet this same cardiologist looked less than awesome after a party at the end of the program when Sarjit and her classmates came upon him standing drunk near an elevator with a felt hat pulled down over his eyes, sticking out his tongue and blowing raspberries.

Jackie and Sarjit saw that the veterans, for all their seeming assurance and occasional high spirits, were cautious in the presence of a professor such as Alan Brown, the Canadian authority on pediatrics. He was always formally dressed, turned out in spats, which added to a persona that seemed distant and autocratic. He imperiously shut the classroom door on anyone who arrived late. On one occasion when he was late himself, some of the veterans locked him out, a nervy prank. Sarjit watched as Dr. Brown knocked from the outside, and everyone, even the boldest, sat still, afraid to turn the lock and be the first to greet him. When he did get in, he threatened not to teach the class any more, but calmed down enough to be satisfied with an apology signed by everyone. The class, of course, was worth an apology. Sarjit was sufficiently impressed by Brown to decide to make pediatrics her specialty.

Brown may have been a major influence, but when the time came, Sarjit chose to do her specialization under the energetic John F. McCreary – Jack to his colleagues. He was in his midthirties in 1945 when he came back to his large family practice in Toronto after three years overseas in the medical branch of the Royal Canadian Air Force. In the last stages of the war, he had accepted an assignment under the Supreme Allied Command that brought him face to face with the malnutrition and disease of children in western Holland and Belgium, and with the desperate condition of survivors in the Belsen concentration camp. He had been among the Allied officers decorated by the Dutch government for his service to the civilian population as the war drew to an end.[12] Back in Toronto, he resumed teaching at the medical school as well as his family practice. Jackie and Sarjit got to know him as a warm, upbeat, engaged, and abundantly congenial medical professor. Later, in 1951, he moved to Vancouver as head of pediatrics at the new UBC medical school. That move made it possible for Sarjit to come home to do her post-graduate studies with him.

Kapoor and Besant Kaur kept in touch with their daughters via weekly phone calls and letters. He would write partly in English and she in Punjabi: commenting on the weather, describing developments in the Sikh community, especially any infighting between factions, mentioning any concerns or plans at the mill or lumber camp, reporting on the dog Prince – adding sometimes for Jackie's benefit, because she was the leading animal lover in a family of animal lovers, "Prince sighs for you" – and signing off "with love from Daddy, Mommy and Prince." And they might add a Punjabi Sikh greeting, "Sat Sri Akal," for Mrs Wallace or Auntie Velma as Jackie and Sarjit knew her. Occasionally, Kapoor would fold a few dollar bills into the envelope with instructions that the girls go out to a favourite eating place.[13]

Jackie and Sarjit had been in Toronto for only a few weeks when he wrote to them about a big fire at Shawnigan Lake that had swept up a narrow valley consuming all the trees in its path as well as a large quantity of timber that had been felled and piled for transport. The fire had burned out when it reached green timber at higher elevations and stopped three kilometres short of the logging camp. The estimated loss to the Kapoor Lumber Company was $200,000.[14] Halfway through their second year at Toronto, Kapoor phoned about another disastrous fire, one that gutted the Barnet mill in its eighth year of operation and cost his company $500,000. It had begun with a spill of molten metal during repairs to an edger saw and quickly got out of hand when the hot metal landed on sawdust and grease. The mechanics had reached for water pails only to find them frozen solid.[15] Jackie and Sarjit worried that they might have to give up their medical studies. But the lumber business was good in the 1940s; the Kapoor Company carried on, and Kapoor never needed to say that he was in financial difficulty.

The girls always came home for Christmas, Easter, and the summer holidays, but they spent their spring term weekends with Auntie Velma at her summer cottage in the woodlands country northeast of Toronto. (When they did this, Sarjit drove Auntie Velma's car for her.) With summers and holidays at home, and the regular letters and phone calls from their parents while they were in Toronto, Jackie and Sarjit avidly followed what was happening in Vancouver, and especially the continuing struggle for the vote. In Ontario, once they reached voting age, they could have voted had there been an election. Their cousin Ajaib, who was a few years their senior, had voted in the federal election of June 1945 when he was employed as a mechanic at the US Air Force refuelling stop at Whitehorse in the Yukon.[16] "You can vote here," someone told him, so he did. British Columbia was the only place in Canada where such was not the case, and it had been the unfortunate truth for nearly forty years, since 1907 when its legislative assembly disenfranchised immigrants from India as it had earlier disenfranchised those from China and Japan.

Jackie and Sarjit had been high school students when they attended the great mass meeting at the Orpheum Theatre, which agitated for the vote. They were in their second year at UBC when the speaker of the legislative assembly ruled out of order a bill to give South Asians the franchise, and a prominent member of the government said some extremely insulting things about South Asians. The speaker ruled on a procedural technicality, but that was after passionate opposition to the bill by the provincial secretary who was also the minister of labour. His name was George Pearson and he was the legislative assembly member for the Vancouver Island town of Nanaimo. Pearson was himself an immigrant, like so many British Columbians of his day, and like nearly every other immigrant from Britain, he took his own political rights in Canada for granted. He was a coal miner's son from the English Midlands who had immigrated in 1899 at the age of nineteen and settled in Nanaimo, starting humbly as a grocery clerk and rising to notice in the town's social structure as wholesale grocer. In his late forties he had plunged into politics and he had represented Nanaimo ever since. And he had been a fixture as minister of labour for more than a decade, with a generally rational and progressive record except when it came to Asians.

For years Pearson's department had kept a tally of the industrial jobs held by Asians, a kind of report card on the provincial government's effectiveness in keeping them out.[17] In 1942 Pearson had been a powerful influence in the removal of the Japanese from the coast, with no respect for the rights of Japanese Canadians born and raised in Canada.[18] And in March 1944, in reaction to a private member's bill that would have given South Asians the vote, he generated headlines with his claim that no group caused his department more trouble than the "Hindus," chiefly because their presence – he insisted – undermined the standard of living for everyone in the province.[19]

In this outburst he called South Asian employers and the South Asians who worked for them "unreliable, dishonest, deceitful and non-cooperative." He did not name Kapoor and Mayo, whose lumber operations were in the riding next to his, but he might as well have. A few months later, he tried feebly to make amends by proposing that Asians who had served in the armed forces should get the vote. Many British Columbians found Pearson's original tirade distasteful and his subsequent idea inadequate. Public opinion was moving against him and that was evident in April 1945, when a legislative assembly bill to give South Asians the franchise fell short of passing by just two votes.[20] Nonetheless, Pearson still had a large popular following, and in the first provincial election after the war, in October 1945, he carried his working-class Nanaimo riding decisively.[21]

By then, Jackie and Sarjit were attending the University of Toronto. Thanks to their father, they followed the development of the franchise campaign as it began to move forward during their second year at Toronto. Dr. Durai Pal Pandia, the Indian National Congress activist and one-time lecturer for the Theosophical Society, was back in BC and leading the franchise fight. This was the same Dr. Pandia who had been so effective in negotiating an amnesty for over two hundred illegal immigrants in 1939. A group of community leaders – headed by Kapoor, Mayo, and Kapoor's friend and manager at the Barnet mill, Kartar Singh – had telegraphed him in Port of Spain, Trinidad, where he had been working for South Asians in the West Indies. They wanted him to redirect his energy to improving things for South Asians in Canada.[22]

Pandia understood that the Sikhs of British Columbia were ready to work together – he knew they had fierce factions – but he had not been in Vancouver for more than a few days when a delegation of fifteen or twenty of them arrived at his door. They included the incoming and outgoing presidents of the Vancouver gurdwara, bitter opponents who were at odds over the gurdwara's account books and making charges and countercharges of extortion and misspent money. They had already launched criminal and civil cases against each other. Pandia got them to drop their complaints by promising to review the accounts himself. For this purpose, he created a committee consisting of himself, Kapoor, and two Punjabi Hindus, Pundit Balmakand of Skrooli and Munshi Ram from Bilga, four ostensibly neutral parties. Balmakand had once been Kapoor's business partner and was a superintendent at Sooke. Kapoor, who did his best to stay clear of disputes like this, wrote optimistically to Jackie and Sarjit that perhaps the committee could bring community peace in the future.[23] For the moment, Pandia had convinced gurdwara factions to shelve their differences for the good of all.

Several of the Sikhs who had recruited Pandia spoke English – Kapoor, Kartar, Ishar Singh, Nagindar Singh, and Mayo. But less-educated men, such as Gurdit Singh Bilga, the old activist who was now the Vancouver gurdwara president, were also key contributors and organizers. All of them were behind Pandia, valuing him because he was highly educated, articulate, experienced, and well connected to the Indian National Congress party in India. They were Punjabi Sikhs and he was a Tamil from Chennai, but they wanted him to represent them to the Canadian public and in meetings with Canadian politicians and bureaucrats, trusting him to make a polished, diplomatic, and forceful presentation. They supplied the information and the arguments, which Kartar more than anyone had at his fingertips, but they looked to Pandia to put across what they had to say. Kartar and Kapoor together had been fighting this battle since before the First World War, and they were more than ready to have a man such as Pandia speaking for them.

As a group, Kartar, Kapoor, and the other leaders of the South Asian community had never resigned themselves to the treatment they received as immigrants; nor had they been quiet about it. From the time they arrived in Canada, they had campaigned and agitated, and they had been effective in keeping their tiny community – around eighteen hundred at the end of the Second World War – from slipping from view, either in Canada or in India.[24] To that end, they had brought in a succession of high-profile champions, people associated with Gandhi and the Indian independence movement who had the stature and celebrity to command public attention as well as to speak directly to the Canadian prime minister or the provincial premier and their cabinet colleagues.

In 1940 the acclaimed social activist and film actress Kamaladevi Chattopdhyay went to Ottawa with Pandia. This was during her six-month stay in the US – a stay that included tea with the president and a personal tour of the White House conducted by Eleanor Roosevelt.[25] She was almost too well known. In 1942 she flew from Seattle to Vancouver and found herself at a special luncheon hosted by an apologetic mayor, who was trying to make up for an incident at the airport. Upon her arrival at Vancouver airport, immigration officials had rejected her as a dangerous radical, and she had spent hours sitting on a bench, refusing to be sent away.

Also in 1942 Henry Polak, the English-born Gandhi disciple, trekked to Ottawa and then to Vancouver and Victoria at the end of his lecture tour in eastern Canada. In the spring of 1945, the venerable Indian nationalist and parliamentarian Pandit Harday Nath Kunzru stopped in British Columbia after a conference in Virginia City. And in the fall of 1946, another prominent Indian nationalist, publicist, and author, Kodanda Rao, made his way to the West Coast after an International Labour Organization committee meeting in Montreal. This was his second trip to Vancouver in a decade. Most of these occasions demanded a great effort by Kapoor and his family, assisting with the arrangements, offering a dinner party at a hotel or a luncheon at York Avenue, or hosting the guest in their home. Each of these visitors commanded public notice and got access to the most important politicians in the province or the country. None achieved change, but all served to prepare the ground.

Kartar, Kapoor, and the others finally brought Dr. Pandia to BC as their advocate, and he established himself in the province's capital of Victoria and later in Vancouver, where he stayed at the Hotel Vancouver. He spoke to service clubs and church groups, on radio and to the press, and directly to Premier John Hart and the provincial cabinet. Fortuitously, the legislative assembly had already struck a committee to review the Election Act, and when it met for two days in the fall of 1946, Pandia was there along with a delegation that included the lumbermen Kapoor and Mayo, the journalist, activist, and intellectual Kartar, the businessman and flying enthusiast Ishar Singh, the Malwai spokesman Nagindar Singh, and his gurdwara opponent Gurdit Singh Bilga from Doaba. The socialist opposition, the CCF, strongly supported the South Asian cause, and encouragingly, members of the government coalition were coming around; and the mainstream newspapers as well.[26]

In his *Vancouver News-Herald* columns, Elmore Philpott sought to shake up readers who thought they had nothing in common with defeated Nazi Germany. How could they laugh at a Disney cartoon lampooning Hitler and the master race yet treat their own tiny Sikh minority so atrociously?[27] He was not alone in asking that, but his column reached a lot of people. And he chose an effective time – the moment of victory against the Nazis – to ask Canadians where they stood. By that fall, public opinion had shifted so decisively that, when Pandia, Kapoor, Kartar, and the rest of the delegation entered a meeting room in the legislative assembly, the battle had been largely won. The seven-member committee on the Election Act, under pressure from Chinese Canadians as well as East Indians, agreed that these two Asian groups should get the franchise. (Japanese Canadians, whose home country had been an enemy during the war, had to wait another year.)

Pandia stayed in his Victoria hotel until the Election Act change passed in the legislative assembly. His strategy, as he lobbied members of the assembly, was to keep the South Asian case separate from that of the Chinese. Like Kartar, Kapoor, and the other Sikhs around him, Pandia thought that the South Asians had a more powerful case than the Chinese because they were British subjects who had come from a British country.[28] In fact, his argument had just lost much of its value because the Canadian Citizenship Act that came into force in January 1947 defined Canadians inclusively and not just as British subjects. Had Pandia and the others thought about this, they might have joined forces with the Chinese during the second reading of the Election Act to object to an amendment that disqualified anyone who spoke neither English nor French – taking away with one hand some of what had been given with the other.

Even with this amendment, the South Asians and the Chinese had a great triumph to celebrate on 2 April 1947 when the legislature passed the act by a vote of forty-six to zero, with only two members absent. After thirty-five years in Canada, Kapoor was at last a fully acknowledged Canadian, or nearly so. So were his compatriots, except for those who could not speak English or who did not have landed status. And another hugely important day arrived four months later, on 15 August, when the British left India and Kapoor's home country finally became independent. "There could have been not greater joy," his daughter Sarjit later wrote in her notebook.

However, Pandia's work was not over. South Asians could vote federally if they had the provincial franchise, so that issue was settled. But they did not have the right to vote in municipal elections in British Columbia; and immigration was a big issue because Canada continued to exclude all immigrants from India, except for spouses and children; and the 218 illegal immigrants on the amnesty list that Pandia had negotiated back in 1939 were still not legally landed and not allowed to bring over their families. Kapoor well understood what that meant because his younger brother, Tara, was one of those illegal immigrants, and his family was stranded in Kharoudi. In the fall of 1946, soon after arriving in British

Columbia, Pandia had gone to Ottawa and convinced immigration officials that letting people stay without permitting them to bring their closest family members was absurd. After his visit, the government moved faster than anyone expected, changing its policy in late August 1947, coincidentally, a week after Indian independence.[29] Of the 218 men who at last were landed and entitled to sponsor their children and wives, about a hundred had wives in India. Tara soon left to collect his wife and children.

Pandia, Kapoor, Kartar, Mayo, and the leadership of the Vancouver and Victoria gurdwaras then turned to the municipal franchise. In September 1947, they went to the annual three-day convention of the Union of BC Municipalities held that year at Harrison Hot Springs, a resort town east of Vancouver. Kapoor and Mayo paid the expenses, but more importantly, just by being there and mingling with the delegates, they reminded everyone that the South Asian community had some very successful individuals who employed hundreds of people, owned valuable property, and paid a lot in taxes.

Pandia made sure that no one missed this point when he was twice given the chance to speak from the podium. He remarked that Kapoor and Mayo had white employees who could vote, while they could not. And Pandia painted a larger picture by applauding the high principles of the new United Nations, as well as Britain's withdrawal from the Indian subcontinent and the just achieved extension of the federal and provincial franchises to South Asians. The world was moving forward, and British Columbia's municipalities should not be left behind. No one at Harrison Hot Springs argued with him; the delegates from municipalities throughout the province were now all behind the municipal vote for South Asians. The city of Vancouver – with its own separate charter – quickly fell in line after Pandia, Kapoor, Kartar, and Ishar attended a Vancouver council meeting in late October 1947. That cleared the way for an amendment to the Municipal Act, which was passed in the provincial legislature in the following April.[30] With that, a half century of exclusion from full citizenship in Canada ended. Kapoor and his friends knew how much they had been helped by a remarkably rapid post-war shift in public outlook. But they also took pride in what they had achieved through their own hard work. Their victory had not been given to them. They had fought long and hard for it.[31]

Throughout the winter of 1947-48, Pandia went on pressing the federal government to soften up on immigration. He was ambitious, but even in his most conservative expectations, he thought that Canada could at least match the US. He knew that Anup Singh Dhillon and fellow South Asian lobbyists in Washington, DC, had finally obtained a tiny annual quota of 100 immigrants from India to the United States. President Truman had signed this into law in July of 1946, in the belief, held by most Washington politicians, that it would help American relations with India. Like Kartar and Kapoor, Pandia thought that Canada should see the advantage in relaxing its own immigration rules. In Ottawa he met with Arthur Jolliffe, the director of immigration, and Hugh Keenleyside, the deputy minister to whom Jolliffe reported. Both men knew the South Asian file well – Keenleyside from his years in External Affairs and Jolliffe from a long career in immigration. Both knew British Columbia intimately: it had been Keenleyside's boyhood home, and Jolliffe had spent most of a decade in the Vancouver immigration office. Keenleyside had always been sympathetic to Asians, but Jolliffe was less so.[32]

In hindsight, Pandia thought that he had laid the groundwork for the tiny but significant concession that Ottawa made three years later, an annual quota of 150 immigrants from India, along with smaller quotas for Pakistan and Ceylon. When he had first spoken with Jolliffe and his department, they had opposed any concession – however well argued – because they expected it would lead to more demands, not just from South Asians, but from the Chinese and other Asian groups as well. And Prime Minister King was unwilling to make a move that ran ahead of public opinion, so he was exerting no pressure on his bureaucrats to open things up. In Pandia's favour was Indian independence and what it meant for Canada-India relations. The Canadian cabinet did look at his proposal in June 1948, just after he left the country. At the time, King and his ministers did not reject it outright – they simply deferred making a decision – and when King's government eventually introduced a tiny quota in 1951, it was thanks in part to Pandia's effort.[33]

Pandia's mission ended in May 1948 when the first Indian high commissioner, H.S. Malik, took up his post in Ottawa. The commissioner arrived from the Pacific, landing in Victoria days before Pandia's departure from Halifax on the Cunard liner *Mauretania,* which sailed to the English port of Southampton. Pandia was not travelling alone. While in Victoria he had met Muriel Holloway, a CCF activist. She had been lobbying for the rights of pacifist minorities, Hutterites, Mennonites, and Doukhobors, while he was lobbying for the South Asians, and she had added some of her energy to his cause. She was thirty-six and he forty-one, not a great difference in age, but they were worlds apart in background, a highly educated and travelled Indian and an English-Canadian woman whose working-class parents had brought her to Canada at the age of two. Her early life had been divided between Vancouver and the English industrial town of Wolverhampton, where she had been born and where her family returned for five years while she was growing up. Her father was an engineering tradesman, her grandfather a coal dealer, and her oldest brother a driller in a shipyard before he joined the Canadian army.

Through Pandia, Muriel entered the Siddoo family social circle. And by marrying her, Pandia ensured that he would return to Canada sooner or later, although neither he nor Muriel realized how much of their lives would be spent in Vancouver. When they left Halifax in 1948, they intended to make India their permanent home. Muriel was one of those rarities, a Canadian immigrant to India. En route, they had a long stopover in London, where their daughter Aruna was born, but they did eventually reach New Delhi. There they unpacked their bags at the leading address in the country, Government House, the palatial 285-room residence vacated by the last viceroy, Lord Louis Mountbatten, in June 1948. Pandia, Muriel, and baby moved in as guests of the new governor general of India, Chakravarti Rajagopalachari, who welcomed Pandia as a fellow Tamil from Chennai (Madras) and as a servant of India who had spent many years working for Indians overseas. Clearly, a vital career in government was in the cards for Pandia. Unfortunately, both Muriel and baby Aruna became ill, and by 1954 they were all back in Vancouver to stay.

In British Columbia, a marriage like Pandia's was almost unheard of. In 1943 an ethnographer from Columbia University, Marian W. Smith, interviewed a number of Sikhs in the province, including the Siddoos at their York Avenue home and at the Barnet mill. Smith asked about mixed marriages and learned that in forty years, only three Sikh men had married Canadian women. Moreover, none of the young Sikh women who had grown up in Canada – there were then fifteen or twenty including Jackie and Sarjit, all very westernized in appearance – had married Canadians.

About 150 married couples and their four hundred children made up the South Asian community, plus about seven hundred men living as bachelors in bunkhouses or cooking together in shared rooms or houses.[34] Many of the "bachelor" men had wives in India, but many others were unmarried. These unmarried men had limited opportunity to meet Canadian women because, away from work, they had little social contact with other Canadians. Even the few who were educated and employed in white-collar jobs said they had difficulty making friends with white Canadians outside work. This was not true for everyone, because Jackie and Sarjit's cousin Ajaib always had many white friends, due to his outgoing personality as a high school student and to both his personality and the absence of prejudice among the whites he knew later in Saskatchewan and the Yukon.[35]

Back in 1908, a twenty-six-year-old educated Sikh named Munsha Singh, from the village of Kandola in the foothills bordering the Punjab plain, had married Annie Wright, an attractive widow in her late thirties, with a nine-year-old daughter. As far as anybody knew, this was the first marriage in British Columbia between a white woman and a South Asian. The couple were married at St. James Anglican Church, Vancouver, by a rector who had once been a churchman in Kolkata (Calcutta), and eight months later they married again in a ceremony at the Vancouver gurdwara performed by Prof. Teja Singh.[36] At the Christian ceremony, Munsha Singh added the surname Joseph, and at the Sikh ceremony, Annie received the name Labh Kaur and her daughter Winnie became Prem Kaur. Together, Annie and Munsha kept a store at the home she had purchased with her first husband on Salisbury Drive in New Westminster. The marriage lasted for fifteen years until her death at the age of fifty-two. Munsha was long active in the Vancouver gurdwara, and a photograph taken during Rabindranath Tagore's visit in 1929 shows him standing behind Tagore and between C.F. Andrews and Kartar Singh. His was one marriage that everyone in the community still remembered in the 1940s.

In 1936 Rakha Singh came back from Texas with his Mexican wife, Maria. And in 1940, Ishar Singh Banns, the Flyer, returned from a wedding sojourn in Kingston, Jamaica, with Ida Muriel Mongol, his young Jamaican-born wife from Highgate just outside Kingston. They had met by chance in Washington, DC, when Ishar Singh and Dr. Pandia were looking for South Asian food and had been directed to a restaurant run by her family. She was South Asian but Christian by faith and did not speak Punjabi. Perhaps when Sikhs spoke to the ethnologist Marian W. Smith, they were not thinking exclusively of marriages to white Canadians. Whatever they meant, few marriages had taken place outside their Punjabi community. But by 1947, there was one more to count, because when Dr. Pandia married Muriel Holloway, Kartar married Helene and moved into her suburban home close to the sea in the Dundarave area of West Vancouver. This was after Kartar had lived for many years at Barnet with Alice Curtis, the motherly companion who had come to Vancouver with him. Kapoor's family felt sorry for Alice and privately criticized Kartar. But he was a long-time friend and inevitably part of a unique social set that included Ishar and Ida, Dr. Pandia and Muriel, and Kartar and Helen.

In the autumn of 1947, not long after Indian independence, Besant Kaur went home for the first time in fifteen years. She travelled with another Sikh family from the Jalandhar District, and they sailed from San Francisco on the *Marine Swallow,* a converted American troop ship built at the end of the war. The small ship lacked stabilizers, so the crossing to India was long and rough. What the shipping company advertised as the luxury of a floating hotel was a mealtime ordeal for a strict vegetarian such as Besant Kaur. When she reached Punjab by train from Mumbai, she found order had finally been restored after the terrible Hindu-Muslim violence that had racked the country for months, culminating that August and September. But she was still a witness to a country in shock from a savage breakdown in civil society, a direct consequence of the precipitous withdrawal of the British and the division of Punjab between India and the new Muslim country of Pakistan. Of course, this was not why she had come. Her destination was Aur and her purpose was to see her mother – Jackie and Sarjit's Grandmother Sandhu – now eighty-eight and still in the village home she had come to as a bride.

For the month she spent in Aur, Besant Kaur kept close to the Sandhu family home and the adjacent lanes she knew so well, with forays into the market when necessary. But she saw evidence everywhere of the brutal passage that the country had just experienced. Aur was an ancient market town, a meeting place for trade between the hill country and the plains. Over the centuries, its market function had drawn a mixed population of Hindus, Sikhs, and Muslims, who had long lived together in peace. During the violence of August and September, Aur had become a gathering place for Muslims who sought refuge and security before they made a mass exodus to Pakistan, leaving behind abandoned homes and shops. Already, their places were being filled by Hindus and Sikhs who had fled from Pakistan.

The Sandhu home that had once been a *jagirdar*'s fort was now just a central courtyard with adjoining small buildings, all of which ran up against neighbouring homes. Cooking and caring for Grandmother Sandhu were Karam Singh and Gurmit, a husband and wife from the hill village of her youth. Besant Kaur spent several months with her mother, trying to persuade her to come to Canada, but she would not. Before leaving, Besant Kaur attended to a final bit of business, which was to pack the last of the gold jewellery she had left behind in her mother's home. Years before, she had given some to Kapoor for his passage when he first emigrated. Later, she had converted some to cash when she finally joined him in Canada and she had taken most of the rest when they visited India in 1932-33. Now she picked up what remained. Kapoor estimated that, when they married, the jewellery was worth 18,000 rupees, or $5,600, a considerable sum for the time and an indication of the Sandhu family's past worth. When she took the last pieces from Aur, she was accepting the fact that life was moving on.

When Besant Kaur returned from India in January 1948, Kapoor, Jackie, and Sarjit drove down to San Francisco to meet her. They were shocked to see how thin she was, for the India trip had been trying. And Kapoor had his own ill-health to confess to her. With Jackie and Sarjit in Toronto while their mother was away, Kapoor had been on his own for the first time in twenty-five years. He always could cook, but left alone he had indulged heavily in *panjiri*, the fried Punjabi sweet, heavy in butter, sugar, nuts, seeds, and dried fruit, left behind by Besant Kaur as a treat. Instead of lunch, he would have two or three helpings of this. By the time she returned, he had developed the full-blown symptoms of diabetes.

At that point in his life, aside from the bad news about his health, Kapoor took great satisfaction in the direction in which his world was moving. He had nurtured such a strong sense of Indian nationalism in his daughters that they had dreamed of becoming Gadarites and fighting for India's freedom. Now that the British had gone, thankfully they could set that ambition aside. He had made a home in Canada with faith in the future, and with the achievement of the franchise, that faith was being realized. As he looked forward, he began to speak confidently about Canada as a real United Nations in practice. This was something he felt deeply: his adopted country was living up to its potential, which was what he had always expected. Despite the two fires, his business was doing well and giving him the means to support advocates for his people, individuals such as Pandia and, over a longer period, his old friend Kartar, who was drawing salary at the Barnet mill while devoting much of his time to community service. Kapoor was understandably proud of what his daughters had achieved in school and pleased to be able to tell people such as the ethnologist Marian Smith that they were studying medicine. But he and Besant Kaur still wanted them to go to India as doctors, a plan that Jackie and Sarjit fully understood.

13
Lessons about India and Spirituality

As young adults, Jackie and Sarjit were proud of their parents' homeland and its history, traditions, and culture. It helped that they spent their early years in a Canadian mill town owned and run by their father and his partners, a multicultural world where they felt secure and comfortable with themselves. It helped even more to hear their father talk of the antiquity of India and its spiritual teachings, and to listen to their mother's stories from the Sikh and Hindu traditions. And it helped further to witness India's achievement of independence under the saintly leadership of Mahatma Gandhi. But India was an abstraction for them, more so than they realized. The year they had spent there as small children was fading in their memories, and they knew much less of India than they could have guessed. Their ideas of the country were romantic images built on what they heard from their parents, aunts, and uncles, or in Theosophical Society lectures, or in the speeches of visiting Indian VIPs, much of which emphasized India's special moral and spiritual purpose in the world. Many people shared this vision, both in the West and India itself.

Their feelings for India got a big boost when VIPs from their newly independent homeland made a point of visiting them in Canada. Within two years of Indian independence, Vancouver Sikhs had twice entertained Sardar H.S. Malik, India's first ambassador, or high commissioner, to Canada ("high commissioner" is the term used within the British Commonwealth). High Commissioner Malik had passed through Victoria and Vancouver on his way to Ottawa in the spring of 1948 and then returned early in 1949. His second visit was for a Gandhi memorial a year after Gandhi's assassination. Kapoor and Kartar Singh had attended a small formal reception given for the high commissioner and his wife, and the Siddoos had enjoyed the honour and responsibility of taking the Maliks to their camp at Shawnigan Lake where Mrs. Malik declared to everyone's gratification that the meal served by Mrs. Warren, the Swedish cook at that camp, was the best she had ever had.

They welcomed Malik with extra warmth because he was a fellow Sikh, one who was bearded and turbaned and who had distinguished himself in many fields: he was a First World War Royal Air Force fighter pilot who – wearing a specially designed helmet over his turban – shot down eight German aircraft; an experienced civil servant and diplomat under the British and under Nehru, who possessed the polished English of his British public school and Oxford University education; and also a famous sportsman, a cricketer and golfer, sought after as a speaker by the Vancouver cricket club when he came to town. Malik's first visit had been heralded by motorcades, marching bands, and great gatherings at the Victoria and Vancouver gurdwaras.[1] At the end of his stay in Victoria, Sarjit drove him to the ferry with a police escort in front and behind, and she relished the chance to speed with the police clearing her route. Malik's visits were exciting. But when Sikhs learned that Prime Minister Nehru was coming, they prepared themselves for something historic, a moment in their lives they expected never to forget.

Nehru was in North America as the guest of the American president, Harry Truman. His talks in Washington had not gone well. He wanted food aid for India without strings; the Americans wanted a committed Cold War ally; both sides parted in mutual disenchantment.[2] But he carried on with a North American tour, criss-crossing the United States and speaking to attentive campus audiences in New York, Knoxville, San Francisco, and Madison. He took a side-trip to Ottawa but visited no other Canadian city until the end of his tour when he landed in Vancouver on a US Army transport plane with an American security escort to protect him. With him were the American ambassador to India, the White House chief of protocol, and Nehru's own entourage: his sister Vijaya Lakshmi Pandit, his daughter Indira Gandhi, his minister of external affairs Girija Shankar Bajpai, and his staff. Any local reporter who wished to learn about the arrangements had to ask the American consul-general in Vancouver for information. Everything was in the hands of the Americans. No one seemed to notice or be bothered by the absence of Canadian government officials, federal or provincial, although the mayor and city were involved as hosts.[3]

After Nehru's plane touched down at 2:00 on a Wednesday afternoon, he went straight to the gurdwara on Second Avenue to meet an admiring crowd of Sikhs – men, women, and children – who had been gathering for hours. Speaking briefly, he told them that he had come on their account and that he had turned down invitations from Toronto, Montreal, and Winnipeg (which had no Indo-Canadian communities). The next day the *Vancouver Sun* quoted both Kapoor and Besant Kaur. In the gurdwara, she had placed a garland of flowers around Nehru's neck and given him an envelope of money collected by Indo-Canadian women for starving children in India. When approached by a journalist, she had said how proud all the women and children were to see Nehru, "our great leader." Kapoor, standing beside her, spoke of the good he expected to come in Canada-India relations and of Nehru's qualities as a leader who followed Gandhi. The journalist was himself a Sikh, Malkit Singh Parhar, recently returned from India where he had stayed during the war. He was a regular contributor to publications in Punjab, and the *Vancouver Sun* had recruited him to write about Nehru's visit and gave him prominent space in its second section. At the end of his article, he said what many Vancouver Sikhs – proud and successful as they were – must have been feeling, "Now that Vancouver people have seen Pandit Nehru perhaps they will no longer look down on us."[4]

From the gurdwara, the whole Sikh crowd took chartered buses to the Denman Arena and Auditorium – once the home of Vancouver's earliest professional ice hockey team – to hear Nehru speak at greater length. Whites were welcomed, but Indo-Canadians had organized the event, and the person presiding was one of their best-known personalities. This was Ranjit Mattu, a UBC graduate who was a little older than Jackie and Sarjit and a renowned local athlete and coach in both rugby and soccer (his junior rugby team had won a national title and gone to the western Canada finals four times).[5] In the gurdwara, Nehru heard Sikhs say that everything was not right for them in Canada: they faced widespread prejudice when they looked for jobs and were not able to bring over their relatives as other Canadians could. Having said that at the gurdwara, they kept the second, more public, event on a positive note, saying how much they valued his visit and how long they would remember it.

The first day ended with a civic dinner hosted by the mayor, and the next day began with a military parade along streets cordoned off by the city's motorcycle police. Jackie had finished her studies in Toronto earlier that year and was now a junior intern at Vancouver General Hospital. She walked over from the hospital – about a block – to join the crowd when the parade broke up and when everyone gathered at the steps of City Hall, where Nehru spoke again. It was an assembly mostly of Sikhs, men both turbaned and bareheaded, and women wrapped in autumn coats but with dupattas (headscarves) and a very few with saris. A great many in the crowd were waving the Tiranga, the tricolour flag that India had adopted at independence two years earlier. An aircraft hired by the Sikh community released flower petals that wafted down as Nehru prepared to speak. Jackie had a movie camera and was filming the event – the footage unfortunately since lost – and she got very close to Nehru, so close she was surprised that nobody stopped her.[6]

Kapoor avoided the podium at these events but was still at the centre of the action. He was a guest at a luncheon given for Nehru at the Canadian Club on the second day of the Indian prime minister's visit. The joint hosts were the Canadian Club, the Board of Trade, and the Junior Chamber of Commerce, with the introduction of Nehru falling to the president of the Canadian Club, Brigadier William Murphy, a Vancouver lawyer who had commanded the Fifth Canadian Armoured Brigade in the Italian campaign during the past war. A black-and-white photograph of the luncheon captured Murphy in uniform, Indira Gandhi rearranging the corner of her sari over her shoulder, and Kapoor beside her in dinner jacket and white tie – all in one shot. This was the first of many meetings that Kapoor and his family had with the woman who would be India's third prime minister.

Nehru had been in Ottawa earlier on this tour, with the result that the Canadian government finally decided to make a goodwill gesture. Over the next few months, the Canadian and Indian governments shaped an agreement; when it came into effect on the first day of 1951, this was exciting news in British Columbia. What it amounted to was an annual quota of 150 immigrants from India, a stingy number considering India's population of 360 million but a significant gain for Sikhs and other Punjabis in BC (now numbering about nineteen hundred). This was mainly a quota for them, or for the relatives they could help to immigrate. Until then, they had been limited to bringing over spouses and dependent children. Now they could also sponsor adult children, parents, grandparents, brothers, sisters, grandchildren, cousins, nephews, in-laws, brides, and grooms if they could get them onto the quota list; and they immediately began to work on it.[7] By lobbying members of parliament and spending money on lawyers and agents, they managed to monopolize a majority of the quota places. (One politician who helped them a lot was James Sinclair, whose young daughter Margaret later married Canada's fifteenth prime minister, Pierre Elliott Trudeau.)[8] A few independent immigrants and their families from Bengal, Gujarat, and other parts of India – engineers, architects, aero-mechanics, teachers, university lecturers, and businessmen – did get in as quota immigrants but not many. The Punjabis of BC grabbed a majority of the places for their own relatives.[9]

The quota system affected roughly two hundred pioneer Canadian Punjabi families at a critical time. These families had been in the country for fifteen, twenty, or thirty years, contemporaries of Kapoor and Besant Kaur in a broad sense. In 1951 many of their children were old enough to marry or were reaching that age, and – given their ideas about suitability – the pool of possible matches in Canada was too small. In any case, with scarcely an exception, Punjabi parents wanted their sons and daughters to marry spouses born and raised in Punjab, who would be powerfully motivated to do what they could to maintain Punjabi culture. And they also believed it was their duty to arrange their children's marriages before they were too old, which, for girls in village society, had been soon after age fifteen, although a boy could be older. In the past, Canadian families had sent young – and not so young – men home for a year or more to negotiate a suitable match, celebrate a wedding, and bring a wife back to Canada. Now parents could arrange the marriage from a distance with the help of relatives in Punjab and then bring out a quota immigrant as a bride or groom for their son or daughter. Young men still went back to India to get married, but in the 1950s, a handful of fiancés started to arrive, and a round of marriage ceremonies began in the local gurdwaras.[10]

Such was not the case for Jackie or Sarjit, who reached their midtwenties free of parental pressure to marry. In their family, medicine was the desired career, not being a housewife. In this, Kapoor and Besant Kaur were unusual among Sikhs and, in fact, in general Canadian society. For Besant Kaur, whose brother and uncle were unani doctors, practising a medical tradition with ancient roots in India, healing was a family calling. And both parents felt that India needed doctors more than Canada did, so serving in India remained the great goal. Kapoor also told his daughters that they should serve Canada but in a field other than medicine. This responsibility to his adopted country was something he felt alone. Besant Kaur was inclined definitely toward India.

In the summer of 1951, Jackie was finishing her second internship year at Vancouver General Hospital, and Sarjit was at the end of her first at Toronto General. To reward them, Kapoor took the family on a great nine-month trip to India by way of the US and Europe. Twenty years earlier, they had travelled across the Pacific, and now they were completing a circle around the world. Kapoor and Besant Kaur had an agenda because they were thinking that the girls should be ready to settle in India and run a hospital. Kapoor had already purchased the land; and Jackie and Sarjit could not miss their mother's fervent wish that they would decide to stay in India and start the work right away. But the trip was also recognition of what Jackie and Sarjit had accomplished and a break after years of study.

Kapoor had upgraded to an Oldsmobile, after buying Chevrolets for years. In mid-July they packed the Oldsmobile and, after stopping at Cousin Kashmir's to drop off Prince, the aging family dog, they drove south to the border to follow an American route east. On 29 July, they were at the port of New York, loading the Oldsmobile onto the luxury liner *Queen Elizabeth* and settling into their first-class cabins. Five days later, they docked at Southampton on the English south coast. They all had enjoyed the Atlantic crossing, the sumptuous meals in the dining room, and the long walks around the first class decks, except for a couple of patches of rough weather when Besant Kaur and Sarjit were in their beds feeling sick. From Southampton they drove north to Scotland for the opening of the fourth season of the Edinburgh Festival, and then back to London, taking in all the sights. At Dover they boarded the channel ferry for Calais, France.

On the French side of the channel, Sarjit was at the wheel of the Oldsmobile as they left Calais. In England and Scotland, they had driven without incident on the left side of the road, but now, driving on the familiar right, they immediately had an accident. Just ahead of them, a parked car suddenly lurched into their lane. Defensively, Sarjit swung left to avoid it, only to be hit by an oncoming vehicle. It too had four passengers. "By the Grace of God no one has been seriously hurt," they all said, after surveying the damage, but their car was too smashed to drive. Kapoor and Sarjit got a ride into the nearest town to ask for help, while Jackie and Besant Kaur sat in the wreck of their car, waiting for several hours until the other two returned. They all took a train into Paris, arriving that Saturday night long after their travel agent, Thomas Cook and Sons, had closed for the weekend. That left them without any guidance about a hotel. They learned later that Thomas Cook had booked them into the luxurious George le Cinq off the Champs Élysées. On their own that night, they secured rooms near the Arc de Triomphe but in a third-rate place.

Kapoor decided to buy another car and luckily found an Oldsmobile of the same model and colour (blue) as the last one. When they left Paris about a week later, he insisted that Sarjit drive. "You have to do it now," he said, "or you'll be nervous in the future." In retrospect, she was grateful. They took a circular route through Switzerland, Liechtenstein, Austria, Italy, and back through France. In Geneva they visited their old friend Sadhu Singh Dhami – their frequent guest at Sooke Lake – and his young German Jewish refugee wife, Ida (Wreschner), from Montreal. This was a chance to catch up with Sadhu Singh and Ida's extraordinary story. His career with the International Labour Organization (ILO) had begun in Montreal at its wartime headquarters on the McGill University campus. He had met Ida a little earlier, when she was an undergraduate and he a PhD student at Toronto, and they had married after he joined the ILO and before it moved back to Geneva.[11] She had encouraged him to take the ILO job to "broaden his perspective," although the two of them already brought together an extraordinary combination of traditions.

After leaving Sadhu Singh and Ida, Kapoor and family came upon a terrible accident in the mountains east of Interlaken, and they stopped by the road so that Sarjit and Jackie, the two doctors, could help with the injured. Their tour took them to Venice and Rome as well as Paris and Geneva. But the one moment that stayed with them from their travel on the Continent was the crash at Calais. Back in England, they drove to the Tilbury docks in East London, where they sailed on the Peninsular and Oriental liner *Chusan* for India.

The passage took seventeen or eighteen days. From Port Said in Egypt onward, the temperatures were intense, but the wall of scorching heat that hit them when they docked in Mumbai in October was something else again. For the first time in her life, Jackie saw the backs of her hands sweating. Sarjit said that doing anything in that heat was like carrying a ton of bricks on her back. And when they offloaded the blue Oldsmobile, they had a trying time with officials and red tape – not the first or last travellers to India to do so. Sarjit, always quick to speak up, acted as the spokesperson for the family, a role that Kapoor let her take for her education and experience. She recalls becoming impatient with the shuffle from official to official and losing her temper several times before finally securing the last document and signature that released the car into their possession. Kapoor had to tell her a number of times, "This is India and you'll have to get used to it."

In Mumbai they stayed with Sarjit's Parsi friend from Toronto Medical School, Zinet Currimbhoy, who lived in the posh Nepean Sea Road area, where the neighbours were leading industrialists and bankers from Mumbai's successful Gujarati, Jain, and Parsi communities. Zinet generously showed the Siddoos around the city, went with them on the hour-long ferry ride across the harbour to the sculpture caves of Elephanta Island, and took them to the historic city of Pune, 170 kilometres away. When they left her, they drove toward Punjab but diverted from the shortest route to see the ancient Buddhist caves of Ellora and Ajanta, the shrine of Hazoor Sahib in Nandad – one of five most revered shrines for Sikhs – the great palace of Man Mandir at Gwalior, and the Taj Mahal in Agra. Despite the magnificent sights, Jackie and Sarjit found themselves shocked by the poverty they encountered, and the filth and flies – as well as the blood they thought they saw men spit in the streets, which they eventually learned was betel juice.

Reaching Besant Kaur's village of Aur took more than a week. On the last two-hundred-kilometre leg north from Delhi, they were on the Grand Trunk Road, which, had they continued, would have taken them across the post-1947 international border to the old Punjab capital of Lahore in Pakistan. But their destination was well short of that. When they reached the town of Phillaur, they turned east on a much smaller road. At that point, Aur was just twenty kilometres away. Initially, they were on a paved single lane that dropped steeply on either side. Halfway, the surface turned to dirt; and with the rain it was muddy, slippery, and dangerous – almost impossible for them to negotiate. They backtracked to Phillaur, where they left the car with an acquaintance and caught the rickety banged-up bus that regularly ran to Aur. Given the condition of the road, the bus too was frightening. They had had visions of driving into the village in their big North American vehicle, but they ended up walking in from the point where the bus put them down.

From then on, whenever it rained, they left their car with friends in Phillaur. Even when it was dry, they could not manoeuvre the car through the village. Instead, they parked it on the outskirts at the elementary school and walked, picking their way carefully through narrow lanes, put off by the smell and the dirt, avoiding the animal droppings in the middle and the shallow open sewer gutters on each side, and constantly on the watch for sudden spills of water or urine from above. As curiosities from abroad, "Canada-wallahs" as the villagers called them, they attracted too much attention: families gathered to watch from rooftops as they went by, and sometimes a crowd of giggling children followed behind, making sly remarks about Jackie and Sarjit's outfits, the slacks and shirts that these children had never seen women wear. Their family home, the qila, which

Jackie and Sarjit scarcely remembered from their childhood, but which they had built up in their imaginations from their mother's stories, now appeared before them stripped of all romance – a big bare courtyard surrounded by low functional room-sized masonry buildings for cooking, sleeping, and storage, with no electricity, no running water, and no plumbing or sewage system.

Grandmother Sandhu was now ninety-two and looking her age. Jackie and Sarjit had not seen her since they were children, but she had always written letters, and as the years passed she increasingly expressed the hope that they would soon be married. In preparation for their visit, she had laid in supplies and had filled a storage room with wheat for flour in the expectation that they would marry in Aur and that the family would host a gala event with many guests and many chapattis to make. Kapoor and Besant Kaur had to tell her that there would be no marriages.

After their initial dismay, they settled into the rhythm of their grandmother's home. Aur became their base as they travelled around Punjab and into the mountains, sometimes by train and sometimes by car. With a village elder from Aur as a guide, they looked down on the rushing Ganges from the hanging Lakshman Jhula footbridge at Rishikesh, and a short distance downstream they watched pilgrims bathing in the river's icy water at Haridwar. And another travelling companion sometimes joined their excursions – a lady doctor, Harbans Kaur, who had stayed with them when in Vancouver on official business. She had just purchased a beautiful house in the pleasingly intact old British hill station and garrison town of Kasauli, and Sarjit and Jackie visited her, driving the Oldsmobile up a road that climbed two thousand feet into the hills. More ambitiously, they and their parents drove from Jammu through the Shivalik Hills to the Kashmir Valley and Srinagar on Dal Lake, expecting breathtaking scenery, only to be disappointed by the bare brown hills they thought no match for the green mountains of British Columbia. People later told them that, had they had gone to higher altitudes above Srinagar, they would have seen wooded areas, so they realized that they had not seen everything.

Around New Year, Sarjit came back from a trip with infectious hepatitis – from something she had eaten or drunk several weeks earlier – and it kept her housebound with high fever, jaundice, and severe weight loss over the next two months. Her illness kept everyone at home, and that was the note on which their stay in India ended. They tried to persuade Grandmother Sandhu to return to Canada with them, but she would not go, and Jackie and Sarjit had seen nothing to make them remain in India.

As they said, their "idyllic bubble had burst" and they had become hypercritical. They had dreamt of India as a land of spiritual giants exemplified by Mahatma Gandhi. This was the country they had grown up loving and wanting to serve, but the India they experienced contradicted that absolutely: the wealth that people with power enjoyed amidst poverty, the luxurious homes of the politicians, and their cars, chauffeurs, and entourages of servants, aides, and sub-aides.

They also found that achieving even the simplest thing was too difficult. Getting the car through customs had been an aggravating introduction to that fact. There was too much bureaucracy and inefficiency, too much complication and waiting in little offices. Nothing was straightforward; even a trip to the bank for a small withdrawal required going from one desk to another – endlessly, it felt – while indifferent clerks passed bulky register books among themselves for initials and inked-in double entries. Late in February, the family left Aur for Mumbai to board a small Polish liner, the *Batory,* which had just forty-six first-class passengers, although many more in tourist class. By 15 March 1952, they were back in Southampton and a week later on the giant Cunard liner *Queen Mary,* heading into the Atlantic. On 27 March, they claimed their car on the docks at New York and began driving home, relieved to be on their way to Vancouver.

Jackie and Sarjit had offers of graduate posts – for Jackie in hematology with Dr. Harry Perry and for Sarjit in pediatrics with Dr. J.F. McCreary – both in Vancouver. The sisters had never thought of pursuing careers in private practice in Canada; income from medicine had not been their goal, so they went back to study while they put India aside for the moment and tried to forget it. Two years later, after thinking about what they had seen there and how they had reacted, they decided that their own attitude was a problem and would have to change. Their friend from Toronto, Lakhshmi Rao, had predicted that they would not last five years in India, and she had been absolutely right. They had given up before they started. If they were to carry out their parents' ambition, something in themselves must change.

In the meantime, they were at home with their parents and involved in what they were doing. Kapoor and Besant Kaur supported and attended the gurdwara on special occasions, and could be counted on for large donations for special projects when gurdwara spokesmen came to the house or the mill for money. But, as in the past, Kapoor did not involve himself in gurdwara politics. Two months after the family returned from India, the gurdwara split into two groups. One group walked out of the old Khalsa Diwan gurdwara on Second Avenue and bought a church building on Eleventh, which it renamed the Akali Singh gurdwara after the Sikh nationalist movement that had forced the British regime to surrender control of historic Sikh shrines in Punjab. The split began with personal differences that had festered for years but exploded when a majority wanted to put clean-shaven Sikhs on the gurdwara management committee. Kapoor and Besant Kaur knew the people on both sides of the issue, but they found it most natural to remain with the old gurdwara and its more inclusive outlook, embracing all Sikhs whatever the form of their practice.[12]

While Jackie and Sarjit were doing post-graduate work at Vancouver General, Kapoor continued to take them to Theosophical Society lectures. There they would see their family doctor, Washington Wilks, still a mainstay of the society, and hear lecturers such as the American Thomas Boyd Kuhn, who explained his radical and – to most Christians – bizarre idea that the Christian story was purely symbolic, not historical, and based on the ancient wisdom and mythology of Egypt.[13] For Jackie and Sarjit, what was attractive in Theosophy was the suggestion of an essential truth that was deeper than the perspective of a single faith. They also got involved with their parents when distinguished Indian visitors came to town. At the end of their second year of post-graduate study, the visitor was Swaran Singh, the Indian minister of housing, works, and supply, on his way home after a UNESCO meeting in Geneva. Kapoor hosted a special luncheon for him in Vancouver and the next day went to Victoria with Jackie and Sarjit for a reception given for Swaran Singh at the Empress Hotel. A *Victoria Times* press photographer captured the sisters with Swaran Singh in a shot taken at the Empress. And for the luncheon in Vancouver, Kapoor had invited one of his daughters' medical professors. In all things, the family worked as a unit.[14]

In the fall of 1954, the sisters decided to go to Montreal for more post-graduate work – Jackie at the Montreal Neurological Institute and Sarjit at the Montreal Children's Hospital.[15] They started in the fall of 1955. In Montreal they met Swami Sivananda Radha. Before that time, they had never met such a person – a disciple of a "real guru." They had observed the religious devotion of their parents and especially their mother, and once at Shawnigan Lake, they had seen a guest meditating. This was Pandit Khushi Ram, who was in BC as a Theosophical Society speaker and whom Kapoor had invited to the lumber camp for a quiet retreat. He sat motionless in the cottage while doing his spiritual exercises, and Sarjit, who had never seen meditation before, was moved. Otherwise, her knowledge of spiritual matters, like Jackie's, was intellectual, from lectures and reading. Sarjit acknowledges her sister as the leader, the passionate reader on mystical-philosophical subjects and the spiritual searcher. She simply followed in her wake. On the *Chusan,* going out to India, the family had listened while Jackie read passages from the *Gospel of Sri Ramakrishna,* the story of the Bengali mystic whose teachings had attracted a dedicated following in the West. At Christmas of their year in Montreal, Jackie had given Sarjit this book, the *Autobiography of a Yogi,* and three books by the English mystic and teacher Paul Brunton. Sarjit found something compelling about these books, even their exteriors. By itself, the orange cover of the *Autobiography of a Yogi,* with its picture of Swami Yogananda, gave her a "spiritual shock."

They met Swami Radha in March 1956 thanks to a lab technician at the Montreal Neurological Institute who had to work one evening and gave Jackie her two tickets to a lecture at the YMCA. Swami Radha, the lecturer, had just returned from India. She was a remarkably attractive middle-aged German woman, whose name until then had been Ursula Sylvia Hellman.[16] As a young woman, she had been a solo ballerina in a troupe that performed on the great stages of Europe. Traumatically, she had been twice widowed before she emigrated to Montreal in 1951, by which time she was a professional photographer and dance teacher. She had discovered her guru, Swami Sivananda Saraswati, while leafing through books in a Montreal bookstore, where she found a photograph of him that matched an image she had visualized during meditation. In the fall of 1955, she had gone to his ashram in Rishikesh for six months' training in hatha yoga, and he had initiated her as a *sanyassin,* a renunciant dedicated to a life without possessions or attachments. At the beginning of March 1956, she returned to Montreal with plans to introduce hatha yoga classes there. At the lecture attended by Jackie and Sarjit soon after her return, she wore what they immediately spotted as a ready-made sari in saffron orange – the colour of Indian sages – with drapes stitched and elastic around the waist, which was practical but quite contrary to Indian tradition. She spoke English with a compelling German accent, and the sisters felt that she emanated a power.

Impressed and spellbound, they stayed after the lecture to talk to her and began to visit her apartment for meditations, to hear her glowing stories of her guru, and to see her coloured slides of him. During meditations, sitting in the lotus or half-lotus position, she would fall into a deep stillness and she told them that, if she ever went off into another realm, they were not to disturb her but simply whisper "om, om" in her ear. Sarjit was skeptical, but she too would be caught up in the moment and only afterward feel some reservations. Swami Radha was a vegetarian, so for the first time, the sisters became vegetarians themselves. Of all the meats, Sarjit found chicken most difficult to give up – the greatest sacrifice for her palate – but she did it right away. Jackie began to talk of becoming a sanyassin herself. Both she and Sarjit spent all their free time with Swami Radha and were neglecting their studies. Kapoor and Besant Kaur, following these developments from Vancouver, became increasingly alarmed. Kapoor was still phoning once a week, and both parents would come on the line. They told their daughters not to accept Swami Radha as their guru until they themselves had met her. Then they sent her a plane ticket to come to Vancouver so they could check her out.

Swami Radha arrived at the end of June for eighteen packed days in British Columbia, using the Siddoo household as her base. She had a press and television reception there on the day she arrived. By the third day, the Siddoos had taken her to Duncan, where she spoke in the Sikh gurdwara. They took her to their Shawnigan Lake cabin and to Victoria, where she lectured at its gurdwara. Within a week and a half, she had generated enough publicity to fill a vaudeville theatre in Vancouver with a seated audience of 450 and another 100 standing. It became evident that she could fill larger venues, so she lectured twice on Yoga and Vedanta at the Vancouver gurdwara and twice more at a major city auditorium. Her instant celebrity won her an interview with Jack Webster, then a pioneer radio talk show host. And she still managed to lecture to small groups in private homes. By this time, Dr. Pandia and his wife, Muriel, had been back from India for two years, and Swami Radha came to their home to teach a group of South Asian boys on the "Principles of Divine Life."[17] For all this activity, she needed volunteers to contact the media, line up venues, arrange transportation, and look after her basic needs. Jackie and Sarjit discovered that this was what they were expected to do and it was Sarjit especially who did not like it.

Kapoor and Besant Kaur became convinced that Jackie and Sarjit should break off with Swami Radha. They felt that they themselves had been the targets of her efforts to hypnotize and that she had used hypnotic power on their daughters, which was not what they expected or respected in a spiritual teacher. In the York Avenue living room, when Kapoor and Besant Kaur were out of the house, Jackie had become speechless in Swami Radha's presence, with tears rolling from her eyes which looked fixed and were unblinking. Sarjit was witness to this.[18] The trigger for Jackie had been the line of a Hindi devotional song playing on the record player. The line meant, "Today, God has come to my house." Body and mind disappeared for Jackie as joy and light flooded in; for her, this was a deep mystical experience, but her family was not so sure. And Besant Kaur observed three signs or omens that Radha was not the right guru or even the right person for her daughters. The most memorable was at Shawnigan Lake when Radha had dropped a box of matches, which ignited upon hitting the floor. If their daughters had reservations about their parents' advice, these were wiped out when they got back to Montreal and were obliged to take back a gift.

When Swami Radha became a sanyassin, she committed herself to teaching yoga and living by faith without working and without possessions, and to do this in Canada as well, where one might assume such a way of life would not be understood or supported. She launched herself on this path while she was in India by giving her guru everything she had there and giving her roommate back in Montreal everything she had left behind. After this, from the moment she landed at the Montreal airport, the world miraculously provided for her. A stranger paid for her taxi from the airport; people she met in the next few days – fellow travellers on the spiritual path – learned what she was trying to do and took over the cost of her groceries. Within a short time, she met Jackie and Sarjit, and within three months was flying to Vancouver with a return ticket provided by Kapoor and the opportunity to expand her following and the reach of her teaching.

To get around in Montreal while they were doing post-graduate studies, Kapoor had provided Sarjit and Jackie with a car, which – in their infatuation with Swami Radha and her teaching – they employed to take her around, sometimes on recreational drives into the countryside. She admired the car and, in an impetuous mood, Sarjit had offered it to her. Radha accepted with undisguised delight. When they were in Vancouver, Sarjit told her father what she had done and learned immediately that he neither approved of it nor accepted it. His uncompromising point was that Sarjit had not earned the money that bought the car and could not make a gift of it. He put it bluntly: "You have no right to give this car away and you shall not do it." Sarjit pleaded in vain with him. When she and Jackie got back to Montreal, they had the unhappy task of explaining this to Swami Radha. They found her staying at a friend's house, and given their notions of a sanyassin's life of denial, they were surprised to discover that the friend was a man. The encounter went badly. After an effusive greeting, they told Swami Radha they could not give her the car. Her face flushed scarlet, which they interpreted as an uncontrolled expression of inner anger. And when she reached into her pocket for a rosary that their mother had given her as a going-away present, and when she put it around her neck, they took that as a signal that they had been dismissed, so they said their goodbyes and left. Had they ever doubted their parents' assessment of Swami Radha, this was largely corrected by her behaviour regarding the car. Neither of them saw her for more than twenty years.

Swami Radha settled in British Columbia in 1959 and within a short time found a large property on Kootenay Lake in the southeastern interior of the province, where she built an ashram that has flourished thanks to a committed following drawn to her teaching. In 1978, while attending a lecture by the physicist-philosopher David Bohm, Sarjit was surprised to see Swami Radha sitting at the next table. She said nothing and had the unmistakable feeling that Radha preferred not to recognize her. When Jackie and Sarjit had parted with her in Montreal, they were thankful to their parents for their insight and guidance. But they still had lingering questions about the spiritual value of her teaching. When they were in India a couple of years later, they went to see her guru, Swami Sivananda Saraswati, near the Lakshman Jhula bridge in Rishikesh. They remembered how, when they first met her, she kept referring to "My guru, my guru," so they decided to go and see him, the real thing. On this expedition they wore Indian clothes, and as long as the swami took them to be just two more Indian women, he seemed to ignore them. Only when he discovered that they were foreigners from Canada, potentially with money, did he pay them a lot of attention. So they ended up disillusioned not just with Swami Radha, but with her guru as well.

Agnes Ramcharan, one of the Trinidadian Indian sisters whom Jackie and Sarjit knew in Toronto, was another friend who understood how hard it was to go back to one's roots after living abroad, and she imagined it would be even more difficult for Jackie and Sarjit, who had been raised in Canada. "In my mind," she later wrote to Jackie, "it does not really matter what is your original nationality. What counts is where you were brought up."[19] When Jackie and Sarjit graduated in medicine, they remembered little of the India they had seen as children, but they had a strong attachment inspired by their parents. When Nehru visited Vancouver, he seemed to exemplify the country and culture as they imagined it, the land of Mahatma Gandhi and of profound spirituality and philosophical insight. And then their ideas of India had collapsed on their first encounter with it as adults.

In a strange way their attraction to the Indian spiritual tradition resurrected itself in Montreal thanks to Swami Radha, a foreigner – a German woman freshly returned from Rishikesh and full of the teachings of her guru. When they began meditating with her, they entered an experience that they had read about but not known for themselves. Their open-minded parents had encouraged them to search widely and freely for spiritual direction, and within their own Sikh community they saw respect and hospitality toward teachers of other Indian traditions – as when several Sikh gurdwaras opened their doors for Swami Radha to lecture on hatha yoga. But Canadian Sikhs seldom saw living gurus or people who presented themselves as such. From time to time, a sant, or holy man, visited from India, but this happened so infrequently that Jackie and Sarjit grew up without knowing what to expect. Their parents encouraged them to search for a guru, while understanding – with an insight that was second-nature for them – that most so-called gurus were bogus. They decided that the guru whom Jackie and Sarjit had found in Montreal was not the right one for them, which left these young women with a taste of something profound but still searching for a path to it.

Unless otherwise noted,
the photographs have been provided by Sarjit K. Siddoo

Kapoor, 1929.

Kartar Singh Hundal and C.F. Andrews in front of Hart House, University of Toronto, March 1929.

Sikhs greet C.F. Andrews (centre) at Vancouver's CNR Station, 3 April 1929.

Rabindranath Tagore (centre) with the welcoming delegation at the Empress Hotel, Victoria, 5 April 1929. Standing at left are C.F. Andrews, Munsha Singh, and Kartar Singh Hundal.

Kartar, Kapoor, Pandia, and Mayo celebrate winning an amnesty for illegal immigrants, 1939.

Sarjit with her parents at the New York World's Fair, 2 July 1940.

The Kapoor mill at Barnet, 1955.

A photograph staged at the Barnet mill office in 1944. Kapoor locates his new timber tract on Vancouver Island while Kartar looks on.

The Indian high commissioner, M.A. Rauf, tours the Barnet mill in 1955. From left to right are Tara, High Commissioner Rauf, Kashmir, Kapoor, and D.P. Pandia.

Facing page

The Vancouver Sikh temple on Christmas night, 1943. In 1936 Kapoor donated the mosaic of Guru Nanak on the front gable. *Vancouver City Archives*

In the Vancouver temple office in 1946, Nagindar Singh conducts a meeting of activists – old and young – in the campaign for the vote. *Vancouver Public Library*

SIKH TEMPLE

Facing page

The painter Lawren Harris (third from right) and his wife, Bess (in jacket), in Vancouver in 1949. Between them is Kartar and behind is a painting by Harris. Kapoor and High Commissioner Malik stand at the left, and Ishar Singh Banns and his wife, Ida Muriel, are on the right.

Nehru leaves the Vancouver Sikh temple after an enthusiastic reception, 2 November 1949. *Vancouver Public Library*

Nehru's audience outside Vancouver City Hall, 3 November 1949. *Vancouver Public Library*

FACING PAGE

Kapoor, Indira Gandhi, and Brigadier William Murphy during Nehru's visit to Vancouver, Canadian Club luncheon, November 1949.

Kapoor, Jackie, and Besant Kaur, Switzerland, summer 1951.

Jackie and Sarjit at Shawnigan Lake, 9 January 1943.

The hospital in Aur, March 2006. *Photographed by author*

Waiting room, Kapoor hospital, Aur, 2006. *Photographed by author*

Alfred Tremeer with the Siddoo clan at the Vancouver airport in 1965. Jackie (centre) and Donny (in white coat) were leaving after their first visit as a married couple.

Besant Kaur with Chanda, flanked by Tashi and Tiny in their home in Vancouver, 1968.

Indira Gandhi, Sarjit, Chanda, and Avtar, West Vancouver, 1980.

Chanda, Avtar, and Sarjit in their home in West Vancouver, 1988.

Krishnamurti with students and staff at Wolf Lake School, April 1978.

Krishnamurti during his visit to the Wolf Lake School, April 1978

14
The Hospital at Aur

Kapoor believed that great good could come from the marriage of Western science and technology with Indian spirituality. He had an understanding and affection for two countries, Canada and India, that only an emigrant could possess, and he felt that he and his family should do their part in bringing the best of the two together. His involvement with the small circle of Theosophists in Vancouver was a natural one – an opportunity to see westerners taking up the great Indian spiritual traditions, and his daughters grew up understanding and believing that this was something worthwhile. They also knew that their parents wanted them to serve India by bringing Western medical care to villagers in Punjab. But when the moment arrived, they had found it too daunting. India was not what they had expected.

Still, their encounter with Swami Radha brought Jackie and Sarjit unavoidably to a moment of truth. All through their post-graduate years, their mother had asked about the hospital in India and when they were going to start it. Within a few months of their brief infatuation with Swami Radha (when they had neglected their studies), she put her foot down and told them that they had been students long enough. They did not argue and left at Christmas along with their parents, flying the Pacific route to Tokyo and Kolkata. They took the train from Kolkata to Punjab and arrived at Aur on 1 January 1957. Their grandmother had recently passed away at the age of ninety-six, and the house felt empty without her, although it soon filled with new friends and neighbours.

This time they wanted to look at India with fresh eyes, without being critical, but it was a challenge. To start with, the family home in Aur was very uncomfortable for two young women from Vancouver. Like the rest of the village, it had no electricity, running water, or sewage system. Servants still carried buckets of water from the hand pump in the courtyard well; they still heated bathwater over an open fire; and they still cooked with firewood in the partial enclosures of mud-baked stoves. During that first January, temperatures fell to a few degrees above freezing, and to keep warm, they closed the windows of their cold masonry house, and everyone huddled around portable mud-baked stoves, on guard against being overcome by fumes from the coals. There was nowhere to sit, except on the floor, which for Jackie and Sarjit, who were not used to squatting, was most taxing until someone produced two small stools. And their usual diversions were missing. They had no telephone or regular newspaper and depended on a small transistor radio for news of the outside world. With the summer came heat and humidity. A village friend constructed a ceiling fan for them, operated by pulling a string, which would give them momentary relief until he fell asleep and stopped pulling.[1]

In the afternoons, Jackie, Sarjit, and Kapoor walked from their gate through fields of sugarcane, *bajra* (millet), and wheat that stretched toward the next village. A curiosity, they attracted a gaggle of children and even adults. Through observation, reading, and conversation, they knew that rural Punjab was in the process of change. Village by village, land consolidation was going ahead, sponsored by the Punjab government and designed to divide village fields into larger and more economic parcels; the electrification of the countryside was moving forward; the great Bhakra dam was rising in the Shivalik Hills fifty kilometres northeast of Aur, promising more irrigation and electric power in the future; and land already under irrigation was expanding, fed by dug wells put in by a combination of village labour and government subsidies.[2]

All this was preparation for Punjab's dramatic Green Revolution of the 1970s. But in 1957, the change was not obvious. Much of the countryside remained dry and dusty, including a large area east of Aur. In villages such as Aur and Kharoudi, where wells provided irrigation, the water reached the fields by shallow channels, which were fed by Persian water wheels with their squeaking buckets. The wheels were turned by oxen, blindfolded so they could not see their master slip away to leave them endlessly circling. This was a country without machinery, with harvesters wielding hand-held sickles or threshing by beating rice stocks with sticks, by treading wheat under oxen hooves – or in a modern adaptation, by putting sheaves on a tarred road for passing vehicles to roll over. Each morning at 3:00 a.m., the village woke to the sound of women in every household grinding wheat on the stone cylinders of their *chakkis*. It seemed timeless, even though Jackie and Sarjit were aware of the modernizing developments under way.[3]

Aur was no longer the village that it had been when Besant Kaur was growing up, or when she had gone back in 1931. Three communities had once lived there in peace, Hindu, Sikh, and Muslim. In fact, Aur had been a major centre for Muslims until 1947 when gangs had roamed the countryside murdering Muslims and when the survivors evacuated to Pakistan. Their places in Aur had been taken by Hindu and Sikh refugees who fled from equally murderous gangs in Pakistan. The village was full of transplanted people, and though Besant Kaur knew its lanes, buildings, and surrounding countryside, she was a stranger to most of its inhabitants.

Even so, many of the refugees had roots in Aur because in 1947 they had headed for the village where their parents or grandparents had once lived. This was the case with seventeen-year-old Krishna Sharma, her parents, and her ten siblings, who lived down the lane from the Sandhu qila. They were Brahman Hindus of the Sharma clan. Her grandfather had left Aur for Lyallpur Punjab (now in Pakistan) to work as a manager for another Hindu, Sri Ganga Ram, who owned cotton, peanut oil, and mustard factories. Her grandfather, the manager, was well off and the main support for an extended family. Her parents had stayed in Pakistan after Partition despite the urgings of her mother's brother to get out. They had listened to one of her father's relatives, who said, "No! No! There will be no bloodshed." But Krishna herself, at the age of seven, had hidden in ditches and heard shots and seen a marauding gang approaching and blood in the streets while she was on a last-minute errand for her mother – cloth for the baby – before they made their escape to India. They had been separated from her father and only after a harrowing train journey across the border were they reunited with him at the station in Phillaur.[4]

From then on, Krishna and her family lived in Aur, where her father ran a small shop that sold all kinds of items such as combs, notebooks, and trinkets. As a small girl, Krishna had often run up the lane to see Jackie and Sarjit's grandmother, who liked young people and liked her. When she was older, and when the Siddoos arrived from Canada, she naturally attached herself to them, spending most of her time with them, with the encouragement of her father but to the annoyance of her sisters and her mother, who complained that she was escaping work at home. When Besant Kaur, Jackie, and Sarjit made excursions into the market for household supplies and food, Krishna went with them – an extra pair of hands to carry things, a guide to the best shops, and a savvy haggler at getting the best prices. About two weeks after arriving in Aur, Besant Kaur and Sarjit made the long bus trip to Jalandhar to buy a car. On the Grand Trunk Road, they found Masand Motors, where they purchased a tiny four-door green Fiat, the last of the Italian-built models available: the last because a Mumbai factory had started manufacturing Fiats under licence the year before. This Fiat was the first car owned by anyone in Aur, and whenever it returned from an outing, a gang of children, small and large, charged to greet it. Krishna would be in the lead.

Krishna's family had a close friendship with the elderly Mehar Chand, another Brahman, who had been a classmate of Krishna's grandfather in Aur and who had also spent many years away from the village, although not set in Punjab but in the mountains in Simla, where he was the postmaster during the days of the British Raj. Mehar Chand was one Aur resident whom Besant Kaur knew well. They felt some affinity in spiritual matters, and she called him her dharam brother. Kapoor knew him from previous visits and had kept up a correspondence with him from Vancouver. When they spent time with him as adults, Jackie and Sarjit also became fond of him and began calling him Uncle. He spoke excellent English and came around daily for a chat; when complimented on his fluency, he explained that on rainy days he read Hazlitt, Chaucer, and Shakespeare. When the sisters complained about life in Aur, he would say, "When in Rome, do as the Romans do." As a constant companion, he was party to their discussions about the hospital and in their complete confidence.

Their most prized help came from Bhai Piara Singh Langeri, Kapoor's old friend from the days when they emigrated together – the freedom fighter who had been twice imprisoned under the British and then elected to the Punjab Assembly in the last year of the British regime. Years before, he had obtained a site for the Kapoor hospital in seven *ghumas* (acres) of land on the outskirts of Phagwara, a city centred on a railway junction forty kilometres northwest of Aur. The land still had to be registered in Kapoor's name, although that was done without delay; it was being cultivated by tenants who would have to be removed; and access was a problem. The property was near the Grand Trunk Road on the Jalandhar side of Phagwara, but it was cut off by a strip of private land and by the main railway line that ran from Delhi to Amritsar and on to Pakistan.[5] The owner of the private land was willing to sell, but his hands were tied by three nephews who had taken out mortgages. Without government help, the Siddoos could not build an access road. Also, people were telling them of severe shortages and rationing of building materials, bricks, cement, iron, and steel, so they realized they would have to apply to both the state and central governments for the railway crossing, a right of way, and building materials. While they took the measure of these problems, they had the delightful company of Bhai Piara Singh, who, during one quiet day at the end of January, told Jackie and Sarjit the story of his brutal capture by police in 1915 and of his hard years in the Kalapani Cellular Jail in the Andaman Islands.

To get moving on the hospital, they started at the top, seeking an audience with the most powerful politician in Punjab, Chief Minister Pratap Singh Kairon. To get appointments, they wrote to Kairon and followed up with telegrams. Aur had a post office and a telegraph office but no telephones, so telegrams were the fastest option, and to speed up the exchange – even though they were dealing with the government – they prepaid the cost of the replies. But replies did not come. When they became impatient, they drove over the rough road to the town of Nawanshahr, twelve kilometres away, to phone Chief Minister Kairon. Even that was not simple; the first time Sarjit did it, she booked her call at the Nawanshahr Public Call Office and waited for two hours to be connected, only to be told that the lines were out of order. Bhai Piara Singh belonged to the opposition Akali Party, but he was able to help through a very good friend of his, Giani Kartar Singh, who was in the Punjab cabinet. By that route they tried again to get the attention of Chief Minister Kairon.

They did two things while they waited. The first was general research for the hospital, and the second was to see some of India's sacred sites and shrines, such as Rishikesh and Haridwar, which they had visited before, and others that were new to them. For guidance on setting up a hospital, they wrote to the US Department of Health and received a great stack of literature with plans far more complex than anything they could hope to attempt. They went to look at a thousand-bed hospital under construction in Punjab's new capital, the striking modernist garden city of Chandigarh, which was rising on the sites of fifty-eight villages that had been expropriated and razed only eight years earlier. And they visited a small village hospital at Narangawal, west of Ludhiana, run by the Christian Medical College in Ludhiana. They called on their friend from Toronto, Lakshmi Rao, who was now dean of the Christian Medical College, and they talked to her about ways they could collaborate.

Sarjit's professor and mentor, the pediatrics specialist J.F. McCreary, arrived in India about a week after they did. He was based in Delhi and travelling frequently, visiting child health facilities throughout the country and meeting people who counted in the medical field. Jackie and Sarjit drove down to see him in Delhi late in January and again in March. Just as in Vancouver, he took them on medical rounds in several Delhi hospitals, and he introduced them to people he thought could be helpful. One was the minister of health for India, Oxford-educated Raj Kumari Amrit Kaur, a member of a Punjab princely family and the first woman in Nehru's cabinet, appointed in 1947. She told them not to bury themselves in a village hospital but to serve India by teaching in a medical college. But, as they later explained, their minds were set on doing what their parents wished.

Kapoor was going back to Canada in June, and they decided to make a major pilgrimage before he left. Their destination was the ancient and holy shrine of Badrinath, high in the Himalayas near the Tibet border, a site important to Hindus and Buddhists alike that was snowbound half the year but accessible from the beginning of May. Elderly Uncle Mehar Chand, cane and all, came along and they drove to the foothills at Haridwar, where they parked the Fiat. A rattling bus took them 150 kilometres by narrow mountain road to Joshi Math, a pilgrim centre and staging point for the thirty-kilometre hike along the higher reaches of the Ganges to Badrinath, which lies in a valley over three thousand metres above sea level. Badrinath is now accessible by bus, but in those days the hike took most of a week, unless one was young, fit, and athletic. At night they stopped at rest houses, or *chatties,* where they threw their bedding on the floor and slept beside strangers. By day they followed the centuries-old footpath, with its steep ascents and sudden drops, which was wide enough for no more than two or three to walk abreast and crowded all the way with pilgrims dressed in every kind of garb, who chanted as they went, or chatted, or walked in silence. The pilgrims jostled with mules, horses, yaks, and goats that were loaded with their paraphernalia or with goods – fabrics, rations, flowers – for the shops at Badrinath. Kapoor hired porters to carry their luggage and a few horses for luggage or to ride when someone got tired, and for Besant Kaur especially he hired a *dandi,* a primitive sedan chair slung from poles and carried by four men. He and Jackie walked most of the way, but Sarjit and Uncle Mehar Chand (who was a heart patient) took to the horses. On the way, the roar of the tumbling Ganges accompanied them. And they had spectacular scenery – hills covered with red and white rhododendrons, thickets of white roses, meadows carpeted with alpine flowers, and on all sides the glaciated peaks of the higher Himalayas. They felt they were in God's country.

They spent two nights in a Badrinath hospice while visiting the temples where pilgrims received darshan (blessing) from resident gurus. Jackie and Sarjit were shocked by bold posters in English advertising *pujas* (prayers) for anyone who paid – so much for this puja, or so much for that one, and five thousand rupees for the ultimate one, which gave *mukti,* or salvation. Because the signs were in English, they had to explain them to their mother. She paid no attention, simply saying "Okay," giving the hundred rupees she would have given anyway, and then performing her own "universal" prayer.

On the third day, with a storm brewing, they began the several-day descent. Some distance down, a sudden landslide washed out the trail, sending huge rocks crashing into the canyon of the Ganges. Kapoor and Jackie, walking ahead, were past the washout but Besant Kaur, Sarjit, and Uncle Mehar Chand were above it until, like the pilgrims ahead of them, they risked crossing it, with porters coaching on either side, shouting "Chalo, chalo!" (Go, go!). Farther down the mountain, Jackie and Sarjit came upon a husband and wife sitting on the path with broken legs. They injected them with morphine, but with a storm pressing behind and panic in the air, they carried on, trusting that the porters they spoke to would have help sent up from the next village. At Joshi Math, all the chatties were full. Thanks to the persuasive efforts of Uncle Mehar Chand, a shopkeeper let them onto an upper veranda, where they sat on bedrolls – without room to stretch out – while a storm raged throughout the night and lightning and thunder shook the building. They woke up to a beautiful day and took the bus to Haridwar, where they picked up the Fiat and drove home to Aur.

Their excursion had taken three weeks, and no news had come while they were away. Kapoor began to think that he should give the Phagwara land and a chunk of money to the government and let it build and run the hospital. Uncle Mehar Chand seemed most upset. "Blazing mad," was the way Sarjit put it in her diary. He told Jackie and Sarjit that if they gave up and left for Canada, they would be shirking their duty. He was, of course, vigorously expressing what their mother thought, and they knew it.

This was their state of mind in the last week of May just before they got an appointment in Chandigarh with Chief Minister Kairon. Their 31 May interview with him seemed to go well. "Excellent," Sarjit noted in her diary, although in the months that followed, they wondered what that interview had really achieved. For good measure, they had already written to Prime Minister Nehru. They got a telegram from his office calling them to Delhi on 3 June, and the four of them drove there to present themselves at the gates of Teen Murti Bhavan, once the palatial home of the British commander-in-chief and, since 1947, Nehru's official residence. (It now houses the Nehru Memorial Museum and Library.) They sat wide-eyed in the expansive waiting hall, watching the back-and-forth of uniformed servants and aides, and whispering to each other when they saw a prominent member of Nehru's government descend a winding staircase and leave by the front entrance.

An aide showed them into a small study, which Nehru entered after a few moments. He listened attentively to Kapoor's explanation of what the family wanted to do, and to Sarjit's list of the difficulties they faced, before telling them not to be so quickly discouraged. And, thinking of people who could provide practical advice, he gave them the names of a doctor and an engineer who were building a rural hospital in a village seventy kilometres southwest of Delhi. Having said this, he left the room, asking them to wait a few minutes. A servant brought cold lemonade before Nehru returned with Indira Gandhi. "Let me introduce you to my daughter," he said, using her familiar name of Indu. The interview turned to small talk, to a description of their trip to Badrinath, encouraged by his display of interest and his questions. Besant Kaur gave him prasad (holy food) from Badrinath, and they had a few minutes alone with Indira Gandhi, whom they found very pleasant and who told them to contact her whenever the need arose. They left feeling much better, although not entirely reassured.

Kapoor flew to Canada ten days later, and Jackie went with him, having decided to return to her post-graduate work under her supervisor, Harry Perry. Her parting words to Sarjit were, "If you can build this hospital, I'll come back. Otherwise, forget it." But things did seem to be happening at last. Just before Kapoor and Jackie flew out of Delhi's Palam airport, the family had two good meetings in the capital with one of the people Nehru had mentioned, the doctor who was building a hospital in the village of Dhanora, southwest of Delhi. His name was Pandalik D. Gaitonde and this was the beginning of a much-appreciated relationship. And they saw Indira Gandhi again. After her father and sister had gone, Sarjit drafted a hospital proposal for the Punjab government, based on what Gaitonde told her. She sent this to Chief Minister Kairon and saw him in early July, along with Punjab's director of health services. A couple of weeks later, she finished a full proposal and sent it to Kairon, followed by a description and sketch of the property at Phagwara. Then came a lull when nothing much happened.

The plan was for a thirty-bed hospital, mostly for the poor, to be built on the Phagwara land that Kapoor would donate to the government along with 200,000 rupees. Jackie and Sarjit would run the hospital without salary, and it would be named the Kapoor Singh Family Hospital. In return the family wanted help from the Punjab government to draw up plans, build and equip the hospital, and put in an access road through the private property and over the railway. And the government could also find an organization like the Red Cross to provide ambulance service and could set up linkages with public health services and with a large government medical centre. To maintain the hospital and pay a staff of nurses, pharmacists, and orderlies, Sarjit proposed an annual subscription paid by local villages. Her calculations assumed that fifty thousand people could be covered at the annual rate of one rupee per person. A board of governors made up of fifteen leading Punjabis would control the funds. Sarjit suggested to Kairon that this could be a pilot scheme, a model for others to imitate across rural Punjab.[6]

She spelled out for Kairon what was most urgent: a road and railway crossing, a government architect to draw up plans, help with construction (especially in getting materials), sanction for a transmission line to deliver electricity to the hospital, and – in the midst of these concerns – a commitment from Kairon to lay the cornerstone.

Chief Minister Kairon was a fifty-six-year-old driving force for change in Punjab, a man of immense energy and vision, and a guiding hand behind remarkable initiatives – electrification, industrialization, irrigation, land consolidation, education, and the creation of an agricultural college – all preparing rural Punjab for an economic revolution. He had been the minister responsible for the relief and rehabilitation of refugees in 1947. But perhaps he is best understood in the light of his American experience. In the 1920s, he had studied economics and political science at Berkeley and Michigan, supporting himself by working on fruit farms in California. What he saw of agriculture in California made him ambitious for rural development in Punjab; and after independence, he found himself in a position to lead.[7] He was decisive by nature but also inclined to take charge of everything, which meant that a project such as the Kapoor hospital had to wait on his time.

Before he would sanction an access road and railway crossing, Kairon insisted on seeing the hospital site for himself, but he did not do so right away, and that effectively stopped the project before it started. (Although the railway division of the central government in Delhi would decide about the crossing, Kairon could decisively influence its decision.) Late in August, he set a time and place to meet Sarjit – 9:30 a.m. on 11 September at the Phagwara Rest House – so she could take him to the site, but then he cancelled. Not until the second week of December did he finally meet her by appointment on the Grand Trunk Road, outside Phagwara. They drove onto the property in a government jeep, and he approved the most direct of three possible routes for an access road. After that, weeks passed without further communication – no government approvals for the key elements of the project. In his letters to Sarjit, Kairon had initiated a familiar form of address, "Dear Daughter," and she began to reply "Dear Uncle," but without action on his part, the familiarity seemed empty. A week after he had cancelled the September meeting, Sarjit sent him a very frank handwritten confidential letter. "We are vegetating in this place," she complained. And she felt worse as she approached the end of a full year in India with nothing to show for it. In her diary she quoted Milton's sonnet about the late spring of his life in which "no bud or blossom showeth." And she added, expressing deep discouragement, that Milton had been twenty-three when he wrote that, and she was already thirty.[8]

She could excuse Chief Minister Kairon when she considered what he had on his plate. He was currently dealing with a huge Hindu agitation over language. This had started that summer after the national government, trying to please Sikhs, had expanded Punjab's boundaries and promised that Punjabi alone would be the official language of the enlarged state, instead of Hindi and Punjabi. Over her transistor radio, and in the newspapers she read when she travelled out of Aur, Sarjit learned of mass demonstrations in the cities, with Hindu nationalists shouting "Save Hindi" and physically attacking Sikhs and their symbols.[9] The Sikhs countered with their own *morchas,* or marches, which Sikh shopkeepers supported with *hartals* (strikes), but that summer and fall it was mostly Hindus in the streets, led by fundamentalists of the Hindi Raksha Samiti. Sarjit knew that this trouble was consuming Kairon's time. She said as much when he proposed meeting at the Phagwara Rest House, and she replied to confirm that she would be there. Her family had been afraid, she wrote, that the hospital project would have to be abandoned because of "that useless *Samiti* movement."[10]

But Sarjit began to think that the chief minister was in no hurry, even though he seemed sympathetic and even apologetic when they met. Early on, he had referred her to Punjab's director of health services and to the

Punjab Medical Council, but those officials were in no hurry to help.[11] On the bottom of a letter that she eventually received from health services, she wrote impatiently, "Strange country where one has to wait six months for a reply!"[12] Incidentally, this letter did not answer her question; its facts were incorrect; and it was addressed to the Phagwara hospital site instead of to Aur and delivered to the farming family that was renting and tilling the land. (The overseer took a long bus ride to bring it to Sarjit.) Moreover, when she talked to Jagdish Singh, the director of health services, and Hans Raj of the medical council, they cynically implied that her family was motivated by potential profit and that she and Jackie wished to practise in India because they were not good enough professionally to be doctors in Canada.

Chief Minister Kairon had spoken to his wife about the Kapoor hospital, and Sarjit got an earful from her in May 1958. This was a month after Sarjit and her mother decided – finally – to build in Aur instead of on the outskirts of Phagwara, and to proceed without involving the government. Bringing along Bhai Piara Singh for support, Sarjit and Besant Kaur went to see Kairon at his official residence in Chandigarh's elite Sector 2, only to discover that he was ill and in bed. Mrs. Kairon, a tall and intimidating woman, came out to speak with them. She was familiar with some of the details, but her version of the story was very partial. Her tone made Sarjit feel like a schoolchild being scolded by a headmistress. She did not believe that the Siddoos would ever build a hospital and said that, though they talked about locating at Phagwara and Aur, they were obviously not serious about either. Unable to get a word in edgewise, Sarjit finally stood up impatiently and walked out. Her mother was shocked. "You should not get so mad," she told her. In her diary Sarjit described the encounter as a showdown.

Two weeks later, on 20 May 1958, with construction underway in Aur, Sarjit and her mother held a ceremony. They had invited Chief Minister Kairon to lay the first brick, but his office had not replied, so Bhai Piara Singh did the honours, while Uncle Mehar Chand acted as master of ceremonies. A thousand people from Aur and neighbouring villages attended. The Aur School Boys' Band paraded through the streets along with local women singing bhajans (hymns) and joined by a boys' band from the village of Urapur, a few kilometres to the east.

Back in January 1957, when the Siddoos arrived from Canada, the villagers at Aur had viewed them as curiosities and shown no interest in the hospital project. After a few months, however, they began taking notice and complaining, and soon they were pressuring Besant Kaur to locate her hospital there. But she and Sarjit had a ready response: the village had no electricity, so it could not have a modern hospital. That changed in late August 1957 when an advance team from the Punjab State Electricity Board showed up, promising electricity within three months. In fact, it took over a year to arrive, but the prospect of electricity made putting the villagers off more difficult.[13] In truth, the idea of a hospital in her home village appealed to Besant Kaur, but she did not say so openly, expecting that once she did local landowners would inflate the prices of potential sites. And Phagwara was the place for a large hospital, so she and Sarjit continued to focus on that.

But the villagers kept pressing their case. In early November, thirteen members of the village *panchayat* (council) plus two officials from the district capital of Jalandhar took mother and daughter to three possible village sites and asked them to choose. None appealed, but Sarjit and Besant identified a barren property near a Muslim graveyard as more suitable than the others. The owner of this land, who had been awarded it for gallantry in a war under the British, expected a lot of money for it, and that ended that. As Sarjit put it, "We were not going to be made utter fools of."

As November passed, the village initiative seemed to wane, but at the end of the month, as Besant Kaur and Sarjit were eating their evening meal upstairs at home, they heard drums beating in the alley below, in the time-honoured way of making announcements. Besant Kaur intuited what it was all about: "Those drums are beating for us." From the rooftop, Sarjit heard criers calling villagers to a meeting at the Hindu *dharamsala* (hospice-temple) just down the alley. After nightfall, she and Besant Kaur heard a great crowd outside, excited voices and loud knocking at their gate. Uncle Mehar Chand came hurrying up the exterior concrete steps to the second floor, out of breath due to his bad heart. "Bibi ji (Sister ji)," he said, "the whole village has come to persuade you to build the hospital here." In their courtyard under a starry sky, Besant Kaur found a great crowd of men carrying lanterns and seated on *charpois* (string-beds) and wooden chairs, or standing in such numbers that they filled the yard and spilled into the alley. They offered Besant Kaur a chair and then fell into what Sarjit described as "an awful silence." It was Uncle Mehar Chand, his voice breaking with emotion, who answered her questions while others nodded. Yes, they wanted her to build at Aur, and yes, they could find her a suitable property.

The next day, the chief officer of the village panchayat and his assistant took Besant Kaur and Sarjit one and a half kilometres outside the village to see land that had been owned by Muslims before 1947 and was now held by the government department of the custodian-general of evacuee property. They explained that a government officer in the next village could do all the paperwork for transfer of ownership. Moreover, the owner of the adjacent land would swap it for some that Besant Kaur's family had elsewhere. (This was a good deal for him, giving him land that was more fertile and triple the value.) Together, the two pieces added up to ten acres, with a long frontage on the main road. The Muslim portion had an attractive cluster of tall trees in the centre, a well, and two brick tombs of the kind found all over Punjab – square or hexagonal domed mausoleums for Sufi saints, or fakirs, with entrances on the south side. (The fakir would have been laid out with his feet to the south and his head turned to face Mecca in the west.) Besant Kaur and Sarjit had driven by the property many times, but when they walked through it, they felt an immediate attraction and agreed that it was an ideal location for a hospital.

They saw this property a few days before Sarjit – after months of waiting – met Chief Minister Kairon on the Grand Trunk Road and got his decision on an access road to the Phagwara site. Besant Kaur was now agonizing about what to do, having given her promise at Phagwara and feeling the pressure at Aur. A telephone call to Kapoor would have helped, but it was difficult enough to get Chandigarh on the line, let alone Vancouver. With Sarjit she sought out Bhai Piara Singh, and after chasing from village to village during one of his busy afternoons of various meetings, she caught up with him as he dismounted from a lorry on which he had been hitch-hiking. She wanted his opinion and he gently turned the question back to her. He said he had the highest respect for her, and whatever she decided would be alright with him. Her solution was to build at both places, a big hospital at Phagwara and a small one at Aur. Having two hospitals was fine with Aur, except it wanted the bigger one. It might also have been fine with Chief Minister Kairon and his bureaucrats in Chandigarh, except they again lapsed into silence.

After putting up with the silence for so long, Sarjit now found it excruciating, and she was devastated when her mother, who had never been ill, passed out on New Year's Day 1958, and again five weeks later after a night at the Swiss Hotel in Old Delhi, this time with all the symptoms of a grand mal seizure. In tears, Sarjit begged her to go back to Vancouver, but she adamantly refused – she had a hospital to build and she was going to do it. To Sarjit she said, "If you are so anxious to return, you go." They never spoke of it again, and she never had another attack.

Those few days in Delhi during February 1958 were the turning point: the beginning of action. They had come to Delhi to see Dr. Pandalik D. Gaitonde and Sri Sivasubramanian, the doctor and engineer whom Nehru had recommended. They had already met Gaitonde, and they were meeting Sivasubramanian for the first time. One day after Besant Kaur had her seizure, she determinedly accompanied Sarjit on the seventy-kilometre drive to Dhanora, where Gaitonde and Sivasubramanian had constructed their village hospital. The hospital was a fine building, although functioning poorly because the village elders were fighting among themselves. More importantly, Besant Kaur and Sarjit found Sivasubramanian, like Gaitonde, to be someone who gave generous help with no expectations of a return.

Gaitonde was a Goan, living in New Delhi during the last days of Portuguese rule in Goa. He was both a political activist and a distinguished surgeon – a staff member at one of Delhi's premier teaching hospitals and a leader in exile of the Goan National Congress. His friend Sivasubramanian, who was from Chennai (Madras), was an executive engineer with the public works department of the Indian government. They lived near each other in Rabindra Nagar, a government housing enclave populated by bureaucrats. Besant Kaur and Sarjit were immediately impressed with Sivasubramanian, both professionally and as a human being, whom they got to know in his home with his large lively family, sharing his delicious South Indian food. He started working on hospital plans immediately and without any fee, making weekend trips to Aur by car or going by train as far as Ludhiana, where they would pick him up. By the end of February, he had paced and measured the site at Aur and taken specifications. On 9 April, he arrived with two sets of plans, asking Besant Kaur and Sarjit to choose one, which they did before he left.

Sivasubramanian, or Sivaji, as Besant Kaur and Sarjit began calling him, found a contractor for Sarjit because he judged her too gullible to find an honest one for herself. By 1 May 1958, his chosen contractor was on the job, an uneducated man in baggy Peshawari pants and loose knee-length Peshawari shirt, who turned up with his brothers and spoke no English but proved keen and energetic. His name was Sohan Lal, and he and his family were refugees from the Peshawar area of what became Pakistan. They lived on the outskirts of Delhi, and Sivaji, who had worked with him over the years, vouched for his reliability. Under Sivaji's direction, and with labourers brought up from Delhi and others recruited locally, he did all the work. Late that summer, with the work going slowly and Sohan Lal disappearing frequently – perhaps on a drinking binge (they had seen him drunk), perhaps away recruiting labourers from Delhi, or perhaps visiting his family – Sivaji wanted to fire him, but Besant Kaur and Sarjit said no. They were impressed by his sincerity.

The plans called for the destruction of one of the Muslim tombs on the site, and in the second week of May, that brought Sohan Lal and his workers to an impasse. None of the men would do it. Lal himself was too respectful, or too superstitious and fearful, to start demolishing the ancient mausoleums of once revered holy men. In his work gang – families whose men did the shovelling and cement work and laid the bricks, whose women carried earth, bricks, cement, sand, and gravel, and whose small children played nearby – there was one fearless young woman from Aur named Harbhajan. She took up a *hathaura* (a heavy-headed hammer) and delivered the first blows against the fakir's resting place. In her notes Sarjit wrote, "Harbhajan turns out to be the heroine for a day." The next morning, Sarjit woke up with a fever and sore throat, which villagers attributed to the assault on the tomb. Two months later, as the hospital rose from its foundations, a story flashed through the village that one wall had collapsed – the front wall facing the ruins of the tomb. It was not true.

Harbhajan began demolishing the tomb on 12 May 1958, four days after Sarjit had her showdown with Mrs. Kairon in Chandigarh, and eight days before Bhai Paira Singh laid the ceremonial corner bricks. By then, Besant Kaur and Sarjit were set on building at Aur only and keeping the Punjab government out of it. They had seen enough of how its machinery worked. Their challenge was to get construction materials without paying black-market prices. Armed with a letter from Indira Gandhi – with whom they had met several times and who continued to be encouraging – they drove here and there, requisitioning what they needed. They also had a letter from the minister of steel and mines, Swaran Singh, whom they had first met four years earlier in Vancouver and Victoria when he was on an official visit to Canada and they had entertained him for lunch.[14] They drove to Ropar for bricks, gravel, sand, and shovels, to Dehra Dun for limestone, and to Delhi for steel and to commission the woodwork, with mother and daughter operating as a team and going everywhere together.

They were up to their necks in house renovation. From the beginning of August, Sohan Lal and his gang worked at the hospital site and in their home – the qila. At the qila they were replacing original bricks, extending the second floor to add a bathroom and to make more living space, installing plumbing, preparing for electricity, and doing the plastering and painting. In August and early September, they rushed to get the job done before Kapoor and Jackie arrived after more than a year's absence. Of course, the renovations were not finished when they arrived and would not be for many months. To take one aspect: electricity reached the village on 30 September; electricians came to the house on 8 November; in January the house still had no power and the flush system was useless because it needed an electric pump; and as late as June everything was not right because when Sarjit tried to take a shower she got a terrific shock to her elbow because something was wrong with the way the electric power had been grounded to the water line. These renovations added another level of stress. When Kapoor and Jackie disembarked at Palam airport in Delhi in late September 1958, it was Sarjit's appearance, not her mother's, that shocked them. Her weight was down to 92 pounds from a normal 115.

This time, Kapoor and Jackie's visit to India lasted about three months. They were back in Vancouver by early January 1959, and Kapoor was speaking with lawyers about a charitable foundation to fund the hospital. Acting on their advice, he cabled Besant Kaur and Sarjit, calling them home to approve and sign documents; and they took a flight within a week. They had become accustomed to the Indian sun, and it rained non-stop for weeks in Vancouver, but Sarjit gained seven pounds in the first seven days. They had contemplated leaving Sohan Lal in charge, but this seemed unwise, so Bhai Piara Singh supervised while they were gone. The trip doubled as a vital shopping expedition. On her stopovers in Hong Kong and London, Jackie had looked at equipment for the lab – German-manufactured Leitz and Zeiss microscopes – which Sarjit checked out when she followed their route a month later.[15] In Vancouver, the sisters bought an x-ray unit, an electrocardiograph machine, a centrifuge, and other lab equipment, and arranged for shipment by American Express. When the Siddoos returned to Aur late in May, they were disappointed by Sohan Lal's lack of progress. In his defence, the delivery of materials had been delayed, but he needed to pick up the pace because they were committed to a specific date that fall. Two days after landing in Delhi, they had gone to see Indira Gandhi and invited her to the hospital opening on 7 October. They had also invited Nehru to be guest of honour but were pleased to leave with a definite promise that she would come.[16]

They had scaled back their project, starting small and saving the possibility of expanding for later. Sivaji had designed a twelve-bed hospital with male and female wards, an operating theatre, an outpatients' department – waiting room, treatment room, consulting rooms, dispensary, and labs – and with an x-ray room and darkroom in a separate building because the emissions from x-ray machines back then were so strong. Behind the hospital were staff quarters for eight. In consultation with Sivaji, the Siddoos had decided to put in a formal lawn and flower garden, a large vegetable garden, and barns for dairy cattle to supply milk. With a great push throughout the summer, the site was looking complete by opening day. Their first shipment of equipment from Canada arrived in the monsoon season, badly damaged by rain. (Their brokers in Mumbai had been careless about repacking after customs had opened everything.) Thankfully, the x-ray equipment came intact and undamaged in the next shipment. During the last two months, they rushed to purchase drugs for the dispensary and equipment for the labs, and with the help of the Christian Medical College, they trained staff, including one of Krishna's brothers, who was to become a lab technician.

They had confirmation of attendance from two eminent guests, Indira Gandhi and the Canadian high commissioner to India, Chester Ronning.[17] Their old friend Elmore Philpott, who was coming as a columnist for the *Vancouver Sun* (planning to go on to Dharamsala for an interview with the young Dalai Lama), was travelling with his wife and a friend, a Mrs. DesBrisay from Vancouver. Members of the Indian press would be there, and with such a high-profile event in the offing, the Punjab health department descended on the village to tidy it up, beating drums in the alleys to warn villagers to clean up their trash and filth, spraying DDT and pouring phenol to disinfect the open drains, and poisoning the village's gaunt and mangy strays – its pye-dogs – many of whom escaped death because villagers hid them. Sarjit hired a famous twenty-two-member police band from Jalandhar, and from Chester Ronning she obtained the sheet music for "O Canada," which she gave to the band and the Aur high school students. She went to hear the students rehearse on a Friday morning two weeks beforehand. And the High Commission had sent by express-post a large Red Ensign, the old Canadian flag with the Union Jack in the corner, and sixty paper flags for children to wave.[18]

The day of the opening – at the tail end of the monsoon season – was perfect, with beautiful clear sky. The village was clean and festive. Crossed Indian and Canadian flags hung over the hospital's front entrance, and the Philpotts and Mrs. DesBrisay emerged on the roof to survey the scene, after their night in a special suite at the top of the hospital. High Commissioner Ronning and his wife were driving from Delhi by car, and Indira Gandhi was on her way. Children with paper Canadian flags lined the entrance road, and people from villages as far as thirty kilometres away crowded along the main road and stood everywhere on the hospital grounds. Someone estimated fifteen thousand of them. The Ronnings arrived precisely on time at 3:00 p.m. and Indira Gandhi shortly after. The band played and the students sang the Canadian and Indian national anthems. Chester Ronning spoke and Indira Gandhi officially opened the Kapoor Singh Canadian Hospital. A late-afternoon tea followed, with Punjabi food – *dal,* roti, *saag, raita* – for the special guests and, as it turned out, for an uninvited collection of ravenous Indian journalists. After a group photo, the Ronnings and Indira Gandhi left, and by 5:00 it was all over. Elmore Philpott settled down to write his stories so that Sarjit could drive to Ludhiana the next day to cable them to the *Vancouver Sun.*[19]

That was 7 October. They still had equipment to install and staff – nurses, technicians, pharmacists – to find. They were discovering that qualified people did not want to work in villages and made extraordinary demands, and as they were to find out, would not stay long. They were to learn it was best to train local people, who were at home in the village, who understood its inhabitants, and who would stay three or four years before the young women got married and the men went to the city. On 9 November, the first day of work at the hospital, eleven patients showed up. For many months, some had come to see the young Canadian doctors in their home, but the opening of the hospital, with all its fanfare, produced no new rush. In the first three months, until February 1960, they saw only 417 patients, 10 or 15 a day. This was at a hospital where patients paid no fees, had free lab work, and paid nothing for their medications. Within a few months, Sarjit and Jackie found a third doctor to stay year-round while they split their time between Canada and India. But even before he joined them, they spent hours playing tennis on the hard surface of the driveway, putting in time while waiting for patients to appear. Their mother was philosophical. "Never mind," she said. "If you see one patient a day and give proper medication, that is enough."

Part of the problem was their receptionist, their elderly cane-wielding friend Uncle Mehar Chand, whose company they so much enjoyed. Only after his death did they realize what a negative presence he had been. In the fall of 1960, after a trip to Vancouver for hospital supplies, Jackie and Sarjit returned to Aur with skis and thoughts of taking a break on the Himalayan slopes of Kufi, a little north of Simla. On what turned out to be Uncle Mehar Chand's last day, he arrived at the hospital with Sarjit. As they mounted the four steps to the entrance, Sarjit pointed to the big wooden boxes of ski equipment and said, "Look, Uncle, this is how we get around in Canada." "Yes," he said, and then collapsed and expired.

The next day everyone noticed a big increase in patients. For all his learning, Uncle had been a Brahman mired in the caste system, and he had been rude to low-caste and out-caste people – shouting at them if they sat down on the benches in the waiting room – so they had stayed away.

After his death, more patients came, but the numbers remained disappointing. Theoretically, the hospital served twenty villages, whose people would otherwise have gone to Ludhiana for modern hospital treatment.[20] But many were afraid of any hospital, preferring their own natural remedies or the traditional *ayurvedic* or *unani* medicine of local physicians or *hakims* and relying on the services of midwives – Aur had a very good midwife, a Muslim woman who had married a Sikh to avoid evacuation in 1947 – and if they wanted antibiotics, they could get them from a pharmacy without a prescription. Pharmacies were not licensed to issue painkillers, but with marijuana, or *bhang*, growing freely on the roadsides, the sisters themselves would advise its use for anyone suffering unrelenting pain. In the beginning, the Kapoor Singh Hospital was mainly a last resort for the desperately ill. The sisters realized this just two days after the opening ceremony when relatives brought in a man who coughed blood, had jaundiced eyes, and was extremely weak. His family had no money and would not take him to Ludhiana for fear he would die there and the Ludhiana hospital would charge two or three hundred rupees to give the body back.

According to the wisdom of the village, Western medicine might have merit, but the doctors who practised it were not to be trusted; and as Jackie and Sarjit judged, Aur had good reason for thinking this way, given the standards of many doctors in rural areas. The only good doctors, villagers seemed to assume, were the ones who stayed in the cities, a prejudice that the sisters struggled to overcome. In time they did overcome it. It helped that they spoke Punjabi. One old man spoke for many when he said to Sarjit, "Now you have come, you can give me salt pills and I can get better." Trust was everything. Eventually, patients began coming regularly from as far as the Shivalik Hills, and Jackie and Sarjit were affectionately known to their clientele as Bibi ji (Sister ji) rather than formally as Doctor Sahib. But building that feeling and relationship took several years.

After the hospital opening, a friend from Toronto Medical School, Amala Ramcharan (one of the Ramcharan sisters from Trinidad), had written to apologize for not attending. She was visiting Kolkata but had a three-month-old baby, which was why she had not come. She wondered why "Canadian" was part of the hospital's name.[21] Why was it the Kapoor Singh *Canadian* Hospital? Her question was a fair one because initially the name was to be the Kapoor Singh Family Hospital, which made sense for a genuine family enterprise. "Canadian" was added because the family was Canadian. In addition, the name sounded natural in Punjab, where people commonly identified themselves by the place they came from, as with Piara Singh Langeri, who was from the village of Langeri. Over the doorways of village homes, one could see names like Harjinder Singh Malaya or Darshan Singh Canadian or Bhag Singh Canadian, which declared the overseas experience of the occupant. If any Punjabi emigrant had the right to be called Canadian, it was Kapoor Singh Siddoo through choice, achievement, and service. And the name expressed a great deal: it said that the hospital was the gift of someone who did well as an emigrant and who was proud to belong to Canada.

15
Finding a Teacher and Losing a Father

Canada was home for Jackie and Sarjit, although India was where they spent much of each year from 1959 onward. They were the products of a special and protected upbringing, but it had taken place in Canada, where they were educated, where they formed lasting childhood friendships, and where they had bonded instinctively and viscerally with the Pacific Coast landscape. In adulthood, they remained closely attached to their parents, whom they loved and respected so much that they dedicated themselves to service in Punjab because their parents wished it. This love and loyalty remained integral parts of their nature even as they matured as strong-minded and capable women, international in outlook and experience, independent in action, and insistent on making their own choices on subjects that mattered most to them. One thing that mattered a lot was holding on to a semblance of their family life in Canada.

While Jackie and Sarjit were medical students, Kapoor assigned a majority of the shares of Kapoor Sawmills to them, intending that they should eventually take over the management. He had no doubt that they could run it as well as any man. He thought that one of them could oversee the mill and forest operation in Canada while the other ran the hospital in India. They could alternate, one in Canada while the other was in India and vice versa. But the sisters had grown up as close as twins, and they did not want to be separated. So he decided, as the hospital rose on its foundations and as he passed his seventy-fifth birthday, that he had to let the business go. He sold it to the giant forestry company BC Forest

Products in January 1959 and a year later liquidated Kapoor Sawmills as a legal entity. With the sale he gave up the mill at Barnet and saw its buildings and machinery dismantled and removed from the site, and he gave up the lumber camp and equipment at Shawnigan Lake, as well as much of the forest that he owned on Vancouver Island.[1] With an eye to his family's future, he kept five thousand acres of timber at Sooke Lake, but after half a century, his career as a lumberman was over. This was a life-cycle change, and his daughters regretfully realized too late that when they let him sell the business, he lost some of his vitality.

With the opening of the hospital, the entire family began staying in India from September to June and coming back to Canada for two summer months. At the hospital, Sarjit and Jackie saw much the same cases as they would have treated in general practice in Canada, although with some exceptions. Patients of all ages arrived at the gates by foot, bus, bicycle, and bullock cart, and sometimes on horseback – and in later years by scooter and occasionally by car – with colds, flu, asthma, allergies, hypertension, heart disease, anemia, arthritis, peptic ulcers, diarrhea, hookworm, and tuberculosis. Less frequently, they suffered from measles, mumps, malaria, amoebiasis, scabies, bronchitis, pneumonia, typhoid fever, urinary disorders, pelvic inflammatory disease, hepatitis, cirrhosis, osteomyelitis, leukemia, cancer, epilepsy, and depression. And from time to time, Sarjit and Jackie encountered a mother-in-law declaring that something was wrong with her daughter-in-law – "She is not having any children" – while the young woman, scarcely more than a child, sat in silence. The sisters did not mince words in explaining that the problem could be with the son. They never got over their dismay at this attitude, and predictably, after they had spoken so directly to the mother-in-law, they never saw her again.[2]

Cases of tuberculosis were much more numerous than in Canada, sometimes appearing as galloping consumption, which Jackie and Sarjit had previously seen only in textbooks. With TB patients, whose village environment they understood, they gave careful instruction on personal hygiene for the sake of their families and others around them: to use a separate set of dishes; never to sleep with anyone, pick up a child, or hold a child near their mouth; never to cough in anyone's face or spit on the ground; to spit into a special container, with soil in the bottom that they could bury. Because the hospital gave free medication, it attracted TB patients from a distance, and Jackie and Sarjit impressed on all of them the importance of taking their medication every day for the full six months of treatment.

Their hospital routine had just begun, and they were seeing only a few patients, when Gandhi's spiritual heir, the saintly Baba Vinoba Bhave, arrived in Punjab on his *pad yatra* (walking tour). He was covering twelve kilometres a day, setting off in the cool of the morning, and reaching the next village at 8:00 a.m. for breakfast. In midmorning, villagers would gather and he would talk. He rested during hot afternoons, and in the evening he and his party retired to the village school or a dharamsala (hospice-temple). Their bedding had been carried from the last village by jeep, and they had walked unburdened. Vinoba Bhave had been walking throughout India for eight years and was to continue for another decade until he was seventy-five, seeking donations of land from the rich for the poor. When Sarjit saw him in February 1960, she was profoundly impressed and jotted down in her diary "frail body but gigantic genius spiritually."[3]

Jackie joined his walking tour at Phillaur, twenty kilometres from Aur, and she stayed with it from December to April.[4] Sarjit and her parents drove every day to hear him at his next village, and Jackie wrote about her experience in an article for the magazine section of the *Chandigarh Tribune.* One consequence of this was a letter from a recently graduated doctor from Kerala, K. Phillip, a Christian Indian full of missionary zeal who was moved by what she had written and who decided to come to Aur to work full-time in the hospital, which he did for many years before emigrating to Australia.[5]

What Jackie joined on the pad yatra was a procession of about forty bare-legged disciples dressed in white homespun and led by Baba Vinoba. Each morning they recited Sanskrit verses before setting out at 4:30 a.m., keeping silence for the first segment of the walk. Later in the morning, Baba Vibnoba gave interviews, for which there was a protocol. One made an appointment through one of his chief disciples and then moved ahead to talk to him while walking. When the interview ended, one fell back to the main group. He would meet the great or the lowly, but only if they came to him. He did not go to anyone. While he was in the vicinity of Aur, Sarjit drove to the railway station at Ludhiana several times to pick up VIPs. Once it was the famous Gandhian socialist and pacifist Jayprakash Narayan, who was bringing Pakistan's high commissioner to South Africa for a personal meeting with Baba Vinoba.

The sisters persuaded Baba Vinoba to route his walk through Aur, where he planted a mango tree and addressed two thousand people. He spent the night at the hospital, and the Siddoo family took darshan from him, seeing him, being in his company, and experiencing the deep blessing of his presence.[6] He gave a paperback book to each of the sisters, and he knew them well enough by then to have their natures pegged. Inside Jackie's book, he wrote "The silent one," and inside Sarjit's he wrote "The talkative one." For their mother, he had a gift of food, *sattu,* the red lentil and chickpea porridge from Bihar – he was a Bihari – that was served cold and had a cooling effect in hot weather. A few lines in Sarjit's diary expressed her profound feelings about meeting Gandhi's leading disciple. "A living Christ," she wrote, "a living Buddha, a living Guru Nanak, walking on this very earth today, and only a handful are able to recognize this fact."

Two of Baba Vinoba's disciples were Brahman brothers, Swami Sachidananda and Swami Brahmananda, youthful-looking men in their forties, with an approachable nature and sweet manner. On the walking tour, Jackie particularly got to know Swami Sachidananda, who had a master's degree from Lahore, spoke perfect English, and had committed himself to Baba Vinoba. Her conversations with him and the example of Baba Vinoba himself revived feelings from her time with Swami Radha in Montreal. She began to urge her parents to turn the hospital over to Vinoba's movement, and she briefly stunned them by announcing that she planned to follow Sachidananda's example and become a renunciant. She said this one evening as she was leaving the qila for the hospital, where she had made the guest suite her residence. After she went out the door, Sarjit and her parents sat in silence until Kapoor asked, "What does she think? We put her through medical school to renounce the world and sit by the Ganges?" He did not believe it. Nor, in the end, did Jackie, though she was still searching for a teacher.

Sachidananda gave Jackie an introduction to the Sikh artist Sobha Singh, whose moving portrait of Guru Nanak has become a defining image for many Sikhs. Sobha Singh lived in an artistic community that had gathered around the elderly Irish actress Norah Richards in the village of Andretta in the Shivalik Hills. It lay a nine-hour drive from Aur, and the Siddoos went to see him for what turned out to be the beginning of a long friendship. He was then nearing his sixtieth birthday with his greatest fame yet to come. Sarjit remembered him with a flowing white beard and hair that was "kind of fluffy." He was not a "cut-and-dried Sikh" and wore no turban. On this visit he took them up the local funicular for a spectacular view of the mountains, and as he walked with them, discussing spiritual things, his wife stayed in the background, evidently not enthusiastic about another round of visitors. "I don't know why she is upset," he said, "a cup of tea is only a couple of *paisa*."

Among the books in Sobha Singh's home was *Life in Freedom,* by Jiddu Krishnamurti, published in 1928 and no longer in print. When Jackie and Sarjit began reading it, Sobha Singh said, "That is the man you are looking for. He is now in Delhi and giving lectures." Krishnamurti had been lecturing in India for the past year and was about to leave for Ojai, California, via Europe. As young people, Jackie and Sarjit had heard of him through their father's Theosophical friends, especially Kartar Singh, but had never given him much thought. More recently, Sachidananda had talked of him. Krishnamurti's book and what Sobha Singh said about him prompted them to go to Delhi, where they found themselves in an audience of four thousand at the Civic Centre near Connaught Circus, listening to Krishnamurti speak with such power that they were glued to every word. They immediately wanted to know him better.[7]

He was staying with his old Sanskrit teacher (by then a prominent journalist and politician) Benegal Shiva Rao and Rao's Austrian wife, Kitty. She invited the sisters to intimate talks by Krishnamurti at their home in Lodi Estate, near the Mughal ruins of Lodi Gardens. They sat with the other guests on the living room floor with the furniture removed so that, when Krishnamurti entered, he naturally sat on the floor with everyone else. Jackie and Sarjit were too shy to speak in his presence, even though Krishnamurti was not the dominating personage here that he had been when he gave his public address. He was in fact a very reserved man without much casual conversation. But when he spoke, Sarjit says, "He pounded you with the truth." And the truth was that people did not need gurus: "I am not your guru. I am just sitting here for convenience." With other spiritual teachers, the sisters felt intimidated, but with him there was no fear. They imagined that this was how it was with Guru Nanak, with Christ or with Buddha.

Benegal Shiva Rao had been close to Krishnamurti for fifty years. He had known him from the moment that Charles Webster Leadbeater, the Theosophist and clairvoyant, noticed Krishnamurti on the beach at the Theosophical Society headquarters at Adyar, near Chennai (Madras). Krishnamurti was then fourteen, looking undernourished and uncared-for, and speaking little English, but Leadbeater thought he saw perfect clarity in his aura and decided that he was the coming Lord Maitreya, the World Teacher, the Bodhisattva, the Christ, all comparable in Leadbeater's vocabulary. Krishnamurti was living at Adyar because his Brahman father, a retired district magistrate, was working for the Theosophical Society as an assistant secretary. The family occupied a rundown cottage just outside the society compound. Young Shiva Rao was at Adyar because he had left a teaching position in Benares to assist in recording Leadbeater's psychic research. His role as a tutor for Krishnamurti developed because he was there and available. With the support of the society's president, Annie Besant, Leadbeater took over the education of the boy he believed had so much to give the world. After a highly publicized custody battle with the boy's father, Leadbeater removed Krishnamurti to the seaside resort of Bude in north Cornwall so he could be westernized and groomed for his future. He brought Shiva Rao to Bude to instruct him in Sanskrit. This continued for three years until Rao returned to India to edit Annie Besant's daily newspaper *New India,* in Chennai.[9]

Nearly a decade later, Shiva Rao and Krishnamurti were sailing to Colombo and sharing a cabin when Krishnamurti received the traumatic and unexpected news of his brother Nitya's death. And four years later, Rao remained a loyal friend when Krishnamurti rejected the role and purpose that Leadbeater had imposed on him – that of the coming World Teacher. From then on, Krishnamurti taught that there was no single path to truth and no teacher or organization that could lead anyone to Truth without becoming a crutch for them or a cage. With that insight, he had resigned from the Theosophical Society and disbanded the Order of the Star, the organization that the Theosophists had formed to prepare for his appearance as the World Teacher. Through all this, Shiva Rao's attachment to him had continued, and after Jackie and Sarjit met Rao's wife, Kitty, they found themselves rubbing shoulders with Krishnamurti's oldest friends and intimates.[9]

Jackie kept a diary of her encounters with Krishnamurti – making a note of everything, consequential and inconsequential, that their conversations covered – which she eventually published as *Listening Is the Guru.* When they first met, and she had a private moment with him on the lawn of the Raos' walled garden, she told him about her mystical experience with Swami Radha and got some confirmation from him of what it was. In her spiritual searching, he became a tremendous point of focus, and from then on, she went to every talk of his that she could. Although Sarjit frequently accompanied her, she did not share the intensity of Jackie's passion. Sarjit wrote about this to Sobha Singh in February 1962. In reply to what he called her "enchanting letter," he had some advice: "So you have become regular listeners of Krishnaji, but I must tell you my child, that you are tiring yourself unnecessarily. What is [it] you lack? Should you run feverishly to every spiritualist whether he be Vinoba bai or Krishnamurti? Never try to know a person too [well] for everything loses its charm when fully known."[10] But Krishnamurti did not lose his charm for either sister.

Not many months after this, Kapoor suffered a major heart attack. This happened in Aur on 9 September 1962, and for the next year and a half he needed constant supervision, with his frailness compounded by the diabetes with which he had been contending since 1947. He badly wanted to see Canada again, and his family took him back to Vancouver for two months the following summer. Everyone understood that this was probably his last look at a country that meant so much to him, where he had lived most of his life and achieved such success despite great challenges. He loved the West Coast and especially the forest and lakes of his company's property on Vancouver Island. And he felt Canadian. As a young man he had chosen to be Canadian, and as far as he was concerned, he had been right.

He valued his friendships outside the Punjabi community, especially with Jim Armstrong, the real estate and insurance agent who had helped him purchase the mill property at Barnet and who had been a close companion ever since. Armstrong was the kind of friend who would come to the airport to greet him whenever he returned from India. Through such people, Kapoor had access to the best professional and legal help in the province. As a failing invalid in the summer of 1963, he was concerned about the future financing of the Aur hospital. He wanted tax-free credit from the Canadian government for the funds that his foundation would be transferring to India. The lawyer he sent to Ottawa to negotiate, successfully, with the tax department was Walter Owen, a past president of the Canadian Bar Association and a future lieutenant governor of BC. The immigrant who had once been rejected at the Canadian border at Blaine had come a long way.

While Kapoor passed his last summer in Canada, Krishnamurti gave ten lectures in the Swiss alpine village of Saanen, a short distance downstream from the international resort of Gstaad in the same picturesque valley. This annual event was Krishnamurti's main meeting for all Europe. He gave his lectures on rented land beside the rushing Saane River in a great domed tent designed by Buckminster Fuller, and that summer Yehudi Menuhin and his family attended as did Charles Lindberg and his wife. Jackie felt compelled to go, not for the company around Krishnamurti, but for the teacher himself and his teaching. She flew to Geneva and took the bus to Gstaad, where she booked into the venerable Park Hotel while Sarjit, with mixed feelings, stayed behind in Vancouver to care for their father. After one of Krishnamurti's talks, Jackie saw him by appointment and asked him about the states of mind she experienced during and after his lectures. She had her own analysis, which followed his teaching about self-observation, stripping away layers of consciousness and reaching a point beyond time and thought without duality. He assured her that she was on the right track. As she left, he asked what she had been doing since he last saw her in Delhi. She told him that her father had had a heart attack, and Krishnamurti was very sorry to hear that.[11]

In September, when the Siddoos left Vancouver for Delhi, they took their little dog, a red Pomeranian called Tiny, which had once belonged to their neighbours on York Avenue. Jackie and Sarjit saw Tiny as the kind of dog that would be good company for their father. The dog's owners were moving into an apartment, so Jackie and Sarjit adopted it. It quickly became an experienced traveller. Jackie wanted her father to have Krishnamurti's darshan (the heightened blessing and experience of being in his presence), so they broke their flight in Geneva and drove the 115-kilometre road to Gstaad and the Park Hotel. Krishnamurti was staying on in Gstaad after his Saanen talks and living in Chalet Tannegg, a large furnished house rented to him by one of his great friends, the aristocratic Italian widow Vanda Scaravelli. Jackie and Sarjit drove to the chalet with their parents and the dog, and asked at the door if Krishnamurti could see them. He graciously came out and said to Kapoor, "How do you do, sir." Kapoor, who was very ill by then, just smiled.

Five months later, on 16 February 1964, Kapoor died at their village home in Aur. Tiny was licking his fingers when he released his last breath. Her father's death, as Sarjit later wrote, left a great chasm in the family. She and Jackie felt both the loss of his moral support and the weight of his many responsibilities, which they now had to take over. Sarjit immediately found herself discharging some of her stress in a frustrating encounter with Indian bureaucracy. The local police station had reported Kapoor's death to the district authorities in Jalandhar, but a low-ranking local police officer, a *jamedar,* had filled out the form without checking with anyone. He had given Kapoor's age as ninety, although Kapoor was in fact only seventy-nine.

Sarjit discovered the mistake when she went to get a death certificate from the office of the surgeon general in Jalandhar. Getting it changed proved impossible, although she drove back and forth from Aur to the local police village, to the subdistrict capital of Nawanshahr, and to Jalandhar. She spoke to everyone she could think of – the jamedar, the *sarpanch* (village head), the *tehsildar* (chief official) in Nawanshahr, the surgeon general in Jalandhar, government attorneys, and the district deputy commissioner himself. The highest officials said they could not change what the jamedar had done; it was up to him; and the jamedar would not change anything without their express instructions. She presented the government attorneys with her father's Canadian passport, which listed his date of birth, but got a runaround without escape after the Nawanshahr tehsildar refused to accept anything but a birth or school certificate. After five weeks, she gave up and took the death certificate as it was, asking her lawyers in Canada to settle her father's estate with the inaccurate paperwork. Then she wrote a letter to Indira Gandhi describing at great length what had happened. "I can only thank God," she wrote "that it is not everyday that we have to meet these officials." She did not expect a reply and she did not get one.[12]

Kapoor's closest family in Canada were his younger brother, Tara, still in his Albert Street house near the demolished Barnet mill, and his nephew Kashmir, Bhagwan's son, who had managed the Barnet mill and then turned successfully to building apartments. But when the *Vancouver Sun* reported Kapoor's death, the person who supplied a statement for the obituary was his old friend, associate, and employee, Kartar Singh Hundal. Kartar Singh had left his job with Kapoor more than fifteen years earlier. This was after his marriage to Helene, the former wife of a UBC professor, when he was fifty-six and she much younger. They had children but the marriage did not last, and when Kapoor died, Kartar was living with his nephew Talminder on Adanac Street and maintaining his accounting office downtown on Granville Street.[13] He had many common causes with Kapoor and a shared political and philosophical perspective, but for the newspaper obituary he chose simply to speak of his qualities: "a very fine man ... an example to all of us ... quiet and humble ... said only what he meant ... you could turn to him for any sort of advice at any time."[14]

Back in 1959, Kartar Singh had written to Kapoor about Punjab's politics. Kartar Singh had never stopped crusading, but he was feeling his age and nursing tremendous disappointment with the current Sikh leadership in Punjab, both religious and political. He had been collecting documents on one case that illustrated the ugliness of the situation – the unbecoming schemes and conspiracies of the people at the top – and he wished to share this with Kapoor. He wrote his letter after Kapoor had returned from a visit to India, and he wanted to see him before Kapoor returned to India permanently. Kartar Singh no longer had a car, so he was using the mail to set up a meeting before undertaking the trip across town. Kapoor kept the letter and when his daughters read it years later, it seemed a sad testimony to the unhappiness of an activist who had lived to see the future and found it less than he had hoped for.[15]

In 1959, as Kapoor wound up his business in Canada and set up a charitable foundation to support the hospital in India, the Sikh community in Canada was entering a new age. The yearly quota of 150 immigrants that Pandia, Kartar, Kapoor, and their countrymen had wrested from the Canadian government in 1951 had made a difference. And with Pandia's leadership, they had managed to get it doubled in 1958. In 1963, just before Kapoor died, the quota disappeared altogether, and by 1967 Punjabis and other Indians were enjoying the same rights of entry as immigrants from Europe or the United States. Although a quota of 150 or even 300 immigrants does not seem like much, for a tiny community that had survived years of severe immigration restriction, it was something to celebrate. It meant that the Punjabi community was secure in Canada for the future.

In July and August of 1959, a British anthropologist, Adrian C. Mayer, taught summer school at UBC. He was already the author of several studies of Indians in India and Fiji; and each day of his summer course, when his class was over, he spent hours talking to Sikhs and other South Asians at their temples and their homes. At the end of the summer, he wrote a report and showed it to Marian Smith, the American ethnologist who had done a similar study back in 1943. In the telephone directory, Mayer found at least 108 and perhaps as many as 113 South Asian addresses in the Greater Vancouver area, most of them in Vancouver itself. Tiny as this population was, it was the greatest concentration of South Asians in the country. Remarkably, the addresses that Mayer mapped were not in a cluster or enclave but spread across the city.

He discovered that when South Asians bought homes and chose neighbourhoods in Vancouver, they looked mainly for value and also for closeness to work or school, and did not worry about being near other South Asians. They had cars and did not mind driving fifteen minutes or half an hour to see friends and relatives. Mayer, who had spent most of his life in London, where people had different priorities, observed that this behaviour was typical in Vancouver and not confined to South Asians. He noticed that Vancouverites generally had little to do with their neighbours. But the South Asians he met told him they got on well with the people next door or across the street, whether white or Chinese. Their children played together – as Jackie and Sarjit had done with their neighbourhood friends in the 1930s and 1940s – and adjacent households helped each other and visited at Christmas and New Year's. This they managed across cultural barriers. As one Sikh father told Mayer, he doubted that his children's playmates knew they spoke a different language at home. They were friends at one level and strangers at another.[16]

Mayer was conscious of two elements among the South Asians he met, one westernized and removed from village culture, and one not. Education, whether in India or Canada, made a big difference in westernization, and family life was producing a generation of Canadian children who drew their parents into the wider Canadian community. But Mayer got the impression that many Indian-born men, both old-timers and new arrivals, behaved as if they were still in rural Punjab, except they had more money, comfort, and freedom. These men brought village society with them, more or less intact. He saw an example of this at a picnic he attended with a group of Punjabis – a boisterous scene of card playing, rough wrestling sports such as kabadi, trials of strength, drinking, loud talking, and comments shouted (in Punjabi) at passing white girls. On the periphery were a number of educated men, immigrants from India who were teachers or civil servants and who spoke excellent English. Mayer noticed that they stood apart from the noisiest of their countrymen except to intervene occasionally to try to calm them down. The intervenors were aware, as the noisemakers were not, of the disapproving looks of the white picnickers around them.

Mayer did not interview Kapoor, who had gone back to India that May, but he did paint a picture of the Punjabi community in British Columbia at the moment of Kapoor's retirement. It was growing, although very small and still predominantly male, which helps explain what Mayer saw at his picnic. Kapoor had been a leader in this community for nearly half a century, and he had been a major part of its remarkable survival. He had always reached out to other Canadians, and it is unlikely that he would have enjoyed an equal business success otherwise. But he had helped to open Canada for other Punjabis. The people who benefited most came from his part of Punjab – when Mayer went through the pages of the Vancouver Island phone directory, he discovered that the majority of villagers listed there were from the Doaba area. These people had been drawn to Canada through village and family networks around Kapoor, Mayo, and their business partners. And the connection would strengthen in the decades that followed as more Doaba families came to Canada. In Kapoor's lifetime, most Canadians were barely aware of the Sikhs in their midst; his success helped to change that, even though he did not see it happen in his own lifetime.

16
Marriages and Losing a Mother

In Punjab, Jackie and Sarjit were neither insiders nor outsiders. They belonged to Punjab through their parents and through their family; and they spoke their mother's authentic rural dialect, a sweet, courteous, idiomatic (*theth*) Punjabi, although it was both refined and antiquated to the ears of native Punjabis who generally spoke bluntly, without graces and formalities. They had grown up abroad, and locals spotted them as foreign by their speech, manners, body language, and clothes. Around Aur they were known as the Canadian sisters who ran the "Canada-wallah" hospital. When they first built the hospital, the villagers did not expect them to stay and expressed surprise when they actually came back after their first summer's absence. Over time they proved their seriousness about serving in the hospital. And as the years passed, their roots in Punjab strengthened, although they never became Punjabis like the people around them.

Five months after her father died, Sarjit married a Punjabi, and sixteen months after that, Jackie did as well. They had not had men as friends before, other than their father or their cousins and uncles, and in their late thirties, they had not expected to marry and did not think they wanted to. At one time, Sarjit had imagined having many children – she liked the fun her cousins had in their large families – but that ambition had long passed. A friend of their father had once suggested a few possible matches, but the sisters had not been interested. When they did choose to have husbands, they surprised themselves. Jackie was six months past her fortieth birthday, seven years older then their mother had been when she came to Canada to join their father.

The man whom Sarjit married – taking that step ahead of her sister – was Avtar S. Atwal, an associate professor of zoology and entomology at the Punjab Agricultural University in Ludhiana, who was almost her age and still a bachelor. She met him shortly before her father died. Sarjit remembered it as follows: She used to go to Ludhiana to buy fruit and vegetables, happy to seize any excuse to go shopping in town. And she would buy medications for the hospital at a chemist shop on Pindi Street, the main medicine bazaar in Ludhiana and in all Punjab. Significantly, she was accompanied on these expeditions by a companion who had a knack for matchmaking, for fanning the slightest suggestion of romantic interest. This was Krishna Sharma, now Krishna Bharadwaj, the neighbours' daughter – now twenty-three and married – who had attached herself to the Siddoo family years before. When Avtar saw Sarjit and Krishna at a fruit stall in the Ludhiana bazaar, Sarjit caught his attention, with her short foreign hairstyle, lack of makeup or jewellery, and print dress worn over wide salwar trousers, a practical but unusual outfit for the time, mixing East and West. "I must have been an odd sight," Sarjit says, but she attracted Avtar nonetheless. After that, he brought a Canadian associate to see the Aur hospital, and there were more meetings, with encouragement from Krishna, leading to their marriage on 25 June 1964.

This was Sarjit's version of the story, as she told it without making much of it. Avtar remembered it a little differently but also gave a very plain account. The Siddoos still owned the seven acres of land in Phagwara that they originally intended for a hospital. They were farming it and having a problem with pests. And they had a large orchard, garden, fields, and milk cows on the hospital property in Aur. They came to Avtar's department several times for advice, and he helped by sending his people to examine the pest infestation at Phagwara and by directing them to experts in the university's horticultural department and veterinary clinic. The most vivid moment for him was his first meeting with Sarjit and her father, near the end of 1963 when he was temporarily an acting dean. Someone came running with the news that a very important person from Canada had arrived at the university entrance, so Avtar went out to introduce himself to Kapoor and Sarjit. He showed them around the grounds and gave them tea in his office. Kapoor, who was not well, spoke with such difficulty that Avtar kept the conversation short, not to tire him. Two months later, Avtar read in the paper that Kapoor had passed away, so he went to Aur to offer his condolences. With the encouragement of Krishna, the go-between, he saw more of Sarjit, and without fanfare or drama they decided to marry.

They were married in a quiet Sikh ceremony in the courtyard of the qila at Aur, with the prescribed Sikh verses and the singing of the *lavan* hymn while they circled the holy book, *Guru Granth Sahib.* After the service there was the traditional lineup of guests, who congratulated the newlyweds and gave them gifts of cash. The wedding did not require much organization. Avtar's brother-in-law attended as did other members of his family; and Kapoor's old friend Bhai Piara Singh helped with arrangements, expressing his great pleasure in the marriage. Sarjit had asked her mother if she should get married, and she had said, "It is up to you." After the ceremony, Sarjit and Avtar went back to his home in Ludhiana on the university campus for a party with his family, which Sarjit found a bit overwhelming. The next day she returned to Aur and the home she shared with her mother now that Jackie had taken up residence in the doctor's suite in the hospital. There was no honeymoon. Avtar had his work at the university and Sarjit had the hospital and they carried on with that.

Sarjit says that she was drawn to Avtar because he was a professor who spoke fluent English and had an educated mind and an international outlook. Ironically, he did not like to hear her speak Punjabi, because she sounded so rural. He would rather she used Hindi – like many urban Punjabis – or kept to English and sounded educated. He had studied abroad and knew Australia and Canada well. But what impressed Sarjit was his dedication to his work and his country. He had ignored the lure and the pay of the West and had come home to serve Punjab.

Avtar's family was from the village of Pharala, twenty kilometres northwest of Aur.[1] His grandfather had been a lambardar (tax collector) and a zaildar (headman) under the British, collecting government taxes in Pharala and the surrounding villages; and Avtar's family still owned land in Pharala. But Avtar himself was born in Khanewal in what was to become Pakistan, in the Multan District of West Punjab. His father was a veterinary assistant surgeon in government service, and Avtar's early memories were of the ten-acre walled grounds of the veterinary hospital in Khanewal, where his family lived and where the main work of the veterinary service seemed to be the castration of bullocks brought in by local farmers. His father, an assistant to the director, was often away travelling. This ended when his father lost his eyesight overnight due to cataracts and retired to the thriving British-built industrial city of Lyallpur (now Faisalabad), where Avtar's oldest brother was working and studying at the Agricultural

College. (His father later regained the sight in one eye.) In Lyallpur, Avtar completed his secondary schooling and went on to the Agricultural College. He wrote his final exams at the age of twenty in March 1947 when his normally peaceful student life was increasingly unsettled by reports of terrible disturbances throughout Punjab, intercommunity violence that pitted Hindus and Sikhs against Muslims. He got his results before Partition, when they were published in the *Lahore Civil and Military Gazette.* He was a gold medallist, standing first in the college.

Like everyone else in Punjab, his family could only guess at the probable location of the India-Pakistan border, which was not announced until midnight on the eve of Partition. They had wondered whether Lahore, the provincial capital, would go to India, but they had no doubt that Lyallpur, where they lived, would be in Pakistan. Fortunately, that spring and summer, they remained undisturbed in their own neighbourhood. But they did not feel safe. From the roof where they slept on hot summer nights, they heard the nearby shouting of a Muslim crowd. That was the cause of a nervous encounter with the police after their Sikh landlord had fired a shot into the dark night air. That encounter made his father and many in the family decide to leave immediately the next day, loading everything they could – clothes, supplies, furniture, firewood, two cows and a calf – onto a railway wagon, while taking seats themselves on passenger carriages.

Avtar stayed behind in Lyallpur to help his brother finish his master of science thesis on the agronomy of cotton. Avtar did the drawings for the thesis, completing them on 10 August, five days before Partition, which gave him three days to pack before leaving by train. Two days after Partition, his brother followed by bus with his wife and two children, and they made it safely to the Indian side despite a threatening brush with a Muslim crowd in Lahore. Avtar had another, unmarried, brother in Lyallpur, who was delayed by a bout of chicken pox but who managed to get out on a private plane that flew daily from a makeshift military aerodrome. Once in India, Avtar made for the old village home of Pharala. This experience left him with a lasting memory of the speed with which a peaceful countryside could descend into barbarity and chaos. And he saw it on both sides of the border. Adjoining Pharala was the vacated Muslim village of Beharam. Its people had left their homes without a fight, just as he had left his, and for weeks after Partition, he could see them and Muslims from other villages waiting in temporary camps for military escorts to take them to Pakistan. On a bus to Jalandhar, where his older brother had resettled, Avtar saw the gruesome remains of a riverside Muslim camp laid waste by a flash flood that had swept away the occupants and their livestock – a natural disaster compounding one made by man.

Avtar's education gave him an advantage in finding work in a country choked with refugees. He went to the improvised offices of the Relief and Rehabilitation Department in Jalandhar and spoke to the director general. With the huge influx of refugees, this department had become a growth area of government. The director general had many openings and could have made Avtar an officer's assistant on the spot. But he also told him that the British tradition of India's public service was that the top student in a graduating class automatically got a government job. He thought that Avtar should use that to obtain a post in agriculture, the subject he had studied. Avtar took his advice, and after a struggle with the bureaucracy, got a position in Jalandhar in the Department of Agriculture as an assistant researcher on the control of insects. Entomology had been his specialization during his last year at college.

His superiors assigned him to research the use of the new commercial insecticides DDT and BHC. But within a few months, he transferred – within the Department of Agriculture – to a fledgling agricultural college in Ludhiana, where he joined a nucleus of faculty and students from his old college in Lyallpur, all refugees. The college opened in 1948 in rented high school buildings, and he began on its first day as an instructor. Three years later, he won a scholarship for research in Australia, taking leave from his college. Under the newly instituted Colombo Plan – which had begun as an exclusively British Commonwealth development program – Australia was offering scholarships to students from India, Pakistan, and Ceylon. Avtar and three of his colleagues from Ludhiana applied in the first year, and they were successful. His first-place standing at Lyallpur made the difference. His three colleagues had also finished first in their years. The scholarship took him to Adelaide and the Waite Agricultural Research Institute, where by the end of 1953, after two years, he had earned a PhD for research on the reproduction of the cabbage worm. He found the institute a congenial place, helped by its compact and intimate layout, and a tradition of morning tea that brought everyone together socially once a day. Australia still maintained a "whites only" immigration policy (with South Asian students a recent exception), but the people he knew at the institute did not like the policy. Any mention of it embarrassed them.

A few months after returning to India, he won a post-doctoral fellowship from the National Research Council in Canada. This put him in the prairie town of Lethbridge, Alberta, at the largest of the federal Department of Agriculture's many research stations, which had a staff of about a hundred, including fifty research scientists. His project, focusing on moth damage to stored grain, required tracking the winter temperature conditions under which grain moths survived. He made good friends with the administrative officer at the station, a Dutch Canadian of about his age named Cleophus (Cleo) Gubbels, who was from a large family of brothers and sisters in Victoria. Lethbridge would have been hard to manage without a car, and Gubbels encouraged him to spend some of his fellowship money on a 1951 Chevrolet. (In Australia he had squeezed enough from his scholarship to buy a shiny new Czech-built maroon Jawa motorcycle, and the exotic image of a bearded and turbaned Sikh on his bike in full riding gear had warranted a picture in the Adelaide paper.)

Avtar's Chevrolet was more reliable than Gubbels' car, and together they used it for a lot of winter driving, including a memorable Christmas trip through the mountains to Vancouver with two colleagues, all four taking turns at the wheel. Avtar had the names of some Sikh families in Vancouver, called one of them, and got a place to stay. While in Vancouver, he visited the old Khalsa Diwan Society gurdwara built by the first Sikh immigrants and the breakaway Akali Singh gurdwara, which was still in a converted church. He met some of the old-timers such as Balwant Singh, who had worked with a horse and plough levelling Vancouver's Hastings Street before the First World War; and he made connections in the local Sikh community, both with those who had done well and an isolated group who had not made much money and who were living – as he saw it – humble lives. Altogether, when he looked back, he remembered his two years in Canada as a good time.

In 1957, on his return to India, Avtar found himself in a private war with the Punjab Department of Agriculture. The department expected him to take up his old position as an instructor at Ludhiana, but with no promotion or salary increase – no recognition of his Australian PhD or his postdoctoral work in Canada. He defiantly took a senior position in entomology elsewhere, at a college in Hoshiarpur that was affiliated with Punjab University in Chandigarh. Once he had settled in at Hoshiarpur he persistently refused orders to report back to Ludhiana. Then came a letter from the government secretary threatening "discipline" and advice from an experienced colleague that "they now mean business." Late in 1958, he returned to Ludhiana, but with some satisfaction because he was now an assistant professor. His intransigence had won him a promotion.

He was there to take part in a great expansion of the college in Ludhiana, to see a beautiful campus emerging on six hundred hectares of semi-arid land that had been vacated in 1947 by Muslim villagers. The first permanent building went up in 1958, the year he returned. A canal brought water for the demonstration farm and for the general greening of the campus. American aid money brought in equipment – although the college had to use bullocks for three years until it got its first tractor. American experts visited to give advice to senior faculty, and either Punjab's minister of agriculture or the government secretary phoned daily to check on progress. The Department of Agriculture steadily transferred its own research capacity to the college, and the Public Service Commission elevated it to a post-graduate college in 1958 and a university in 1962. It was on its way to becoming one of the finest agricultural research institutions in Asia.

Young foreign-trained PhDs like Avtar were critically important in turning a small undergraduate college into a large research institution. They knew it and were disturbed when less-qualified people with more seniority got promotions ahead of them. This happened to Avtar twice in quick succession. His department had gained two professorships in entomology, but neither went to him, although he was supervising most of the graduate students. After the first disappointment, opportunity delivered an extraordinary session with the chief minister, Pratap Singh Kairon. This was before Avtar knew Sarjit or of her contact with Kairon. Avtar's opportunity came because he knew Kairon's son Surinder. He had been called by Surinder for an informal discussion with Kairon. They met in a government rest house near the campus, and Avtar biked over to answer Kairon's questions about the college, the progress of its buildings, its equipment, the role of the American experts, the faculty who had been trained abroad, the development of its academic infrastructure, and what must be done to start agricultural industries such as poultry farming, milk plants, and fertilizer outlets. Then came a question out of the blue: were the right people being chosen for the right positions in a fair way? Avtar's body language gave him away. He did not think so, and Kairon quickly got him to speak of his own case. "Come and see me," Kairon said, "before you are interviewed for the next position."

Because the college was under the Department of Agriculture and its staff were civil servants, its appointments came under Punjab's Civil Service Commission. This would change when the college became a university and was run like a North American university. Kairon knew the change was on its way, which encouraged him to help Avtar. It was also Kairon's nature to get involved. For his part, Avtar was nervous about speaking to the chief minister, even with an invitation, because the civil service code barred lobbying ministers, let alone chief ministers, for promotion. Gathering his courage, he saw Kairon before his interview for the second professorship, and he went back again upon learning that he had not received it. This time, Kairon called the chair of the Civil Service Commission and asked for an explanation of its decision, with Avtar in the room. The explanation was that the other candidate had more seniority, to which Kairon replied, "If that is all you are looking at, I don't need your commission. I could do the appointments myself."

The commission had made a decision and Kairon left it alone, but he ordered a state appointment for Avtar, making him the state entomologist and locust control officer while leaving him in his academic position and putting him into the headship of his department. Avtar was now a leader of the team of agricultural scientists whose work would enable Punjab's Green Revolution of the 1970s.

With locust control, he had a dramatic start. He assumed the job at the precise moment a long-expected locust swarm entered Punjab, the culmination of a cycle of locust infestations that had spread from Africa over the previous eighteen months. The Indian government was prepared with the purchase of two Canadian Beaver aircraft for aerial spraying, and Avtar's first duty was to make the long drive to New Delhi and its old Safdarjang airport to requisition one of the Beavers. He expected no more than to have a look-see at the cockpit, but to his surprise the pilot took off once he was seated and flew all the way to Ludhiana, circling to find an empty patch of ground and then landing. As a consequence, Avtar was able to sleep in his own bed that night, and the next day he launched the first aerial spraying campaign in Indian history, using an abandoned military airfield at Sangrur, south of Ludhiana. He coordinated the support of the civil authorities and the police, requisitioned drums of insecticide and the trucking needed to bring it to the airfield, and flew with the pilot on low sorties over swarms that could stretch for four or five kilometres, clipping the tops of trees and landing with leaves tangled in the aircraft wheels. The pilot liked to fly lower than necessary to impress his passenger. In three intensive weeks, they brought that cycle of locust infestation to an end.

Avtar had been head of his department for four years when he married Sarjit, and he was firmly established in Ludhiana with a residence at the university. But Ludhiana was near enough to Aur for Sarjit to live on the campus and work at the hospital. They hired a driver, which made the commute easier, although he was a chain-smoker and in that respect less than ideal. She was thrilled to be in a university environment while simultaneously serving her patients at Aur, and felt at home in both places. Since starting medical school in Toronto, she had spent her life in hospitals and at universities. Marriage, she later wrote, was a difficult adjustment, especially at the age of thirty-seven. She was not a typical Indian wife and found the expectations of her husband, in-laws, and their friends extraordinary and foreign. Yet, when she decided to get married, she became determined that Jackie should follow suit. And she did her bit to make it happen.

Her matchmaking began with the green Fiat purchased back in 1959. For honest maintenance, the Fiat dealer had recommended a repair shop in Jalandhar managed by Donny Luther, a Punjabi Christian. Sarjit looked after the car, so she got to know Donny in his role as auto-shop manager, always costumed in a blue smock like a doctor's. He was more than friendly and invariably sent out for *pakoras* to share whenever Sarjit turned up. On the day she told him she was getting married, he looked shocked. Subsequently, she was inspired to "put a bee in his bonnet" by telling him she had a sister.

Donny was one of three siblings from an evangelical Christian family, members of a tiny minority in Punjab's population and Christians by conversion two generations before. One of his grandfathers had been a Muslim Pashtun from Afghanistan, and the other was a Sikh of the Bedi clan – the clan of Guru Nanak, founder of Sikhism. Both grandfathers had converted, for which they paid a stiff price. Their Muslim and Sikh families had not accepted it and had broken off with them, although Donny's Pashtun grandfather had eventually reconciled with his family after it fell on hard times and came to him for help and shelter. This grandfather had married the daughter of an Anglo-Indian missionary and his Burmese wife, a branch of the family tree that connected Donny to people of prominence among Punjab's Christians.

Sarjit told Donny that she had a sister just before leaving for Vancouver with her mother. He lost no time in going to the hospital at Aur and asking for Jackie. And he accomplished his mission by igniting a friendship from the moment she came down from her suite to meet him. Early in this friendship, they took a trip to Dalhousie, the hill station that had been the summer capital of Punjab under the British and that was enjoying a recent revival as a tourist destination. They brought Sarjit's dog Tashi and Jackie's dog Tiny, and while they were waiting at a construction roadblock, Tashi crawled out the open car window and disappeared. In

Vancouver, Besant Kaur and Sarjit learned of this in two telegrams that arrived in reverse order. The first read "Tashi found" and the second "Tashi lost." Donny had recovered the dog in a nearby village. Tashi strayed again when Donny and Jackie took a trip to Chandigarh. There, Donny stayed in a Radhaswami *dera,* a temple-hostel in which anyone, Christian, Sikh, or Hindu, was welcome. Tashi absconded and Donny found him by chance on the street.

These stories about Tashi alerted Besant Kaur and Sarjit that Donny was becoming a feature in Jackie's life. When they returned from Vancouver that fall, Donny came down to meet them at the Ashoka Hotel in Delhi, where they always stayed the first night before travelling to Punjab. This was his introduction to Besant Kaur. She never said to Jackie, "You cannot marry him," even if she worried that he would try to convert her to Christianity. Instead, she reached out to him by exercising her penchant for changing people's names. A few of the names had stuck. She called him Inderjit, although he preferred Donny, which is what he stayed. But he was willing to give up his last name and legally changed it from Luther to Siddoo, so he was Donny Siddoo when he married Jackie. This was in October of 1965 in a Sikh ceremony – like Sarjit and Avtar's – in the courtyard of the qila.

Donny did not share Jackie's interest in Krishnamurti and objected to her attendance at his lectures. In July 1966, she managed to take him to Gstaad for a holiday and she spotted Krishnamurti on the main street while they were walking Tiny. She ran across the street with the dog to greet him. A year later Donny finally relented, and she was back at the Saanen lectures. As she has said, she simply could not stay away. After that, Donny always went on the annual pilgrimage to Switzerland. He ignored the lectures but loved the place and the local Swiss townspeople, whom he got to know well.[2]

The next year in July, Sarjit gave birth to a girl at Grace Memorial Hospital in Vancouver. She had timed her return from India so that the baby would be born in Canada. Besant Kaur hired an English nanny for her after Sarjit declared herself "hopeless" at looking after a newborn. The nanny happened to be both buxom and blond, which meant she was left behind that fall when Sarjit, Besant Kaur, and baby went to India. The nanny was disappointed, but Sarjit was adamant. She thought that such a voluptuous blond would be trouble in a country full of Indian men with expectations – from everything they had heard – that Western women were free and available.

Besant Kaur named the baby Chandramapatti, which means "the moon has risen in our home." Everyone settled on Chanda for short. Chanda grew up familiar with homes on either side of the world, the York Avenue house, the qila in Aur, and her father's home on the Ludhiana campus. Until she was nine, the most constant and influential person in her life was her Maji, her grandmother Besant Kaur, who was with her constantly, in Canada and in India, telling her the stories she knew so well and teaching her marvellous things. When she was five, she started school in Vancouver. Avtar wanted her to attend an elite private school in India, but Sarjit insisted that she have a Canadian education.

A private Catholic school in Vancouver was the compromise, so Chanda was enrolled as a very small girl under the instruction of black-habited nuns at the Convent of the Sacred Heart, an all-girls school.[3] After two years, Sarjit moved her to St. Anthony's Elementary School in West Vancouver, a co-educational Catholic school, where the nuns did not wear habits. When the family went back to India each year – some time after Halloween when Sarjit would put on a big party for Chanda's class – Sarjit brought books and lessons from the nuns, and she tutored Chanda at home in Aur and make her do homework. But the difference between one environment and the other was huge. St. Anthony's meant regimentation and discipline; and life in Aur and in her father's home at Ludhiana meant liberation. Each year, Sarjit made sure that they returned to Canada before school closed for the summer so that Chanda would be eligible to go into the next grade.

Chanda liked the children at St. Anthony's but not the atmosphere and especially not the religion class, where the nun said that only good Catholics went to heaven. Chanda asked, "What happens if you are a good person? Do you still go to heaven even if you are not a Catholic?" "No," the nun answered, "you go to purgatory." After school, her little friend Jane Trojan, from a skeptical Catholic home, offered the advice not to worry, it was all garbage.

When Chanda was in grade six, Sarjit and Jackie began planning a Krishnamurti school on Vancouver Island. It opened the next year on a spectacular oceanfront property on Swanwick Road, half an hour's drive from the centre of Victoria, with three cabins and a main house in a setting of forest, field, orchard, and garden. Chanda, aged eleven, was the youngest of ten students at the school, which, with the cook, grounds-keeper, handyman, and teachers, had a staff as large as the student body. A few students were from Victoria, others from Alberta and California, and all were children of parents who followed Krishnamurti. Chanda found the school exciting, and she embraced the principles that Krishnamurti had set out – allowing students to develop in their own direction at their own pace, with no competition and no comparison between them.

The school was Jackie's idea, and she insisted that it be created. "You have a daughter and you have to do something for her," she told her sister repeatedly.[4] Together, they bought the property and paid most of the cost of staffing and running the school. Avtar, who was not involved, expressed great doubts, which Krishnamurti must have sensed. In Ojai, California, when Jackie and Sarjit talked to him about the school, he said, "Your husbands may not be interested. How will you manage that?" Nonetheless, he gave the school his blessing and came to Vancouver Island to walk in the Kapoor forest at Wolf Lake, where the sisters first wanted to build. They dropped that idea after their architect told them that developing the location would be too expensive. Still, they kept the name Wolf Lake for the school they started on Swanwick Road.

Later, when Krishnamurti visited the school, Jackie and Sarjit found themselves complaining that their teenaged students were out of control. (In one escapade, three boys took Sarjit's car for a midnight ride; they pushed it up the road to get out of earshot before starting it up; and then they ran into the police who happened to be out looking for escapees from nearby William Head Prison.) Krishnamurti heard of that kind of behaviour and called for a piece of paper, "No, a big one," and sitting on the edge of his bed dictated rules for students at the school, including no meat eating, no smoking, no drugs, and no sex. In making rules, Sarjit observed, he set off shock waves among his friends and followers around the world, who exclaimed, "How did he do that? It's against his principles." But experience and age seemed to be reshaping his thinking.[5]

The Wolf Lake School had attracted several young teachers and students imbued with the youth culture of the post-sixties world. When Chanda was fourteen, Jackie and Sarjit closed it down after learning of one teacher's year-long affair with a student and his open advocacy of sex to relieve frustration, of another teacher's assumption that describing her sexual adventures to her class was appropriate, of the boldness of six boys and girls who had slept together, and of the conduct of a boy who brought marijuana into the school.[6] Sarjit was appalled, more so than Jackie, who shared some of Krishnamurti's tolerance of sexual goings-on. But neither of them were willing to perpetuate the situation. After discussing it with Krishnamurti at a meeting in Ojai, they shut the school down. This was not the environment that Sarjit wanted for Chanda.[7]

After this, Sarjit sent Chanda to Brockwood Park, the Krishnamurti residential school in rural Hampshire, England. At Brockwood Park, the seventy to one hundred students were very international; most came from Western Europe, but every major continent was represented. Krishnamurti spent part of the year in residence and took his meals at the head table in the dining hall. Chanda and the other students used to meet with him, and from the perspective of youth, he seemed old, tired, and sometimes irritable. Chanda had had a real taste of alternative schooling at Wolf Lake and found Brockwood Park rather standard: "Here is your lesson, now recite it back." She asked Krishnamurti how such regimented classes could accord with his vision, but he did not seem to think she had much of a point. Education, he seemed to say, was just something you had to get on with.[8]

Chanda's years at the Wolf Lake School and Brockwood Park came after Besant Kaur's death in Aur at the age of eighty-five on 20 January 1975. A year and a half earlier, she had developed a chill and pneumonia while travelling to India. She was at Orly airport in Paris, parked in a wheelchair – because of her arthritis – and waiting for Sarjit and Avtar while they got a visa for Avtar for a night in transit in Paris. During the hour they left her, she collapsed. Staff took her to emergency at the airport and paged Sarjit, who called Jackie in Gstaad. The doctors at Orly wanted to hospitalize her for observation, but on Jackie's advice, Sarjit took her to Gstaad, where they could look after her together. This seemed the right decision, for she was much better after twenty-four hours. But she was frail from then on.

In December 1974, Jackie phoned from Aur to tell Sarjit that Besant Kaur was asking for her. She and Chanda flew out of Vancouver the next day, and when they reached Aur, Besant Kaur seemed to rally. Avtar was then the vice-chancellor in charge of planning a new agricultural university in Jammu and serving as adviser to the government of Jammu and Kashmir. He asked Sarjit to come to Jammu, and feeling they had passed a crisis with her mother, she went. A few days later, when she returned to Aur, her mother was dying and refusing all nourishment. Sarjit felt tremendous guilt for being away at that last critical time, but she was with her sister by her mother's bedside before the end.

Besant Kaur's life began and ended in the qila at Aur, although she had lived half of it in Canada, from her early thirties until she was nearly seventy, travelling back and forth after that. In Canada and India, she possessed an honoured and respected place among her own people, earned by her personality and demanded by her position. She was a jagirdar's daughter, proud of her family's past and protective of the next generation – her daughters and their cousins. And she was a pioneer among Indo-Canadian women as well as a guide and arbiter in a small Punjabi society far from home. She had travelled widely with her family and had entertained swamis, sants, diplomats, scholars, her husband's professional and business associates, her daughter's teachers, friends and family, and neighbours, especially their children. One neighbour, the widower and retired merchant seaman Alfred Tremeer, she had taken into her house and incorporated into her family for several years. All this she managed without ever learning much English but helped by a deeply religious spirit that embraced all humanity.

The stories told by the family about Besant Kaur illustrate what they admired in her. When she was about eighty, Avtar happened to be in the York Avenue house when three Sikhs came by appointment to see her. She asked him to be present, so he sat quietly in a corner. They wanted her to contribute to a building fund for a new Vancouver gurdwara to replace the historic one on Second Avenue, which dated from 1908, and they expected her to make the largest donation. The new gurdwara, designed by the internationally famous BC architect Arthur Erickson, opened on Ross Street in 1970, but the occasion that Avtar witnessed occurred a few years before. The three Sikhs, two bearded and one clean-shaven, had come as a group to show that modernists and traditionalists were now working together. They had anticipated a positive response to their request. And indeed, Besant Kaur said she would contribute "if you are all together." But when she left the room to write a cheque, one of the visitors became a little aggressive. Avtar was wearing a turban, as always, but he had groomed his beard, contrary to the strictures of the traditionalists. The aggressive one said, not very subtly, "What is the use of Sikhs today, they trim their beards." He would never have said this in Besant Kaur's presence, though she overheard a few of his words as she re-entered the room. Nonetheless, she said nothing, presenting the cheque as promised. For Avtar, this episode illustrated the quiet strength of her personality and her firm but motherly role in the community.[9]

A little earlier, when Chanda was still a baby and the family was in Aur, one of Avtar's relatives telephoned with the news that Avtar's eldest brother was seriously ill. Even though he was in Ludhiana and it was the middle of the night, Sarjit felt that she must go immediately. Besant Kaur did not like this, but said that if Sarjit went, she and the cook boy would go with her. On the way they encountered *dacoits* (robbers), who stepped out of a cornfield with rifles or shotguns and signaled them to stop. When the *dacoits* came up beside the car and saw Besant Kaur sitting in the front passenger seat, they hesitated. They knew her, and out of respect for her they stepped aside and waved the car through.[10]

For Sarjit, facing down dacoits on a dark road was her mother as she had always been. Months earlier, upon learning of an intruder in the back yard at York Avenue, Besant had fetched a gun and plunged into the night to see who it was. But the encounter with the dacoits was also an example of her gift of premonition: she knew she would be needed, and she was right.

Besant Kaur often seemed to anticipate future events or to sense danger to her relatives, even when they were on the other side of the world. But she made little of it and was not a believer in fortune tellers, astrology, or evil spirits. When friends told her of their occult experiences, she insisted she had never seen anything like that and told them that fear could be dispelled by centring oneself in the recitation of God's name. To her final days, she maintained her daily prayers and her continuous telling of the beads of her mala. In her last words with her daughters, she thanked them for the care they had given her, told them to take good care of Chanda, whom she loved, and said that all must leave this earth when their moment came. Nobody wished to go, she said, but none had a choice.

As far as family or friends could see, nothing unsettled Besant Kaur's essential nature or her understanding of life. After she emigrated, she remained unchanged, with the same acceptance of other faiths and the same comfort with her own. She taught her daughters a love of Hindu and Sikh traditions, and a natural respect for those of others. Where she drew the line and became protective was at the moment when someone began seeking converts. According to her indisputable logic, all paths led to the same truth, so conversion was not required, an approach that kept her centred on what she knew and had always known. In keeping a tight rein on her daughters and in her unwillingness to see them mix with the opposite sex, she was a typical Punjabi mother. But her expectations of them were far from typical. Under her influence, Jackie and Sarjit grew up as unconventional women – whether from a Canadian or a Punjabi perspective – and when they eventually married, they made their own independent, and especially with Jackie, unconventional choices. They found husbands in Punjab without guidance or direction from their mother, but she was in the background as the woman who had shaped their choices from childhood.

17
Canada and India

December 2012 marks a century since Kapoor entered Canada in Victoria after being turned back at the Blaine border crossing. He joined an expatriate South Asian community that numbered 2,300, according to the Canadian census. Soon, he saw it shrink to about 700 and then watched it take forty years to build back to 2,150. It shrank because immigrants experienced such difficulty in entering the country, because some lost their Canadian jobs and went home, and because so many of them answered the Gadar call to arms in 1914, returning to India for the failed Gadar rebellion. Then the community slowly regained people after the First World War when Ottawa began allowing wives and children to immigrate.

Kapoor witnessed all this during his first forty years in Canada, and in the dozen years before his death, he saw the beginnings of tremendous growth in the Indo-Canadian population as the main sources of Canadian immigration became truly global, shifting from Europe to Asia, the Caribbean, Africa, and South America. He would be amazed and gratified by the ethnic and racial diversity of present-day Canada, including the more than 1,250,000 people who trace their roots to the Indian subcontinent, who have built temples, mosques, and gurdwaras across the country, who are served by their own TV programs, radio stations, and periodicals, who patronize their own shops and shopping areas, who support their own vibrant cultural programs and organizations, and whose presence has so enriched Canadian culture. But he believed that such was Canada's future, and he did what he could to make it happen.

He might be surprised at the great diversity of present-day Canada's South Asian population, with people from many regions of India, Pakistan, Bangladesh, and Sri Lanka, as well as from overseas Indian settlements in the Caribbean, the South Pacific, Africa, and the United Kingdom. He would be impressed by the multitude of languages, customs, group stories, and religious traditions from South Asia now expressed in Canada. Even so, his people, the Punjabis, and especially the Punjabi Sikhs, have a special place in the country as the largest single group from South Asia with the longest history and the greatest presence. And among the Punjabis, the core community is still from Doaba and Malwa, the families whose Canadian pioneers – like Kapoor – arrived before the First World War and who eventually set in motion an immigration of offspring, siblings, cousins, brides, and grooms that continues to the present. He would have been a proud observer in the past twenty years as his community began exercising its political muscle, taking full advantage of its ability to organize its concentration of votes in a few metropolitan ridings in British Columbia, Alberta, and Ontario, and its possession of aspiring politicians with complete command of English and a ready understanding of the Canadian political system.[1]

Individuals from his part of Punjab have been in the forefront of a most successful Punjabi entry into Canadian national and provincial politics – nine Punjabi MPs were sent to Ottawa in 2009, in BC seven Punjabi MLAs were elected in 2005, and in Alberta five won their seats in 2007. No other visible minority has done so well. The four Punjabi Canadians who have achieved the greatest prominence, Moe Sihota, Ujjal Dosanjh, Herb Dhaliwal, and Wally Oppal, are from Doaba families. In a BC political career that began in 1986, Sihota became the first Indo-Canadian elected to a legislative assembly and the first to hold cabinet office. Dosanjh was premier of BC for fourteen months and a federal minister of health for two years. Dhaliwal, the first Punjabi and first Sikh in the federal cabinet, held his place there for six years until his party was voted out of office. And Oppal, who was BC's attorney general for four years, enjoyed a distinguished career as a provincial Supreme Court judge before that. The family villages of Dosanjh, Dhaliwal, and Oppal lie within twenty or twenty-five kilometres of Aur, a proximity that suggests the small size of the area from which most of Canada's Punjabis have come.[2]

This area, in the centre of India's Punjab, including part of Malwa and all of Doaba, extends no more than fifty to a hundred kilometres from Aur. It is contained within the boundaries of just six of Punjab's seventeen districts. There the influence and affluence of overseas Punjabis – in Britain and the United States as well as Canada – is readily seen, in the grand homes they build for retirement in their native villages, in the wedding palaces, with great banquet and reception halls, that serve them when they return for family weddings, in the gleaming new temples and shrines to which they have contributed and that dot the landscape, and in the depopulation of villages as their relatives follow them overseas. The Punjab government is well aware of the benefits that flow from emigrants overseas, who are commonly referred to as NRIs (non-resident Indians). It listens to their organized lobbying, especially regarding their property rights in Punjab, has special bank branches for them, and has promised fast-track courts and special police stations to deal with their cases – one police station for each district concerned: Jalandhar, Hoshiarpur, Kapurthala, Moga, Nawanshahr, and Ludhiana.[3]

Overseas Punjabis maintain an influence in their homeland out of proportion to their numbers, just as they did in Kapoor's day. That influence can promote modern improvements in Punjabi villages, and it can be the source of turmoil and upset, both at home and abroad. On the latter point, the money and moral support that many overseas Sikhs gave to the Khalistan movement of the 1980s and early 1990s was a large factor in the descent into violence, lawlessness, and criminality that gripped their state for over a decade. Ordinary Punjabis, caught in the middle between the police and Khalistani militants, terrorized by both, were generally relieved by the peace that settled in the countryside when the Punjab police finally got the upper hand. And expatriate Sikhs, whether they tried to stay on the sidelines or were actively involved, were themselves profoundly affected. They were apprehensive for their relatives at home and generally nervous about going back themselves. In those years, the number of Punjabi marriages arranged between Canada and India dropped precipitously. Only after the troubles were over did the full social and economic exchange between Canada and Punjab return to normal and then blossom as never before.

The years of trouble were difficult for Jackie and Sarjit. They continued their service in the hospital at Aur, their visits to Canada in the summers, and their stops in Switzerland for Krishnamurti's annual European lectures. Even after Indira Gandhi became prime minister, they tried to see her whenever they passed through Delhi. Gaining an audience with her was not so extraordinary, because she regularly made herself available to a long line of supplicants and well-wishers, rich and poor. When they first met her, they found her natural, approachable, and very helpful. But she changed as her time in office stretched on and she obviously became accustomed to the exercise of power. One visit took a strange turn. This was after June 1975 and during the twenty-one months of her "Emergency" rule when she had arrested her political opponents, suspended elections, and assumed dictatorial power. When Jackie and Sarjit went to see her, she looked worried and asked them for money. How does one react when the prime minister of India makes such a request? Sarjit had $3,000 in cash, which she had just withdrawn from the bank for travel expenses. She gave it to Mrs. Gandhi, who reached for her cloth shoulder bag and tucked the money into it without explanation or comment.

Indira Gandhi was back in power when Jackie, Sarjit, Chanda, and Avtar went to see her in the summer of 1980. The family has a photograph of this occasion. This was after she lost the election she called in 1977 and then rebuilt her popular base and returned to power with a huge majority. She was beginning her fourth and last term as prime minister, the one that ended with her assassination at the garden gate of her official residence, her life ended by pistol and machine gun at the hands of two of her Sikh bodyguards. In 1980 one could not have predicted that she would be an enemy to nearly the whole Sikh nation. But that is what she had become in early June 1984 when the Indian army, on her orders, carried out a full-scale assault on the Sikhs' Golden Temple in Amritsar – in pursuit of Sant Jarnail Singh Bhindranwale, the charismatic priest entrenched there with armed followers. The hundreds who died in the assault, code-named Operation Bluestar, and the sight of the Indian army's destruction of sacred and historic buildings in the Golden Temple complex, left even those Sikhs closest to Indira Gandhi feeling apprehensive, angry, and disconnected from their own country. From that moment, it was expected that some retaliation would come from some element of the Sikh community.

Chanda and Sarjit were present in India at the time and witnessed the national trauma that followed Gandhi's assassination. Chanda at eighteen had finished her schooling at Brockwood Park and had come to Delhi for a year to study the sitar, motivated by Avtar, who had introduced her to the instrument and who used to play his tapes of live performances for her. She was also somewhat unenthusiastically taking classical Indian vocal training, her mother's idea for improving her musical ear. To study the sitar, she went to the home of a Bengali professor who also taught at Delhi University and who performed internationally. For voice lessons, she had a diminutive but otherwise unmemorable Muslim teacher who came to her small rented flat and who was always late, with a different excuse each time. Her social life involved two aunts – her father's sisters

– and their families in Delhi, villagers from Aur who visited regularly, and two friends from the West, a schoolmate from Brockwood Park who turned up for a few weeks and a Canadian boy she met through the Canadian High Commission and saw a lot of.

Sarjit learned of Mrs. Gandhi's assassination a day after it happened. The news reached Aur on the radio, and Krishna Bharadwaj, her village friend and companion, told her about it. Sarjit's first question was whether a Sikh had done it. She knew there would be riots in the capital, but with no idea of what she could do about it herself she went on with a planned drive to Phagwara to see a cousin. When the news about Mrs. Gandhi simultaneously reached Avtar in Ludhiana, he sent a university car and driver to find Sarjit and to tell her to come to him immediately – no time to pack or gather a change of clothes. And when she reached his office, he told her to take a train to Delhi that night; he was worried about Chanda. Sarjit was annoyed that he was not going with her, but she understood better later on. He drove her to the station and as she remembered "literally pushed" her onto the train without a berth or reservation and with three instructions: don't speak Punjabi in Delhi; don't hire a Sikh taxi driver; and don't take a straight route to Chanda's flat. Having witnessed the violence of Partition in 1947, he knew what terrible things to expect. She did not, but once she got to Delhi she was thankful for his sake that he had not come.

So it was that Sarjit and Chanda witnessed the rioting, killing, and arson that raged throughout Delhi for ten days – Hindu mobs targeting Sikhs, unrestrained by curfew or by the army, the latter not firing a round to stop the violence or even showing itself for the first forty-eight hours. When Sarjit reached the New Delhi railway station in the early morning darkness, she found it packed with Sikh families gathered together for safety. She got a taxi operated by two clean-shaven "boys," but in her great apprehension forgot to tell them to take a round-about route and headed straight for Chanda's flat in Sarpriya Vihar in the south of the city. The pre-dawn streets were empty. On the far side of the Safdarjung Bridge she wanted to stop for a "beautiful young Sikh" who was standing by his taxi and waving for help, but her taxi driver and his front seat companion refused. They had not gone much further when a gang of fifteen *gunda*s (hoodlums) blocked the road shouting what everyone called the Sikhs, "Sardar, Sardar." Sarjit covered the Sikh bangle on her wrist while they looked in the car and trunk. She realized then that if Avtar had been with her, he would have been murdered on the spot.[4]

She was in the midst of a terror hidden from most of the country – unmentioned in the press or on television, where all attention was on Indira Gandhi and the endless procession of mourners filing past her body as she lay in state. And Chanda was not in her flat. The previous afternoon, Chanda had gone to play tennis with a twenty-year-old cousin who lived nearby in South Extension. When they became aware of the danger in the streets, she stayed with his family through the afternoon and evening, first in their house, and then, after a nerve-wracking dash by car, at another aunt's house, getting reports of approaching mobs armed with metal rods and gasoline cans and using voters' lists to locate Sikh residences. From the roof and in the full moonlight, Chanda and her aunt's family could see the red glow of fire in all directions, on the horizon and close at hand. In their chilling drive from one aunt's house to another, Chanda had glimpsed a fire-blackened shell of a bus and a donkey cart removing a charred corpse that trailed an unwound turban.

In the early morning, when they thought that even the gundas would be asleep, Hindu friends arrived to take Chanda, her aunt, uncle, cousin, and driver to their home on Pandara Road, a residential enclave for government employees and a safer place to shelter. These friends were a Brahman Hindu journalist and his wife. That was where Sarjit eventually found Chanda, reaching Pandara Road in a hired three-wheeled taxi driven by a Christian Indian. She had given up her first taxi at Chanda's flat, but she now had company – Krishna's son (a Hindu) from Aur, who was visiting Delhi and whom she found in the flat. They all stayed several days at the Pandara Road house until, feeling they were imposing too much, Sarjit sent a servant to find a taxi, which took him some time. Then she and Chanda braved the largely deserted midnight city, where truckloads of gundas still roamed, menacing and shouting, and set off for Chanda's flat. A block before they reached it, a gang stopped them and opened all the doors and trunk before letting them go. Again, they were certain that, had a Sikh male been with them, he would have been murdered.

When it was over and Sikhs slowly and cautiously emerged from hiding to take up their lives against a dark backdrop of burned-out cars, buses, scooters, and buildings, Chanda declared that she never wanted to be in India again. In fact, she stayed for the balance of that year and has been back frequently, but what she felt then was anger toward a country that fell so brutally short of its tolerant ideals. That anger was still with her two years later when she sat down at a typewriter in her father's Chandigarh home and wrote a fictionalized account of what she had seen, felt, and experienced.[5] This proved cathartic and though she put the finished manuscript in a drawer, it served its purpose.[6] In her account, she portrayed her relatives as divided about Indira Gandhi's death, her young cousin elated and her aunt worried. She put herself in her cousin's camp, saying at one point that "justice had been done" when Indira Gandhi was shot. This was directed towards a woman her family had met personally many times. In spite of her international upbringing, education, and friendships, Chanda had spent enough time in Punjab to assimilate the outrage felt by Sikhs after the attack on the Golden Temple, and she naturally identified with her Sikh heritage. And during the ten days of rioting, she believed she was seeing a spontaneous and general Hindu eruption against Sikhs. What she read later in the reports of independent investigators eventually convinced her that the rioting was the orchestrated work of unscrupulous politicians, functionaries, and paid thugs, and harrowing as it was, she eventually put it into perspective.[7]

In the turbulent decade after the assault on the Golden Temple, the assassination of Gandhi, and the Delhi riots, Jackie and Sarjit kept returning to Punjab, as did Chanda. It helped that Avtar held his post at the university in Ludhiana until 1986 and then joined the State Planning Board in Chandigarh where he served up to his retirement three years later. As an academic, he often had reasons to travel to North America, and after retirement he was free to go back and forth annually with Sarjit. Generally they flew with Jackie and Donny. But these were not easy times to travel. In Punjab, acts of terrorism – bombings, murders, shoot-outs with the police – were such a threat that normal civil government was suspended for over five years in the late 1980s and early 1990s, with the central government in Delhi running the state under the president's rule. It was war between Sikh militants from home and abroad and the Indian government. The bombing of Air India Flight 182 out of Montreal on 22 June 1985 was the most terrible moment of this war, but far from the end. All Sikhs abroad were affected because they had family in Punjab and because Indian officials viewed them with suspicion when they applied for passports or visas to go home.

In the worst of the troubles, Jackie and Sarjit had difficulty getting permission from the Indian government to enter Punjab. Without Avtar and the connections he had as dean of post-graduate studies at Ludhiana, and then as a full-time member of the State Planning Board, they might well have been kept out. And once they were in Punjab they found police and road blocks everywhere. Just in their regular coming and going from Aur, they were regularly stopped by police. And people from the cities and from outside the state were afraid to visit rural Punjab. It all made the normal life of the hospital impossible. The company that serviced the x-ray machine was in Kolcuta. When the troubles started, that company refused to send technicians to Punjab, and when the sisters had problems with the x-ray machine they had to send patients into Nawanshar. By then they had eliminated the wards and operating room and converted to an outpatient hospital only. Whatever dream they had of full hospital service died in these years, but they kept going with what they could do, which was to serve up to four hundred patients a day (in peak season), supplying them with free medicine and referring those they could not help to Ludhiana.

By the time Punjab returned to peace in 1993-94, Jackie and Sarjit were in their late sixties. They were not tempted to restore the hospital to its full original purpose, but they remained committed to serving there as their parents had wanted. Nearly a decade later, they were still spending several months a year in Aur and employing a full-time staff, including a doctor, year-round. But as Sarjit approached eighty and Avtar's health became a concern, she stopped attending the hospital, although she and Avtar went to India every year, spending the winter months in his house at Chandigarh. But into her eighties and up to the writing of this book, Jackie has continued to see her patients in Aur.

What the Siddoo sisters have done in Aur has won them great respect in that part of Punjab, especially among those who attempted to do anything similar. In the last few years this group has grown, but such was not always the case. In the closing years of the twentieth century, nearly all the money spent by expatriates in their native villages went to projects like building elaborate gateways at a village entrance, or temples, shrines, and monuments – which some critics in Punjab have dismissed as ego satisfaction for the donors, showing how well they have done overseas. But in the early years of the twenty-first century, expatriates have begun to direct significantly more money to socially beneficial projects, education, health care, sports facilities, and village improvements such as paved streets, sewerage, and drainage.[8] They are manifesting the political and social awareness of the earliest emigrants who, even before the First World War, were raising money for education. These included Kapoor and Bhai Piara Singh Langeri, who collected for village schools in the Doaba area and for a Khalsa high school in Jalandhar while they were still in California. And this sort of effort continued throughout the years among first- and second-generation emigrants in Canada and the United States, who sent money home to build schools or repair school roofs, or as the years passed, to bring in electricity, buy a water pump, or install toilets.

The idea of doing something for one's own village has always existed in Punjab. In the 1970s, in a great expansion of post-secondary education in Punjab, colleges were starting up or expanding at Mahalpur, where Kapoor had gone to school, at Garshankar, twenty kilometres to the south, at Banga, a half-hour drive north from Aur, and at Sang Dhesian, the same distance to the northwest. All these colleges sent fundraisers to Vancouver, Victoria, and other Punjabi settlements in North America. And as the overseas population has grown and prospered, the money it has raised for villages in Punjab has increased accordingly. But a lot did go for show.

That makes post-1999 developments in Kapoor's native village of Kharoudi most remarkable. In three years of concerted activity, the village installed concrete streets, solar street lighting, a covered sewer line to every house, a formal public park, and a secondary sewage treatment plant producing clear, safe water for a fish farm. This project, which transformed Kharoudi into a model village with an infrastructure to be envied by most of Punjab and India, owes its existence to two village expatriates – Dr. Gurdev Singh Gill, a retired medical doctor from New Westminster who was the first Indo-Canadian in private practice in British Columbia, and Ragbir S. Bassi, a vice-chancellor of Alaska Pacific University in Anchorage.

Chancing to visit Kharoudi at the same time, Gill and Bassi sat together over a drink one winter evening, sharing their dismay at the smell of sewage and the flies and mosquitoes around them – an environmental decline from the days of their youth. The downside of recent village progress had been the introduction of indoor plumbing and of an abundant water supply to many houses, without a covered sewerage system to carry it away. All would be clean and dry within the walls of a home, but not beyond. In the monsoon rains, the village was awash with sewage. Dr. Gill was all too aware of the diseases that bred in this environment, especially typhoid, hepatitis, and hookworm. He and Bassi contributed substantially themselves and raised about $2,500 each from thirty-one of Kharoudi's expatriate families, and then negotiated funding from the government of Punjab, overseeing the project themselves and firmly keeping government bureaucrats out of it. Dr. Gill judged that it was not just money that he and Dr. Bassi brought to the project but their knowledge and experience. And it was their knowledge and experience that made it go ahead.[9]

The more one travels in Punjab, the more one sees recent good work by expatriates. Former federal cabinet minister Herb Dhaliwal has followed the Kharoudi example in launching a development project in his ancestral village of Dhingrian. A sports stadium in Bhai Piara Singh's village of Langeri was built with money raised among Langeri-ites in Canada. The little village of Daulatpur, just a few kilometres northeast of Aur, has a new school, stadium, and auditorium as well as school buses and computers for its students thanks to the efforts of Kehar Singh Thandi, who raised funds among other village expatriates in Canada and the United States. The village of Kultham has a school with nearly four hundred students built year by year by a single retiree from Canada, Tara Singh Bains, out of his own pocket after a lifetime of working in BC sawmills. A new college has recently arisen at Chabewal, only ten kilometres from Mahalpur, through the efforts of a past president of the Vancouver Khalsa Diwan Society, Surjit Singh Singhpuria, and his brother. Many annual sports tournaments across Punjab depend on the endorsements of overseas Punjabis. One, in the village of Hakimpur, owes its existence entirely to the Purewal brothers of Pitt Meadows, BC.

A Nargis Dutt mobile hospital, based in Jalandhar and servicing Punjabi villages, has been paid for by Punjabis in Vancouver. In Banga, one finds a modern 250-bed hospital in the midst of rural countryside, one as fine as any city hospital, with a nursing school affiliated with the University of British Columbia. The thirty-two-acre complex includes trauma and detox centres as well as a large secondary school, all the dream – now realized – of a villager from near Banga, Budh Singh Dhahan, who worked for nineteen years in British Columbia before beginning his great project in 1984. Much of his funding comes from Canadian Punjabis through a registered society in Vancouver. Since laying a foundation stone in 1988, the Grewal family of Sarabha village in the Ludhiana District has developed an impressive medical college and hospital there, which combines ayurvedic training and modern medical treatment. Grewal family members in Britain, Canada, and the US have all contributed, with management currently in the hands of Avtar Singh Grewal of Toronto.[10]

In the heart of the Ludhiana District, one might also chance upon a bookmobile that calls twice a week at six villages. The only mobile library in Punjab, it was conceived, created, and paid for by Jaswant Singh, a retired librarian who immigrated to study in Canada many years ago and resettled in Michigan. Books and education are the great equalizer, he believes, and a library more important in a democracy than a church or gurdwara. He wished to see a library service for all Punjab, but failing that, is doing what he can himself.[11]

More developments are occurring than anyone can easily track, not even the NRI Sabha Punjab, the expatriate association that facilitates and records what Punjabis abroad are doing for their homeland. The NRI Sabha Punjab recently listed thirty-nine overseas-funded village projects in the Doaba area – in Jalandhar, Hoshiarpur, Nawanshahr, and Kapurthala – while conceding that complete information was hard to get.[12] Typically, these projects are launched by villagers who have settled in Canada, the United States, and Britain but whose first loyalties are to their own families, villages, and localities. Because they almost exclusively work through their own village networks in India and abroad, summarizing their projects requires a lot of investigating, phoning, and asking. But there is no doubt that the spirit and values that inspired Kapoor, Besant Kaur, and their daughters have manifested themselves among later emigrants. The Siddoos set an example that others are now following, consciously or unconsciously.

Kapoor always told his daughters that they must give to both Canada and India – to the country of their birth and the country of their ancestry. His former partner Mayo Singh contributed generously to hospitals and charities on Vancouver Island as well as to projects in his native village of Paldi, and in this respect, he and Kapoor had more in common than either easily admitted.[13] Kapoor's daughters took his words to heart. Their own personal and professional experience made health care and education priorities for them, so they funded scholarships in medicine, forestry, and ecology at UBC, and donated generously to several major hospitals in the Vancouver area, as well as to local charities. Their main mission in Canada, however, has been the Krishnamurti Educational Centre of Canada, which they have maintained since 1977 on Swanwick Road as a school and then a spiritual centre. When they closed the Wolf Lake School in 1981, they turned the property, with its six-bedroom main house, its auxiliary cottages with another six bedrooms, and its tennis court and swimming pool, into a spiritual retreat for groups and individuals – offering silent retreats, discussions, and lectures. When Jackie first drove Krishnamurti through its gates, his comment was, "This is like an English manor."[14] He appreciated the beauty, peace, and quiet of the setting, qualities that have helped it function admirably for nearly three decades, except for a temporary closure from 2004 to 2007. Krishnamurti's teachings lie at the core of the Swanwick Centre, where viewing and discussing his videotaped lectures form part of the daily program. The atmosphere is open-minded, consistent with Krishnamurti's teaching about freeing the mind to make it fresh and creative.[15]

For all these years – except during the closure – Jackie and Sarjit have maintained a staff of at least four to run the property and the retreats. When they need to feed large numbers, they bring in a cook. The food is vegetarian, a rule dating from the establishment of the centre, and one approved by Krishnamurti. The thirty-two-acre waterfront property includes a small farm with an apple, pear, and cherry orchard, vegetable garden, fields and meadow, and two milk cows and chickens (not for eating) – a counterpart to the farm on the hospital grounds at Aur. A staff member handles the farm work, and during retreats guests help with outdoor chores. During breaks, they can walk the nature paths in the woods or through wild broom bushes by the ocean, where they can enjoy the view across the water to the snow-capped mountains of the Olympic Peninsula in Washington State twenty-five kilometres away.

One of the speakers that Jackie and Ssrjit brought many times to the Swanwick Centre was Dr. Allen Anderson, senior professor of religious studies at San Diego State University. His eighteen videotaped dialogues with Krishnamurti – first aired on the American public television network in 1974 – are now classics, the most sold and listened-to Krishnamurti tapes ever made. Although Anderson had taught courses on Eastern religion for many years, he met Krishnamurti just once before making the tapes. In part, Sarjit appreciated them because, as the dialogues progressed, Anderson's understanding of Krishnamurti's thought deepened. In his numerous visits to the Swanwick Centre, Anderson was drawn to Chanda and became something of a spiritual mentor for her. They had many long-distance phone conversations on serious subjects. Krishnamurti's endorsement of Anderson deepened Chanda's respect for him, because, while Krishnamurti complained many times over the years that no one understood what he taught, he did once or twice concede that Anderson was an exception.[16]

Another who gave many seminars at Swanwick was Mark Lee, the founding director of the Krishnamurti school in Ojai, California. His connection with Krishnamurti went back to Switzerland in 1965 when Lee was a twenty-four-year-old American in search of a spiritual guide. After that, for eight years until the early 1970s, Lee taught English at the Krishnamurti junior school in South India's Rishi Valley, northeast of Bangalore. He became principal of that school, and in 1975 Krishnamurti asked him to start the school in Ojai, so Lee moved there with his Indian wife, Asha. They have remained at Ojai ever since, active with the Krishnamurti Foundation of America. Other special visitors included Mary Cadogan, the secretary of the Krishnamurti Foundation in England, and Dorothy and Montague Simmons, who built up and ran the Krishnamurti school at Brockwood Park.

The centre also entertained Krishnamurti's close friend David Bohm, the American-born quantum physicist from Birkbeck College, London, and Bohm's British-born wife, Saral. By the time the Swanwick Centre opened, Bohm had been part of Krishnamurti's circle for over twenty years, and the two men had recently collaborated on their book *The Ending of Time*. Chanda got to know Bohm well during her years at Brockwood Park, and like Allen Anderson, he was a great source of easily shared advice and wisdom. Bohm was the person that Jackie and Sarjit thought of first when Krishnamurti asked what they were doing to make their Krishnamurti Education Centre known in Canada. In 1978, Bohm agreed to give a lecture tour and with Sarjit doing all the driving and with Saral coming along, Bohm covered Canada coast to coast, speaking to Canadian university audiences about physics, philosophy, and the new Krishnamurti school on Vancouver Island. Sarjit found the Bohms delightful and formed a lasting friendship with them.

The main beneficiaries of the Swanwick Centre were members of the Theosophical Society in Victoria, plus a diverse and inquiring collection of visitors from far and wide variously studying Buddhism, yoga, Sufism, and human potential, and who felt kinship within a Krishnamurti environment. One speaker who did not come to Swanwick after it became an adult spiritual centre was Krishnamurti himself. When he visited the Wolf Lake School in 1978, he was already protesting that travel was too taxing for a man of his age, although he continued globe-circling from Gstaad to Ojai and to Madras. Somehow, the trip to BC seemed farther than the others. And he told Sarjit that his visit would simply give everyone a temporary boost, which would evaporate after he left. Sarjit asked him again two years later when he was eighty-five years old, and he told her that he was having to cut down on his talks: it was taking him two days to recover from each one of them. This conversation was in Gstaad, in the chalet that his old friend Vanda Scaravelli maintained for him. She was not there, and another old friend, Mary (Taylor) Zimbalist, the widow of movie producer Sam Zimbalist, was looking after Krishnamurti. She was very protective of him and said immediately that, when Jackie and Sarjit set up their foundation in Canada, everyone had understood that Krishnamurti would not be able to come there.[17] Neither Jackie not Sarjit took this amiss. They had no illusions about belonging to the inner circle of Krishnamurti's friends or having any special call on him.

Despite his protests, Krishnamurti kept up an energetic pace of 120 lectures a year until he was over ninety. Jackie and Sarjit still attended his Saanen lectures every July and August, generally staying in the background without trying to get his personal attention. Their many trips to the area nourished their deep attachment to it, and they sometimes visited it just for recreation. That was why Jackie and Donny were in Gstaad in February 1986, when Jackie learned that Krishnamurti was very ill in Ojai. She called Sarjit, who immediately flew to California in time to to have a last meeting with him. On 17 February, Jackie herself was preparing to fly to Ojai for a last darshan with him when Sarjit phoned to say that he had died that day at the age of ninety-one.[18]

As he got older, Krishnamurti became increasingly concerned about how his teaching would carry on. (Earlier he had said it did not matter; when he was gone, it would be over.)[19] This concern, which he began to express several years before Jackie and Sarjit established the Swanwick Centre, revolved around the several Krishnamurti schools in India and those at Brockwood Park and Ojai, as well as his publications and the continuing dissemination of his teaching – how to keep it fresh or, using his word, how to ensure that its "fragrance" lingered after his death. His solution was to entrust the future of the Krishnamurti tradition to Krishnamurti foundations that he and his closest friends established in England, the US, and India. These foundations all remain active today, and the teachings also live on through Jackie and Sarjit's Krishnamurti Educational Centre of Canada.

With the Krishnamurti Centre and with the Kapoor Singh Canadian Hospital in Aur, Jackie and Sarjit have served the vision of their immigrant parents. They have donated their time, talent, and resources to projects in two countries, bringing the best of each to the other. Their work has been localized, but the spirit and motivation behind it are large, and they have expressed in their lives the positive things that can happen when doors are open and people free to enter.

18
The Span of a Century

Although it did not occur to them, Jackie and Sarjit could have celebrated the one hundred and first anniversary of their father's arrival in North America when they reopened the Swanwick Centre in 2007. (A hundred and one is an auspicious number in Indian culture.) This would have been appropriate because they were still fulfilling their parents' expectations through the hospital at Aur and the centre at Swanwick. They were continuing to live a family evolution from business success to philanthropy and service.

Sikhs have many scriptural verses and many common proverbs about selfless service (*seva*) and charity (*dan*) for the poor and needy. Judging by the guidance they gave their daughters, these were values that motivated Kapoor and Besant Kaur. And there was another influence in their background that made it natural for them to share with those who had less. They were from the landowning gentry of rural Punjab, and were distinguished among landowning families by their *jagirdar* ancestry. Their families had always had a village clientele – relatives, servants, and retainers – that they looked after. Punjabi commentators do describe a less attractive side to giving among Punjabi villagers: vying for status and prestige through largesse.[1] But Kapoor and Besant Kaur stayed clear of that. If Kapoor had wanted a monument to himself in his native village, he should have built the family hospital in Kharoudi. He and his family did put a hospital in Besant Kaur's village, but they did so only after finding it impossible to build in the town of Phagwara. They were not doing it to enhance their reputation in either village.

Kapoor seemed to have little nostalgia for the village of his birth. It certainly did not have the importance for him that Aur did for Besant Kaur; and that is understandable. His mother died when he was still in primary school, and he had lived in his aunt's village while attending high school. Then he had gone to business college in Kolkata and had emigrated almost immediately afterward. Once abroad, nearly a quarter of a century elapsed before he returned. When he did come back for an extended visit, he spent it in Aur. But, though he seemed to have lost any emotional attachment to the physical village of Kharoudi, his relatives and fellow villagers from there and from the surrounding Mahalpur area were with him throughout his life.

After all, Kapoor had achieved success in North America in the company of other Mahalpur emigrants. That was the story of his leaving India, his years in California, his beginnings in Canada, and his entry into the lumber business. The influence, brotherhood, and sharing of his Mahalpur companions were critically important in advancing his own settlement in a new world. In his search for opportunity in North America, he had more eyes than his own and the benefit of more experience, observation, energy, and capital than he could have acquired by himself. To the people around him, he was always special by virtue of his command of English, his education, and probably his quiet, thoughtful, and balanced personality. Their respectful title for him – Babu – which even his brother Tara used, signified that. But his early progress as a budding immigrant entrepreneur depended on his partnership with them.

As an immigrant, Kapoor had saved enough after a few years to invest in real estate and a small business, but his true success as an entrepreneur came after he decided to settle permanently in Canada. Most of his countrymen eventually did what they had planned from the start and went home. In choosing to stay, Kapoor joined a minority that made a critical difference by maintaining a foothold in Canada that relatives and other Punjabis could take advantage of later on. Shaving, cutting his hair, and discarding his turban symbolized his decision to stay, a path he chose during a moment of crisis when the hostility of white Canadians had reached its peak and when divisions between Sikh militants and moderates had taken a violent turn. His explanation (of a complex reaction to a many-sided situation) was simply that he chose to stay in Canada and be a Canadian.

For Kapoor, becoming Canadian did not mean abandoning India. He thought he could do more for his native country from abroad than by going home as an armed revolutionary. And from abroad, he did what he could to help people such as his friend Bhai Piara Singh Langeri, who did go back and who ended up in a British-run jail. When Mahatma Gandhi emerged as a leader in India's independence movement, Kapoor subscribed to his non-violent philosophy and spoke publicly as a Gandhian. But he never lost his admiration and sympathy for revolutionaries like Bhai Piara Singh, who paid for their patriotism with jail terms or with their lives. Listening to him speak of this, Jackie and Sarjit ambitiously decided to be militant Gadar revolutionaries themselves. That was how his non-violent ideals and his nationalist feelings added up in their minds. To an outsider, this may seem paradoxical, but it was not so to them. They had absorbed the logic of people who had been subjected to foreign rule and who identified with anyone who was trying to throw it off.

Kapoor knew the bitterness felt by Punjabis and other South Asians regarding the treatment they received during their early years in Canada, painfully exemplified for them by the *Komagata Maru* episode of 1914. But he did not seem to nurse the hurt of it, and it did not affect his relations with white Canadians. In fact, he treasured his friends outside the Punjabi community, although he was sometimes required to overlook their ethnocentricity. He and his family were surrounded by a majority culture that knew very little of India, and though he could be gently ironic about it, he was also philosophical. With the support of Besant Kaur and her inclusive view of the world, he raised his daughters to be Canadians without reservation and not to make the past a barrier to the present.

Kapoor had played a positive role in his community by supporting a determined and persistent campaign for fair treatment. Publications, petitions, and delegations were all part of this effort. Small as his community was, it managed over the years to recruit a succession of highly educated and articulate individuals – notably Prof. Teja Singh, Dr. Sundar Singh, Sadhu Singh Dhami, Anup Singh Dhillon, and Dr. Pandia – to make its case in Ottawa and Victoria. Victories came very slowly but progressively: the admission of wives and children, an amnesty for illegal immigrants, the federal, provincial, and municipal franchises, the concession and subsequent increase of an immigration quota, and finally the elimination of racial and national considerations in immigration policy. In the post–Second World War years, Canadian public opinion shifted decisively from the old "whites only" attitude, a change that made complete acceptance possible for Kapoor's people. But he and his generation could rightly tell themselves that they had earned their place in Canada. It had not been handed to them; they had struggled for it.

Kapoor and his friend Kartar Singh Hundal always received encouragement from friends in white Canadian society. And among these, none were more welcoming than the Theosophists, who as students of Eastern spirituality, had taken Kartar Singh into their midst as a brother and offered a perspective on religion that Kapoor found meaningful. In the words of his family physician, Washington Wilks, a leading Vancouver Theosophist, the Theosophical Society had no creeds, beliefs, or dogmas but existed from its inception to bring truthseekers together in "free and fearless investigation."[2] This attracted Kapoor and it might have interested Besant Kaur had she been able to follow the English-language lectures at Theosophical meetings. Neither of them believed that any religion possessed exclusive truth. That was their sense of the teachings of the Sikh Gurus; and it was with this outlook that they had grown up in the Sikh faith. They reflected an acceptance of religious variety that earlier generations in their families and villages had also possessed. The religious nationalism that was on the rise among Sikhs in their lifetime was not something to which they subscribed. And with the same thinking, they quietly put off Christian missionaries when they came seeking converts.

Kapoor did not simply invite Jackie and Sarjit to attend Theosophical Society lectures – he made sure that they went. He believed it was an important part of their education; and while he was not telling them what spiritual path to take, he expected them to work on the spiritual side of their lives. They were inclined to do so anyway, given his example and, more powerfully, their mother's. This influence eventually led them to Krishnamurti, though before they found him, their searching caused their parents moments of anxiety. Kapoor and Besant Kaur had opposed Swami Radha because they did not take every spiritual teacher at face value. And they also believed that striking a balance in life was necessary, so when Jackie spoke of becoming a religious recluse, a sadhu, Kapoor was most upset. On the other hand, what he and Besant Kaur learned of Krishnamurti after their daughters began to attend his lectures let them trust his teaching. And when Jackie and Sarjit opened the Krishnamurti Educational Centre at Swanwick, they were certain that their parents would have approved.

In carrying out their parents' wishes, especially with the hospital, Jackie and Sarjit encountered difficulties for which, looking back, they should have been prepared. Sarjit especially (as the one who got the hospital built) was not ready for the trials and distress she had in dealing with officials and politicians, or for the attitude of villagers and officials that no one from abroad would come to serve in India if they were any good, or that they would come without the idea of making money. And neither she nor Jackie were prepared – which makes it more impressive that they did not abandon their project – for the long struggle to win the trust of those whom they had come to serve. When few patients materialized, the sisters might have been forgiven had they quit and gone home. It was their mother, who had shown the greatest determination throughout, who refused to accept discouragement. She might be called an existentialist for her advice that, if one patient appeared and received the right treatment, that was enough. One lives through action, not results. She needed no knowledge of Western philosophy to embrace that perspective. It was present in the Sikh and Hindu traditions with which she was so familiar.

Over the course of a century, with all its drama and change and with all their own willingness to welcome adventure, the Siddoos never lost their connection to Punjab. Kapoor's position of leadership in the BC Punjabi community helped keep him active within an Indian and Punjabi world. He was able to meet every visiting Indian of note, from Tagore to Nehru, and he was close to remarkable Punjabis such as Bhia Piara Singh Langeri and Anup Singh Dhillon, whose lives and careers bridged Canada and India. It was inevitable, given the influence of Kapoor and Besant Kaur, that their daughters would strongly identify with India. They did so while completely accepting their Canadianness. They lived in a city neighbourhood, where they were surrounded by Canadians of mostly British and European background, and they attended city schools and went on to universities in Vancouver, Toronto, and Montreal as the only Indo-Canadians in their classes. And they did so without feeling self-conscious about it. Their early years were so Canadian that, despite everything they had been told – or perhaps because of it – they were unprepared for India when they first visited it as young adults. But they returned to India and made themselves a part of it. As a consequence, Sarjit's daughter, Chanda, is a child of both British Columbia and Punjab.

The years have transformed beyond recognition some of the important places from the family's past in Canada. The lumber village at Mayo Siding is gone. All that remains is the gurdwara (where services are still held) and Mayo's house, which is now empty and seems to be abandoned. The Siddoos own 2,447 hectares (6,047 acres) of managed forest at Sooke Lake, but the buildings and equipment at at their village of Kapoor at Sooke Lake have long since been removed, and the site has returned to wilderness. The site of the Kapoor mill at Barnet is now a marine park. A three-story condominium stands on the lot at York Avenue, where

Kapoor and his family lived for so many years. But in India, the story is different. The Siddoo sisters still own the qila at Aur as well as fields in Aur and Kharoudi. They retain property held by their family for generations, which gives them a personal and visible connection to their roots. In their deep attachment to the forest and mountain setting of Canada's Pacific Coast, and to the Canadian way of doing things, the sisters are British Columbians and Canadians, and in their sense of history and their ownership of family property at Aur and Kharoudi, they remain Punjabi.

Notes

Chapter 1: Pioneers

1 Art McKenzie, "Modest Millionaire." *Vancouver Province,* 20 October 1956, magazine section.

2 Official American figures show that 5,697 South Asians were admitted from 1901 to 1910. Most of these entered the US from British Columbia and are also counted in the official Canadian figure of 5,185 arriving in Canada up to 1910. The need to make allowance for this in calculating the total entering North America explains my estimate of seven to eight thousand. See W.P. Dillingham, *Reports of the Immigration Commission: Immigrants in Industries,* pt. 25, *Japanese and Other Immigrant Races in the Pacific Coast and Rocky Mountain States,* vol. 1, *Japanese and East Indians,* 61st Congress, 2nd Session, Document 623 (Washington, DC: Government Printing Office, 1911), 327-29.

3 Intelligence Bureau, Home Department, Government of India, comp., *The Ghadr Directory: Containing the Names of Persons Who Have Taken Part in the Ghadr Movement in America, Europe, Africa and Afghanistan as Well as in India* (New Delhi: Government of India Press, 1934; repr., Patiala: Publication Bureau, Punjabi University, 1997).

4 Inspector W.C. Hopkinson of the immigration department toured the province in January 1910 and estimated that there were 2,500 South Asians in BC. An American congressional report in 1910 estimated 5,000 in the Pacific Coast states. The 1920 US census counted 1,898 in Washington, Oregon, and California, and the 1921 Canadian census counted 951 in BC. For Hopkinson's estimate, see his "Report on Hindus," 10 February 1910, Governor General's Numbered Files, Record Group 7, G 21, vol. 206, file 332, and vol. 3(a), Library and Archives Canada, Ottawa.

5 Note the observation by Marian W. Smith with Hilda W. Boulter, "Sikh Settlers in Canada," *Asia and the Americas* 44 (August 1944): 363.

6 Quoted by Sarjit Siddoo, conversation with author, 8 December 2006.

Chapter 2: *Jagirdar* Families

1 For information on historical ground- and surface water resources, crops, and climatic zones on the Punjab plain, see Avtar S. Atwal et al., eds., *Land and Water Management in the Indus Basin,* 2 vols. (Ludhiana: Indian Ecological Society, 1978).

2 Ram Das, former *sarpanch* (village head), Kharoudi, interview by author, 16 March 2006.

3 Tara Singh Siddoo, interview in Punjabi by Avtar Atwal and Sarjit Siddoo. 9 February 1977, transcript in English. The other village in Nihal Singh's jagir was Fatehpur, also in the Hoshiarpur District.

4 James K. Nichol, "I Visited Canada's West Coast Sikhs," *Star Weekly,* 29 August 1953. Nichol, who interviewed Kapoor, writes that Kapoor and Besant Kaur were engaged for eleven years before their marriage.

5 For speculation about the origins of the Jats, see J.D. Cunningham, *History of the Sikhs* (1849; repr., Lahore: H.L.O. Garrett, 1915; New Delhi: S. Chand, 1985), 4, 300; Khushwant Singh, *A History of the Sikhs,* vol. 1, *1469-1839* (Princeton: Princeton University Press, 1963), 13-16; and W.H. McLeod, *The Evolution of the Sikh Community: Five Essays* (Oxford: Clarendon Press, 1976), 10-11.

6 A handwritten letter in Urdu by Kapoor was reproduced in the Punjabi edition of *India and Canada: A Journal of Interpretation and Information* (January 1932).

7 Kapoor's attendance at the business college is mentioned in "Canadianization of the Hindu," *Witness and Homestead* (Montreal), 16 October 1918; repr. in *India and Canada: A Journal of Interpretation and Information* 2, 1 (March 1930): 17. It is also mentioned in Art McKenzie, "Modest Millionaire," *Vancouver Province,* 20 October 1956, magazine section.

8 Sarjit Siddoo, "Kapoor Singh, Timeline VI" (draft manuscript, c. 2002), 8; Jagdis Siddoo interview in Harry Pride, ed., *Burnaby Centennial Anthology: Stories of Early Burnaby* (Burnaby: City of Burnaby, 1994), 478-80. Neither Sarjit nor Jagdis Siddoo knew their mother's age, but the ship's manifest for the *Queen Mary,* which sailed from Southampton to New York in March 1952, gives it as sixty-one and Kapoor's as sixty-six.

9 Quoted in Nichol, "I Visited Canada's West Coast Sikhs."

Chapter 3: Emigrant *Jathas*

1 Jagdis Siddoo, "Biography of Kapoor Singh Siddoo" (typescript, August 2001), 3.2 *San Francisco Chronicle,* 6 April 1999, 10.

3 William Lyon Mackenzie King, *Report of the Royal Commission appointed to inquire into the Method by which Oriental Labourers have been induced to come to Canada* (Ottawa: King's Printer, 1908), p. 7.

4 Script for CBC Radio broadcast, "New Homes for Old," Toronto, 30 July 1941, Ian Smith, producer, Allister Grosart, writer.

5 Tara Singh Siddoo, interview by Avtar Atwal and Sarjit Siddoo, 9 February 1977.

6 See interview of Paldi emigrants in Archana Verma, *The Making of Little Punjab in Canada: Patterns of Migration* (New Delhi: Sage, 2002), 99-100.

7 See Sarjeet Singh Jagpal, *Becoming Canadians: Pioneer Sikhs in Their Own Words* (Madeira Park, BC: Harbour, 1994), 39-43.

8 Shipping column, *Vancouver Daily News-Advertiser,* 17 October 1906, 5. Look also for the *Empress of Japan* in the shipping column, *News-Advertiser,* 28 May 1907, p. 3, 25 June 1907, p. 3.
9 P.H. Bryce, chief medical officer, to W.D. Scott, director of immigration, with a plan of the detention hospital, 8 June 1906, Department of Immigration, Record Group 76, vol. 351, file 379496, pt. 1, Library and Archives Canada, Ottawa.
10 "The Hindu Problem," *Vancouver Daily News-Advertiser,* 19 October 1906, p. 5.
11 The seven and nine hundred ships were mentioned by Lashman S. Thandi in an interview by Avtar Atwal, 11 November 1982.
12 "City Officials Move to Assist Hindus," *Vancouver Daily Province,* 17 November 1906, p. 1.
13 Tara Singh Siddoo, interview by Avtar Atwal and Sarjit Siddoo, 9 February 1977.
14 Ibid. When Tara's son recounted this episode in 1994, he got it slightly twisted and located the encounter in Canada. Verma, *The Making of Little Punjab,* 115.
15 The Pacific Mail Steamship Company and the Occidental and Oriental Steamship Service were two of the services available from Hong Kong to Yokohama and San Francisco.
16 Kapoor told elements of this story to CBC script writer Allister Grosart in 1941. The November date of arrival is from Piara Singh Langeri, "Inquilabi Yadan: Bhai Piara Singh Langeri di Atam-Katha," which dates from 7 November 1955 and was subsequently published in *Desh Bhagat Yadan,* August 1963. *Desh Bhagat Yadan,* a magazine produced by the Desh Bhagat Yadgar Committee, was edited by Munsha Singh Dukhi. This article was identified and translated for the author by Sohan Pooni.
17 See W.P. Dillingham, *Reports of the Immigration Commission: Immigrants in Industries,* pt. 25, *Japanese and Other Immigrant Races in the Pacific Coast and Rocky Mountain States,* vol. 3, *Diversified Industries,* pt. 5, *Immigrants in the Lumber and Shingle Industries of Washington and Oregon,* 61st Congress, 2nd Session, Document 623 (Washington, DC: Government Printing Office, 1911), 354, 356. For Kapoor's wages, see Art McKenzie, "Modest Millionaire," *Vancouver Province,* 20 October 1956, magazine section.

Chapter 4: Settling in Canada

1 Shipping columns, *Vancouver Daily News-Advertiser,* 1906-7.
2 W.P. Dillingham, *Reports of the Immigration Commission: Immigrants in Industries,* pt. 25, *Japanese and Other Immigrant Races in the Pacific Coast and Rocky Mountain States,* vol. 1, *Japanese and East Indians,* pt. 3, 61st Congress, 2nd Session, Document 623 (Washington, DC: Government Printing Office, 1911), 325-37; Joan M. Jensen, *Passage from India: Asian Indian Immigrants in North America* (New Haven: Yale University Press, 1988), 30-40.
3 Hugh Johnston, "The Surveillance of Indian Nationalists in North America," *BC Studies* 78 (Summer 1988): 22; telegrams intercepted by CPP Telegraph and forwarded by the immigration department to chief commissioner of Dominion police, Ottawa, and chief press censor, RG 6, E, vol. 524, file 150-D-1, Library and Archives Canada (LAC), Ottawa.
4 Teja Singh's movements were reported in W.C. Hopkinson to W.W. Cory, 18 May 1909, RG 7, G 21, vol. 322, vol. 2(3B), LAC.

5 "Mystery and Power of Teja Singh," *Vancouver Daily Province,* 12 December 1908, magazine section; Darshan S. Tatla, *Sant Teja Singh, a Short Biography* (Jalandhar: Punjab Centre for Migration Studies, 2004), 1-38; Teja Singh, *Jeevan Katha: Sant Attar Singh Ji Maharaj* (Patiala: Bhasha Vibhag, 1981), 290-386.

6 *Vancouver Daily Province,* 21 December 1908, 3; Tatla, *Sant Teja Singh.*

7 The case of "Mr. Kapur Singh" was cited in a memorial from British India subjects residing in the US. See Lewis Harcourt to Lord Grey, 9 February 1911, with attached, RG 2, Series 1, PC 704, vol. 759, LAC. An identical memorial was addressed to Sir Wilfrid Laurier and received by the Department of Immigration on 22 September 1910, RG 76, vol. 384, file 536999, pt. 3, LAC.

8 The cheque made out to Laboo was for $507.50 on the Government Street, Victoria, branch of the Bank of Vancouver and dated 29 July 1913. The cheque for Lall Singh, $243.30 on the same branch, was dated 20 November 1913. Both cheques are in the possession of Sarjit Siddoo.

9 Sarjit Siddoo's personal papers include four pages of income and expenditure for the dairy recorded in her father's hand and written on Guru Nanak Mining and Trust Company stationery. She also has a one-page chronology of her father's income/savings from 1907 to 1946 in his hand and written about 1951. The dairy is included there.

10 Copies of *Sansar* survive in the National Archives of India, among descendants of pioneer Punjabi immigrants to Canada, and in Canadian immigration files (RG 76) housed in Library and Archives Canada. Pages from *Sansar* are reproduced in Sohan Surindar Singh Sangha, *Kainedeean Sikhan da Itihaas* (Vancouver: Khalsa Diwan Society, 1999), and in Kesar Singh, *Canadian Sikhs and* Komagata Maru *Massacre* (Surrey: published by author, 1989). Kapoor's and Piara Singh Langeri's involvement with *Sansar* is mentioned in the police biography of them that appears in Intelligence Bureau, Home Department, Government of India, comp., *The Ghadr Directory: Containing the Names of Persons Who Have Taken Part in the Ghadr Movement in America, Europe, Africa and Afghanistan as Well as in India* (New Delhi: Government of India Press, 1934; Patiala: Publication Bureau, Punjabi University, 1997).

11 Tara Singh Siddoo, interview by Avtar Atwal and Sarjit Siddoo, 9 February 1977.

12 For a description of the original gurdwara, which no longer stands, see Walter W. Baer, *Canadian Courier;* repr. *Aryan,* November 1912.

13 "Meeting in Victoria," *Sansar,* 20 July 1913, 1, facsimile copy in Sangha, *Kainedeean Sikh,* 187.

14 Hundal put much of what he remembered of Kartar into a letter that he wrote to Sarjit Siddoo on 23 September 2004.

15 Talminder Singh Hundle to Sarjit Siddoo, 23 September 2004; Talminder Singh Hundle interview by Ranjit Johal, 21 October 2000.

16 US Immigration Service, Minutes of Board of Inquiry re Sundar Singh, 1 November 1910, RG 7, G 21, vol. 201, file 332, vol. 5, LAC.

17 A.E. Armstrong to W.L. Macrae, 25 June 1915, Presbyterian Church in Canada, "Presbyterian Mission to the Hindus," United Church of Canada Archives, Toronto; W.C. Hopkinson to W.W. Cory, 11 October, 1912, RG 7, G 21, vol. 201, file 332, vol. 3, LAC.

18 Individual cases re South Asian immigration to Canada, #55, RG 76, vol. 384, file 536999, pt. 4, LAC; W.C. Hopkinson to W.W. Cory, 17 February, 10 March, and 23 March 1911, RG 7, G 21, vol. 201, LAC.

19 Rajah Singh mentions his service in "Correspondence: An Appeal to Sikhs at Home," *Vancouver Hindustanee,* 1 January 1914, 6.

20 Sundar Singh's words from *Aryan,* December 1911, 1. Canadian Club address in "The Sikhs in Canada," *Aryan,* January 1912, p.1; Empire Club address in *The Empire Club of Canada Speeches, 1911-1912* (Toronto: Empire Club of Canada, 1913). An account of the Labour Temple address is given in "Labor Men Discuss the Hindu Question," *District Ledger,* 24 February 1912. For a clipping from *District Ledger,* see RG 76, vol. 384, file 536999, LAC.

21 See quote from *Toronto World* in Isabella Ross Broad, *An Appeal for Fair Play for the Sikhs in Canada* (Victoria: Victoria Society of Friends of the Hindu, 1913), 8. Sundar Singh claimed to have the president of the University of Toronto, Robert Falconer, the lawyer and amateur astronomer John A. Paterson, the Presbyterian missionary John Wilkie, the lawyer H.E. Irwin, and J.K. Macdonald, John Firstborn, and Thomas West on a committee looking into the claims of the Sikhs.

Chapter 5: Trouble in British Columbia

1 Sundar Singh, "Address to Empire Club of Canada, 25 Jan., 1912," in *The Empire Club of Canada Speeches, 1911-1912* (Toronto: Empire Club of Canada, 1913), 112-16.

2 Richard Wilbur, *H.H. Stevens, 1878-1973* (Toronto: University of Toronto Press, 1977), 3-25; "Insulting the Hindu," *Sansar,* 20 July 1913, 1, facsimile copy in Sohan Surindar Singh Sangha, *Kainedeean Sikhan da Itihaas* (Vancouver: Khalsa Diwan Society, 1999), 187.

3 "Meeting in Victoria," *Sansar,* 20 July 1913, in Sangha, *Kainedeean Sikhan da Itihaas,* 187.

4 Teja Singh, *Jeevan Katha: Sant Attar Singh Ji Maharaj* (Patiala: Bhasha Vibhag, 1981), 380-81.

5 Isabella Ross Broad, *An Appeal for Fair Play for the Sikhs in Canada* (Victoria: Victoria. Society of Friends of the Hindu, 1913), 1-16, RG 76, vol. 385, file 536999, pt. 8, Library and Archives Canada (LAC), Ottawa. Biographical information from her death certificate, dated 17 January 1919 in Victoria, her marriage certificate dated 10 October 1919 at Balsam Grove, Ontario, and her 1901 census entry, showing her residence in Grey County, Ontario.

6 *Vancouver Daily Province,* 30 June 1909, 12; K.S. Akali (Kartar Hundal), 630 Speed Avenue, Victoria, to [A.E. Armstrong], 1 April 1914, Presbyterian Missions to Hindus, United Church of Canada Archives, Toronto.

7 W.L. Macrae quoted in S.S. Osterhaut, *Orientals in Canada* (Toronto: United Church of Canada, 1929), 192. See also Ruth Compton Brouwer, "A Disgrace to 'Christian Canada,'" in *A Nation of Immigrants: Women, Workers, and Communities in Canadian History, 1840s-1960s,* ed. Franca Iacovetta, Robert Ventresca, and Paul Draper (Toronto: University of Toronto Press, 1998), 374.

8 *Victoria Daily Times,* 7 June 1915, 6.

9 Bhagwan S. Gyanee, "Brief Sketch of Life Lived by Bhagwan Singh," copy of part of a letter from Bhagwan Singh Jakh to the consul-general of India at San Francisco, October 1958, Famous Ghadarites, http://www.sikhpioneers.org/.

10 See T.R.E. McInnes to Robert Borden, 2 December 1913, Borden Papers, MG26-H., LAC.

11 Confidential statement to immigration authorities by informers Bela Singh, Baboo Singh, and Ganga Ram, January 1915, RG 7, G 21, vol. 206, file 332, vol. 13(a), LAC.

12 Statement by Piara Singh Langeri, in Chain Singh Chain, ed., *Gadar Lahr di Kahani: Gadri Babian di Zavani* (Jalandhar: Desh Bhagat Yadgar Committee, 2002), 143, identified and translated for the author by Sohan Pooni.

13 See "The Sansar," *Hindustanee*, 1 June 1914, 6, RG 7, G 21, vol. 211, no. 332B, LAC.

14 Bela Singh, Baboo Singh, and Ganga Ram were named at a meeting in the Vancouver Sikh temple on 27 December 1913 in connection with Jakh's deportation. Statement by ten men given 27 December 1913; see also translated *Gadar* article on Bhagwan Singh Jakh attached to Malcolm Reid to H.H. Stevens, 30 December 1913. Both items are in H.H. Stevens Papers, Add. Mss., no. 69, City of Vancouver Archives, Vancouver.

15 "Directors of United Indian Association" (translated from Punjabi), *Sansar,* 20 December 1913, 1, facsimile copy in Singh Sangha, *Kainedeean Sikhan da Itihaas* (Vancouver: Khalsa Diwan Society, 1999), 211. The 5 January 1914 issue, with a translation of the lead page, is in the H.H. Stevens Papers, Add. Mss., no. 69, City of Vancouver Archives. The 25 April 1914 issue is mentioned in "The Sansar," a hostile article in Husain Rahim's paper the *Hindustanee,* 1 June 1914, 6, RG 7, G 21, vol. 211, no. 332B, LAC.

16 Khalsa Diwan Society Minute Book, entry for 9 January 1914, identified and translated for the author by Sohan Pooni.

17 Piara Singh Langeri, "Inquilabi Yadan: Bhai Piara Singh Langeri di Atam-Katha," *Desh Bhagat Yadan,* August 1963, 43-44.

18 Harish K. Puri, *Ghadar Movement: Ideology, Organization, Strategy* (Amritsar: Guru Nanak Dev University, 1993), 77-88.

19 Translation of articles from *Gadar,* 23 December 1913, Colonial Office Papers, CO 42/985, Public Record Office, London; translated *Gadar* articles attached to Malcolm Reid to H.H. Stevens, 30 December 1913, H.H. Stevens Papers, Add. Mss., no. 69, City of Vancouver Archives.

20 Memorandum of a conversation with Sunder [sic] Singh, 29 May 1914, Loring Christie Papers, MG 30, E 15, vol. 2, file 4, LAC.

21 His June 1914 arrival in Toronto is mentioned in W.L. Macrae to A.E. Armstrong, 16 June 1915, Presbyterian Missions to Hindus, United Church of Canada Archives.

22 Battan Singh to Kartar Singh Hundal, 21 September 1914, letter in the possession of Sohan Pooni, Surrey, BC. This Battan Singh was from Sarhala Kalan in the Hoshiarpur District. For biographical information on him, see Intelligence Bureau, Home Department, Government of India, comp., *The Ghadr Directory: Containing the Names of Persons Who Have Taken Part in the Ghadr Movement in America, Europe, Africa and Afghanistan as Well as in India* (New Delhi: Government of India Press, 1934; Patiala: Publication Bureau, Punjabi University, 1997).

Chapter 6: Refuge in Ontario

1 Art McKenzie, "Modest Millionaire," *Vancouver Province,* magazine section, 20 October 1956.

2 Kartar Singh, "The Canadian Crucible," *India and Canada: A Journal of Interpretation and Information* 1, 1 (June 1929): 1.

3 A photograph of Sundar Singh, Teja Singh, Rajah Singh, and the Reverend Louis W. Hall, taken about December 1911, shows Sundar Singh, like the other two Sikhs, with full beard and turban. Six months later, in a photo taken outside the construction site of the Victoria gurdwara, his beard and turban are gone. See Sohan Surindar Singh Sangha, *Kainedeean Sikhan da Itihaas* (Vancouver: Khalsa Diwan Society, 1999), 211, 259, or Kesar Singh, *Canadian Sikhs and* Komagata Maru *Massacre* (Surrey: published by author, 1989), 66, 87.

4 An official statement can be found in "*Komagata*'s Return," *Comrade* (Delhi), 10 October 1914.

5 Sarjit Siddoo, "Kapoor Singh, Timeline VI" (draft manuscript, c. 2002), 29.

6 See "Rosebank from the Lake" (1920), photograph #96-01632, found in the Pickering East Shore Community Association Collection, "Historical Photographs of the Frenchman's Bay Area," Pickering Public Library. Available online in the Pickering-Ajax Digital Library, http://www.pada.ca/.

7 Obituary of Reverend James B. Moore, *Watford Star*, 3 September 1931. See the 1901 (http://www.archives.ca/02/020122_e.html) and 1911 (http://www.collectioncanada.ca/archivianet/1911/index-e.html) manuscript census entries for William Moore at his Toronto address.

8 Khalsa Diwan Society, *Report on Dominion, Provincial, and Municipal Franchise for Hindus in British Columbia* (Victoria: Khalsa Diwan Society, 1947), 4.

9 George McMurtrie was the Toronto Theosophical Society's book steward for a number of years. See *Canadian Theosophist, 1, 12* (15 January 1921): 184, and *Canadian Theosophist*, 6, 6 (15 August 1925): 92.

10 Moore's appointment with the Toronto Railway Company is reported in the *Tillsonburg Observer*, 30 April 1903, Tillsonburg Public Library, Tillsonburg, Ontario.

11 The Union Station job is mentioned in Intelligence Bureau, Home Department, Government of India, comp., *The Ghadr Directory: Containing the Names of Persons Who Have Taken Part in the Ghadr Movement in America, Europe, Africa and Afghanistan as Well as in India* (New Delhi: Government of India Press, 1934; Patiala: Publication Bureau, Punjabi University, 1997), 159. The Toronto-Newmarket reference is from Cecil Scott, "The Saga of Kapoor," *Vancouver Province*, 21 October 1943, and from a Canadian Press story of 31 December 1929 reprinted in *India and Canada: A Journal of Interpretation and Information* (March 1930): 11.

12 Harish K. Puri, *Ghadar Movement: Ideology, Organization, Strategy* (Amritsar: Guru Nanak Dev University, 1993), 94.

13 Sarjit Siddoo, "Raja or Fakir" (draft manuscript, c. 2005), 20.

14 Lahore Conspiracy Case, III, First Supplementary Case, accused number 60, 347, National Archives of India.

15 Piara Singh Langeri, "Inquilabi Yadan: Bhai Piara Singh Langeri di Atam-Katha," *Desh Bhagat Yadan*, August 1963.

16 Piara Langeri's own memoir confirms much of the testimony at his trial.

17 Jagdis Siddoo, "Biography of Kapoor Singh Siddoo" (typescript, August 2001), 6.

18 Kapoor Siddoo to William Moore, 6 October 1945, letter in the possession of Sarjit Siddoo.

19 Khalsa Diwan Society, *Report on Dominion*, 4.

20 "Albert E.S. Smythe," *Canadian Theosophist* 1, 2, April 1920, 281.

21 A.E. Armstrong to W.L. Macrae, 25 June 1915; A.E. Armstrong to John McKay, 14 April 1915, Presbyterian Missions to Hindus, United Church of Canada Archives, Toronto.
22 "Samuel Beckett," *Canadian Theosophist* 7, 2 (15 January 1928): 260-61.
23 "The Canadian Crucible," *India and Canada: A Journal of Interpretation and Information,* 1, 1 (June 1929): 1; "Bliss Carman," *India and Canada: A Journal of Interpretation and Information,* 1, 2 (July 1929): 6.
24 George L. McDermott, "Frontiers of Settlement in the Great Clay Belt of Northern Ontario and Quebec," *Annals of the Association of American Geographers* 51, 3 (September 1961): 261-73.
25 W.H. Moore, *The Clash! A Study in Nationalities* (London/Toronto: J.M. Dent and Sons, 1918), 146-48, 162-67.
26 Siddoo, "Kapoor Singh, Timeline VI," 29; Scott, "Saga of Kapoor"; McKenzie, "Modest Millionaire."
27 Eric Smith, interview by author, 1 February 2007.
28 Kapoor's one-page financial summary, in his own hand, takes his history up to 1951. It shows that (in an unspecified currency) he accumulated 20,000 from 1906 to 1912 and another 17,000 from 1913 to 1914. If they referred to dollars, these figures would be unbelievably high. Kapoor's summary makes sense if one assumes that he is calculating in rupees. From 1951 to 1952, he took a trip with his family to India, and an attempt to explain his finances to a relative there was probably the occasion for making this summary in a currency the relative would understand. The Indian rupee then exchanged at the rate of 13.5 rupees to the pound, the pound was worth US$2.80, and the US dollar was between Cdn$1.02 and Cdn$1.06. This means that a rupee was worth roughly 20 cents to the Canadian or American dollar. Assuming that Kapoor has given his figures in rupee, we must divide them by five to convert to dollars. Rs20,000 equals $4,000 and Rs17,000 is $3,400. Kapoor's total income from the dairy would be $1,000, which would accord with the $88 a month his dairy accounts show. His profit on the sale of a house at the corner of Balsam and York in the late 1940s, which he gives as (Rs)3,000, would be $600.
29 See "Private Buckam Singh: Discovering a Forgotten WWI Hero," SikhMuseum.com, http://www.sikhmuseum.com.
30 *Toronto Star,* 9 August 1916.

Chapter 7: The Lumber Business

1 Joan Mayo, *Paldi Remembered: 50 Years in the Life of a Vancouver Island Logging Town* (Duncan, BC: Paldi History Committee, 1997), 3.
2 Ibid., 3-4; Sohan Surindar Singh Sangha, *Kainedeean Sikhan da Itihaas* (Vancouver: Khalsa Diwan Society, 1999), 393. Archana Verma, *The Making of Little Punjab in Canada: Patterns of Migration* (New Delhi: Sage, 2002), 116-18. Each of these three books draws on interviews with old-timers, as well as newspapers and surviving documents. Their sources are inconsistent, but one can work out the main outlines of the story from them. Kapoor came back to BC earlier than Sangha and Mayo say.
3 W.C. Hopkinson to W.D. Scott, superintendent of immigration, 11 July 1911, RG 7, G 21, vol. 201, file 332, vol. 4, Library and Archives Canada (LAC), Ottawa.

4 Mayo, *Paldi Remembered,* 5, 7; Sangha, *Kainedeean Sikhan,* 394; Verma, *The Making of Little Punjab,* 122.

5 The original cheques, written on the Vancouver branch of the Bank of Ottawa, are in the possession of Sarjit Siddoo. Kapoor dated them 25 and 27 January 1916, forgetting that the year had changed, but the bank stamped them 26 and 29 January 1917, when they were cashed.

6 The mill at Strawberry Hill, at Mosher Siding, fifteen miles south of New Westminster, had been owned by Markham Lumber.

7 The other three partners in the Mayo Lumber Company, when it was formed on 16 October 1916, were Shiam Singh, Doman Singh, and Jawalla Singh. Jawalla was also known as Amar Singh Sangha. Their names and the date and terms of the original partnership are given in a legal document of 16 October 1917, which transfers some shares from Shiam Singh to a sixth partner, Jello. A carbon copy of this document is in the possession of Sarjit Siddoo.

8 *BC Lumberman: Fraser Valley Supplement,* August 1930. Kapoor came back to BC earlier than Sangha and Mayo say.

9 R.E. Gosnell, *The Year Book of British Columbia 1911* (Victoria: Government of British Columbia, 1911), 247-63, 289; *BC Lumberman,* June 1930, 24.

10 Verma, *The Making of Little Punjab,* 122, 142. Verma cites two documents in the possession of Mayo's son-in-law, Joe Soroya: a "State of Title Certificate" and an anonymous memo "The Mayo Group: Its History and Potential." Kapoor went to the CPR head office in 1924 to negotiate cutting rights on a thousand acres, and over the years the company expanded its cutting rights on railway land to fourteen thousand acres. See Mayo, *Paldi Remembered,* 34.

11 Virtual Museum Canada, "From Camp to Community: Cowichan Forestry Life," http://www.camptocommunity.ca.

12 "History of the Canadian Lumber Industry," *BC Lumberman,* February 1940, 43-44; Mayo, *Paldi Remembered,* 12.

13 *Cowichan Leader,* 28 April 1955; Mayo, *Paldi Remembered,* 12. On Carlton Stone, see "Sikh Communities: Hillcrest," *India and Canada: A Journal of Interpretation and Information* 3, 1 (1936): 6.

14 Tansor ceased operation in 1924 but was formally dissolved as a company in 1932. See dissolved Registrar of Companies files, reel B05154, file BC0004954, BC Archives, Victoria. Balance sheets for the Tansor Lumber Company for 1923 and 1924 are in the possession of Sarjit Siddoo.

15 Sangha, *Kainedeean Sikhan,* 378-82; *Ghadar Directory (Punjab Section, Revised),* vol. 4, *1913-15* (Lahore, 1916; repr., New Delhi: Gobind Sadan Institute for Advanced Studies in Religion, Gadalpur, Mehrauli, New Delhi, 1996), 64.

16 See the material on Mahton and Manhas Rajputs from the 1883 and 1892 census reports for Punjab as presented in H.A. Rose, *A Glossary of the Tribes and Castes of the Punjab and North-West Frontier Province* (Lahore: Punjab Government Printing, 1919; repr., New Delhi: Nirmal Publishers and Distributors, 1997), vol. 3: 49-53, 67; see also Verma, *The Making of Little Punjab,* 20-55.

17 Hugh Johnston, "Patterns of Sikh Migration to Canada," in *Sikh History and Religion in the Twentieth Century,* ed. Joseph T. O'Connell et al. (Toronto: University of Toronto, Centre for South Asian Studies, 1988), 304.

18 W.H. McLeod writes of a hierarchy of Malwais, Majhails, and Doabis in that order but one that had lost much of its meaning by the time he made his observations. McLeod, *The Evolution of the Sikh Community: Five Essays* (Oxford: Clarendon Press, 1976), 98-99.
19 In addition to Balwant Singh Khurdpur, the seven included Uttam Singh Hans (from Ludhiana), Bir Singh Bahowal (Hoshiarpur), Ishar Singh Dhudike (Ferozepur/Moga), Jawand Singh Nangal Kalan (Hoshiarpur), Jagat Singh Sursingh (Amritsar/Tarn Taran), Baboo Harnam Singh, Kahri-Sahri (Hoshiarpur).
20 "Note on the Hindu Revolutionary Movement in Canada," Department of Immigration, March 1919, RG 76, vol. 386, file 536999, pt. 2, LAC.
21 Members of this committee are listed in Malcolm Reid to W.W. Cory, 28 January 1921, RG 76, vol. 388, file 536999, pt. 2, LAC.
22 Malcolm Reid, special immigration officer for western Canada, to W.W. Cory, acting deputy minister, Immigration and Colonization, 7 April 1921, RG 76, vol. 388, file 536999, pt. 2, LAC.
23 Descriptive chronology of Vancouver Khalsa Diwan Society Minutes compiled by Arjan Singh Chand, who was president of the society in the early 1950s. The chronology is now in the possession of Sohan Pooni.
24 R.K. Das, *Hindustani Workers on the Pacific Coast* (Berlin/Leipzig: Walter de Gruyter, 1923), 27.

Chapter 8: Women and Children at Mayo Siding

1 Amarjit Hundle, Kartar Singh Hundal's nephew's son, conversation with author, 30 May 2006.
2 Figures tabulated from the annual reports of the superintendent of immigration contained in the "Reports of the Department of the Interior" up to 1917 and subsequently in the "Reports of the Department of Immigration and Colonization," in *Sessional Papers of Canada*, 1906-24.
3 A summary of gurdwara society minutes concerning the girl Karam Kaur is given in Mahinder Singh Dhillon, *A History Book of the Sikhs in Canada and California* (Vancouver: Shromani Akali Dal Association of Canada, 1981), 141-42. A facsimile of the record of Annie and Munsha's 4 April 1909 Sikh wedding, as written by Teja Singh, is given in Kesar Singh, *Canadian Sikhs and Komagata Maru Massacre* (Surrey: published by author, 1989), 43-50. The Anglican ceremony of 21 August 1908 is reported in *Vancouver Daily Province*, 21 August 1908, 1. Munsha's village was Kandola, which is near the main road from Hoshiarpur to Jalandhar.
4 The Bhag Singh Bhikhiwind and Balwant Singh Khurdpur families each had a child born in Canada.
5 See Sohan Surindar Singh Sangha, *Kanedeean Sikhan da Itihaas* (Vancouver: Khalsa Diwan Society, 1999), 154-56, 188-89, which reproduces articles from *Sansar*, the *Victoria Daily Times*, and the *Victoria Daily Colonist*.
6 Sarjeet Singh Jagpal, *Becoming Canadians: Pioneer Sikhs in Their Own Words* (Madeira Park, BC: Harbour, 1994), 90-91.
7 Sarjit Siddoo, conversation with author, 22 May 2006.

8 W.D. Scott, superintendent of immigration, to Dr. W.J. Roche, minister of the interior, 22 September 1915, and W.D. Scott to Sir Joseph Pope, deputy minister of external affairs, 22 September 1915, RG 76, vol. 385, file 536999, pt. 9, Library and Archives Canada (LAC), Ottawa. Also see Norman Buchignani and Doreen Indra, *Continuous Journey: A Social History of South Asians in Canada* (Toronto: McClelland and Stewart, 1985), 65.
9 See, for example, various Anglo-Canadians quoted in *Canada and India: A Journal of Information and Conciliation* (July 1915). See also Reverend R.P. Mackay to W.D. Scott, 23 October 1917, RG 76, file 536999, pt. 10, LAC.
10 J.A. Calder, minister of immigration and colonization, to governor-general-in-council, 27 November 1917, RG 76, vol. 388, file 536999, pt. 1, LAC; J.A. Calder to governor-general-in-council, 25 November 1918, RG 76, vol. 386, file 536999, pt. 11, LAC; F.C. Blair to Sir Joseph Pope, under-secretary of state, 25 July 1922, RG 76, vol. 386, file 536999, pt. 14, LAC.
11 Figures on arrivals, with a breakdown by nationality, gender, and travel class, can be found in the "Reports of the Superintendent of Immigration" in the "Annual Reports of the Department of Immigration and Colonization." In *Sessional Papers of Canada*, The South Asian women who came in 1921, 1922, 1923, and 1924 all travelled steerage class, like the men.
12 Episode described by Sarjit Siddoo, conversation with author, 17 January 2008.
13 Jagdis Siddoo, "Biography of Kapoor Singh Siddoo" (typescript, August 2001), 7.
14 Sarjit Siddoo, "Raja or Fakir" (draft manuscript, c. 2005), 23.
15 Dhan Kaur Johl, interviews by author at her Vancouver home, 14 March and 19 May 1988.
16 From the memory of Sarjit Siddoo and from her family photographs. See photographs in F 36, Joe Soroya Fond, Simon Fraser University Archives, Burnaby, and the descriptive passages and photograph in Joan Mayo, *Paldi Remembered: 50 Years in the Life of a Vancouver Island Logging Town* (Duncan, BC: Paldi History Committee, 1997).
17 Kartar Singh Hundal quotes the following figures for Mayo employees in early 1930: Chinese 181, South Asians 97, "Canadians" 73, and Japanese 41. *India and Canada: A Journal of Interpretation and Information* 2 (March 1930): 17.
18 A family picture of about 1931 shows Tara's son Lukhbir in the arms of his mother, Balwant Kaur.
19 Bing Chong is mentioned in Harnam Kaur Gill, interview by Avtar Atwal and Sarjit Siddoo, 4 November 1982.

Chapter 9: Village Life in Canada and India

1 *BC Lumberman: Fraser Valley Supplement*, January 1930, 72, and *BC Lumberman*, May 1930, 19; Tansor Lumber, file BC004954, and Maroka Lumber, file BC0007641, Registrar of Companies, BC Archives, Victoria.
2 "Since the New Year," *India and Canada: A Journal of Interpretation and Information* 1, 2 (July 1929): 1, 29, 7-8.
3 "Tagore," *Canadian Theosophist* 10, 2 (15 April 1929): 77-78.
4 See *Poems from Tagore; With an Introduction by C.F. Andrews* (Calcutta: Macmillan, c. 1920).

5 See C.F. Andrews, *Mahatma Gandhi's Idea; Including Selections from His Writing* (London: G. Allen, 1931).
6 "An Address Presented to Sir Rabindranath Tagore," *India and Canada: A Journal of Interpretation and Information* 1, 1 (June 1929): 3.
7 "Kartar Singh," *Canadian Theosophist* 9, 3 (15 May 1929): 95.
8 *Canadian Theosophist* 9, 11 (15 January 1929): 338.
9 Rajkumar Hans, "Punjabi Press and South Asian Immigrant Culture of British Columbia during the Inter-War Period" (paper presented to the "Seminar on Indian Immigration to Canada," Centre for Canadian Studies, M.S. University of Baroda, 25-27 March 1996).
10 *India and Canada: A Journal of Interpretation and Information,* 29 May 1929, 1, weekly Punjabi edition; Intelligence Bureau, Home Department, Government of India, comp., *The Ghadr Directory: Containing the Names of Persons Who Have Taken Part in the Ghadr Movement in America, Europe, Africa and Afghanistan as Well as in India* (New Delhi: Government of India Press, 1934; Patiala: Publication Bureau, Punjabi University, 1997), 226-27; Avtar Atwal, interview by Lashman S. Thandi, 11 November 1982.
11 *India and Canada: A Journal of Interpretation and Information,* 30 October 1930, 1, weekly Punjabi edition.
12 Intelligence Bureau, *The Ghadr Directory,* 152.
13 The figure comes from Sohan Pooni's assiduous research, published in his *Canada de Gadri Yodhe* (Amritsar: Singh Brothers, 2009), 241.
14 *BC Lumberman,* June 1930, 26.
15 *BC Lumberman,* October 1930, 14, 10, 22, and August 1931, 8, 15, 23; Ajaib Siddoo, interview by Avtar Atwal, 4 November, 1982.
16 "History of the Tank at Aur" (four-page translation by Sarjit Siddoo of a history in Urdu by Guari Skaṇkar Shastri of Aur that had been translated into Punjabi by Puran Singh).
17 They returned from Hong Kong on the *Empress of Canada,* embarking on 1 February 1933, stopping in Yokohama on 6 February and Honolulu on 14 February, and arriving at Vancouver on 20 February.
18 Harnam Kaur Gill, interview by Sarjit Siddoo and Avtar Atwal, 4 November 1982.
19 Moore's predictions are the subject of a story in the *Vancouver Sun,* 13 October 1933.
20 Sadhu Singh Dhami and Anup Singh Dhillon to Hugh Keenleyside, 1 July 1937, copy in the possession of Sarjit Siddoo. For biographical details on Dhami, see Harjot Oberoi, "Imaging Indian Diasporas in Canada," in *Culture and Economy in the Indian Diaspora,* ed. Bhikhu Parekh, Garharpal Singh, and Steven Vertovec (London: Routledge, 2003), 187. See also S.S. Dhami, *Maluka: A Novel* (New Delhi: Arnold-Heinman, 1978).
21 Sadhu Singh Dhami, "Maluka's Quest" (manuscript, Geneva, 1989), 253.
22 For biographical details, see Intelligence Bureau, *The Ghadr Directory,* 12. During a 13 November 1982 interview by Avtar Atwal, D.P. Pandia mentioned Anup Dhillon's efforts in Ottawa. During a 4 November 1982 interview by Avtar Atwal, Ajaib Singh Siddoo mentioned the visits of both Sadhu Dhami and Anup Dhillon to Kapoor. Sarjit and Jagdis Siddoo remembered them as well.
23 During her 4 November 1982 interview by Sarjit Siddoo, Harnam Kaur Gill, who travelled with Ajaib, read out the dates recorded in her passport. It had been stamped Calcutta 6 December 1929 and Victoria 24 January 1930. The passport was issued in Lahore on 13 February 1929.

24 Ajaib Siddoo, interview by author, 19 May 2006; Ajaib Siddoo, interview by Avtar Atwal, 4 November 1982; Daleep Kaur Siddoo, interview by Sarjit Siddoo, 14 October 1982; Harnam Kaur Gill, interview by Sarjit Siddoo and Avtar Atwal, 4 November 1982.
25 G.S. Sangra, interview by author, 24 September 1987; Mahinder Singh Dhillon, *A History Book of the Sikhs in Canada and California* (Vancouver: Shromani Akali Dal Association of Canada, 1981), 285.
26 Joan Mayo, *Paldi Remembered: 50 Years in the Life of a Vancouver Island Logging Town* (Duncan, BC: Paldi History Committee, 1997), 65.
27 Sarjit Siddoo, conversations with author, 14 March 2004; Mayo, *Paldi Remembered,* 105.

Chapter 10: Ending a Partnership: Life in the City

1 *BC Lumberman,* 19 January 1935, 44; *Cowichan Leader,* 28 April 1955; Sarjit Siddoo, "Kapoor Singh, Timeline VI" (draft manuscript, c. 2002), 50-51.
2 L.C. Lytton to Kapoor Siddoo, 5 November 1934, and Kapoor Siddoo to L.C. Lytton, 8 November 1934, in the possession of Sarjit Siddoo.
3 Tara Singh Siddoo, interview by Avtar Atwal, 25 October 1982 (translated from Punjabi).
4 L.C. Lytton to Kapoor Siddoo, 5 November 1934, and Kapoor Siddoo to L.C. Lytton, 8 November 1934.
5 Minutes of a Mayo Lumber Company shareholders' meeting held in the offices of Mayo Brothers Timber, 6 November 1936, in the possession of Sarjit Siddoo.
6 Walter Jacklin to Kapoor Siddoo, 10 April 1954, in the possession of Sarjit Siddoo.
7 See Gurcharan S. Basran and B. Singh Bolaria, *The Sikhs in Canada: Migration Race, Class and Gender* (New Delhi: Oxford University Press, 2003), 138-43.
8 Sarjit Siddoo, interview by Ranbir Johal, 14 October 2000.
9 Ajaib Siddoo, interview by author, 29 May 2006.
10 *Vancouver Daily Province,* 29 March 1938.
11 Kapoor's copy of the court stenographer's notes.
12 Society membership as reported in *Canadian Theosophist,* 10, 1-10 (1929-30).
13 For a post-Blavatsky definition of Theosophy, see "About Theosophical Principles," *Canadian Theosophist* 12, 3 (15 May 1931): 97; for Wilks' views, see his "Is Theosophy a Definite Philosophy?" *Canadian Theosophist* 42, 6 (January-February 1962): 137-44. For a sympathetic biography of Blavatsky from within the Theosophical circle, see Sylvia Cranston, *HPB: The Extraordinary Life of Helena Blavatsky the Founder of the Modern Theosophical Society* (New York: G.P. Putnam's Sons, 1993).
14 For an example of the advice Kartar Hundal received, see "Kartar Singh," *Canadian Theosophist* 9, 11 (15 January 1929): 338.
15 On Ethel Wilson, see Anjali Bhelande, *Self beyond Doubt: Ethel Wilson and Indian Philosophical Thought* (Mumbai: SNDT Women's University, 1996), 14; on Emily Carr's interest in and eventual rejection of Theosophy, see Stephanie Kirkwood Walker, *This Woman in Particular: Contexts for the Biographical Image of Emily Carr* (Waterloo: Wilfrid Laurier University Press, 1996), 113-15, 180n10; on Harris, Carr, and Theosophy, see Dennis Reid, *Atma Buddhi Manas: The Later Work of Lawren Harris* (Toronto: Art Gallery of Ontario, 1985), 21, 26, 44.

16 Copies of "Return of Shares" for Modern Sawmills and Kapoor Sawmills Limited, filed with Registrar of Companies, BC, 12 September 1938 and 2 October 1939, in the possession of Sarjit K. Siddoo.

17 Eric Smith, "Kapoor Sawmills Ltd." (two-page handwritten history by Kapoor's former employee, April 2004); see also Jim Wolf, "North Pacific Lumber Company, 1899-1914"; Jim Wolf, "Barnet Lumber Company, 1825-32"; Sarjit K. Siddoo, "Kapoor Sawmills Ltd., 1938-64," all in *In the Shadow by the Sea: Recollections of Burnaby's First Village*, ed. Harry Pride (Burnaby: City of Burnaby, 2004), 13-74; Tara Singh Siddoo and Kashmir Singh Siddoo, interview by Avtar Atwal, 25 October 1982.

18 *Vancouver Daily Province*, 15 January 1948, 33; *Vancouver Daily Province*, 21 October 1943; *Vancouver Daily Province*, 6 February 1969, 8.

19 Marian W. Smith mentions without naming a Sikh woman whose cow was such a pet that it would put its head on her shoulder while it walked. Smith, with Hilda W. Boulter, "Sikh Settlers in Canada," *Asia and the Americas* 44 (August 1944): 363.

20 Diljeet Teja Dimock, interview by author, 21 May 2006; Diljeet Teja Dimock's recollections in Pride, *In the Shadow by the Sea*, 69-72.

21 Jagdis Siddoo's recollections in Pride, *In the Shadow by the Sea*, 64-68.

22 *India and Canada: A Journal of Interpretation and Information* 3, 1 (September 1936): 1.

23 Sarjit Siddoo, interview by Ranbir Johal, 14 October 2000.

Chapter 11: Citizens without Votes

1 Biographical information from Ajaib Siddoo, interview by author, 29 May 2006, and Ajaib Siddoo, interview by Avtar Atwal and Sarjit Siddoo, 4 November 1982. Reference to BC Mobilization Board from "Memorandum for the Undersecretary of State for External Affairs concerning the Position of the South Asian Group under Dominion and Provincial Legislation," 10 August 1945, 5, Department of Immigration, Record Group (RG) 76, vol. 387, file 379496, pt. 17, Library and Archives Canada (LAC), Ottawa.

2 Harnam Kaur Gill, interview by Sarjit Siddoo and Avtar Atwal, 4 November 1982.

3 F.C. Blair, Memorandum for File, 19 September 1939, Department of Immigration, RG 76, vol. 387, file 536999, pt. 16, LAC.

4 Copy of petition on behalf of Ganda Singh addressed to the minister of immigration by six leading citizens of Duncan, 24 August 1927, F 36, Joe Soroya Fond, Simon Fraser University Archives, Burnaby.

5 F 36, Joe Soroya Fond includes Bishen Singh's passport and letters from the Canadian immigration department related to his case.

6 Blair, Memorandum for File, 19 September 1939, 6.

7 For a first-hand account of Malwai-Doabi antagonism, see Bachan Singh Guan, interview by G.S. Basran, 15 July 1985, Indo-Canadian Oral History Project, http://www.multiculturalcanada.ca/icohc.

8 F.C. Blair, Memorandum for File, 11 July 1939, Immigration Department, RG 76, vol. 387, file 536999, pt. 16, LAC.

9 Barbara Roberts, *Whence They Came: Deportation from Canada 1900-1935* (Ottawa: University of Ottawa Press, 1988), 38, 159-88.

10 D.P. Pandia, interview by Sarjit Siddoo and Avtar Atwal, 1 November 1982.

11 For information on Pandia's tour, see *Canadian Theosophist* 20, 3 (15 May 1939): 92; 20, 4 (15 June 1939): 111, 122; 20, 5 (15 July 1939): 130, 140; 20, 6 (15 August 1939): 177; 20, 7 (15 September 1939): 210; 20, 8 (15 October 1939): 250, 244-45. The Canadian immigration department confirmed Pandia's claim to have been a secretary to Gandhi. A.L. Jolliffe to J. Farr Simons, 12 May 1941, Department of Immigration, RG 76, vol. 387, file 379496, pt. 16, LAC.

12 "A Hindu Aviation Club in BC," *India and Canada: A Journal of Interpretation and Information* 2, 2 (April 1930): 3, 6; also information collected and shared by Ishar Singh Banns' adopted son, Paul Singh Banns.

13 Tara Singh Siddoo, interview by Avtar Atwal and Sarjit Siddoo, 9 February 1977.

14 Tara Singh Siddoo and Kashmir Singh Siddoo, interview by Avtar Atwal and Sarjit Siddoo, 25 October 1982. The passenger list for the *Empress of Japan,* sailing from Hong Kong on 16 November 1934, shows Kashmir on board and returning on a Canadian passport after last residing in Canada from 1928 to 1931. He was born in 1911. See his obituary in *Vancouver Sun,* 11 September 2005.

15 "Control of War Effort Now," *Vancouver News-Herald,* 11 April 1942, 3.

16 Khalsa Diwan Society, *India's Victory in Canada* (Victoria: Khalsa Diwan Society, 1947), 5.

17 Sarjeet Singh Jagpal, *Becoming Canadians: Pioneer Sikhs in Their Own Words* (Madeira Park, BC: Harbour, 1994), 125-28; Darshan Singh Sangha, interview, 3 April 1985, Hari Sharma, Summary, Indo-Canadian Oral History Collection, http://www.multiculturalcanada.ca/icohc.

18 "Minister Sees Difficulty of East Indian Vote: Religious Barrier Stands in Way of Franchise," *Vancouver News-Herald,* 10 October 1942; Nagindar Gill's age in 1934 is given as twenty-two or twenty-three in Intelligence Bureau, Home Department, Government of India, comp., *The Ghadr Directory: Containing the Names of Persons Who Have Taken Part in the Ghadr Movement in America, Europe, Africa and Afghanistan as Well as in India* (New Delhi: Government of India Press, 1934; Patiala: Publication Bureau, Punjabi University, 1997), 202. When he immigrated in 1931, he carried a passport giving his date of birth as 1914, but his family says that his true birth year was 1908.

19 *Vancouver Province,* 3 March, 1943; Sir Robert Erskine Holland, *Changing India: The Empire Club of Canada Speeches 1937-1938* (Toronto, Canada: The Empire Club of Canada, 1938) pp. 271-287.

20 "1200 Urge Franchise for East Indians in Province," *Vancouver News-Herald,* 18 Jan, 1943.

21 "Mass Meeting at Orpheum Theatre," *Vancouver Sun,* 18 Jan. 1943.

22 "Minister Sees Difficulty of East Indian Vote: Religious Barrier Stands in Way of Franchise," *Vancouver News Herald,* 10 Oct., 1942.

23 "East Indians Expect Action," *Vancouver Province,* 3 March, 1943.

24 Fred J. Lawrence, Queen St. South, Kitchener, Ontario, to Kapoor Singh Siddoo, 20 Nov., 1959, letter in possession of Sarjit K. Siddoo.

Chapter 12: A Real United Nations in Practice

1 There were thirty-five students in Sarjit's grade eleven-twelve class, seventeen boys and eighteen girls. On the back of her class picture, Sarjit got the signatures of most of the

girls (Eunice Wardle, June Hepburn, Sue Perkins, Anne Munn, Dorothy Keller, Yvonne Martin, June Butler, Doreen Watson, Helen Rosengren, Vivian Wong, Betty McAlpine, Judy Seymour, and Audrey Sherlock) but none of the boys.

2 Diljeet Teja Dimock, interview by author, 22 May 2006.

3 *Vancouver Daily News-Advertiser,* 9 May 1945.

4 *Vancouver Sun,* 10 April 1945.

5 *Canadian Theosophist* 25, 9 (15 November 1944): 292-94.

6 Kapoor Siddoo to William Moore, 6 October 1945, in the possession of Sarjit Siddoo; *Canadian Theosophist* 26, 6 (15 August 1945): 176.

7 "Office Notes," *Canadian Theosophist* 26, 6 (15 August 1945): 177.

8 Alvyn J. Austin, "Edward Wilson Wallace and the Canadian Educational Systems of China," in *Canadian Missionaries, Indigenous Peoples: Representing Religion at Home and Abroad* (Toronto: University of Toronto Press, 2005), 112-32.

9 Jagdis Siddoo, "Biography of Kapoor Singh Siddoo" (typescript, August 2001), 13.

10 Lyn Harrington, "The Proud Sikhs of British Columbia," *Saturday Night,* 20 November 1948, 26.

11 Robert Douglas Gidney and W.P.J. Millar, "Medical Students at the University of Toronto, 1910-1940: A Profile," *Canadian Bulletin of Medical History* 13 (1996): 29-52.

12 John F. McCreary, "The Condition of Civilians in Western Europe at the Conclusion of the German Occupation," in *The Empire Club of Canada Speeches 1946-1947* (Toronto: Empire Club Foundation, 1947), 228-44; "John Ferguson McCreary: A Man for All Seasons," *Canadian Medical Association Journal* 5, 1 (12 January 1980): 123-24.

13 Sarjit Siddoo, "Raja or Fakir" (draft manuscript, c. 2005), 60; Kapoor Siddoo to his daughters, 8 September 1946, in the possession of Sarjit Siddoo.

14 "Flames Sweep Holdings Near Shawnigan," *Victoria Daily Times,* 9 October 1945.

15 "Mill Fire," *Vancouver Daily Province,* 15 January 1947.

16 Ajaib Siddoo, interview by Sarjit Siddoo and Atvar Atwal, 4 November 1982.

17 These were published annually in "Oriental Activities in British Columbia," and in "Annual Reports of the Deputy Minister of Labour," *British Columbia Sessional Papers.*

18 Ann Gomer Sunahara, *The Politics of Racism: The Uprooting of Japanese Canadians during the Second World War* (Toronto: Lorimer, 1982), references to Pearson in chap. 2.

19 "East Indians Say Pearson Attack Unfair," *Vancouver Sun,* 9 March 1944; "Hindu Vote Ruled Out," *Vancouver News-Herald,* 10 March 1944.

20 *Vancouver Sun,* 14 March 1945; "City Sikh Attends Frisco Conference on India," *Vancouver News-Herald,* 2 May 1945; Khalsa Diwan Society, *India's Victory in Canada* (Victoria: Khalsa Diwan Society, 1947), 5.

21 On Pearson's proposal and reactions, see *Vancouver Daily Province,* 12 March 1945. In the 1945 election, Pearson received 54.24 percent of the vote and his CCF rival 44.22 percent.

22 See the mention of D.P. Pandia in Kris Rampersad, *Finding a Place: IndoTrinidadian Literature* (Kingston, Jamaica: Ian Randle, 2002), 213.

23 In his letter of 8 September 1946, Kapoor names Gurdit Singh Bilga, who was the new gurdwara president, and Surain Singh Muhim, the old one. Some of this matter appears in Mahinder Singh Dhillon, *A History Book of the Sikhs in Canada and California* (Vancouver: Shromani Akali Dal Association of Vancouver, 1981), 214-16.

24 Pandia's 1947 population estimate for all Sikhs living in Canada was 1,394, down slightly from 1,465 in 1941. A survey done in the BC community in October and November 1944

produced a higher figure of 1,756. The 1951 census counted 1,937 in BC. See D.P. Pandia to Hugh Keenleyside, 16 March 1948; Dhillon, *A History Book of the Sikhs,* 224-26; and Elmore Philpott, "Citizenship for Sikhs," *Vancouver News-Herald,* 29 January 1945.

25 Kamaladevi Chattopdhyay and D.P. Pandia to W.L. Mackenzie King, addressed from the Chateau Laurier, 27 May 1940, copy in RG 25, vol. 1891, file 60N, Library and Archives Canada, Ottawa; see also reference to Pandia and Chattopdhyay in Gary Hess, "The 'Hindu' in America," *Pacific Historical Review* 38 (1969): 71; D.P. Pandia, interview by Avtar Atwal and Sarjit Siddoo, 13 November 1982; Jamila Brijbhushan, *Kamaladevi Chattopdhyay: A Biography* (New Delhi: Abhimav, 2003), 98.

26 A *Vancouver Sun* editorial of 1944 revealed that the paper was not ready to endorse the franchise for South Asians, but a year later a *Vancouver Province* editorial came out in favour of it. "Don't Forget the Past," *Vancouver Sun,* 16 March 1944,; "Votes and Citizens," *Vancouver Province,* 28 March 1945.

27 Elmore Philpott, "Hitler Is Losing in Europe but Not Everywhere," *Vancouver News-Herald,* 15 March 1944; "Citizenship for Sikhs," *Vancouver News-Herald,* 29 January 1945.

28 D.P. Pandia, interview by Avtar Atwal and Sarjit Siddoo, 13 November 1982.

29 "Domicile Rights Granted to East Indians," *Vancouver Daily Province,* 22 August 1947.

30 "Civic Vote Allowed East Indians," *Vancouver Daily Province,* 30 April 1948.

31 Khalsa Diwan Society, *India's Victory in Canada* (Victoria: Khalsa Diwan Society, 1947), 9.

32 F.M. Bhatti, "South Asian Immigration into Canada, 1905-1973" (PhD diss., University of Surrey, 1974), 415-18.

33 L.B. Pearson to John Kearney, 12 August 1848, in Ministry of External Affairs, *Documents on Canadian External Relations* (Ottawa: Queen's Printer, 1967), 14, 84.

34 Marian W. Smith with Hilda W. Boulter, "Sikh Settlers in Canada," *Asia and the Americas* 44 (August 1944): 363. Figures quoted are calculated from tables on "population of Hindu racial origin" in *Census of Canada, 1941.*

35 Ajaib Siddoo, interview by Avtar Atwal and Sarjit Siddoo, 4 November 1982.

36 The Anglican rector was H.G. Fiennes-Clinton, who had been the principal of Bishop's College, Calcutta. Munsha Singh was from the village of Kandola in the Shivalik Hills, north of the present city of Chandigarh.

Chapter 13: Lessons about India and Spirituality

1 "Entry Right Sought by Indians," *Vancouver News-Herald,* 29 January 1949, 3; "India Looks Ahead to Era of Progress," *Vancouver News-Herald,* 3 February 1948; Harbans Singh, ed., *The Encyclopedia of Sikhism* (Patiala: Punjabi University, 1996), 2, 231-32; Pushpindar Singh, "Flying Ace and Pioneer," http://www.sikhchik.com/.

2 Michael Brecher, *Nehru: A Political Biography,* abridged ed. (Boston: Beacon Press, 1962), 163.

3 "Nehru to Arrive Nov. 2," "Ticket Sale For Luncheon to Nehru Set," "Nehru to Arrive with US Escort," *Vancouver News-Herald,* 11, 14, 15 October 1949.

4 "Nehru Told of Racial Bias," *Vancouver Sun,* 3 November 1949, p. 1; Malkit Singh Parhar obituaries, *Vancouver Sun,* 19 August 2006, and *Vancouver Province,* 19 August 2006; Malkit Singh Parhar, interview by author, September 1983.

5 "East Indian Women Adjust Selves to Canadian Life," *Vancouver Sun,* 29 October 1949.
6 Jagdis Siddoo, "Biography of Kapoor Singh Siddoo" (typescript, August 2001), 11.
7 The quota immigrants are identified individually by name, file number, immigrant status, and date of arrival in a handwritten list kept in the immigration department from 1951 to 1967. See RG 76, vol. 714, Library and Archives Canada (LAC), Ottawa.
8 See references to James Sinclair in C.E.S. Smith to deputy minister, 13 July 1955, RG 76, vol. 714, LAC.
9 C.E.S. Smith, director of immigration, "Resume of East Indian Immigration to Canada Showing Concessions Granted since 1945," c. 21 January 1958, RG 26, vol. 127, file 3-33-15, pt. 2, LAC.
10 For registered marriages in the Vancouver temple, see tables 3 and 4 in Michael Ames and Joy Inglis, "Conflict and Change in British Columbia Sikh Family Life," *BC Studies* 20 (Winter 1973-74): 24-25.
11 Sadhu Singh Dhami mentions his first meeting with Ida (identified as Anna Wertheimer) in his autobiographical manuscript novel "Maluka's Quest" (Geneva, 1989), 224.
12 Mahinder Singh Dhillon, *A History Book of the Sikhs in Canada and California* (Vancouver: Shromani Akali Dal Association of Canada, 1981), 273-78.
13 Kuhn spoke to the Vancouver Theosophical Society in April 1953. "Notes and Comments by the General Secretary," *Canadian Theosophist* 34, 4 (15 June 1953): 56. For a book that has recently attempted to revive an interest in Kuhn and his ideas, see Tom Harpur, *The Pagan Christ: Recovering the Lost Light* (Toronto: Thomas Allen, 2004).
14 *Victoria Daily Colonist,* 18 August 1954; *Victoria Times,* 18 August 1954; G.F. Strong to Kapoor Siddoo, 17 August 1954, letter in the possession of Sarjit Siddoo.
15 In Montreal, Sarjit worked in pediatric pathology with Fred W. Wigglesworth.
16 Swami Sivananda Radha, *Radha: Diary of a Woman's Search* (Toronto: Timeless Books, 2003).
17 "A Swami's Calendar, 1956," in "Radha's Life of Service, Part II," *Lightwaves,* 26 October 2007, http://www.lightwaves.cc/.
18 Jagdis K. Siddoo, *Listening Is the Guru: A Diary of Conversations with J. Krishnamurti* (Ojai, CA: Edwin Publishing House, 2005), 8.
19 Agnes Ramcharan to J. Siddoo, Montreal, 18 September 1959, letter in the possession of Sarjit Siddoo.

Chapter 14: The Hospital at Aur

1 Sarjit Siddoo kept a sketchy diary of ten pages from January 1957 to May 1960, which documented the hospital story as it unfolded, and an even more cryptic diary chronology with two columns filling a single legal-sized page. She has also kept some of her correspondence, written up the experience in several draft manuscripts over the years, and spoken about it to the author.
2 Gurcharan Singh Kalkat, former director of Punjab Agricultural Services, interview by author, 22 March 2006.
3 *Handbook of Agriculture,* rev. ed. (1961; repr., New Delhi: Indian Council of Agricultural Research, 1980).
4 Krishna Bharadwaj, interview by author at Rosebery Avenue, West Vancouver, 17 July 2006.

5 Sarjit Siddoo to Jagdish Singh, director of health services, Punjab, 19 July 1957, copy in the possession of Sarjit Siddoo.
6 Sarjit Siddoo to Pratap Singh Kairon, 10 July 1957, draft in the possession of Sarjit Siddoo.
7 E.N. Mangat Rai, "Pratap Singh Kairon," in Harbans Singh, ed., *The Encyclopedia of Sikhism* (Patiala: Punjabi University, 1997), vol. 3.
8 Sarjit Siddoo to Pratap Singh Kairon, 10 July, 7 August, 28 August, 18 September, 10 October, and 9 December 1957, and Pratap Singh Kairon to Sarjit Siddoo, 24 August 1957, 23 December 1957, copies and originals in the possession of Sarjit Siddoo.
9 Sarjit Siddoo to Popaji and Sis, 25 August 1957, original in the possession of Sarjit Siddoo; Paul R. Brass, *Language Politics and Religion in North India* (Cambridge: Cambridge University Press, 1974), 329; Khushwant Singh, *A History of the Sikhs*, vol. 2, *1839-1964* (Princeton: Princeton University Press, 1966), 297.
10 Sarjit Siddoo to Pratap Singh Kairon, 28 November 1957, copy in the possession of Sarjit Siddoo.
11 Sarjit Siddoo to Jagdish Singh, 19 July, 7 August, 13 August, and 28 August 1957, 12 February 1958; Jagdish Singh to Sarjit Siddoo, 9 August, 14 August, and 30 August 1957, 8 January and 6 February 1958, copies and originals in the possession of Sarjit Siddoo.
12 Gurdev Singh, Office of Director of Health Services, to Surjit [sic] Siddoo, 20 January 1958, copy in the possession of Sarjit Siddoo.
13 Sarjit to Popaji and Sis, 26 August 1957; Sarjit Siddoo to Pratap Singh Kairon, 10 October 1957, copies in the possession of Sarjit Siddoo.
14 G.F. Strong to Kapoor Singh, 17 August 1954, original in the possession of Sarjit Siddoo; "Pleased with Countrymen's Lot," *Victoria Daily Colonist*, 18 August 1954.
15 Jackie to Mommaji and Sar, 15 January 1959, original in the possession of Sarjit Siddoo.
16 While she was in Canada, Jackie followed the progress of the hospital in detail. Jagdis to Mommyji and Sar, 22 January 1959, original in the possession of Sarjit Siddoo.
17 Sarjit Siddoo to Chester Ronning, 18 September 1959; Chester Ronning to Sarjit Siddoo, 1 September 1959, copies in the possession of Sarjit Siddoo.
18 Sarjit Siddoo to K. Reid, Information Section, Canadian High Commission, 10 October 1959, copy in the possession of Sarjit Siddoo.
19 Hope Philpott to Besant Kaur, 15 October 1959; Elmore Philpott to Mr. and Mrs. Kapoor Singh, 23 October 1959, originals in the possession of Sarjit Siddoo.
20 Sarjit Siddoo, "Summary of Particulars of Kapoor Singh Canadian Hospital," c. 1960, copy in the possession of Sarjit Siddoo.
21 Amala Ramcharan to Sarjit Siddoo, 13 November 1959, in the possession of Sarjit Siddoo.

Chapter 15: Finding a Teacher and Losing a Father

1 Modern Sawmills, 139 pages of records, Registrar of Companies, microfilm reel B5498, Royal BC Museum, Victoria.
2 Minutes of the Kapoor Singh Foundation: Reports of President on Hospital, 1995-2002, files of Kapoor Industries; Sarjit Siddoo, interview by author, 13 March 2006.
3 Jagdis K. Siddoo, *Listening Is the Guru: A Diary of Conversations with J. Krishnamurti* (Ojai, CA: Edwin Publishing House, 2005), 8-9.
4 Ibid.

5 J.K. Siddoo, "A Day with a Saint," *Chandigarh Tribune*, 27 March 1960.
6 Bhave was in Aur in February 1960.
7 *The Collected Works of J. Krishnamurti* (Dubuque, Iowa: Kendall Hunt, 1991), 11:367-69.
8 C.W. Williams, *Jiddu Krishnamurti, World Philosopher, 1895-96: His Life and Thoughts* (Delhi: Motilal Banarsidass, 2004), xvi.
9 Mary Lutyens, *Krishnamurti: The Years of Awakening* (New York: Avon Books, 1975), 25-26, 89, 228-33, 260-97; Mary Lutyens, *Krishnamurti: The Years of Fulfilment* (New York: Avon Books, 1984), 1-15.
10 Sobha Singh to Sarjit Siddoo, 3 March 1962, letter in the possession of Sarjit Siddoo.
11 Siddoo, *Listening Is the Guru*, 24-25.
12 Sarjit Siddoo to Indira Gandhi, 23 March 1964, copy in the possession of Sarjit Siddoo.
13 Kartar Hundal's office was in the landmark Leigh Spencer Building on 553 Granville Street.
14 Kapoor Siddoo's obituary, *Vancouver Sun*, 18 February 1964.
15 Kartar Singh Hundal to Kapoor Singh Siddoo, 17 March 1959, original in the possession of Sarjit Siddoo. The case involved North American fundraising for the Sikh nationalist party in Punjab. Kartar thought that too much money was sticking to the fingers of the fundraisers.
16 Adrian C. Mayer, *A Report on the South Asian Community in Vancouver* (Vancouver: Institute of Social and Economic Research, 1959), 37.

Chapter 16: Marriages and Losing a Mother

1 Avtar Atwal, interviews by author, 17 July 2006, 11 December 2006, and 24 January 2007.
2 Jagdis K. Siddoo, *Listening Is the Guru: A Diary of Conversations with J. Krishnamurti* (Ojai, CA: Edwin House Publishing, 2005), 31.
3 Chanda Atwal, interviews by author, 13 and 20 November 2006 and 11 December 2006.
4 Sarjit Siddoo, interview by author, 16 October 2006.
5 Krishnamurti's rules for the school are given in Siddoo, *Listening Is the Guru*, 139-42.
6 Ibid., 168.
7 Ibid.
8 Ibid., 148; Chanda Atwal, interview by author, 20 November 2006.
9 Avtar Atwal, interview by author, 17 July 2006.
10 Sarjit Siddoo, interview by author, 20 July 2006.

Chapter 17: Canada and India

1 See analysis by Andrew Matheson, "Seeing Inclusion: South Asian Political Representation in Suburban Canada," *Electoral Insight*, December 2006, Elections Canada, http://www.elections.ca/res/eim/.
2 Dosanjh is from the village of Dosanjh Kalan, Oppal's family is from Oppal Khalsa, and Dhaliwal's paternal and maternal villages are Dhingrian and Chaheru.
3 "Punjab to Set Up NRI Police Stations," *Times of India*, 6 January 2008.
4 Sarjit Siddoo, interview by author, 6 March 2006.

5 Her account, written in 1986, is a forty-three-page typescript on legal-sized paper.
6 Chanda Atwal, interview by author, 8 December 2006.
7 *Who Are the Guilty? Report of a Joint Inquiry into the Cause and Impact of the Riots in Delhi from 31 October to 10 November 1984* (Delhi: People's Union for Democratic Right and People's Union for Civil Liberties, 1984), 46.
8 Satnam Chana, "NRI Investment in Social Development Projects: Findings from Two Sample Surveys in Doaba, Punjab," in *Sikh Diaspora Philanthropy in Punjab: Global Giving for Local Good,* ed. Verna A. Dusenbery and Darshan S. Tatla (New Delhi: Oxford University Press, 2009), 107-19.
9 Author's notes from Gurdev Singh Gill's talk at a workshop on diasporan philanthropy, Lyall Khalsa College, March 2006; Reeta Sharma, "Khushali Comes to Kharaudi," *Chandigarh Tribune,* 23 March 2002; Shipra Saxena, "Model of Cleanliness: A Case Study of Kharoudi Village in Punjab," in *Sanitation for All – Still a Long Way to Go: Compilation for the Second South Asian Conference on Sanitation, Pakistan, September, 2006* (New Delhi: WaterAid, India, 2006), 75-78; Ramesh Vinayak, "Philanthropy Reinvented," *India Today,* 13 March 2006.
10 The author was given a tour of the Shaheed Kartar Singh Sarbha Ayurvedic Medical College and Hospital by Avtar Singh Grewal on 27 March 2006.
11 Ramesh Vinayak, "Words on Wheels," *India Today,* 14 September 2009.
12 See Appendix B2: "Investment by NRIs in Development Projects," in Dusenbery and Tatla, *Sikh Diaspora Philanthropy,* 300-4.
13 For a description of Mayo Singh's benevolence, see Norman Shields, Historical Services Branch, "Mayo Singh (1888-1955)," Report No. 10 (2008) to the Historic Sites and Monuments Board of Canada.
14 Jagdis K. Siddoo, *Listening Is the Guru: A Diary of Conversations with J. Krishnamurti* (Ojai, CA: Edwin House Publishing, 2005), 133.
15 For example, see "On the Old and the New," in J. Krishnamurti, *The First and Last Freedom* (New York: Harper and Row, 1975), 246-48.
16 Siddoo, *Listening Is the Guru,* 152.
17 Ibid., 158.
18 Ibid., 170-71; C.V. Williams, *Jiddu Krishnamurti: World Philosopher 1895-1986: His Life and Thought* (New Delhi: Motilal Banarsidass, 2004), 438.
19 Mary Lutyens, *Krishnamurti: The Years of Fulfilment* (New York: Avon Books, 1984), 193-94.

Chapter 18: The Span of a Century

1 See Verne A. Dusenbery, "'Through Wisdom Dispense Charity': Religious and Cultural Underpinnings of Diasporan Sikh Philanthropy in Punjab," in *Sikh Diaspora Philanthropy in Punjab: Global Giving for Local Good,* ed. Verna A. Dusenbery and Darshan S. Tatla (New Delhi: Oxford University Press, 2009), 79-106.
2 Washington E. Wilks, "The Purpose of the Theosophical Society," *Canadian Theosophist* 36, 5 (November-December 1955): 102.

Index

Printed and bound in Canada by Friesens

Set in Garamond by Artegraphica Design Co. Ltd.

Text design: Irma Rodriguez

Copy editor: Deborah Kerr

Proofreader: Jean Wilson

Indexer: Annette Lorek

Cartographer: Eric Leinberger